INNOVATION POLICIES IN EUROPE AND THE US

The Authors would like to thank the
Austrian Federal Ministry of Education,
Science and the Arts for their generous support.

Innovation Policies in Europe and the US

The new agenda

Edited by

PETER S. BIEGELBAUER
Institute for Advanced Studies, Vienna, Austria

SUSANA BORRÁS
Roskilde University, Denmark

LONDON AND NEW YORK

First published 2003 by Ashgate Publishing

Reissued 2018 by Routledge
2 Park Square, Milton Park, Abingdon, Oxon OX14 4RN
711 Third Avenue, New York, NY 10017, USA

Routledge is an imprint of the Taylor & Francis Group, an informa business

A Library of Congress record exists under LC control number: 2002110615

ISBN 13: 978-1-138-71789-3 (hbk)
ISBN 13: 978-1-138-71785-5 (pbk)
ISBN 13: 978-1-315-19590-2 (ebk)

Contents

List of Tables

List of Figures

Preface

This book raises both general and specific questions of great interest both for scholars interested in public policy and policy makers. What role do new ideas and new theoretical developments play when it comes to shaping changes in policy? Do such changes take place abruptly and radically, or are they rather processes of incremental policy learning? Do they evolve differently in different national contexts or do the similarities dominate when national trajectories are compared?

The contributions to this book analyze how a general tendency, the transformation of technology policy into innovation policy, is reflected differently in different countries. It points to the importance of new theoretical developments such as evolutionary economics and innovation studies as well as to the role of international organizations such as the OECD and the European Commission in diffusing these ideas.

The case studies show that while the direction of change is similar in the different countries, the degree and the form of change are very different. Among the countries studied the clearest change has taken place in the Netherlands and Finland while Austria and the UK seem to be lagging far behind in terms of adjusting to the new policy paradigm.

The analysis brings a new, important, input into the process of international policy learning and its characterization of innovation policy as constituted by the promotion of policy co-ordination, learning and knowledge appropriation, functional flexibility and organizational change is very much to the point. These are three new policy areas where new initiatives meet administrative and political resistance as well as transcending the old theoretical market-failure logic.

In international organizations as in national administrations, the dividing lines between directorates or ministries have become barriers to policy integration and hamper the process of innovation. One striking example is labor market policy that has become very much focused on the 'market mechanisms for buying and selling labor' while neglecting how labor market institutions affect life-long learning processes which are critical to the long term innovative capability of national systems.

Labor markets and labor contracts are among the most important factors for innovation, but for reasons of tradition they are not integrated in efforts to promote innovation.

Learning and knowledge appropriation are not easily integrated into main-stream economics. When they appear, they do so in the misleading sense that they refer to the diffusion of *information* that is the only form of knowledge that can be handled in neo-classical economics. While the distribution of *information* may be seen as a mainly technical problem, the same is not true for learning competences and skills. Here human interaction, trust, and social capital appear as crucial prerequisites for effective learning. This is why innovation policy needs to take into account the social dimension – both as something that conditions policy outcomes and as something that is affected by innovation policy. One of the major problems with policies that speed up innovation is that, if not thoughtfully designed, they may undermine the social cohesion that is necessary to support future learning.

In a standard neo-classical context, firms will always find the best way to organize themselves. Policy makers and management will also tend to regard the choice of organizational form as something that definitely should be left to the firm to define and develop. This contrasts with the view on new technologies and especially information technologies where it is seen as being highly relevant to stimulate their diffusion. All my practical experience from the OECD and all my research make me believe that this represents a serious misallocation of policy efforts. Especially in 'the new economy', the social and private rates of return to new forms of organization and to new ways of enhancing the skills of employees are extremely high. In contrast, the speeding up of diffusion of information technology reinforces the so-called Solow paradox where productivity growth does not correspond to the use of advanced technology.

I strongly recommend readers to study carefully the different cases presented in this book. As indicated by the last few paragraphs, the change from technology to innovation policy has just began. To understand the specific barriers blocking this change and how they have been overcome in some countries may be helpful when it comes to taking the next steps.

Bengt-Åke Lundvall
May 2002

Acknowledgements

The idea for this book was born in 1999, in a seminar held at Guildford, UK, where both co-editors met and soon engaged in discussions about how far different national technology policies in Europe have changed over the last few years. In the Spring of 2000, almost exactly one year after our meeting in England, we organized a seminar at Roskilde University, Denmark, under the auspices of the Danish Social Sciences Research Council, to discuss precisely this topic in a more systematic manner. The seminar was entitled 'The Innovation Policy Turn: Economic Ideas in the Re-Framing of Research and Technology Policy' and 8 papers were presented there. We were delighted by the superb academic response to our call, and by the good atmosphere among participants all through the two working days of the seminar. We would like to thank Marianne Jølby and the other secretaries of the Department of Social Sciences for their invaluable organizational support.

A second meeting with the same topic was held in Vienna, Austria, within the European Association for the Study of Science and Technology and the US Society for the Study of Science and Society's Conference 'Worlds in Transition', taking place from the 27th to the 30th September 2000. The panel was entitled: 'The Innovation Paradigm: The Impact of Economic Ideas on Research and Technological Development Policies' and a total number of 11 papers were presented. The attractive location of the conference did not overshadow the work, since the attendance and the level of discussions were excellent. Due to a number of reasons – not the least of which was the fact that a number of members of our group lived through busy times – the final edition of this book has taken longer than expected. During the three years of working together, we have become indebted to a number of people and institutions. We would first like to thank all of the contributors, for their solid work and for their patience upon our many editing requests. Most of them came to one of the seminars at Roskilde or Vienna, while some others even came to both of them. This book, though, includes also some few selected chapters elaborated upon request. We feel fortunate that such an extraordinary set of authors accepted joining our idea, and that we manage to cover the North-South-East-West dimension of the European geography, plus the US.

We should thank the Austrian Ministry for Education, Science and the Arts for their financial support. We would also like to thank Ashgate for their support at all stages of this project. Special thanks go to Andrew Crabtree, from Roskilde University, who did a fantastic linguistic revision and helped enormously to enhance the clarity and correctness of non-English native authors, including both co-editors. And last, but not least, thanks to Gertrud Hafner from the Institute for Advanced Studies in Vienna, for her invaluable editorial work, and for helping us to turn all the documents into a camera-ready copy.

Peter S. Biegelbauer, Vienna
Susana Borrás, Roskilde

Introduction: Ideas and the Transition from Technology to Innovation Policy

During the late 1970s, most advanced industrialized countries made clear changes in the nature and content of policy measures in a number of fields, the most celebrated of them being the transition from a Keynesian towards a Monetarist strategy in macro-economic policy (Hall 1986, 1989). In research and technological development (RTD) policies, the 1970s featured a striking change too. These new policies became more project funding oriented as opposed to the en-bloc funding which was the norm in the decades following World War II. This was the result of an increased utilization of RTD policy for the purpose of solving wider economic problems (Gibbons, et al 1994; Ruivo, 1994; Biegelbauer, 2000), which was also present in the Eastern Bloc (Biegelbauer, 1998). The economic turbulences caused by the oil crisis, the first signs of the international debt crises, and the new social movements can be seen as some of the factors which underpinned these policy changes at late 1970s.

Currently, a new wave of changes seems to be affecting policy-making. The 1990s have been dominated by an eclectic mix in economic policy, consisting primarily of supply side policies. From the problem-solving approach of the 1970s, RTD policy has moved towards a broader perspective on the innovation process focusing on the systemic nature of technological performance. Consequently, a typical feature of current RTD policies is their integration with other national policies such as: education, competition, regulatory, regional, agricultural, and foreign policies. This goes along three new perspectives deeply interrelated to each other. Firstly, a new understanding of RTD 'infrastructures' that expands beyond the conventional laboratory infrastructures and equipment, and covers a wide range of areas, including, for example, the educational sector, telecoms infrastructure, or IT access and usage. Secondly, the new policy approach generally emphasizes the rise of knowledge as a main factor of production, together with the classical factors namely, land, labor and capital (Valdez 1999).

Hence, the focus has been placed on the expansion of the knowledge-base, and the ability of individuals and organizations to learn and adapt to new conditions (Sulzenko in OECD, 1998; Lundvall and Borrás, 1998). Finally, the RTD policies of the 1990s have endeavored to link the institutions operating in the system, by fostering networks of firms (David/Foray, 1995; Müller, 1996), and by building bridging-institutions (DTI, 1993; OECD, 1998b). These efforts should enhance the communication, the synergy and the flexibility of the innovation system. The financial infrastructure is found to be particularly important in this regard, namely the private risk capital available in the venture capital industry and at second-tier stock markets (like the US' Nasdaq or Germany's 'Neuer Markt').

Some authors have characterized this change as the transition from a technology policy towards an innovation policy (Dodgson and Bessant, 1996), others have describe it as the emergence of a new policy paradigm, the innovation paradigm (Lundvall and Borrás, 1998). The latter characterization indeed seems to fit quite well, as in many instances not only policies and policy tools have changed, but also the policy aims and even the very conception of what may constitute a problem worth solving. One interesting explanation of such a transformation can be found in the rapid development of a new 'policy rationale' for RTD during the 1990s. This rationale is based on new theoretical frameworks in the field of economics. Since the early 1980s, evolutionary and institutional economic theory have devoted a large amount of effort to understanding the role of technological innovation for economic development (Nelson and Winter, 1982; for an overview Valdez, 1999).

Evolutionary and institutional economics introduce a number of changes with regards to the standard models of technical change as understood by neoclassical economics. Clearly the newer models are more dynamic in their evolutionary and endogenous perspectives of the innovation process. Whilst evolutionary and institutional – similarly to neoclassical economics – see technological change as the main driving factor for economic growth, the former include factors such as the level of technology and stock of knowledge, the size and quality of investments into RTD, the skills of the work force, and the complexity of institutional arrangements in the production function. The new models are able to explain phenomena such as spurs and slacks of certain sectors, as these models are not dependent on a constant flow of exogenous technological change to ensure their functioning. On the contrary, these models thrive on fluctuations of the rate of technological change, explaining innovations in terms of the behavior of the archetypal 'Schumpeterian entrepreneur', who is a risk-taker, building and destroying corporations quickly (Schumpeter, 1946; Nelson, 1992).

Perhaps, the most important finding of evolutionary and institutional economics for this study has been the notion that the innovation process is socially and institutionally embedded characterized by a degree of path dependency (Metcalfe and Georghiou 1998). The institutional settings at national and regional level constrain and enable the learning and adaptive processes that drive innovation. This economic theorizing has received so much support in policy-making circles (OECD, 1998) that one might expect it to have had a significant impact on the way RTD policy-making has been re-formulated and designed since the beginning of the 1990s. Trends towards an 'innovation policy paradigm' can be traced through the increased attention given to issues like the appropriability and diffusion of scientific knowledge production, the creation of a positive normative environment, the encouragement of SMEs' participation in collaborative research alliances, and the emphasis on human resources.

This book tries to address the nature and dynamics of this policy transformation. Our empirical research wants to trace the factors that have shaped their respective policy designs and aims to explore signs of convergence between different national RTD policies. Similarly, we expect the comparative study to raise some theoretical debates, critically reviewing the way in which previous authors have defined the process of ideas' institutionalization in the field of political economy. The country sample reflects key variables such as size, income, economic-technological specification and geographic location.

Theoretical framework: ideas and policy change

The theoretical framework of this book focuses on the interplay between ideas, interests and institutions, between framing and institutional processes, between interpretation and interaction in policy change. This, generally speaking, follows the recent 'ideational turn', which has been advanced by several researchers in the fields of comparative politics ('comparative public policy' in the US), political economy and international relations (for overviews see Busch/Braun, 1999; Jacobsen, 1995; Yee, 1996; Blyth, 1997). Social scientists have become more interested in exploring the way in which ideas and knowledge influence politics and policy-making (Edler, 2000; Hall, 1989; 1993; Howlett/Ramesh, 1993; Radaelli, 2000; Sabatier/Jenkins-Smith, 1993). Ideas provide worldviews and cognitive frameworks for the interpretation of the reality, and they might provide as well normative rationales, which directly influence policy design (Campbell, 1998).

Indeed, most of these studies in one way or another are part of the three schools of neo-institutionalism, rational actor based, historical and sociological, which over the last two decades have lead to a new understanding of the relations between state and society. Neo-institutionalism was doubtlessly successful in overcoming the rigid division between structures and functions that characterized a number of classical works in social science from Marx to Parsons, and in more contemporary ones such as the redeployed social systems theory of the 1970s. By identifying the structural components of society as something alive and (inter)active, drawing heavily from such factors as values and norms, it was possible for neo-institutionalism to come up with a more flexible understanding of social change, addressing the conventional dichotomy between actor and structure.

The three schools of neo-institutionalism address the question of social change and institutions differently depending on their premises about actor behavior, on their definition of institutions and on their understanding of structural conditions, resulting in significantly diverse analytical and methodological approaches. It is not our purpose to review them in detail here, since excellent review literature already exists in this regard (Peters, 1998; 2000; Hall and Taylor, 1995; Braun and Busch, 1999). Interesting for us is, however, the role that ideas and cognitive frameworks play in each of them, and their explanatory power when studying social and policy change. In a nutshell, ideas may be a 'hook' for some rational choice theorists, a 'catalyst' or 'lever' for some historical institutionalists or a 'framework' and 'principle' for some authors from sociological and constructivist traditions.

Whilst in rational choice theory, the concepts of ideas have traditionally been seen as resources for societal interactions and negotiations, and hence as instrumental to the material interests of rational and utility-maximizing actors (Busch, 1999), the other schools of neo-institutionalism have tended to ascribe them a role which is much more embedded in social action. For historical institutionalists, ideas are the basis from which the worldview of an individual or group operates. In this view, ideas are often seen as being intricately linked to a set of cognitive frameworks, policy frames and worldviews (Rein and Schön, 1994). Ideas provide lenses through which the world is seen, problems conceptualized, and solutions envisaged. Once the very basis for such a conceptualization changes, it is easy to understand that the policies, which are based on these conceptualizations, almost by necessity have to change too. Peter Hall's work has been very influential in this regard, particularly when studying the advancement of Keynesian ideas in Post War macro-economic policy-making (Hall, 1989).

Another model, which has tried to account for changes on the basis of ideas, is the advocacy-coalition-framework advanced by Sabatier and Jenkins-Smith (1993). They see actors as united by a belief-system addressing a specific issue or policy and thus find enough common ground to form an advocacy coalition. Belief-systems consist of a normative core, resulting from socialization in the course of the actors' upbringing, and a secondary area, which is a result of experiences and learning processes – the latter might be changed more easily in the course of policy learning processes. The advocacy-coalition-framework until now has proven an interesting tool for analyzing a specific set of policy areas: those which are relatively technocratic and depoliticized, such as infrastructure and environmental policies.[1]

Whilst these until now have been arguably the most influential ways to utilize ideas in neo-institutionalism when explaining policy change, another group of authors has a much wider understanding of ideas. The constructivist tradition of neo-institutionalism focuses on ideas as discourses and narratives, into which actors are socialized. Rather than 'explaining' social change, these authors aim at 'understanding' such change by deconstructing the discourses and narratives upon which social action has been self-reflected (Radaelli, 2000). Along this methodological tradition, ideas are not just agents of change devised by rational actors or grasped by policy-makers in need for policy-alternatives, but these ideas are influential enough to integrate actors into public discourses, in which the very way actors conceive of themselves and their interest structures are aligned along the boundaries of the discourse (Gottweis, 1998). Consequently, ideas become the basis of material interests, and not vice versa (Edler in this book).

This book will mostly follow the historical institutionalism approach, and examine the power of ideas in social change, operating as a framework for individual and collective action. For this purpose, we will ascribe to Peter Hall's examination of policy change focused on three interrelated dimensions: the economic, administrative and political viability of the new ideas, as their ability to be introduced into the existing institutional set-up of the country in question (Hall, 1989). As Hall has stated: 'the economic viability of ideas refers to their apparent capacity to resolve a relevant set of economic problems' (Hall, 1989 p.371). The financial instability of the early 1990s, the rapid process of globalization, and the rise of new technologies like biotech and ICT with their impact on industrial organization and on technological change, can be seen as three leading economic problems in this sense. Obviously, each of the national cases in this book presents different experiences, depending on the situation of their respective economies.

The administrative viability of ideas, on the other hand, depends on the administrative traditions of the civil servants, and to what extent the new ideas 'seem feasible in light of the existing implementational capacities of the state' (Hall, 1989 p.373). This is the question of how willing and flexible the administrative-organizational apparatus of the state has been in terms of adopting the new policy rationale, and what has characterized such adoption. Last, but no least, the political viability of the new policy ideas refers to their ability to appeal the broader political discussions held at national level. This again, depends to quite a degree on the specific configurations of the political discussions, particularly of economic nature, and the political ascription of the government in power in each national case examined in this book. All in all, the economic, administrative and political viability of the new policy ideas, serve here as a good and clear analytical framework from which to compare the different national cases exposed in this book.

The changing conditions of the 1990s

It would be too simplistic to understand the 1990s RTD policy changes exclusively in terms of a technocratic adoption of new policy ideas. It is our argument that the 1990s have experienced two very important transformations in the realms of politics and economics that have held a direct impact upon the viability of the new ideas. These are namely the tremendous transformations experienced in the international political economy, and the changing nature of the state. As to the first, the 1990s have been earmarked by an increased internationalization of the world economy, by the new dynamics in international politics signaled by the end of the Cold War, by the increased rationalization of the world economy, and by the notorious acceleration of the innovation process in new high-tech sectors as well as conventional medium- and low-tech ones. These factors are interlinked to each other and have led not only to an unprecedented internationalization of the global political economy both in scale and scope, but also to a more competitive environment. As a reaction to this increased competition, a large number of firms have developed strategic alliances, both within Europe, across the Atlantic, and of truly global reach (Vonortas, 2000). Similarly, governments have recently increased their efforts to cooperate in technological matters, with large international projects like the

ISS (International Space Station), the Human Genome project, and the Hubble Telescope. The governmental cooperative schemes, however, only represent a little part compared with the thrust of private firms' cooperation (Georghiou, 1998; Meyer-Krahmer and Reger, 1999). This means that globalization has brought about new patterns of competition and cooperation between firms and between governments, as means to cope with the increased market pressure at international level (Skolnikoff, 1993; Dicken, 1998).

It is in this later regard that we have to understand the considerable advancements of regional integration in the 1990s. Both in Europe and in North America, the EU and NAFTA projects have transformed the context for national economic development and policy-making. Perhaps the most striking transformations have taken place in Europe with the projects of the Single European Market, the Economic and Monetary Union and the latest enlargement rounds with new member states. These transformations in the political economy of the individual European states have been linked to the rising concerns about the issue of competitiveness in world markets and about the optimization of market size (European Commission, 1995; Lundvall and Borrás, 1998). This former issue has also been present in the USA (Dertouzos et al, 1989; Porter, 1990; D'Andrea Tyson, 1992), and it is interesting to note that on both shores of the Atlantic, the competitive position of the other region has been seen as economically more successful (Krugman, 1996; Strange, 1998). Likewise, the voices advocating further regional economic integration have linked this issue to the challenges and imperatives posed by the globalization process (Rosamond, 2001).

These economic, political and technological transformations have also affected the nature of the state and the public understanding of its tasks in a multifacetous way. This change has been characterized as the transition 'from the welfare to the competition state' (Jessop, 2000; Cerny, 1990; Hirsch, 1995). By this, the changing focus of the state's actions is addressed, from the welfare of the nation via means of broad social, educational, economic, security and other policy programs to the competitiveness of the national economy via means of targeted, but eventually 'deeper' – in the sense of reaching more into society – policy initiatives. Indeed, under the impression of globalization,[2] innovation policy today can be seen as one of the last few areas in which policy action by the state is greeted quite unanimously by all societal interests, regardless of their political predisposition. Likewise, the role of the state in technology matters has changed too. In the post-WW II period, the state was often seen as the prime mover targeting resources at activities such as 'picking the winners' among strategic scientific fields, and among firms in specific industrial sectors. Since the 1990s, the state has transformed its approach, partly by expanding its scope of activities and by changing its governance manner. Consequently, state involvement is now reaching a wider range of areas than before (not just financing scientific research or technological development), it works as a catalyst and facilitator of innovative activities rather than as an innovator itself, and its mode of governance is now much more participatory than previously (Grande, 2000; Simonis and Martinsen, 1995).

Consequently, the new international political economy as part of which the European states and the USA have been operating, and the important transformations of the state in this regard, have provided the basis for re-framing the contents of policies by identifying new problems and searching for new solutions within a given worldview. Evolutionary and institutionalist economic theories opportunistically came up with useful understandings of the complexity of the technological development in a context of accelerated change, thereby aiding the development of a new worldview from which a new policy rationale has emerged. In other words, our main hypothesis is that the prevailing economic uncertainties in the 1990s (related mainly to the acceleration of the innovation process and to the notorious globalization of the economy) paved the way for the emergence of a new policy paradigm (the innovation paradigm) in the national RTD policies of the 1990s. This paradigm turn is related to a new explanatory framework from economic theorizing. However, these assumptions need to be contrasted empirically through systematic analysis of individual case studies.

We do not expect the transition towards an innovation paradigm to take place simultaneously nor homogeneously among the European states and the US. The empirical results shall show important national differences. The institutional settings (in terms of administrative practices, industrial and educational structures, research and technological traditions) differ from state to state. These settings have defined the development of each national system of innovation as historical cumulative processes of institution building (Lundvall, 1992; Keck, 1993; Nelson, 1993). RTD policy forms part of this national institutional setting embedded in the administrative, social and economic dimensions of the system. By and large, changes in policy-making are more likely to take place gradually than abruptly following the constraints and opportunities that the institutions offer. This means that the adoption and institutionalization of the new economic ideas is more likely to happen gradually as well, in a process of interpretation and production of strategies through public deliberation.

Policy-making is in itself a cognitive process of framing and re-framing problem solutions through deliberation mechanisms. Economic ideas might in part be adopted as the overall theoretical rationale behind newly designed strategies, but in these designs there is always room for interpretation. Most importantly, this is the case, because until now neither institutional nor evolutionary economic theories have been developed to a point where clear ex-ante policy prescriptions are discernible; instead, it seems that policy rationales are being formulated ex-post, leaving large margins for manoeuvre in policy design and ex-post rationalization. On this basis, we expect to find large differences in the way in which the individual RTD policies have moved towards an innovation paradigm.

The research questions

From what has been said until now, a number of questions can be derived. Adhering to the concept of policy paradigms, explaining policy change seems to be rather urgent, especially in light of the emphasis of different strands of neo-institutionalism on phenomena such as path-dependencies and institutional inertia, which make it rather difficult to explain policy change. What has then characterized this transition from technology to innovation policy? Four sets of more specific analytical questions arise here. These will define the focus that circumscribes the empirical research of the cases presented here. Consequently, they will serve as guideposts to undertake the comparative study and elaborate the concluding remarks at the end of this book.

The first set of questions relates to the characteristics of the policy change, and *how the institutional set-up has absorbed the new ideas*. Interesting here is to explore to what extent the policy change has taken place in a radical or incremental way. Based on Peter Hall's notion of the administrative viability of the new ideas we shall explore the nature of paradigmatic change as gradual and consensual or radical and conflictive. In other words, whether the Kuhnian notion of paradigmatic change (Kuhn, 1970), applies here, or whether the adaptation into the institutional set-up has been less dramatic and taking place by piecemeal. One important point to examine here will be to what extent the new policy rationale was generally perceived as complementary or alternative to the previous neo-classical conception of 'market-failure'.

The second set of questions deals with *the forces that have enabled change*. By this we will refer to the political actors involved in the process, to the international dimension of the new ideas and the role of international organizations in spreading them, and to the reflexive-symbolic dynamics of this policy in the context of national politics and economics. This will respectively address the question of the economic and political viability of the new policy ideas, in the context of each national case, and the way in which actors and institutions have reacted to them in order to convert them into a valid guideline for policy action.

The third set of questions is related to the issue of *policy learning and policy diffusion.* Learning is a complex social process, where local and national traditions in business and public administration practices have the highest significance. Learning is a collective process where new organizational structures emerge in a way that they become better suited to respond to new market-social needs. Learning is essentially driven by a reflexive process, and anchored in pre-defined patterns of social interactions. Therefore, we expect learning to be essentially nationally-defined and heavily contextually-bounded. This, however, does not hinder to ask the degree of diffusion that innovation policy has acquired the past years. Or in other words, whether the extensive diffusion of the innovation policy among the different case studies examined might allow to identify the simultaneous appearance of a new policy paradigm in Europe and the US, and if so, what dynamics characterize this diffusion process.

Last, the fourth set of questions deals with the *future of innovation policy* in the coming decades. What issues, end of innovation? What context in the EU and international?

The contents of the book

A total of 12 national case studies are presented in this edited volume, in what we believe constitutes an interesting sample of this policy transition in the Western world. Almost all of our cases are European, either European states, or, as in the case of the BRITE program, the EU as such. The USA is the only non-European case in this book, and it diverges significantly from the others by its traditional position regarding industrial and RTD policy. Henry Etzkowitz makes interesting remarks about this, on what he defines 'the secret life of US science policy'. The question of size is also an interesting aspect in our sample, particularly among the European states. Small states are represented by Finland, Denmark, Slovenia and Malta (the later also to be considered as a micro-state). On the other hand, large European countries like Italy, the United Kingdom, and France bring another perspective to our study, with much larger economies and political systems. Smaller medium-sized countries might be interesting as well, such as Austria, The Netherlands or Hungary, all of them centrally located in geographic terms. Beyond size, the sample also provides a West-East political dimension. Transition countries like Hungary and Slovenia provide interesting insights about the depth and speed of policy transitions in a context of overwhelming changes in the political-economic system since the end of the Cold War at the end of the 1980s. Malta joins this set but only when considering the question of its forthcoming EU membership. For the three countries the impact that the EU already has in its policy-formulation during the long negotiation process, should not be underestimated. The North-South dimension is also present in our European cases. Nordic countries like Finland and Denmark constitute a clear 'North' in this regard; and Italy and Greece a 'South' in terms of industrial and economic structure. The large disparities within Italy make this case somewhat of an exception. However, the clear bottom-up dimension of policy-formulation that Fiorenza Belussi suggests, induces us to consider it in a rather decentralized manner. Furthermore, the trans-Atlantic dimension is also present in our book. Jakob Edler's analysis of the BRITE program within the EU, and the USA case bring about this dimension, which has a more decidedly sectorial approach based on specific programs. Yet, both cases illustrate nicely, how policy change takes place in a context of much wider, systemic, transformations.

At the end of this book, when all case studies have been introduced, the conclusions will aim at answering collectively the questions posed in this introduction, and will try as well to elaborate a concise perspective about what the future brings. By this we will aim at taking a quick look at the changes we expect innovation policies to take in the next decade. Will we see a further integration of science, technology, industrial and educational policies? What role can we expect tools as benchmarking to play? What are the chances of seeing a further shift of innovation policy functions from the national to the supranational level (as is the case in the EU)? What new agenda might be evolving at the beginning of the first decade of the 2000s?

Notes

1 For a comparison of Hall's and Sabatier/Jenkins-Smith's concepts, see Hemerijck/van Kersbergen, 1999.

2 And what Ulrich Beck calls 'globalism', the ideology of globalization, see Beck, 1997.

References

Beck, U. (1997): Was ist Globalisierung? (What is Globalisation) Suhrkamp.

Biegelbauer, P. (1998): 'Forschungs- und Technologiepolitik in Slowenien und Ungarn' (Science and Technology Policy in Slovenia and Hungary)', in: Wirtschaftspolitische Blätter 4/1998, p.399.

Biegelbauer, P. (2000): 130 Years of Catching Up With the West – Success and Failure of Hungarian Industry, Science and Technology Policies Since Industrialization. Ashgate Aldershot.

Blyth, M. M. (1997): 'Any More Bright Ideas?' The Ideational Turn of Comparative Political Economy in Comparative Politics (29) 2, pp.229–250.

Braun, D./Busch, A. (1999): Public Policy and Political Ideas. Edward Elgar, Cheltenham, UK.

Campbell, J. L. (1998): 'Institutional Analysis and the Role of Ideas in Political Economy', in: Theory and Society (27), pp.377–409.

Cerny, P. C. (1990): The Changing Architecture of Politics. Structure, Agency and the Future of the State. London, SAGE.

D'Andrea Tyson, L. (1992): 'Who Is Bashing Whom? Trade conflict in High-Technology Industries', Washington: Institute for International Economics.

David, P./Foray, D. (1994): 'Accessing and Expanding the Science and Technology Knowledge Base', OECD, DSTI/STP/TIP (94)15.

Dertouzos, M./Lester, R./Solow, R. (1989): Made in America; Regaining the Productive Edge. Harper Perennial, New York.

Dicken, P. (1998): (3rd ed.), Global Shift, Paul Chapman Publication.

Dodgson, M./Bessant, J. (1996): Effective Innovation Policy: A New Approach London: Thompson International.

DTI (1993): 'Realizing Our Potential – A Strategy for Science, Engineering and Technology', White Paper of the UK's Office for Science and Technology.

Edler, J. (2000): Institutionalisierung Europäischer Politik. Die Genese des Forschungs-programms BRITE als Reflexiver Sozialer Prozeß. (Institutionlisation of European Policy. The Genesis of the BRITE Research Programme as a Reflexive Social Process). Baden-Baden.

European Commission (1995): 'Green Book on Innovation'.

Georghiou, L. (1998): 'Global Cooperation in Research', in: Research Policy 27 (6) 611–626.

Gottweis, H. (1998): Governing Molecules – the Discursive Politics of Genetic Engineering in Europe and the United States. MIT Press, Cambridge, Massachusetts.

Grande, E. (2000): 'Von der Technologie- zur Innovationspolitik – Europäische Forschungs- und Technologiepolitik im Zeitalter der Globalisierung' (From Technology to Innovation Policy in the Era of Globalisation), in: Simonis, G./Martinsen, R./Saretzki, T. (Hg) (2000): 'Politik und Technik: Analysen zum Verhältnis von technologischem, politischen und staatlichen Wandel am Anfang des 21.Jahrhunderts', (Politics and Technology: Analyses of the Relationship of the Change of Technology, Politics and the State at the Change of the 21. Century) in: Politische Vierteljahresschrift, Sonderheft 31/2000, 368–387.

Haas, P. M. (1992): 'Epistemic Communities and International Policy Coordination' in: International Organization (46) 1, pp.1–36.

Hall, P. (1986): Governing the Economy – The Politics of State Intervention in Britain and France. Oxford University Press.

Hall, P. (ed.) (1989): The Political Power of Economic Ideas: Keynesianism Across Nations. Princeton: Princeton University Press.

Hall, P. (1993): 'Policy Paradigms, Social learning and the State: the Case of Economic Policy-Making in Britain', in: Comparative Politics 25 (3), pp.275–295.

Hall, P., Taylor, R. (1996): 'Political Science and the Three New Institutionalisms', in: Political Studies, 44(5), pp.936–57.

Hemerijck, A./van Kersbergen, K. (1999): 'Negotiated Policy Change: Towards a Theory of Institutional Learning in Tightly Coupled Welfare States', in: Braun, D./Busch, A., Public Policy and Political Ideas. Edward Elgar, Cheltenham, UK.

Hirsch, J. (1995): Vom Sicherheitsstaat zum nationalen Wettbewerbsstaat. (From the Security to the National Competition State) ID Verlag, Berlin.

Howlett, M./Ramesh, M. (1993): Policy Instrumente, Policy-Lernen und Privatisierung: Theoretische Erklärungen für den Wandel in der Instrumentenwahl. (Policy Instruments, Policy Learning and Privatisation: Theoretical Explanations for the Change in Policy Instruments), in: Heritier, A. (Hg.): Policy-Analyse: Kritik und Neuorientierung. PVS-Sonderheft 24/1993. Westdeutscher Verlag, Opladen, pp.245–265.

Jacobsen, J. K. (1995): 'Much Ado about Ideas. The Cognitive Factor in Economic Policy', in: World Politics (47), pp.283–310.

Jessop, B. (2000): The State and the Contradictions of the Knowledge-Driven Economy. Knowledge, Space, Economy. Bryson, J. R./Daniels, P. W./Henry, N. D./Pollard, J. London, Routledge.

Keck, O. (1993): The National System for Technical Innovation in Germany, in: Nelson, Richard (1993).

Krugman, P. (1995): Pop Internationalism. Boston: MIT Press.

Kuhn, T. (1970, 1.ed. 1962), The Structure of Scientific Revolutions, Chicago, Chicago University Press.

Lundvall, B.-Å. ed. (1992): National Systems of Innovation. London: Pinter.

Lundvall, B. Å./Borrás, S. (1998): 'The Globalising Learning Economy: Implications for Innovation Policy'. Brussels: European Commission.

Metcalfe, S./Georghiou, L. (1998): 'Equilibrium and Evolutionary Foundations of Technology Policy', in: OECD.

Meyer-Krahmer, F./Reger, G. (1999): 'New Perspectives on the Innovation Strategies of Multinational Enterprises: Lessons for Technology Policy in Europe', in: Research Policy 28 (6) pp.751–776.

Müller, K. (1996): The Austrian Innovation System, Project Reports I–VII, Institute for Advanced Studies, Vienna.

Nelson, R. (ed.) (1993): National Innovation Systems. New York and Oxford. Oxford University Press.

Nelson, R./Winther, S. (1982): An Evolutionary Theory of Economic Change Cambridge: Harvard University Press.

OECD (1998): STI Review Special Issue on 'New Rationale and Approaches in Technology and Innovation Policy' no. 22.

Peters, G. (1999): Institutional Theory in Political Science – The 'New Institutionalism'. Pinter, London and New York.

Peters, G. (2000): Institutional Theory: Problems and Prospects. Political Science Series 69. Institute for Advanced Studies, Vienna, Austria.

Porter, M. (1990): The Competitive Advantage of Nations. New York: Free Press.

Radaelli, C. (2000): 'Policy Transfer in the European Union: Instituitional Isomorphism as a Source of Legitimacy', in: Governance 13(1), January 2000, pp.25–45.

Rein, M./Schön, D. (1994): Frame Reflection. Toward the Resolution of Intractable Policy Controversies. New York: Basic Books.

Rosamond, B. (2001): Discourses of Globalisation and the Social Construction of Europe, in: The Social Construction of Europe. Christiansen, T./Jørgensen, K. E./Wiener, A., London, SAGE.

Ruivo, B. (1994): 'Phases or Paradigms of Science Policy?', in: Science and Public Policy (21), pp.157–164.

Sabatier, P./Jenkins-Smith, H. (1993): Policy Change and Learning. An Advocacy Coalition Approach. Boulder, Co., Westview Press.

Schumpeter, J. (1975, 1946 orig.): Capitalism, Socialism and Democracy, Harper & Row.

Simonis, G./Martinsen, R. (1995): Paradigmenwechsel in der Technologiepolitik? (Paradigm Change in Technology Policy?), Opladen, Leske + Budrich.

Skolnikoff, E. (1993): The Elusive Transformation – Science, Technology, and the Evolution of International Politics, Princeton University Press.

Strange, S. (1998): 'Who are EU? Ambiguities in the Concept of Competitiveness.' Journal of Common Market Studies 36(1): pp.101–114.

Sulzenko, A. (1997), Technology and Innovation Policy for the Knowledge-Based Economy: The Changing View of Canada, in: OECD STI Review, No 22, p.285.

Valdéz, B. (1999): Economic Growth, Great Britain, Edward Elgar Cheltenham.

Vonortas, N./Arvanitis, R. (2000): 'Technology Transfer and Learning Through Strategic Technical Alliances: International Experiences,' The Journal of Technology Transfer, 25(1).

Yee, A. (1996): 'The Causal Effects of Ideas on Policies', in: International Organization (50) 1, pp.69–108.

Chapter 1

The UK-Experiment – Science, Technology and Industrial Policy in Britain 1979–2000

Margaret Sharp

1.1 Introduction

The last twenty-five years of the 20th century witnessed dramatic changes in the UK economy. Traditional industries, such as coal and shipbuilding, have all but disappeared. Other sectors, such as motor vehicles or consumer electronics, once seen as strategic growth sectors, are now almost entirely owned and run by foreign firms. New firms, such as Vodaphone and Astra-Zeneca, unheard of in 1980, have now emerged as world giants.

These developments illustrate well the twin pressures of globalization and technology. Globalization has taken the old, labor-intensive industries to new, lower cost locations and encouraged restructuring and concentration in others, turning what was national into global oligopoly. Technology has reinforced these trends. No major pharmaceutical company, for example, can now operate without an R&D budget of over a billion dollars, a factor lying behind many recent mergers. Technology has also created new industries, such as mobile telephony, the Internet and biotechnology, with firms such as Vodaphone, Microsoft and Amgen as global players.

The UK's policy response to these developments has been unique. The Conservatives who came to power in 1979 rejected both the interventionism and the incrementalism of their predecessors. Theirs was a radical *laissez-faire* agenda, which became more radical as privatization gathered momentum. It was driven both by ideology, and by a desire to limit and control public spending. In this they had a powerful bureaucratic ally – the British Treasury.

When control of the public sector borrowing requirement grew to totem status in the development of public policy, this formidable alliance of Government and Treasury carried all before them. To understand the significance of this response, consider table 1.1, which sets the scene.

Table 1.1: Labor productivity in the UK and competitors – 1950–1996[1]

	UK	US	France	Germany[2]	Japan[3]
Labor productivity growth (percentage per annum)					
1950–96	2.60	1.55	3.70	3.87	4.48
1950–73	2.99	2.34	4.62	5.18	6.11
1973–96	2.22	0.77	2.78	2.56	3.06
Labor productivity levels (UK=100)					
1950	100	195	79	72	39
1960	100	197	95	96	47
1973	100	168	116	119	74
1979	100	154	130	131	79
1989	100	133	137	125	87
1996	100	121	132	129	90

Notes:
1 Value added per hour worked.
2 Former West Germany.
3 The data series for Japan start in 1953.

Source: Crafts and O'Mahony (1999).

The UK emerged from WW 2 as the dominant economy in Europe; Germany was divided, and France, worn down by German occupation, was still a predominantly agricultural economy.

Productivity in all three countries lagged well behind that of the USA. By 1960, both Germany and France had caught up with the UK; and by 1973, they overtook it. UK governments tried many different policies: nationalization, de-nationalization and re-nationalization; French-style indicative planning; a German-style Ministry of Technology. They subsidized capital to encourage investment and penalized services to encourage manufacturing. They gave infant industry protection to telecommunications and computers and forced marriages amongst larger firms to create national champions, which might benefit from economies of scale. Through it all, productivity growth remained obstinately below that of our European partners. Was it really sensible to expose the comparatively weak British economy to the full force of laissez faire? And how successful has that policy been?

This chapter seeks to chart that experiment by following the course of three inter-related strands of policy – science, technology and industrial policy. Section 2 discusses developments in industrial and technology policy and highlights in particular the shift from the high subsidy regime of the late 1970s and early 1980s to the position in the 1990s when less than 0.001 per cent of GDP was being spent on industrial support, most of that going to innovation and small firm initiatives. Section 3 looks at parallel developments in science policy and the tensions posed for scientists in accommodating to 'steady state' science budgets after experiencing real terms increases of 3–4 per cent for most of the post-war period. Section 4 looks at developments since the election in 1997 of the New Labor government under Tony Blair and Section 5 attempts to draw conclusions from the 20-year experiment.

1.2 Industrial and technology policies 1979–1997[1]

1.2.1 The rise and fall of industrial subsidies

The Conservative government of Margaret Thatcher, elected in May 1979, came into office determined, in their own words, 'to get government off the back of industry'. This meant less intervention in the sense both of lower taxes and fewer subsidies. In their eyes subsidies, whether in the form of outright subsidies or tax breaks, frequently came with strings attached and it was this attempt to interfere with industrial decision taking that the Conservatives found offensive. Such changes were easier to contemplate than to effect.

Table 1.2: Overall estimates of expenditures in support of individual firms (£m 1997/8 prices)

	General industrial support	Support for nationalised firms[1]	Regional assistance	Small business support	Total
1975/76	7112	3415	2194	na	12,721
1979/80	9842	3415	1305	na	14,562
1983/84	6775	3318	756	na	10,849
1987/88	178	2523	365	135[2]	3,201
1990/91	136	595	179	183[3]	1,093
1995/96	139	–	126	236	501
1997/98	123	–	141	267	531

Notes:

1 The total attributed to support for nationalised firms for each specific year is the average attributed to that five year period.

2 Refers to financial year 1988/9 not 1987/8.

3 Refers to financial year 1993/4 not 1990/91.

Source: Sharp (2000) Table 1.4.6. Much of the data for the earlier years is derived from Wren (1996 a and b).

As tables 1.2 and 1.3 illustrate, most support in 1979 came from investment allowances and regional assistance, both of which were in effect tax breaks on investment expenditure. The main beneficiaries were the big capital spenders – above all the oil and chemical companies exploiting North Sea oil. Even before the Conservatives came to power this concentration of subsidies had come in for criticism.[2] The Conservatives rapidly dismantled the regional measures, cutting regional assistance severely and switching what was left away from industrial subsidies towards re-generation measures in inner cities. For industry, they retained only 'regional selective assistance' (RSA), which allowed selective grants when jobs were at stake and provided a useful source of funding with which to attract inward investment. Investment allowances were retained until the 1985/6 budget when they were abolished in return for substantially lower corporation (profits) tax.

Two further items in tables 1.2. and 1.3 merit comment. First, the considerable subsidies for nationalized industries detailed in table 1.2.

Table 1.3: General industrial support 1975–1995 (£m at 1997/8 prices)

	Investment allowances	Technology support	Employ-ment schemes	Sectoral support	Firm speci-fic support from NEB & section 8 schemes	Total
	(1)	(2)	(3)	(4)	(5)	(6)
1975/76	7.086	–	17	5	4	7.112
1979/80	8.839	84	272	156	491	9.842
1983/84	6.168	189	198	71	149	6.775
1987/88	–	154	22	2	–	178
1990/91	–	136	–	–	–	136
1995/96	–	137	–	–	–	139
1997/98	–	123	–	–	–	123

Source: Sharp (2000) Table 2. See also the detailed notes attached to that table which give full attribution to Wren (1996 a and b).

The 1974–79 Labor government had brought a number of industries, such as steel and shipbuilding, into the public sector, while the very deep recession of the early 1980s brought huge deficits to these and other nationalised firms including British Leyland and Rolls Royce, blocking privatization. By the early 1990s even British Coal was being privatized. The residual payments recorded in table 1.2 for the 1990s largely reflect the costs of privatization.

Secondly, note the column headed technology support in table 1.3. This reflects a series of programs introduced by the Labor government in the late 1970s to support new technologies, ranging from a general support program called the Product and Process Development Scheme (PPDS) to specific support for developments such as micro-electronics and robotics. Initially the Conservatives backed these programs and in the mid-1980s even embarked upon an ambitious program of support for electronics and telecommunications known as the Alvey Program. In 1988, however, all these schemes were axed as the Conservatives pulled out of 'near market' support[3] arguing that industry itself ought to be meeting the costs of such programs. They argued that help should be concentrated on 'far from market' support, and introduced new programs such as the LINK scheme, aimed at promoting collaborative research with universities. Only small and medium sized businesses (SMEs) were to escape this rule.

1.2.2 Privatization and the rise of popular capitalism

The Conservative administrations between 1979 and 1997 will undoubtedly go down in history for their privatization policies. Yet, although Mrs. Thatcher came to office pledged to curb the rise of state power, the Conservative manifesto of 1979 contained no commitment to privatize the major public utilities. The decisive shift of policy came in 1984 with the privatization of British Telecom. It was a new strategy that emerged more by accident than design.

Until 1981, telecommunications in Britain, as in most European countries, had been run by the Post Office. The rising demand for telecommunications services and the opportunities opened by the digital revolution led, first to the separation of function within the Post Office, and then, in 1981, to the establishment of a wholly separate public corporation for telecoms, British Telecom (BT). Even in 1981 telecoms were still regarded as a classic case of natural monopoly and privatization was not considered. The problem was that in order to realize the wide opportunities opened up by the digital revolution, BT needed urgently to invest large sums in updating Britain's antiquated telecoms infrastructure and any borrowing had to be made through the Treasury and count as part of the Government's borrowing requirements.[4] Cutting the public sector borrowing requirement (PSBR) had become a key success indicator for the Conservative government. Privatization emerged as the practical solution to this dilemma: it enabled BT to go directly to the market to raise funds, while having the fortuitous side effect of bringing an unanticipated windfall into the public sector accounts (and thereby relieving other pressures on the PSBR).

Privatization finally came in 1984, when the government sold off 49 per cent of BT. At £3.5 billion, it was the largest public share offer ever handled by the London market. Fearful that it might flop, the City underwriters insisted on a simultaneous share offering in New York and Tokyo, and an extensive share promotion offer to UK customers. The exercise proved to be a dramatic success. The shares were over-subscribed, and, thanks to a formula which favored small shareholders, widely distributed amongst a population that had not previously held shares.

Thus was created one of the hall-marks of Thatcherism – popular capitalism – the spread of shareholding amongst the population based on the cheap distribution of privatized utility shares. Where BT led, others followed – gas in 1987, the water industry and electricity in 1989/90. The 1990s saw the privatization of two loss making sectors – railways and coal – both of which have continued to cause problems.

In all cases of utility privatization, initially a substantial element of monopoly remained and the industries were subject to regulators whose task was to prevent exploitation of the customer. Relationships were difficult since the regulators had to ensure that profits were high enough to fund the investment while simultaneously paving the way for the emergence of competition. This was slow to develop. It came first in telecoms where the advent of satellite and cable and then mobile facilities began to create tough competition for BT by the mid-1990s. With gas and electricity it was not until the end of the 1990s that smaller commercial and domestic purchasers were offered a choice of supplier.

A key question is whether the change from public to private ownership has brought efficiency gains. Here the evidence is mixed. Helm (1994) rightly pointed to the considerable gains in organizational efficiency stemming from clearer management roles and better practice. Newberry and Pollitt (1996), examining the social costs and benefits deriving from electricity privatization, show that the efficiency gains were largely achieved by switching away from British coal and using cheaper imports (gas and coal) to generate power. The gains to electricity consumers were paid for by the social costs of pit closures. For the utilities themselves, escaping from the Treasury financing rules opened up new financial opportunities which they have only gradually exploited. For the Government, however, with windfall gains for the PSBR, the policy represented a win-win situation – it enabled them both to finance tax cuts and, by selling shares cheaply, to put direct financial gains into voters' pockets.

1.2.3 The 1990s – policy by exhortation

The run down of industrial subsidies and the success of the privatization program meant that by the early 1990s, the Conservatives had achieved much of what they had originally set out to do: withdraw government from industrial decision-making. Their main failure was that they had not improved Britain's productivity performance, which still lagged behind that of our main competitors (see table 1.1) With a prime minister more sympathetic to industry's case came a new push towards 'competitiveness' with innovation a central plank of policy.

The problem was that the very success of the Conservatives in withdrawing from industrial issues had left a distinct gap in policy tools. The Major government issued a succession of competitiveness white papers (UK Government, 1994; 1995; 1996), strong on analysis and weak on prescription. Much was left to exhortation with three words – liberalization, privatization and de-regulation – repeated time and again. Privatization was extended to local government where the distinction between service purchaser and service provider was introduced. The mantras 'value for money' and 'standards of service' opened the door to a plethora of targets and league tables.

The deregulation agenda put emphasis on SMEs and successive attempts were made, without much success, to make bonfires of government regulations. As table 1.2 makes clear, by the mid-1990s, a good part of what was left of government support for industry was targeted at SMEs with the aim of 'helping them to help themselves'. Research had shown that the core of Britain's low productivity lay in the long tail of poorly performing SMEs. Money was channeled to SMEs through locally-based 'Business Links' to provide a few days of free consultancy in the hope that this would inspire further investments by the firm itself in both consultancy and equipment. These were top-down initiatives, run by the local offices of central government, except in Scotland, Wales and Northern Ireland, which had separate regional development agencies. On the whole, the latter were judged more successful, perhaps because they were somewhat more generously funded and often able to leverage extra resources, especially as the EU's Structural Funds grew in importance.

The other main policy area where the Conservatives took a strong, positive stance was *inward investment*. They argued that foreign companies, especially the Japanese, provided good role models with good management, high level skills' training and quality control. The government actively courted foreign investment using grants under RSA to attract major projects. In the 1980s Nissan received £112m towards the cost of its plant in Sunderland and Toyota received some £75m for its plant in Derby. In the 1990s, Ford received grants worth some £80 million towards its engine plant in South Wales, while the planned (but never completed) Lucky Goldstar plant attracted grants of £248m (House of Commons, 1998 p.13). In relation to its spending on other innovation initiatives, these sums were substantial.

The cumulative impact of foreign investment over the past 25 years was considerable. By the early 1990s the UK had become the largest recipient of foreign direct investment (FDI) after the USA, with a stock of capital exceeding £150 billion – twice that of France and Germany combined. (UK Government, 1995 p.161). In the mid 1990s foreign-owned companies operating in Britain contributed over 30 per cent of manufacturing investment and 20 per cent of manufacturing employment. While not knowingly espousing it, the Conservatives were subscribing to the philosophy of Robert Reich when he argued that the ownership of capital and technology was unimportant compared to income from the jobs it created (Reich, 1991). What they failed to understand was that to attract and keep high value-added jobs required complementary investment in human resources and the infrastructure. As a result, many of the jobs coming to Britain were low wage, low value-added jobs, highly vulnerable to cyclical swings (Keep and Mayhew, 1995).

1.3 Science policy in Britain 1975–1997

1.3.1 Science policy in the 1980s – science in a *'steady state'*[5]

To explain the developments in science policy through the 1980s and 1990s it is necessary to appreciate the functioning of the 'dual support system' for funding research in the UK. In the early 1980s the Department of Education and Science (DES) directly funded universities by block grant allocation to the University' Grants Committee (UGC) which then dispersed the funds to the universities to meet teaching needs and, in the case of research, to provide the 'infrastructure' necessary for research, funding laboratory space, equipment and tenured academic staff. In parallel, the DES also provided a block grant to each of the research councils, which in turn made research grants available on a project basis with researchers competing for project funds. Research council funding essentially met the cost of research specific to the project – the cost of any new equipment required and the salary costs of researchers employed (usually on contract). The assumption was that UGC funding would meet the overhead costs. Both the UGC and the research councils were independent of government: they received block grants and their allocation was left to the respective councils.

Tables 1.4 and 1.5 summarize developments in the UK over the period. Table 1.4 details gross national expenditures on research and development (GERD) by source of funding. It is worth noting that by 1996 the government's contribution was half the level of 1981, partly explained by cuts in defense R&D. In the 1980s defense took almost 50 per cent of government spending on R&D but this has now shrunk to 38 per cent – and since most of defense R&D is in development rather than research, these cut-backs have hit the industrial-military complex in the UK. Industry's contribution was also very disappointing, falling in the 1990s.

Table 1.4: UK – GERD as a percentage of GDP, by source of finance

	Government	Industry	Non-Profit	Total
1975	1.3	0.7	0.1	2.1
1981	1.3	1.0	0.1	2.4
1985	1.0	1.3	0.2	2.5
1990	0.7	1.1	0.3	2.1
1995	0.6	1.0	0.4	2.0
1996	0.6	0.9	0.4	1.9

Source: OECD Science and Technology Indicators.

Table 1.5 focuses on the two streams of funding coming through the dual support system. Because the statistical base has been changed rather frequently (see footnotes) the figures have to be treated with caution. The broad picture is clear enough; as a percentage of GDP, government funding of the science base fell marginally from 0.33 per cent in 1980–1 to 0.30 per cent in 1996–7.[6] This table, however, presents only half the story. The figures in all these tables relate to *research* funding, not funding for teaching. Cuts in public expenditure in the 1980s hit the universities disproportionately hard and caused the effective collapse of the dual support system. Universities could no longer be relied upon to provide the infrastructure for research. Basic equipment, technician support and even secretarial time were available only if paid for by project (i.e. research council) grants.

Table 1.5: Government funding of UK higher education R&D (in real terms – £1997/8)

	UGC/ UFC/ HEFC	Research councils	Total	1980/81 =100	Total as % GDP	HERD as % GDP[5]
1977/78	923	750	1.673	93	0.32	0.32
1980/81	1.011	771	1.782	100	0.33	0.32
1984/85	1.121[1]	902	2.023[1]	114	0.35	0.31
1987/88	1.176	9.662	10.838[2]	120	0.33	0.33
1990/91	1.072[3]	1.049	2.121[3]	120	0.31	0.31
1993/94	1.068[4]	1.252	2.320[4]	130	0.33	0.37
1996/97	1.053	1.292	2.345	132	0.30	0.38

1 1982/3 – Humanities added = +£133m.
2 1985/6 – VAT added to RC stream = approximately +£60m.
3 1988/9 – Polytechnics added to UGC/UFC/HEFC stream = approximately £30m.
4 1993/4 – New method of calculating HEFC stream – adds approximately £26m.
5 HERD – OECD definitions relate to R&D performed in higher education sector.

Source: UK Government Annual Reviews of Government R&D/SET Statistics 1987, 1990, 1994 and 1998; OECD for HERD as per cent GDP. For full run of figures see Sharp (2000) Table 1.

The impending collapse of the dual support system led to discussion about how best to allocate the scarce research funds. *A Strategy for the Science Base*, published in 1987 (ABRC, 1987), proposed grouping universities in three categories: R would be top-ranking research universities; T would be those concentrating primarily on teaching; the X group would be 'mixed' universities which had a few specialist areas of research but were mainly teaching institutions. The implication was clear; given a shortage of funds, research funding would be concentrated in the research universities.

The X, R, T proposals were thrown out after a storm of protest from the universities. But the idea did not die. Rather, it provided the basis for a new system for research fund allocation introduced by the other arm of the dual support system, the former UGC, which became the Universities' Funding Council (UFC) in 1989, and then the Higher Education Funding Councils (HEFCs) in 1993. This new system was known as the Research Assessment Exercises (RAE) and measured research performance by evaluating the comparative quality of research in different departments in terms of publications and ability to attract research grants: the higher the ranking, the greater the weighting given to the research element of the UFC grant. It has, as predicted, resulted in an increased concentration of funding in the top-flight research universities and very little for those perceived as teaching institutions.

The development of the RAE can be seen as part of a wider exercise requiring academics to 'account' for their time and activities. The Conservative government, anxious to secure 'value for money' from public expenditures put increasing emphasis on industrially-relevant research. Incentive schemes to encourage collaborative research were strengthened, including the LINK scheme already mentioned, the Teaching Company Scheme (TCS) under which academics were subsidized on an individual basis to work with a company developing a new product or process, and CASE (Cooperative Awards for Science and Engineering) studentships which provided for doctoral students to undertake research on a subject chosen by a firm. In addition an increasing proportion of funding was allocated to 'directed programs' where the research council, not the researcher, chose the topic of research. For the purists, for whom curiosity-led research selected by peer review was by definition the only route to excellence, these developments led to predictions of mediocrity. However, by the 1990s they had become voices in the wilderness. The outcome of the pressures was to increase the share of industrial funding in higher education research in the UK by the mid-1990s to over 8 per cent higher than in any other major European country and, in proportionate terms, even above US levels of funding (OECD, 1998).

Two other developments are worth noting. First, the shift of funding from big science – nuclear and astronomical/space research – to little science. By the 1980s new technologies, especially microelectronics, materials technology and biotechnology, were the new, fast-moving, exciting areas and demanded resources. New money, when it became available, went to new areas while budgets for existing projects were held constant. With inflation running at 4–5 per cent, big science saw a progressive reduction in real terms funding.

Secondly, the growth of European programs by the end of the 1980s began to make an impact on British universities. Britain was second after

France in the number of participations in the Third Framework Program (1989–1993) and top in the Fourth (1994–1998), with higher education establishments the most active sector. Precise figures are not available, but government estimates suggest that by 1996–7 the total contribution of the EU amounted to some £370 million,[7] or about 10 per cent of total government expenditure on civilian R&D (rising from 4 per cent in 1986–7). These figures include support for industrial innovation, but given the active role played by UK universities in successive Framework Programs, it seems reasonable to suggest that by the mid-1990s some 10 per cent of the research being undertaken in UK universities was benefiting from EU sponsorship.

By the early of the 1990s, therefore, a number of trends were apparent: increasing strain on the dual support system; the rise in selectivity (rationing); growing demands for accountability and relevance; and the shift from 'big' to 'little' science. In addition, European science and technology programs were beginning to have some impact. These trends combined to create considerable pressures on the existing institutions of science in the UK. To accommodate them new structures were necessary. The 1990s saw these put in place.

1.3.2 The 1990s – the Waldegrave Report and its effects

The new Conservative administration led by John Major, which took over from Margaret Thatcher in late 1990, was instinctively more sympathetic to science. After the General Election of April 1992, Major created the Office of Science and Technology (OST) with its Minister, William Waldegrave, in the Cabinet. Besides having overall responsibility for science, the OST also took over responsibility for the Research Councils from the Department for Education and Science (DES). It was the first time there had been a voice for science in the Cabinet since 1963 and this in itself was seen as a significant advance, even if the experiment lasted only three years. In 1995, OST was subsumed within the DTI.

Waldegrave's first move as the new Minister for Science was to set in hand a substantial consultation process. Its results were presented in a report entitled *Realizing our Potential: A Strategy for Science, Engineering and Technology* (UK Government, 1993). The report put forward a series of reforms, which in some respects seemed little more than re-ordering and clarifying the roles of the research councils. In the event, the reforms proved more far reaching. What had been a largely self-governing system of science was made subject to clear ministerial control, and embedded within a departmental hierarchy.

Three sets of reforms followed:

1. *The reorganization of the research councils* – the research councils were re-organized to recognize the importance of biotechnology and the life sciences. A knock-on effect was the break up of the former SERC and the separation of 'big science' from 'little science'. The reforms also brought a clear line of command by establishing a Director General for the Research Councils in OST with overall responsibility for their performance. In addition, all research councils acquired mission statements stressing the importance of gearing research to industrial needs.

2. *The foresight exercise* – with the rapid development of new technologies, many countries had conducted Foresight exercises. Waldegrave argued that now was the time for Britain to do the same. Fifteen Foresight panels were set up in areas such as materials, chemistry, food and drink, financial services and communications. Their task was to identify areas where new developments in science and technology were opening up new market opportunities and challenges from competitors. In the minds of those who conceived it the 'process' of Foresight, as much as the message, was important (Martin, 1995). The hope was that involvement would encourage industrial participants to think long term and strategically and, crucially, to increase their spending on R&D. Sadly this did not happen.[8] Foresight did, however, have an impact upon the academic sector. In the aftermath of the White Paper there was a noticeable switch towards more industrially relevant and directed programs – by 1996/7 80 per cent of Research Council funds were going to 'oriented' basic research or applied projects.[9] New initiatives such as Foresight Challenge and the 'Realizing Our Potential Awards' (ROPAs) all channeled research towards industrial relevance.

3. *The privatization of the public research establishments* – the third initiative stemming from the Waldegrave Report was the setting up of an 'efficiency scrutiny' of public sector research establishments (PSREs) which in effect looked to privatizing any which could stand alone. The DTI pushed ahead with plans for privatizing the National Engineering Laboratory, the National Physical Laboratory and the Laboratory of the Government Chemist – all 19th century foundations which had long provided core government scientific services. Freeing

> these establishments from the constraints of public sector status was seen as a major advantage, enabling them to build links with a wider range of 'customers'. The reverse was to leave the government largely dependent on outside scientific research and advice. In 1995, Sir Robert May, Chief Scientific Adviser, conceded that spending cuts in the Ministry of Agriculture in the early 1990s had probably damaged that department's scientific capability at a time when public concern over BSE was rising (Independent, 2 May 1996).

The overall result was more revolutionary than appeared. The research councils were separated from the education ministry and implanted within the department responsible for innovation. Clear priority was given to industrially relevant research. Finally, and, perhaps most significantly, Directors General were appointed with responsibility for both the university and the research council funding streams, each embedded within their respective departmental structures and accountable to ministers. At the same time public sector research establishments were sold off or contracted out. By the end of the 1990s the relative autonomy of the university research sector, a marked feature of the post-war science system, had largely disappeared.

1.4 Science, technology and industrial policy under new labor

How far have things changed with the New Labor government elected in May 1997? They appeared to take the innovation agenda seriously. A new innovation unit was established in the Treasury and successive budget statements have highlighted Britain's productivity gap and the importance of innovation in closing that gap. Five key 'drivers' of productivity performance were identified: investment in physical capital; enterprise and innovation; education and skills; competition and regulation; and public sector productivity (HM Treasury, 1999a). Nevertheless, in spite of their seeming understanding of the issues and recognition of the vital role played by innovation, it is questionable whether Labor have really come up with the new ideas necessary to reform Britain's innovation record. In particular their insistence on following the previous Conservative spending plans for the first two years of their administration (1997–1999) provided remarkably little leeway for new initiatives and prolonged unnecessarily the squeeze on the science budget and much needed renewal of the scientific infrastructure.[10] It was not until the 1999 Comprehensive Spending Review

(HM Treasury, 1998) that new money for science and technology began to make its impact, and much of that new money was dedicated to the renewal of buildings and equipment through a special £800 million Joint Infrastructure Fund established with the Welcome Foundation.[11] Table 1.6 shows how little new spending has in fact been injected into the science, technology and innovation budgets. In real terms spending in 1999/2000 was no higher than in 1995, with the new money, most of it as indicated for capital renewal, only beginning to come through in 2000 and 2001.

Looking at the broader spectrum of measures to promote innovation, there are again many similarities between the policies pursued by the Conservatives in their 'policy by exhortation' period of the mid-1990s and those of New Labor. This is well illustrated in table 1.7 which contrasts the measures put forward in the 1995 Competitiveness White Paper (UK Government, 1995) with measures introduced by New Labor in their Budget (HM Treasury, 2000) and Science and Technology White Paper (OST, 2000) of the year 2000. A glance at the table establishes immediately that New Labor have been more active than their Conservative counterparts in proposing measures, but a more detailed comparison reveals the similarities. Under the *Enterprise and Innovation* heading, for example, the emphasis remains on university/industry links and a succession of 'challenge funds' which require universities and their partners to bid for a limited pot of finance and in most cases bidders to raise co-funding from the private sector. Under SMEs, the most significant new measure is the R&D tax credit, a reform the Treasury had long resisted. The other major innovation under New Labor has been the establishment in England of regional development agencies (RDAs) with (some) recognition of the need for local links with SMEs. But thinking is still centralist: the Treasury controls finances and the RDAs are given little leeway. The new Small Business Service (a conversion of the Conservative Business Links initiative), for example, is run not by the RDAs but by central government regional offices.

Table 1.6: Net government expenditure on science, engineering and technology 1995–2001 in real terms (£m 1999 prices)

	1995/ 1996	1996/ 1997	1997/ 1998	1998/ 1999	1999/ 2000	2000/ 2001	2001/ 2002
RCs	1.368	1.345	1.331	1.346	1.424	1.476	1.501
HEFCs	1.075	1.053	1.033	1.046	1.098	1.145	1.187
DTI	399	365	343	314	324	343	341
of which innovation	187	179	179	180	194	223	230
Total	2.842	2.763	2.707	2.706	2.846	2.964	3.029

Source: 1999 Forward Look (DTI, 1999).

The biggest contrast between Conservative and New Labor thinking is to be seen in education and training. Labor have introduced a series of initiatives aimed at getting the unemployed (and unskilled) into work and/or training. They have targeted in particular the young unemployed, many of them school drop-outs, and this, combined with an attempt to overhaul the vocational education and training system will, they hope, turn around the crucial skills gap. They also put much emphasis on improving school and college standards with a proliferation of performance targets and tough inspection systems. Once again all these moves are led by central government with local authorities and RDAs largely excluded. Like the Conservatives, Labor are putting faith in the private sector, which has for so long been a free rider on training, changing its ways and leading the revolution.

Britain's long term failure to recognize the importance of skill training is probably the most important factor explaining its poor productivity performance. In other respects, the agenda has really changed remarkably little. Thanks to the Wellcome Foundation, the backlog of funding for the science infrastructure is now being addressed, and a small amount of new money is at last beginning to trickle through to research budgets. As a whole, however, the higher education sector has not seen new money from New Labor and university budgets and salaries remain as tightly controlled as under the Conservatives.

Table 1.7: A comparison between conservative and new labor innovation policies

Conservative policies in the mid-1990s	New labor policies in 2000
Enterprise and innovation	**Enterprise and innovation**
Enhance SMART and SPUR schemes (approx £15M p.a.). Build on existing LINK scheme (approx £20m p.a.). Expand Teaching Company Scheme (TCS) (£10m p.a.). Build on Technology Foresight. Introduce Foresight Challenge (£25m). Extend ROPA awards to encourage university-industry science links. Enterprise in HE scheme to encourage entrepreneurial education.	Extend HEROIC (Higher Education Reach Out Into the Community) initiative – £20m p.a. to encourage university links with local industry. Establish new Foresight Fund (£15m). Fund one further round of University Challenge (£15 m p.a.) for early stage funding for research with commercial potential. Extend science enterprise challenge (£ 25 m p.a.) to encourage universities to commercialize research. Extend faraday partnerships between academic research and specialist research organizations. Expand Teaching Company (+£9m) and SMART (+£ 26 m) schemes.
Small and medium sized enterprises	**Small and medium sized enterprises**
Ease capital gains tax on small business. Promote Enterprise Investment Scheme (EIS) giving extra tax breaks on personal investments in new ventures. Stimulate Alternative Investment Market (AIM). Expand (government financed) Business Links consultancy scheme. Maintain Small Firms Loan Guarantee Fund.	R&D tax credit for SMEs on expenditures up to £0.5 m. Tax reliefs on management share options and employee share ownership schemes to encourage start-up firms. Measures to encourage serial (successive) investments through EIS. Venture Capital Challenge (£20m) to encourage the provision of funds for early stage start-ups.

Keep up pressure on banks to make loan finance available to SMEs on more favorable terms.	Tax reliefs for corporate venturing (i.e. big company investments in start-ups). Small Business Service to replace Business Links as 'one stop shop' for SMEs. Cruikshank Report condemns banks' role for SMEs. Support for SMEs to get on-line (£60m). 'Umbrella' fund to encourage investment in regional clusters (£100m to RDAs to help leverage further £900m from private sources).
Education and Training	**Education and Training**
Set national targets for achievements at ages 16, 18 and 21. Use OFSTED to improve school standards. Expand Investors In People (IIP) awards for high quality training. Introduce career development loans. Expand Modern Apprenticeships through Training and Enterprise Councils (TECs). Use TECs to promote skills for SMEs.	Targets for literacy and numeracy in schools. National Curriculum to encourage school links with enterprise. Extend OFSTED to FE sector. Introduction Individual Learning Accounts (ILAs) with discounts on course fees for those pursuing training. (National) Learning and skills council (LSC) and local LSCs to take over from TECs and combine with training responsibilities with those for FE. New deal for young people and connexions service to bring unemployed young people into work and training. Establishment University for Industry (UfI) (distance learning for management skills).

Sources: Conservative Policies derived from the 1995 Competitiveness White Paper (UK Government, 1995). New Labor Policies derived from the Budget Red Book (HM Treasury: 2000) and the Science and Technology White Paper Excellence and Opportunity, published in July 2000 (OST, 2000).

It is too early yet to judge how far the New Labor innovation agenda will be successful. Much depends on the education and training initiatives where in relation to industry and small business, the emphasis remains on encouraging self-help and enterprise, with particular emphasis on new technology start-ups. The newly established RDAs for the English regions, however, have little power and less money. Generally speaking, for all the rhetoric, there has been only modest change.

1.5 Conclusions

This paper has sought to describe the parallel development over the last 20 years in Britain of, on the one hand, industrial and technology policy, and, on the other, science policy. It has mapped the rapid run-down of industrial intervention in the 1980s; the emergence of privatization and the rise of popular capitalism; the growing importance to Britain of inwards investment from global multinationals; and the growing consensus in Britain about the need to promote a more entrepreneurial society. It has described the shift of policy away from large firms towards small, and from science towards technology; and how, when liberalization and deregulation ruled the industrial agenda, the search for relevance and accountability had the opposite effect in the world of academic science and brought instead a plethora of bureaucratic controls and performance indicators. The advent of New Labor for the last three years of the century has to date made little difference. New money has belatedly been injected into updating the buildings and equipment of academic science and greater emphasis is at last being put on education and skills. But essentially New Labor have accepted and reinforced the innovation agenda developed by the Conservatives in the 1990s.

In many respects this innovation agenda mirrors developments in other OECD countries, indeed the influence of OECD is written across it. But there are also important national variations, reflecting the different traditions and institutions in each country. An important part of the British agenda has been the degree to which it has been 'top down', dictated and implemented by central government. While the focus may have shifted to small firms, it was the national government that introduced and orchestrated the initiatives, focusing perhaps too much on venture capital and high tech start-ups to the detriment of the majority of low tech small firms. Again university-industry links have emerged as a result of the top-down agenda imposed on universities rather than, as in the US, growing organically from below. This is an important distinction and helps to explain why British initiatives have found it difficult to take root, for there is little sense of 'ownership' in such policies.

In the introduction to this chapter it was suggested that the British policy response had been unique and more radical than in other countries. Certainly, as illustrated in the second section of the chapter, the shift from intervention to non-intervention was rapid and pervasive. The two really radical policies to emerge over these 20 years were, on the one hand, privatization, and, on the other, the 'hands on' involvement (nationalization?) by government in science policy.

Privatization, as was made clear, emerged almost by mistake, but proved to be one of the 'big ideas' dominating the 1990s. In ideological terms it was swimming with the tide, representing as it did a rejection of all things associated with socialism. In practical terms, it represented as much a popular condemnation of government failure as a questioning of market failure (although in its aftermath there has been a considerable questioning of how far market failures really existed in public utility sectors). Governments had proved themselves too weak in the face of producer interests to be trusted to run large industries effectively. A new set of public intermediaries, the regulators, was required. Institutional change and ideological change went hand in hand.

The 'nationalization' of science policy, while representing a marked switch of policy, was more incremental in implementation. Again there were ideological overtones. The Conservative government of Mrs. Thatcher distrusted academics who, for their part, made little effort to disguise their distrust of her.[12] But there were wide issues at stake. One was accountability. The science budget had by the 1980s grown to around £3 billion and, in a world where public sector expenditure outlays were being examined and questioned in detail, was it right that scientists should continue to exercise autonomy over their own expenditures? Another was the gradual loss of trust by the public in science and scientists. This was to come to a head in Britain in the 1990s in the BSE crisis, in which Ministers used scientific advice as a scapegoat for policy blunders. But earlier incidents in relation to salmonella in chickens and eggs, nuclear power and, not least, the growing debate over genetic engineering had already begun to erode the public's faith in scientific advice. It was not surprising in the circumstances to find the politicians anxious to exert more control.

Finally, it is worth coming back to the question put in the introduction. The UK government, by adopting radical changes in policy at a time when it faced far-reaching challenges within the global environment, was embarking on an experiment. Has it worked? On the face of it, the answer would appear to be 'no'. Trend productivity growth has remained obstinately below that of Britain's competitors and, in spite of all the bullish talk of the new economy, the depressing R&D record of British industry at a time when profits have been running at record levels gives little cause for optimism. There is little doubt that the British economy is now one of the most 'flexible' in Europe – the trade unions have but a shadow of their former strength, national wage bargaining is rapidly disappearing even in the public sector, large parts of industry contract out all but core functions. Britain has also developed a strong venture capital industry and sports more start-up firms in new technology sectors than the other European economies of comparable size.

Why then the poor productivity record? Two possible explanations suggest themselves. First, changes in policy were too 'one-dimensional' and failed to recognize the operation of a 'system of innovation'. In particular, Conservative failures to tackle the endemic problems of skill training or to invest in the science and technology infrastructure (remarkable oversights given their faith in inward investment), will cast a long shadow over current prospects. It has yet to be seen whether new initiatives will be sufficient to make good the deficiencies. Secondly, British experience illustrates well how difficult it is to effect change by changing institutions without simultaneously winning 'hearts and minds'. Britain's 'top down' SME policy, designed at the center for implementation at the local level, is a good example, failing as it does to involve those affected by the changes. Likewise, many of the changes experienced in the education sector have been imposed from the top rather than being allowed to emerge from below. Sadly, to date, New Labor's record indicates that they are no different.

Notes

1 This section and the next section (3) are drawn from a longer and more detailed paper on UK policy. See Sharp (2000).

2 Mainly because at a time of rising unemployment they provided so few jobs. See House of Commons (1977).

3 See 1988 White Paper – UK Government (1988).

4 Under rules concocted by the British Treasury in the 1950s when they were anxious to maintain control over the gilts market. Over time these rules extended to all public sector borrowing, including local authorities. It meant that all borrowing by any public authority

in Britain had to be channeled through the Treasury and counted against the public sector borrowing requirement (PSBR).

5 This is derived from the phrase coined by Ziman (1987) to describe the shift from the pre-1980 period when science budgets had been growing at 3–4 per cent per annum to the 1 per cent per annum growth in the 1980s.

6 OECD figures show the share of HERD actually rising from 0.32 per cent to 0.38 per cent over the same period. These figures however relate to the amount of research being performed in the academic sector, they therefore reflect both the increase in non-profit and industrial financing of research in the UK. They do not show, as does the previous column, the actual proportion of government funding of the science base.

7 This figure is quoted in the 1999 Forward Look (DTI 1999) as the sum 'attributed' to UK expenditures under the EU RTD programs. Under Treasury rules all UK expenditures on EU programs have to be attributed to departmental budgets. Assuming that the UK receives approximately the same sum as it spends, this attributed expenditure would seem to provide a reasonably good estimate of actual expenditures.

8 These hopes have not been fulfilled. The CBI NatWest Innovation Trends Survey in 1996 suggested that a surprising number of businesses were not aware of the Foresight exercise. See House of Lords, 1997.

9 Because definitions changed in 1994–5, it is not possible to make precise comparisons with earlier years. In 1986/7, 50.2 per cent of research was assigned to the Frascati basic category (including both pure and oriented research) and 49.8 per cent to applied categories (DTI, 1998: Table 1.3, 1.4).

10 In their final year of government, in order to help limit the level of public expenditure, the Conservatives had taken some £350 million of capital expenditure (approx. £50 m a year) from the science budget stating that it would be funded instead through the private finance initiative (PFI). As expected, it proved extremely difficult to find private sector backers for such expenditures (mainly building and equipment for university science laboratories) and the result was to delay yet further the already urgent replacement of such equipment (see HM Treasury 1998).

11 The Wellcome Foundation in 1998 offered to put £400 million into renewing the science infrastructure provided it was matched by a similar sum from the government (See HM Treasury 1998). Whether credit for the initiative should go to the Government or the Wellcome Foundation is a moot point.

12 In a famous incident in 1984 Mrs. Thatcher was refused an honorary degree in a ballot of academics at Oxford. Ox ford was her own university and it was customary for serving Prime Ministers to be awarded honorary degrees. But uniquely among British universities, the award of an honorary degree depended not just on the approval of the university senate but on a ballot of university members and they rejected her by 738 votes to 319. According to Hugo Young (1989, Chapter 18) she never really forgave the academic profession for this insult.

References

ABRC (1987): A Strategy for the Science Base, London, HMSO.

Crafts, N./O'Mahony (1999): 'Long Run Trends in Productivity', The New Economy, Vol 6, Issue 1.

DTI (1991) (and subsequent years): The UK R&D Scoreboard. 1991, Company Reporting Ltd, 68 Dundas St, Edinburgh EH3 6QZ.

DTI (1998): Science, Engineering and Technology Statistics, CM 4006, London, HMSO.

DTI (1999): The Forward Look – 1999: Government Funded Science, Engineering and Technology, CM4363, London, HMSO.

DTI (2000): Excellence and Opportunity: a Science and Innovation Policy for the 21st Century. Cm 4814, London HMSO.

Economist (1996): Article on Lucky Goldstar Investments in Wales, 12 December.

Helm, D. (1994): 'British Utility Regulation: Theory, Practice and Reform' Oxford Review of Economic Policy. Vol 10 No 3.

HM Treasury (1998): Comprehensive Spending Review – Modern Public Services for Britain Cm 4011 London. The Stationery Office.

HM Treasury (1999a): Budget 99: Building a Stronger Economic Future for Britain. HC 298 London. The Stationery Office.

HM Treasury (1999b): Trend Growth: Prospects and Implications for Policy. HM Treasury. November. London. The Stationery Office.

HM Treasury (2000): Budget 2000: Prudent for a Purpose: Working for a Stronger and Fairer Britain. HC346 London The Stationery Office.

House of Commons (1977): Third Report Public Accounts Committee. Regional Investment Allowances Session 1977/8 London HMSO.

House of Commons (1998): Third Report of Welsh Affairs Committee, 'The Welsh Office Departmental Report', HC 751 1997/8, London, HMSO.

House of Lords (1997): Innovation Exploitation Barrier, Select Committee on Science and Technology, Report HL62, Session 1996–7, London, HMSO.

Keep, E./Mayhew, K. (1995): 'Training for Competitiveness: Time for a New Persepctive', in: Metcalfe, S. (ed.): Skill Demand and Supply, London, Policy Studies Institute.

Martin, B. R. (1995): 'Foresight in Science and Technology', Technology Analysis and Strategic Management, Vol 7, No 2, pp 139–168.

Newberry, D. M./Pollitt, M. G. (1996): The Restructuring and Privatization of the CEGB: was it Worth it?, Department of Applied Economics Working Paper No. 9607, University of Cambridge.

OST – Office of Science and Technology (1999): Forward Look of Government – Funded Science, Engineering and Technology. Cm 4363 The Stationery Office. 1999.

Reich, R. (1991): The Work of Nations, Knopf, New York.

Sharp, M. (2000): The UK Experiment – Science, Technology and Industrial Policy in Britain 1979–1997. Paper prepared for the Triple Helix Conference. Rio de Janeiro. April 2000. Mimeo obtainable from SPRU, University of Sussex. Brighton. BN1 9RF. UK.

UK Government (1988): The DTI – The Department for Enterprise, Cmnd 278, London, HMSO.

UK Government (1993): Realising our Potential: A Strategy for Science, Engineering and Technology, the Waldegrave Report, CM 2250, London, HMSO.

UK Government (1994): Competitiveness: Helping Business to Win, Cmnd 2563, London, HMSO.

UK Government (1995): Competitiveness: Forging Ahead, Cmnd 2867, London, HMSO.

UK Government (1996): Competitiveness: Creating the Enterprise Centre for Europe, Cmnd 3300, London, HMSO.

UK Government (1997): The Governments' Expenditure Plans 1998–1999, CM3905, London, HMSO.

Wren, C. (1996a): Industrial Subsidies: the UK Experience, London, Macmillan.

Wren, C. (1996b): 'Grant Equivalent Expenditure on Industrial Subsidies in the Post-War UK, Oxford Bulletin of Economics and Statistics, Vol 58, No 2, pp 317–351.

Young, H. (1989): One of Us: a Biography of Margaret Thatcher, London, Macmillan.

Ziman, J. (1987): Science in a 'Steady State': the Research System in Transition, The Science Policy Support Group, London.

Chapter 2

Public Venture Capital: The Secret Life of US Science Policy

Henry Etzkowitz

2.1 Introduction

The U.S. has a knowledge-based industrial policy, a specific role for the federal government in creating and developing industries and jobs, beyond general measures to encourage economic health such as regulating the supply of money and credit. More specific than macro-economic policy for the entire economy, industrial policy is also broader than a measure cloaked in general principles to aid a particular company. When industrial policy is defined as, '...a nation's declared, official, total effort to influence sectoral development,' an American industrial development program may be difficult to recognize (Graham, 1992). While the very idea of government providing 'seed capital' to initiate new firms is anathema to some, a 'public venture capital' strategy can be discerned in post-war U.S. science policy.

Science-based industrial policy takes place on three levels. The first is the formulation of a legitimating theme to guide action, such as the 1945 report Science: the Endless Frontier (Bush, 1945). The second is the creation of a regulatory framework such as the 1980 Amendment to the Patent and Trademark Law, the Bayh-Dole Act, devolving intellectual property rights generated from federally funded research to the universities. The third is the provision of public venture capital to initiate or help grow new firms. Until quite recently, industrial policy referred to support of existing industries, especially those in decline. To save jobs, government might subsidize relocation, equipment and training costs or reduce taxes to address company problems. In many countries industrial policy primarily takes place through direct assistance to traditional industrial sectors and their member firms. The U.S. has taken an alternative approach of assisting the formation of high-tech firms, as well as helping older firms upgrade their technology. Science policy has had a 'secret life' as industrial policy, giving it a new meaning associated with future economic growth.

This chapter argues that 'public venture capital,' the various programs that have been created over the past thirty years to help move technology from research into use, tend to follow a distinctive format, typically involving the university as an intermediary between government and industry. Industry defined as 'small business,' fewer than 500 employees in a firm, is an acceptable target, rather than large corporations that, with notable exceptions, are expected to fend for themselves. The involvement of the university in industrial policy serves two purposes: it deflects ideological opposition to direct government industry relations and, more importantly, it brings longer term, discontinuous technologies, derived from academic research to the market.

2.2 The secret life of US science policy

The United States is often said not to have an industrial or innovation policy, a specific role for the federal government in creating new industries or reviving old ones. Instances such as the bailout of the Chrysler Auto Company in the 1980s were soon forgotten when the resuscitated firm publicized its CEO, Lee Iacocca, as its patriotic savior but then merged into Daimler/Chrysler. Such is the strength of business ideology in the U.S. that the role of government in encouraging innovation is usually not fully recognized. Indeed, many believe that the 1990s economic resurgence was wholly a private sector phenomenon fueled by private venture capital.

Behind the private investment in the development of a biotechnology industry lay decades of public support for biomedical research at universities. The story of the Internet's origins in a Department of Defense communications project during the 1950s and 1960s, that was taken the last steps toward commercialization by the National Science Foundation in the late 1980s and early 1990s, is well known. Nevertheless, the 'private' tip of the iceberg is more credited than the 'public' base of the glacier. The role of universities as an engine of economic growth is becoming increasingly recognized, even when it is attacked as inappropriate. Academic acceptance of government funding for research was an important change in government-university relations from the pre-war to the post-war. However, Vannevar Bush's objective, the promotion of integration between research and utilization was largely lost outside the realms of military, space and health research. Apart from the academic acceptance of government research support, the civilian innovation system was largely unchanged in the early post-war. It was difficult, if not impossible, to institute technological innovations in industries such as housing. Nevertheless, a financial innovation, low cost loans to veterans created sufficient demand to transform suburban housing construction from craft to batch processing production during the post-war. However, research was out of the loop and traditional disconnects between government, university and industry persisted.

Nevertheless, the 1945 Endless Frontier Report represented a turning point in U.S. Science policy. The report legitimated an active role for government in practice while rejecting it in theory. Vannevar Bush, the head of the Office of Scientific Research and Development, created for the duration of the World War II, hoped to resolve the potential contradiction between government support and scientific autonomy during the post-war that had previously led to scientists rejection of federal monies. He united the power of federal funding resources with the private foundation model of peer review developed before the war. However, instead of disbursing private resource to a public end, public resources were to be distributed by private actors, the members of the scientific community. The Endless Frontier model created a 'principal/agent' dilemma over whether the internal democracy of science could substitute for traditional democratic processes. In a recent debate on federal funding of science, a Senator expressed amazement that a funding disbursement arrangement had been established that was seemingly beyond the control of Congress. Of course, there was the important exception of how much resources were to be allocated to the purpose, a hidden issue as long as resources were increasing. Perhaps one reason U.S. S&T policy has tended to focus on the issue of R&D funding is that this had become the only acceptable point of political intervention in the policy process, at least according to the initial version of the Endless Frontier as a linear model.

The original assumption of the linear model is that if you pour in the funding at one end, knowledge comes out at the other and will be picked up by industry. In this mode, government, university and industry exist as relatively separate spheres. Government funds university research. Universities produce knowledge. Industry utilizes it. However, by the late 1960s, it was realized that there was a gap between the knowledge being produced and it being taken up and utilized, which became known after the Biblical image as 'the valley of death.' The Valley of Death is the space in between where traditional public research funding programs leave off and where the market and private venture capital is supposed to pick up.

An appropriate role for government in addressing various 'gaps' has been an issue since, especially given the reluctance in the U.S. to have government directly intervene in the 'private sector.' The European, Korean and Japanese models exemplify direct industrial policy, and at times it is the U.S. model too. For example, the Defense Advanced Research Projects Agency (DARPA) was founded in the aftermath of Sputnik when the perceived technology gap was considered too important not to address directly. Although the U.S. considered an industrial policy of government interfacing directly with industry, it largely rejected that strategy, at least with respect to civilian industry during the Carter administration in the late 1970s. The Advanced Technology Program (ATP), begun as a very small experiment in the late 1980s, is an apparent exception. The ATP grew rapidly during the early years of the Clinton administration and then was sharply reduced when the Republican Party took control of Congress in 1994. The ATP initially emphasized funding consortia, involving several large and small firms, sometimes coordinated by a non-profit research organization. The ATP was seen as subsidizing the research projects of large firms that they could well afford to undertake on their own or perhaps had declined to fund internally. One reason for the establishment of the ATP was to insure that U.S. firms did not move their R&D to Europe to take advantage of the European Union Framework Programs, offering matching funds. Nevertheless, the ATP soon ran into a strong ideological backlash, attacks from the left and the right that it was a form of corporate welfare. These attacks left the ATP in a precarious position even through it emphasized the extent of its involvement with small firms and undertook an initiative to reach less R&D intensive parts of the country.

In 2001, at the advent of the Bush Jr. administration, funding was again cut severely but the ATP was also reorganized as a university-industry program. Previously, universities were allowed to be part of ATP consortia or subcontractors on individual grants.

Under the new requirements, emphasizing the early development of high-risk cutting edge technology, rather than previous objectives such as the transfer of technology from high tech to medium tech industries, all projects must have university partners. The new ATP focus of developing technology collaboratively with academic partners also served to lessen the ideological objection to ATP as a government led industrial program. The new ATP format now coincides with other public venture capital programs, emphasizing small business and university initiated technologies. Following the linear innovation model, but instead of having research only go out from the university through publication, it moves out through consultation, which may take place informally between a professor and former students now located in industry or through formal arrangements organized by a liaison office. Moving from knowledge to technology, intellectual property rights may be put into the form of a patent and licensed by a technology transfer office. Finally, the knowledge and the technology put together with an entrepreneur and made into a firm and sent out form the university through its incubator facility. We have an evolution and differentiation of university-industry relations with all of these modes in place simultaneously.

2.3 The renewal of the linear model

What could be accomplished, in accord with ideological prescriptions, was an indirect policy of government going through the universities to reach industry. This approach is exemplified by the passage of the Bayh-Dole Act, turning over the intellectual property rights from federally funded research to universities. For decades previously, these rights had been building up, relatively unutilized. It was possible as an individual school sign an agreement to transfer over a particular invention to a firm. However, there was a 'free rider' problem. Since these rights were officially owned by the government, many firms felt that even if they could get that agreement, they would think, 'What if I have a great success? Another firm may come along and say, your innovation was funded with taxpayer monies. Why shouldn't I have the rights to it also.' The first firm, thinking of this possibility, then would decide it was too risky to get involved and therefore decide not to make an investment in developing university originated technology. Therefore, the initial firm did not act in the face of this 'free rider' dilemma.

Thus, there was a blockage in the system. The research building up, that was potentially useful, wasn't being put to use. Through a modification to the intellectual property system assigning these rights to the university, ownership was clarified and responsibility was assigned for seeing that these rights were put to use. Since the passage of the Bayh-Dole Act there has been an efflorescence not only of university patenting but also of firm formation activity spreading from a few universities, that were significantly involved prior to the passage of the amendment to the Patent and Trademark Act, across the academic system. The next steps after the establishment of a legitimating theme and regulatory framework are organizational mechanisms to translate intellectual property into economic activity. Various organizational innovations have been introduced into the universities to accomplish this purpose, including technology transfer offices and incubator facilities. In the next section, I shall examine an innovation on the government side, public venture capital. Public Venture Capital Public venture capital comprises various government programs, at the federal state and local levels, which provide funds to entrepreneurs and innovative firms to help them realize economic gain from scientific and technological advance. The federal and state sponsors of public venture capital expect to realize returns for society, in the long term, through new jobs created and new tax returns generated. Although a newly proposed amendment to the NIH Appropriations Act requests the Agency to plan for a more direct return, the federal government has largely abstained from acting as a for profit investor, allowing it to take a longer range view. State government programs, on the other hand, sometimes expect equity in exchange for their investment and operate closer to the private venture capital model, both in time frame and in the making of investment decisions. Public venture capital, in either case, represents a shift from the Endless Frontier model that relied on a self-propelling dynamic of scientific and technological advance to achieve economic growth to a more hands-on approach. While holding to the original premise of activating a science base, it provided a means to bring the technologies that emerged into use. However, the provision of public venture capital can seldom be done directly in the US since it is not believed that government should pick winners. Thus, most public venture capital is made available through programs overtly designed to support scientific research and technological innovation.

However, entrepreneurs have found that these programs can serve dual purposes, product development and marketing as well as research and dissemination. In some cases, such as SBIR, it was the underlying intention of the program founders, if not part of the official announcement to encourage technical entrepreneurship (Etzkowitz, Gulbrandsen and Levitt, 2000). Public venture capital is available through a variety of programs, with initials like (SBIR, ATP, COSSI) that, whether directly intended for the purpose or not, are utilized by knowledgeable entrepreneurs to help fund their start-ups. The federal government gave out $1.2 billion in FY 1999 in R&D funds targeted directly at small firms through its Small Business Innovation Research Program (SBIR). An additional $250 million in pre-competitive research funds was available through the Advanced Technology Program (ATP). Small business has been successful in winning approximately half of the ATP funds in the recent past. The Small Business Administration (SBA) guarantees several billions in loans to small firms each year, although technology firms have problems in accessing these funds. Through the Manufacturing Extension Partnership (MEP), government provides funding for subsidized consulting services to small businesses, delivered through regional and local offices. Through the Cooperative Research and Development Agreements (CRADAS) approximately 700 government laboratories are available as partners on R&D projects to which government can make in-kind contributions of researchers time and equipment. However, 70 laboratories actually undertake most of the partnerships. The Defense Advanced Research Projects Agency (DARPA) spends $2 billion each year on developing advanced technology with military relevance.

There are also various programs, primarily in the Department of Defense (DOD), such as Act II and Mantech, that provide other funding opportunities to take completed R&D work the next step toward production. The National Science Foundation (NSF) currently has an experimental program SBIR 2b, that provides matching funds, 2 parts private to one party government (current maximum is $100,000), for successful Phase 2 awardees who qualify. Dual use programs in various R&D agencies in the DOD offer opportunities to demonstrate the usefulness of civilian technologies to the military and vice versa.

SBIR, a 2 per cent 'tax' on the research programs of agencies that spend more than a certain amount on research, continues to grow in accordance with the increase in R&D spending of its sponsoring agencies. SBIR is set up on the model of applying for basic research grants. However, a startup can also use these funds as the initial capital to start a firm by funding research that doubles as product development or can soon be extended into it. Contrary to the private model it may seem that there is no one to guide the firm. However, SBIR program officers have taken on the mentoring role and are 'hands on' and nurturing in providing advice, much as traditional venture capitalists.

2.3.1 State venture capital

Another development, not new but continuing, is the trend toward increase in state funded S&T programs, currently at the $3.5 billion level. State government programs to assist entrepreneurs and innovative firms. These programs are typically targeted at the needs and special opportunities for technology development within their borders. Many state programs offer entrepreneurs assistance, including small grants, to develop projects that can become eligible for larger federal grants. State programs also help entrepreneurs meet needs for 'bridge' funding which fills gaps in federal programs.

Perhaps, most importantly, in line with state responsibilities for promoting local economic growth and job creation, states can more readily assist entrepreneurs whose projects are closer to the market. This focus on business development complements the virtue of federal programs whose mandate is often targeted at longer range more research-oriented projects. States typically orient their programs to expand research centers at local universities in areas with potential for economic development or to assist entrepreneurs to start businesses in fields which the state wishes to promote.

2.3.2 Public and private venture capital

Public venture capital is rarely the government acting in a similar format to a private venture capitalist. In the U.S. public venture capital programs, government does not usually play a direct role in making decisions. Public venture capital typically is given out by peer review, although peers may include industry experts as well as researchers. There is limited input from program officers, with the exception of some military related programs where a direct role for government is acceptable. Most public venture capital follows a similar application format as a government research grant. Indeed, most of the programs are offshoots of research programs.

Public Venture Capital is typically given out as a grant or contract, with no equity taken. In the US SBIR program an individual can apply for a grant, without having yet formed a firm. An applicant can be in their job at a corporate or academic research laboratory, apply for a grant, get the first grant and even start work on it before even having to think of starting a firm. Much riskier and longer term projects can be funded, especially through the grant format. In Europe where it is much more acceptable for government to play a direct role in supporting industry, there is a tendency to deal with existing firms. It that it is expected that if a firm receives money from government, it should provide matching funding. The effect of this requirement is that only existing, usually large companies can afford to apply for funds. Public venture capital typically follows a basic research funding model where the idea is to support something that is new and risky by definition, even if this concept is not always followed in practice.

Nevertheless, it represents a clear alternative to private venture capital where the focus is on a new wrinkle on a proven business idea, that is accompanied by an experienced management team. The technological areas of interest to government are broader, and often at an earlier stage of development, than ones that private venture capital is willing to consider. Thus, public and private venture capital is complementary, with government playing the role of seeding the private venture capital industry.

Public venture capital is not well known in comparison to private venture capital. For example, a software industry conference recently had two sessions, one on public and the other on private venture capital. Three hundred persons attended the private venture capital session; six persons were present at the public venture capital session, including two presenters and two observers. The rate of success in obtaining public venture capital is in the 10–15 per cent range, the same as the rate for NSF and NIH grants. For private venture capital it is well below 1 per cent of business plan submissions to venture capital firms. Most proposals to venture capitalists do not get a hearing or feedback. By contrast, government programs typically give feedback and encouragement to reapply if a good idea has been introduced without being sufficiently developed.

The growth of the private venture capital industry has made it seem a broader based phenomenon than it really is. Widespread publicity about highly successful firms launched by private venture capital have made a role for government in firm-formation seem superfluous. Nevertheless, despite its growth to a $100 billion dollar industry, most venture capital is still concentrated in a few areas of the country and focuses on a few 'hot' technologies at a time. Although there are occasional exceptions in the very hottest and most competitive areas, private venture capital is seldom available at the early stages of firm-formation. This is where government has creatively stepped in to fill the gap.

2.3.3 New developments in public venture capital

Recently, government agencies have become interested in adapting the private venture capital model to meet their needs, and in one case, the CIA, has actually instituted a quasi-private venture capital firm. Government's interest in the private venture model is not to make money but to meet government's need to improve its access to advanced technology. In past decades, government was seen as a prime source of new technology, in its own laboratories and through the research that it sponsored at universities. So-called 'spin-off' firms, often supported by government contracts, had close ties to the military or NASA.

In recent years, newly founded firms, emerging from previous generations of spin-offs, corporate labs or university research groups often have little or no direct connection to the military or any other part of government. Moreover, private sector R&D has been increasing at a faster rate than public R&D spending. Although government has authorized collaborative mechanisms such as the Cooperative Research and Development Agreement (CRADA), the loosening of anti-trust restrictions allowing firms to collaborate with each other as well as maintain their traditional ties to universities, may be more significant.

These developments have opened up a gap, or at least the perception of increasing distance, between the public and private technology sectors. The traditional role of firms in selling to government is being reversed as government attempts to convince technology entrepreneurs and innovative firms to pay closer attention to its needs.

Nevertheless, private and public venture capital have traditionally operated according to different access models, until IN-Q-Tel.[1] As a venture capital firm sponsored by the Central Intelligence Agency (CIA), IN-Q-TEL is the first government program to explicitly follow the private venture capital model of directly seeking investments, rather than waiting for applicants. The CIA finds that IN-Q-TEL gives it access to firms with technology that they might not previously have learned about. More importantly, as a venture firm, IN-Q-TEL allows the CIA to more easily interact with the venture capital industry. Other venture firms bring potential companies to IN-Q-TEL, as a fellow venture firm whereas they might not have thought of directly approaching the CIA. IN-Q-TEL is a hybrid public/private creature. With initial funding from the federal government, IN-Q-TEL can earn profits and fund its future expansion if its investments are successful. Having authorized this experiment in government-industry interface, it can be expected that Congress will keep a watchful eye on this unique model before authorizing other agencies to establish their own versions of IN-Q-TEL.

2.3.4 Making the transition from public to private venture capital

Public venture capital programs want to meet their goals of gaining the best technology for government while encouraging the development and growth of technology firms. Some assist entrepreneurs and innovative firms to reach private capital markets, with information about private funding sources and by organizing conferences at which they can make contacts. The Internet, which is fueling much current and expected growth, took decades of public support, first from DARPA, and then from NSF, before it was ready for commercialization in the early 1990s.

Most importantly, an SBIR, ATP or other award can serve as a stamp of approval to venture capitalists or other prospective investors that a firm has qualified its technology through a tough vetting process. Although the path from public to private funding can take many courses, a typical approach is to leverage the credibility gained through a public award into private funding.

For example, in the following instance, public venture capital provided the initial capital base and reduced the funding requirement, making the project more attractive to private 'angel' investors. A scientist in a government laboratory who had a project idea founded the firm, based on his research on agency issues, that was not accepted by his supervisor. He became aware of SBIR as a reviewer of proposals for his lab and searched the DOD SBIR solicitation book for a relevant source. He found a precise match in an Army SBIR request for his technology.

Firm formation with public venture capital obtained through an application to SBIR was the chosen route. According to SBIR policy the applicant did not have to leave his job, even temporarily, until after receipt and acceptance of the grant. Indeed, as is now typical, the government laboratory had an entrepreneurial leave program that allowed him to take time off with the option of returning.

The firm founder leveraged the SBIR award with additional government funds from a Department of Energy (DOE) program targeted at cooperation with Russian nuclear research Institutes. With these two government sources in hand, it was then possible to raise private funding. Although the pathway from public to private venture capital is not always as direct as in this case, the search for public venture capital typically beings with an information search.

2.4 The triple helix

The U.S. has developed an industrial policy, based upon university-industry-government relations. There has been a movement from separate institutional spheres, which represent, at least in ideology, the US situation. This has occurred in parallel with a movement away from statist regimes in other countries. There has been a shift from the model of the state encompassing industry and academia, in its strongest form in the former Soviet Union but versions could also be found in Latin American and European countries. Bilateral relations between government and university, academia and industry and government and industry have expanded into triadic relationships among the spheres, especially at the regional level. Academic-industry-government relations are emerging from different institutional starting points in various parts of the world, but for the common purpose of stimulating knowledge-based economic development. Older economic development strategies, whether based primarily on the industrial sector as in the U.S. or the governmental sector as in Latin America, are being supplemented, if not replaced, by knowledge-based economic development strategies, drawing upon resources from the three spheres. A new institutional configuration to promote innovation, a Triple Helix of university, industry and government is emerging in which the university displaces the military as a leading actor. In the U.S. the dynamic of society has changed from one of strong boundaries between separate institutional spheres and organizations to a more flexible overlapping system, with each taking the role of the other. The university is a firm founder through incubator facilities; industry is an educator through company universities and government is a venture capitalist through the Small Business Innovation Research (SBIR) and other programs. Government has also encouraged collaborative R&D among firms, universities and national laboratories to address issues of national competitiveness. This is a different model of the relationship among the institutional spheres either than one in which the spheres are separate from each other and do not collaborate or one in which one sphere dominates the others. This picture, for example, depicts a model in which the state incorporates industry and the university. This would represent the Former Soviet Union and some Latin American countries in a previous era, when state owned industries were predominant.

The model of overlapping spheres is also different from the model of institutional spheres as separate from each other, which, at least in theory is how the US is supposed to work. From each of these previous models, whether it was the state dominating the other institutional spheres or the spheres separate from each other, we are moving to a model of 'Structural Integration' in which the institutional spheres of university, industry and government collaborate and cooperate with each other.

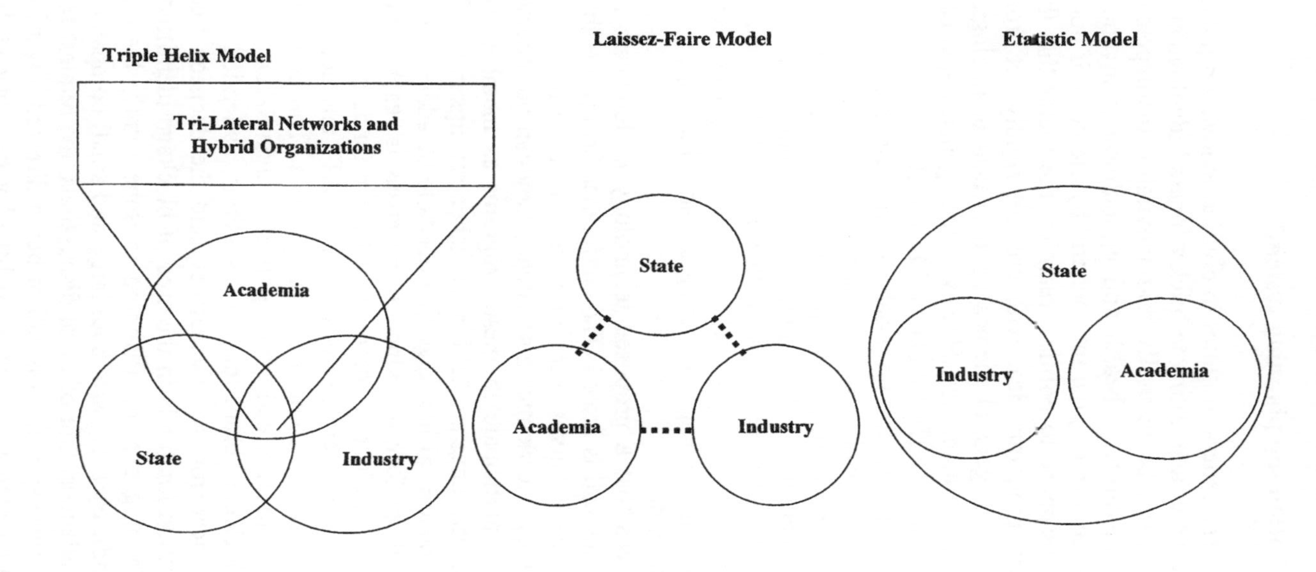

Figure 2.1: From the etatistic to the triple helix model

Source: H. Etzkowitz & L. Leydesdorff, The Dynamics of Innovation: From National Systems and 'Mode 2' to a Triple Helix of University-Industry-Government Relations, *Research Policy*, No. 29, Elsevier, p.111.

2.5 The emergence of a 'bottom-up planning system'

Government can only set very general outlines in civilian innovation policy for fear that it will be accused of attempting to 'pick winners.' Ideologically, government is often perceived as naturally and inevitably incompetent, despite manifest success in military, health and agricultural innovation, exemplified by the Manhattan Project, the Internet and hybrid corn, if not a cure for cancer! Thus, in response to political realities, the topics that the civilian federal technology programs deal with are not rigidly set from above. Certainly they draw for general themes upon critical technologies lists or the interests of program managers. However, the agencies also call meetings on technology themes in different parts of the country.

Although there is an open call for proposals in any relevant area of commercializable science and technology in some federal technology programs, these programs increasingly rely on a more focused approach based upon the critical technologies list. Such lists are hardly unique; virtually the same broad topics can be found on lists in the U.S. Japan in Europe. Nevertheless, within the broad guidelines of the list, government R&D program managers and companies suggest specific aspect of technologies for special attention.

Once the program agrees that a proposed technology is deserving of special attention a conference call is issued. The conference brings together program managers with representatives from companies that are interested in working on the technology. Academics also attend; they can not always initiate a proposal but can participate in these programs as members of company led consortia. The meetings are held in workshop settings in which the discussion focuses on the area of blockage that needs to be addressed to move the particular technology forward. Once a consensus is reached the next step is that the program conducts a competition for the funds in which both technical and business reviews are carried out. In the ATP and dual use programs companies also have to commit matching funds. Through this process government involves itself directly in support of civilian R&D.

These technology blockage brainstorming sessions, attended by government, industry and academic representatives, and the decision that results to mount a competition for funds in the area of blockage identified, constitute an informal planning system. Planning is done jointly by the government side, by the industry side, with both large and small companies participating as well as academics. Out of these discussions, the request for proposals are made much more specific. Instead of being directed toward a general critical technology which is typically so broad a category as be almost meaningless for targeting innovation, the planning process reduces the general category to a particular point, at which the people who are closest to the technology agree, that a blockage exists.

Through this format, instead of a top down planning hierarchy, a bottom up planning process is being created in the U.S. Out of the discussions among people from government, industry and university, the direction of these programs are shaped and the funds then given out. It is a judgment call as to whether a technology program has fallen too long or short of the 'middle range' of market failure that it is considered legitimate for technology policy to address in the U.S.

If results follow too quickly, the program will likely be attacked for entering into the realm of near term industrial R&D and conversely, if they are long in coming, it will be said that the work should more appropriately have been supported by a basic research agency. This planning process is typical of the newer efforts like ATP and dual use programs in the Department of Defense. SBIR is still to a large extent based on the older models of contracts and grants, although conferences and workshop discussions are common in this program as well.

2.6 Conclusion

The linear model is alive and well today but it does not work on its own. A series of mechanisms have been instituted that help make the linear model work. The build up of research and useful results from university to industry did not move by publications alone. As innovation moves outside of a single organization, lateral relationships across boundaries, rather than hierarchical bureaucratic structures, become more important.

To both analyze these developments and guide their future development, a new model of the relationship among the institutional spheres and their internal transformation is needed. A model that takes account of border crossing and the co-evolution between technological and institutional transformation is required. The Triple Helix Model denotes the university-industry-government relationship as one of relatively equal, yet interdependent, institutional spheres that overlap and take the role of the other.

Normative implications

The triple helix model of innovation, with converging institutional spheres of academia, industry and government each taking the role of the other has been read in different ways in various parts of the world. In countries where the interface is well underway, whether occurring from the bottom up, through the interactions of individuals and organizations from different institutional spheres, or top down, encouraged by policy measures, the triple helix can be recognized as an empirical phenomenon. The US has been seen to exemplify the former and Europe the latter mode of triple helix development. Both types of triple helix development may actually be under way in the US and Europe albeit at different rates and with varying emphases.

The role of science in industrial policy becomes ever more important as knowledge-based industries become a greater part of the economy. As the overlap between science and industrial policy increases, innovation policy appears at its interface. Government programs often operate as a 'hidden industrial policy' to deflect opposition. The need to not have government seen as a sole actor has made these programs more efficacious through the involvement of industry and academia, not only in execution but also in formulation of initiatives. As industry becomes more science-based, it is not surprising that the role of the university as a home for science, and government as a regulator of science, becomes more important. Indeed, the relationship among university, industry and government is reconfigured as knowledge based innovation becomes predominant.

In recent years, the movement to eliminate educational inequalities, based on race and class, has given the federal government a greater role in basic education, both through judicial decisions and funding programs. As in other instances of federal involvement in previously local activities, government has become a significant force for change but by no means the predominant actor as is commonplace in Europe. Typically, such initiatives take place indirectly, utilizing a neutral party as an interface in order to deflect controversy.

Such an insulation device allows highly ideologically charged linkages, between the federal government and basic education and the federal government and industry, to be diffused.

Due to ideological resistance, the U.S. often pursues industrial and social policies by indirect means, encouraging other institutions to carry out public purposes. For example, universities have been incentivized to interact with industry since it was expected that academic institutions could more easily interface with firms, without causing the controversy that would be generated by an open government-industry relationship. Since much U.S. industrial policy takes place through indirect means, it does not rise to visibility as part of a general schema. However, if viewed more broadly, a comprehensive US industrial policy can be discerned from more than 200 years of actions supporting invention, development and diffusion of technology. Indeed, the combination of indirect as well as direct interventions suggests that the U.S. has the world's strongest industrial policy, despite a reputation to the contrary.

Note

1 The firm, originally called Inquit, changed its name after protest from Intuit, the financial software firm who thought that the CIA sponsored firm sounded too similar.

References

Bush, V. (1945): Science: The Endless Frontier Washington DC: US Government Printing Office.

Etzkowitz, H./Gulbrandsen M./Levitt J. (2001): Public Venture Capital: Sources of Government Funding for Technology Entrepreneurs. New York: Aspen/Kluwer, 2nd edition.

Graham, O. L. (1992): Losing Time: The Industrial Policy Debate. Cambridge, MA: Harvard University Press. p.2.

Chapter 3

On the French System of Innovation: Between Institutional Inertia and Rapid Changes

Dominique Foray

3.1 Introduction[1]

Since the collapse of the Soviet Republic, only one national system of innovation can still be described as 'mission-oriented' – and this is the French! Research is concentrated in a few high tech sectors and in a small number of firms; government defense and civilian contracts play an important role in this polarization; and the share of public sector in domestic expenditure is the highest in OECD. Mission-oriented policy structures are, thus, still predominant and persistent. There are however a lot of changes and policy experiments around these structures.

In this paper we want to balance and contrast the persistence of a certain kind of policy structure ('mission-oriented') with the institutional changes which are under way. After a short analytical section about the meaning of 'mission-oriented' policy, we will overview some quantitative features and we will discuss more deeply the organizational characteristics of the system. We will finally address the issue of the possible evolution of the system.

3.2 Policy structure

The qualification of 'mission-oriented' (Ergas, 1987) has not the pretence of describing in exhaustive details the institutions which support innovation. It only suggests that the 'mission-oriented' part of the policy is predominant. More precisely, such a qualification suggests that the institutional conditions prevailing in a country – especially as regards economic co-ordination –

involve large technological programs being set up efficiently, while horizontal diffusion-oriented programs will be implemented in less efficient circumstances (Foray and Llerena, 1996). A non-negligible part of technology policy still corresponds to the support of 'radically innovative projects and the building of complex technological systems' requiring centralization of decision making processes and concentration of resources on a few number of targets.

France success in fields such as aerospace, nuclear energy, and transport systems can be attributed to these specific features. These are sectors in which the coherence between public procurement, large-scale research institutions and a few numbers of national champions has played a decisive role. But this model has not produced the same good results in technological fields that are closely tied to the market trends (such as ICTs).

'Mission-oriented' programs are distinguished by:

- The degree of centralization they entail;
- the goals are centrally determined;
- high costs encourage a narrowing in the range of options explored;
- their technical complexity restricts participation in program execution to a few, technologically sophisticated agents.

The consequences are twofold:

- Firstly, mission-oriented programs place a heavy burden on administrative capabilities – their design and implementation typically involve a high degree of administrative discretion. The monitoring of performance relies primarily on administrative processes rather than on market selection processes.
- Secondly, they are high-risk ventures: a few large bets are being placed on a small number of races. This creates the danger that the wrong bets will be chosen and that the large resources devoted to these programs will crowd-out more valuable alternative uses.

There are of course large defense and technological programs in many other countries but either the size of the country is so large that the crowding effect is reduced (this is the American case) or the size of the mission-oriented programs is small. Moreover, Mowery and Rosenberg (1989) have shown how the US system of innovation was slowly shifting from a predominance of the mission-oriented structures towards 'adoption-oriented' policy structures.

3.3 Quantitative picture: the French system of innovation in the late nineties[2]

3.3.1 Inputs

Domestic expenditures on R&D (GERD) amounted to 182 billion (Francs) in 1996 (about 30 billion $). This amount counts for 21 per cent of the total EU R&D expenditures; and 6 per cent of the total OECD. It corresponds to 2.3 per cent of French GDP (just above the OECD average).

In France, as in other major EU countries, research expenditures have tended to level off since the beginning of the 1990s reflecting the economic slow down, high real interest rates and the stabilization or cutbacks in public budget. However, this trend seems to be more persistent in France than in other countries.

3.3.2 Outputs

French scientific performance, as measured on the basis of scientific publication, has been good – even showing some improvements from the beginning of the 1990s. France technological performance is rather more mixed. Its share of patents issued in the U.S. has shown an overall decline since the end of the eighties (this is the same trend for Germany as well as for EU as a whole). France's share of the export market in high tech goods remained roughly constant.

In the ICT field, France's position weakened in the 1990s, like that of European countries. No French firm and very few European firms were among the world's leading electronic and ICTs firms in the 1990s (Tijssen and van Wijk, 1998). In contrast, the French high tech industry performed extremely well in the aerospace industry, as well as in some other less high tech fields such as automobile, and railways.

Some kinds of similarity between the French and the European trends can be highlighted: decline of technological performance that can mainly be attributed to ICT-related sectors. And this similarity suggests that the French institutional factors to which we will move soon does not fully explain France's decline. There is a concern for Europe as a whole. However, the weakness of France in ICTs reveals particular problems. Innovation in ICTs is largely market-driven and probably the link between research and the market seems be the weakest point of the French innovation system.

3.4 Organizational characteristics

3.4.1 French research is concentrated

Half of the French manufacturing industry's R&D expenditures are in the high tech sector (aerospace, telecommunication equipment, and electronic components). The research intensity of sectors is extremely differentiated – especially high in the high tech field and very low in the other sectors. Government defense contracts play an important role in this polarization (see below).

The concentration does not only concern sectors. There is also a concentration of research expenditures on a small number of firms. The 15 major firms that spend most on R&D account for 37 per cent of total expenditures and the 3 leading for 15 per cent.

3.4.2 Government influence remains strong

In terms of funding and performing, the importance of the public sector is higher than in any other OECD countries. The government influences innovation through three main channels:

- Procurement and research contract with firms;
- national laboratories and institutions such as the CNRS (employing more than 20,000 S&T personnel and covering all fields of basic research), the CEA (Atomic Energy Agency) and a range of sectoral research institutions (health, agriculture and food, oceanography, space, transport, and so on);
- a variety of financial incentives mechanisms (subsidies, research tax credit, refundable loans).

3.4.3 The particular structure of government research contract

The total of government research contracts to companies amounted to 23 billion French Francs in 1996, of which twelve related to defense research; eight to five major technological programs (GPT) and three to financial incentives schemas (to which we can add three billion devoted to the R&D tax credit scheme).

Of course this 23 (or 26) billion FF corresponds to a rather small part of the GERD which accounted for 182 billion FF. Half of the GERD was funded by the government (about 87 billion FF). Thus the total of government research contracts to companies amounted for 1/3 of the public expenditures. However, this is a crucial part because it is the only part of the public budget that can be used to define a public policy in the short and medium term (the other 2/3 being mostly pre-affected for the payment of salaries and other costs of the public research institutions). Thus how these 23 billion FF are spent is a good mirror of the logic of the system.

This structure of government research contracts thus exhibits the following features:

- Defense research contracts are predominant;
- a very small number of firms have contracts in mission oriented funding (defense + GPT); 120 firms received 20 billion FF while these 120 firms performed less than the half of industrial R&D (40/109 billion FF);
- 10 industrial groups received: 98 per cent of defense research contracts plus 86 per cent of GPT contracts plus 25 per cent of the resources devoted to financial incentives.

We immediately realize this incredible asymmetry between the 'mission-oriented' contract based funding which accounts for 20 billion and the 'diffusion-oriented' contract based funding which accounts for 3 (plus 3) billion FF. Public resources are monopolized by a few numbers of companies in a few numbers of sectors.

3.4.4 A crucial policy tool: the 'Grand Program Technologique'

The main policy instrument, which generates this concentration and polarization, is the GPT. Initially, there were 5 GPTs: nuclear, aeronautical engineering, space, defense electronics, telecommunication.

The objective of those GPTs is to produce certain complex technological systems in civilian or defense areas that are considered as strategic, for which the government is directly or indirectly the major client and for which concentration of resources is a necessary condition for entering oligopolistic markets. The programs require substantial funding over very long periods of time. They are financed mainly by the government but are carried out by public research bodies and industries to varying degrees.

For each program there is a coherent and strongly connected set of actors: a public agency plus a public research institution plus a small number of large companies (Figure 3.1).

Although not officially labeled as GPT, some other areas of S&T were organized with the same kinds of vertical structures: the high-speed train; biotechnology (called program Bioavenir).

As well as producing successful breakthroughs in technology (in nuclear, aerospace, high-speed train, and telecommunications), these programs have some times resulted in major technical, organizational or commercial failures (computers; perhaps Concorde).

These 5 GPTs constitute a policy instrument, which is very pivotal for the French technology policy. They amounted to almost half of total public funding: (20 billion corresponding to government research contract) plus (21 billion corresponding to resources devoted to the GPTs by the large public research bodies that can only claim for additional costs reimbursement).

As a dominant way of organizing research and innovation, this policy instrument raises many problems:

- GPTs management entails complex bureaucratic organizations; lack of transparency; some bodies are both principal and agent.

- GPTs create distortion regarding industrial competitiveness. Through their large scale, they exert a major influence on the direction of research in the participating firms, and have encouraged them to abandon areas in which technologies are market driven that are less attractive because they are most competitive. As Ergas (1992) wrote some years ago: 'Mission-oriented programs tend to introduce distortions when firms are tempted to direct their research towards mission-oriented policy areas, thus losing sight of the essential issue of finding the best way for developing in line with needs expressed by the market. It is true that mission oriented policies can generate advanced technologies but they can never produce organizations capable of being truly competitive'.

- GPTs create vertical structures which reduce the scope of influence of public funding and these programs create very few spillovers. Why is that a case of low externalities? First, most of the sectors in which the programs are specialized are known as not very much 'knowledge diffusing'.[3] Moreover, most of those programs are organized under principles of access restriction to knowledge, non-disclosure and secrecy (all of them are dealing with strategic issues touching national security). Secondly, the companies which are benefiting from the public contract are very limited in sub-contracting their activities. This is a key point: The possibility of progressively enlarging the scope of a program by introducing more and more SMEs as subcontractors was viewed as an effective way to improve the system without changing the basic policy structures (i.e. keeping the vertical structures). But it simply did not work. The large contracting companies sub-contracted only a minor part of the activity (Bernard and Quéré, 1994).

3.4.5 Diffusion-oriented policy: Incentives to industrial innovation and R&D tax credit

The 'incentives to industrial innovation' schema is a small program as compared with the civilian and defense GPTs. This program has three axes:

- Key technology schema which awards subsidies to business conducting research in certain fields (this is a 'small foresight' activity but implemented in a very 'French' way!);
- funds for technological research (FRT), including Eureka funding, employment of doctoral candidates funding (Ciffre) and regional initiatives;
- the National Agency for the Promotion of Innovation (ANVAR) which essentially provides SMEs with preferential loans to finance innovation (interest free, repayable only if a venture is successful).

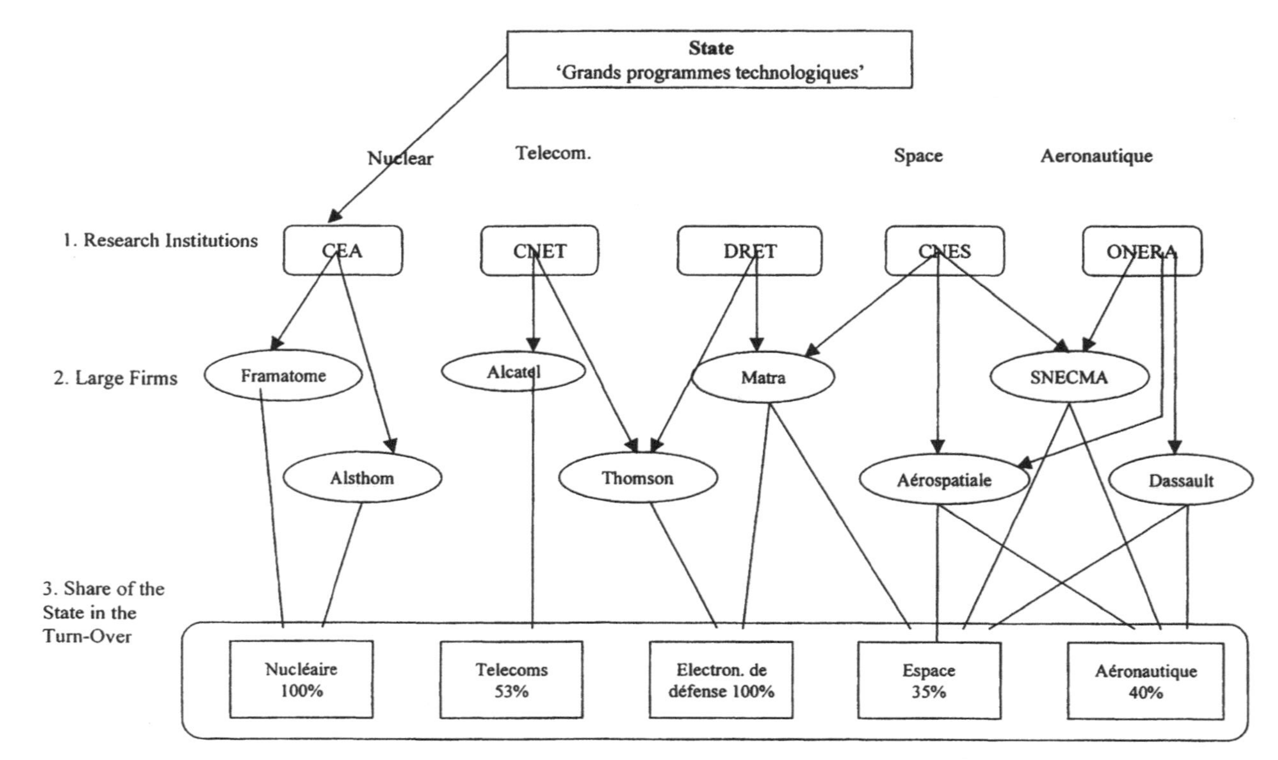

Figure 3.1: Grands programmes technologiques: sets of actors

Source: Serfati: Production d'armes croissance, innovation Economica, 1995.

All these schemas are based on one of two main contractual arrangements: advance repayable in case of success, subsidies. A problem was that repayment rate remained very low, turning the aid into de facto subsidies. The new principles, which are to support feasibility studies and demonstration works, have resulted in an increase of the repayment rate to 70 per cent.

The other side of the diffusion-oriented policy is the research tax credit program, introduced in 1982. This is a horizontal measure, which is non-discriminatory across sectors – aimed at supporting corporate R&D investments by means of tax incentives. The research tax credit fund amounts to 3 billion annually. The tax credit is equal to 50 per cent of the increase in research outlays between the year in question and the average of the two preceding years. In 1996, 3,660 firms claimed R&D tax credit. This is the only program, which is really broad, covering a large number of sectors.

3.4.6 Where are the increasing returns?

To evaluate such a system, it is useful to take up Pavitt's question (1996) about national policies for technical change: 'where are the increasing returns to economic research' within the French system? This is an important issue to be addressed because public expenditures in RTD cannot be evaluated in the same way as public expenditures in physical infrastructures. As is well known, the production of knowledge and the generation of innovation are economic activities, which have the potential to generate massive knowledge externalities. The measurement of social returns to R&D generally gives extremely good results and this is, thus, critical to have an idea about these positive externalities (or spillover effects). Evaluating public policy beyond the achievement of the target (the supersonic aircraft or the super computer) is important. In the most favorable cases – in which positive externalities are important – the public policy can have a big leverage effect, contributing quite significantly to economic growth. Such an issue is also important because the full cost of public expenditures (including the costs of collecting taxes as well as the perverse incentives produced by the excess burden on the economy) requires that a public program needs to produce more than a 20 per cent rate of return to justify its existence (Brown, 1998).

What can be said in the case of the French system? We can argue that most of the parameters describing the organizational structure of mission-oriented policies are not in favor of large externalities:

- Firstly, most of the sectors in which public research contracts are concentrated are weak in terms of externalities – either structurally (aerospace and aeronautics) or because of access restriction problems (nuclear, defense electronics);
- secondly, as already said, the large contractors involved in the large programs do not su-contract very much, and thus impede the possibility of enlarging the scope of the programs by including more and more SMEs;
- finally, France has no explicit and deliberate dual policy, which is a valuable way to maximize spillovers between civilian and defense R&D (Cowan and Foray, 1995, Dagusan et al 2000).

3.5 Relations between public research and industry

The public research sector is rather vast and has even tended to expand in recent years – from 76,000 public sector researchers in 1992 to 81,000 in 1995 (contrasted with a population of 67,000 researchers in the private sector). A major institution is the CNRS (Centre National de la Recherche Scientifique) which is a public research organization set up to produce fundamental knowledge and to disseminate it within society. The CNRS employs 11,470 scientists and 13,930 engineers and technicians. It covers all fields of fundamental research. The size of the sector raises various problems. For an institution like CNRS, the amount of the total budget that goes on salaries is so great (more than 80 per cent) that only a very tiny sum is left over for new projects, for modernizing the stock of scientific instruments, for conducting a real science policy (Foray, 1999).

The second problem is about the industrial transferability of knowledge produced by the public sector. The sector is so large that transferring properly knowledge produced within the public laboratories is a critical issue for the system as a whole. Transferability does not work very well:

- Very few researchers from the public sector move to the industry (50 out of a total of 11,400 scientists at CNRS in 1996);
- royalties from patents and licenses are modest,
- government and industry have relatively few joint research laboratories and the proportion of public research to be financed by industry is significantly lower than in the other European countries.

This is a structural problem for several reasons:

- Firstly, the French research system is strong in fields, which are relatively far from the market and weak in 'transfer science' (engineering);
- secondly researchers have few incentives to transfer their results, because to do so entails efforts that are not much rewarded in their careers. This is of course not a simple issue of dissemination or of being opened to industrial needs. But it entails the problem of who will carry out the developmental phase, which is often extremely costly and not that rewarding for academic researchers.

An assumption made by Zucker and Darby (1998) is that the dominant role of national research institutions (contrasted with research universities) could be a major feature in explaining the weak level of commercial involvement of scientists in countries like France. They wrote, 'The idea of research institutes sounds very attractive. (...) In fact, we ourselves would like to have our research well funded until retirement and the opportunity to build a more permanent research team without the need to train successive generations of graduate students and post-doctoral fellows. Despite the personal attractions, we can also see how that situation might cool the entrepreneurial spirit, particularly if one is seen as a truly full-time employee of the institute and therefore constrained by various conflict-of-interest rules from profiting from any involvement or collaboration with firms'.

3.6 A problematic figure

In this section, we try to figure out the various problems identified above. Weak externalities from the GPTs, low transferability between the public research sector and the private sector, and the high asymmetry between 'mission-oriented' and 'diffusion-oriented' public funding are three basic problems that any new policy should try to overcome.

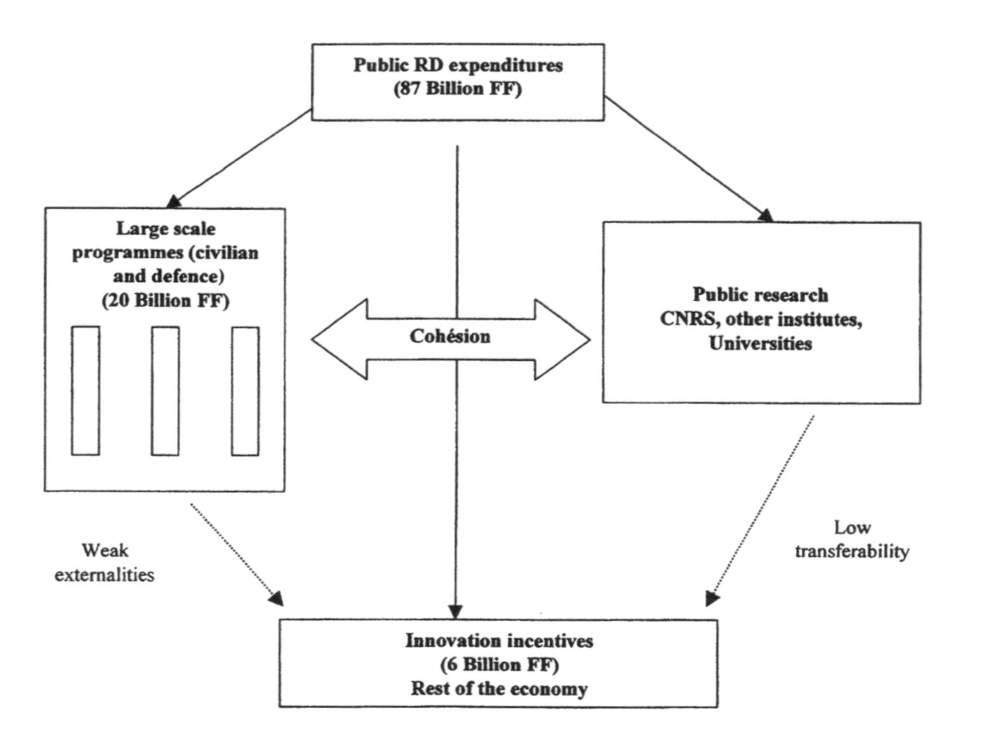

Figure 3.2: The problem of the French innovation system

3.7 Changes and institutional inertia

Of course, the French system is not petrified such as an old dinosaur! Changes are under way:

- The influence of government and defense expenditures is beginning to decline in the field of science and technology policy.

- As a consequence of deregulation and liberalization, some major actors of the public research sector are experiencing strong changes (case for CNET or SNCF). All these research institutions were important national scientific assets, conducting basic research and disseminating their results. They are now moving to competition on the knowledge markets.

- The French government is setting up networks linking public laboratories and enterprises, including SMEs. The idea is to substitute networks to the GPTs. This is probably a good idea inasmuch as the large technological programs 'à la française' are quite inefficient given the huge opportunity costs of public funding. However it is useful to recall that 'the now-fashionable metaphor of 'a network' is not the same thing as a well worked out economic model from which one can legitimately move, by way of institutionally grounded empirical inquiries, towards a fundamental re-orientation of policies to affect the allocation of resources for science and technology. *It is important to remember that an emblem is not a rationale*' (David et al, 1999).

- Major policy actions are conducted for the creation of innovative enterprises (development of venture capital, attractive tax treatment, development of specialized securities markets). If, thus, many actions are launched to increase the supply of capital and to support the expansion of venture capital, remains the 'demand side' problem of having enough projects and people willing to start a business, accepting the risk to leave the comfortable and stress-less public sector.

- Finally, new incentive structures are set up to support the commercial involvement of scientists (innovation bill, seed capital funds). This is a key point for reducing the demand side problem. Researchers of the public sector are now allowed to create or to help to create enterprises without having to break all ties with their research institutions.

> However this easing of the legal framework will only bear full fruit when a new 'culture' of researchers' evaluation will have been developed.

Are these changes sufficiently strong to move the system away from its 'mission-oriented' base? Is this move desirable? We all know that changing systems is costly, not just socially but also in economic terms as well during the transition.

It is interesting to ask why the mission-oriented policy structures have been so persistent? While there are some good reasons to implement them for a certain class of technological systems (nuclear, aerospace, high speed train), it is more difficult to understand what the rationale behind the re-use of this instrument for new classes of technology, such as biotechnology. A factor of persistence deals certainly with a strong consistency between this instrument and the more general structures of the French society. The conditions prevailing in France at the general level of the society (centralization of administrative and political procedures, elitist education and training) involve this kind of policy being set up quite efficiently. And actually, this policy has led to some great successes in nuclear technology (see David and Rothwell, 1996, for a comparison between France and the U.S.), the high speed train, aerospace. Another factor of persistence is that GPTs require extremely high level of competence in public agencies at both managerial and technological levels. GPTs have thus generated a class of high skilled people who are interested in reproducing the same procedures. Last but not least, the evolution of institution exhibits some path dependent features (David, 1992): institutions are like technologies. They are clustering, they keep inter-linked and they are mutually reinforced through functional compatibility. As a result, even if the original context later becomes irrelevant, changing a given institution would interfere with the way in which numerous other operations are carried out and would thus induce substantial readjustment costs. The organizational structure may therefore become locked in to a narrow sub-array of routines, objectives, and future growth trajectories.

Given such fundamental inertia, should we not rather think in terms of complementarity between the old – mission-oriented – part of the system and few new features? However the incentives-compatibility of both institutional structures has not been proved yet.

Notes

1 I gratefully acknowledge comments and suggestions from the participants to the workshop 'Innovation paradigm: the impact of economic ideas on RTD policies' (4S/EASST Conference 2000, September 27–30, 2000 in Vienna), and I am glad to Susana Borras and Peter Biegelbauer for their encouragement to finalize this paper.

2 The data are coming from various sources: OST, 2000; OECD, 1999; Barré and Carpentier, 1998; Serfati, 1998.

3 This is for instance the case of aerospace and aeronautical engineering. This is less true for telecommunication.

References

Barré, R./Carpentier, C. (1998): Les Contrats Publics de R&D Civils Et militaires: une Analyse en Termes de Potentiel de Recherche et de Technologie, Document de Travail, OST: Paris.

Bernard, J./Quéré, M. (1994): 'L'évolution du Financement Public sur L'activité de Recherche des PME-PMI', Revue d'Economie Industrielle, 67.

Brown, K. (1998): Downsizing Science, The AEI Press, Washington.

Cowan, R./Foray, D. (1995): 'Quandaries in the economics of Dual Technology and Spillovers from Military R&D', Research Policy, 24.

Dagusan, J. F./Foray, D./Guichard, R. (2000): Recherche Appliquée et Technologies Duales: Quelles Stratégies pour la FRANCE?, Rapport FRS, Paris.

David, P. (1992): ''Why are Institutions the 'Carriers of History'', SITE Summer Program on Irreversibilities, Stanford University.

David, P./Foray, D./Steinmueller, E. (1999): 'The Research Network and the New Economics of Science: from Metaphors to Organizational Behaviors', in: Gambardella/Malerba (eds.), The Organization of Economic Innovation in Europe, Cambridge University Press.

David, P./Rothwell, G. (1996): Standardization, Diversity and Learning: Strategies for the co-Evolution of Technology and Industrial Capacity, CEPR Publication n°402, Stanford University.

Ergas, H. (1987): 'The Importance of Technology Policy', in: Dasgupta et Stoneman, Economic Policy and Technological Performance, Cambridge University Press.

Ergas, H. (1992): A Future for Mission-Oriented Industrial Policies? A Critical Review of Developments in Europe, OCDE.

Foray, D. (1999): The Economics of the CNRS: In Search for a New Model Between Academic Research and National Laboratory, Working Papers IMRI – WP 99/04.

Foray, D./Llerena, P. (1996): 'Information Structure and Coordination in Technology Policy', Evolutionary Economics, n°6.

Mowery, D./Rosenberg, N. (1989): New Developments in US Technology Policy: Implications for Competitiveness and the International Trade Policy, CEPR Publication, n°166, Stanford University.

OECD (1999): France, Etudes Economiques de l'OCDE, Paris.

OST (2000): Science et Technologies, Édition INDICATEURS 2000, Economica.

Serfati, C. (1998): R&D Militaire, Grands Programs et Capacités Technologiques Nationales: Caractérisation et Indicateurs, Document de Travail OST: Paris.

Tijssen, R./van Wijk, E. (1998): In Search of the European Paradox: an International Comparison, CWTS Working Paper, Leiden.

Zucker, L./Darby, M. (1998): 'The Economists' Case for Biomedical Research', in: Barfield, C./Smith, B. (eds.) The Future of Biomedical Research, The AEI Press, Washington DC.

Chapter 4

Innovation Policy in Finland

Tarmo Lemola

4.1 Introduction

Within a couple of years of the deep recession of the early 1990s, the Finnish economy showed positive growth again, manufacturing reached a growth rate of 12 per cent in 1994. Behind this sudden upturn was the exceptionally fast growth of industries related to information and communications technologies (ICT). Whereas in 1970 the electric and electronics industries represented just 2 per cent of Finnish exports as a whole, the corresponding figure was 11 per cent in 1990, and as much as 30 per cent in 1999. Similarly, the balance of trade in high-tech products changed from a deficit in the beginning of 1990s to a notable surplus by the end of the century.

The economic crisis of the early 1990s has been explained mainly in terms of external factors like the slowdown of the world, especially the European economy, and the collapse of Soviet Union. At its height the Soviet Union accounted for about 25 per cent of Finnish exports. The effect of the external factors was accelerated by internal factors, mistakes in exchange and monetary policies, and uncontrolled deregulation of the Finnish financial markets during the 1980s. The first mentioned lead to an overvalued Finnish mark, and the last mentioned resulted in the evolvement of casino economy.

For its part, the rapid recovery from recession and the growth of industrial output in ICT has been mainly explained by the success of the Finnish company Nokia (Ali-Yrkkö et al, 2000). In the 1990s, Nokia became one of the world's leading telecommunications companies and it contributed significantly to the economic growth in Finland, which has again been one of fastest in Europe. But there is more than just Nokia. The whole Finnish information and communications cluster has expanded rapidly. The positive development, or a significant part of it, has also been explained in terms of an active innovation policy which Finland has pursued from early 1980s. According to this argument, investments in R&D and education, and other policy instruments have gradually created conditions for favorable structural changes in the Finnish economy and industry, and paved the way for the growth and success of Nokia and other Finnish, high-tech companies.

4.2 Phases of Finnish innovation policy

It was not until the 1960s that science and technology or research and development (R&D), and their economic significance crystallised as a topic of debate and became an area of government activity in Finland. This was later than in larger and more developed OECD countries. The late start has been counterbalanced by the fact that the development of innovation policy proceeded quickly in the 1970s and particularly since early 1980s.

The development of Finland's innovation policy from the late 1960s onwards can be divided on the basis of its content into three phases (see table 4.1). Naturally, the phases are by no means completely unambiguous.

During the first phase, which began in the mid-1960s, the emphasis was on the construction of the machinery of innovation policy and its quantitative expansion. The main driver in this phase was the intensifying internationalisation and the liberalisation of trade. This placed new strains on Finland's production structure, which was one-sided (high dependence on paper industry), and its level of technology, which was low compared with Finland's main competitors. Investment in R&D and education were absorbed as important building blocks of Finnish developmentalism.

The focus during the second phase, which began at the turn of the 1980s, was on information technologies and on the development of international R&D co-operation. The factors behind this transition were economic and social. The 'oil crisis' of the mid-1970s led in Finland to a slow-down in the rates of economic growth and to high levels of unemployment and inflation. These were even the years of 'micro-electronics revolution'. Active exploitation of the opportunities opened by microelectronics for the benefit of economic growth and employment became the core of the innovation policy of the 1980s in Finland.

Table 4.1: The phases of Finnish innovation policy

	1970s	1980s	1990s
Main justification	– underinvestment in R&D – technology gap – liberalization of international trade	– technological threats and opportunities – technological competitiveness	– building a knowledge-based society – global competitiveness
Main target	– universities – VTT – enterprises	– large enterprises – co-operative ventures	– SMEs – industrial clusters – national champion
Level of intervention	– national	– national – international (European)	– national – European – global – regional
Types of policies	– financial support of government R&D organizations – direct financial support	– national technology programs – direct financial support – EU research programs	– direct financial support – EU research programs – regional technology transfer initiatives – cluster programs – venture capital

The latest phase began in the early 1990s. Innovation policy involves both scientific and technological development being examined from the standpoint of innovations, taking account of innovation-promoting factors such as science and technology, and emphasising the perspectives of technology transfer, diffusion and commercialisation. The latest transition was also shaped by economic crisis. In the beginning of the 1990s, the Finnish economy experienced a dramatic downturn into a deep economic crisis which was much more severe than the recession of late 1970s. However, the exceptional circumstances did not bring about radical changes in foundations and instruments of the innovation policy of 1980s. On one hand, they strengthened the prevailing orientation towards innovations throughout the national research system. On the other hand, they encouraged the government and the private sector to develop Finland in the spirit of a 'knowledge based society'.

4.3 Construction and development of the innovation policy machinery (1965–1980)

Three important changes occurred in Finland's innovation policy at the turn of the 1970s (Lemola, 1994). Firstly, the capabilities and operating conditions of the *universities* were improved. The measures were targeted directly at the universities' teaching and research appropriations and at the *Academy of Finland* (a system of research councils), which the government started to develop into a new instrument for the planning and funding of university research. Behind these measures was the significant enlargement of tertiary educational establishments as the large post-war generation began to reach maturity, and the desire to 'modernise' university education involving universities in meeting the growing needs of industry.

Secondly, the task of increasing and improving research that would raise the level of industrial technology was undertaken. Above all, this meant the development of the *Technical Research Centre of Finland (VTT)*. VTT was comprehensively reorganized in 1972. In addition, the Ministry of Trade and Industry received an additional appropriation from the state budget for *goal-oriented technical research*. This gave rise to the first 'national technology programs' in the universities of technology and VTT.

Thirdly, the government began to support firms' research and product development directly by means of *R&D loans and grants*. A new fund under the authority of the Bank of Finland, the Finnish National Fund for Research and Development (Sitra), was established for this purpose. In addition, the

Ministry of Trade and Industry began to support the research and product development of firms. The background to these measures was concern about the lack of firms' own R&D. Statistical studies made in the early 1960s showed that, with only a few exceptions, the level of Finnish firms' own R&D was modest by international standards.

These three areas of development can still be regarded as the basic building blocks of Finland's innovation policy. The emphasis placed on them has changed over time, as have their mutual relationships. The main trend has been that of increased co-operation and interaction between them. However, the basic structure itself has remained surprisingly unchanged for over thirty years, and integration of the constituent parts has proceeded quite slowly.

Whereas the turn of the 1970s was a time for constructing the machinery of innovation policy, the main goal for the rest of the decade was the quantitative expansion of the new system. However, the Finnish research system did not progress very far from its starting position of the 1970s. The GDP-share of R&D expenditure did grow from 0.8 per cent in 1969 to 1.1 per cent in 1979, but this was more modest than had been expected. Finland's GDP-share was also at the end of the 1970s lower than the average for the OECD countries. Even though the growth in the corporate sector's R&D expenditure was above average, the intensity of firms' research (the share of research expenditure in the value added of production) did not rise throughout the 1970s. The positive trend of the beginning of the 1970s had slipped into decline in all sectors by the end of the decade.

4.4 Development of information technologies and international R&D co-operation (1979–1990)

A new era in Finland's innovation policy began at the turn of the 1980s. The factors behind the transition from research orientation to technology orientation were economic and social. The 'oil crisis' of mid 1970s led to a slow-down in the rates of economic growth and to high levels of unemployment and inflation. These were even the years of 'micro-electronics revolution', which was recognized as offering new productive and other opportunities, but which, it was feared, would exacerbate social problems. In particular, it was feared that the increase in the use of automation in industry and services, would cause mass unemployment and greater social inequality.

Finding ways out of the potential problems were submitted to a broadly based committee appointed by the government (Technology Committee). 'Broadly based' meant experts representing political decision-makers, the government sector, employers, employees and researchers. The committee's key conclusion was that not even the rapid development of automation would place any restriction on social development in the 1980s. On the contrary, information technology and its application would be a resource opening up new opportunities (Lemola and Lovio, 1988). Indeed, the committee's principal recommendations included the strengthening of innovation policy both quantitatively (increased resources) and qualitatively (allocation of resources).

A national consensus on the necessity for technological development and its basic objectives was reached on this basis, leading to the formation of the National Technology Agency (Tekes) in 1983. The tasks formerly carried out by the Ministry of Trade and Industry (i.e. R&D loans and grants, appropriations for goal-oriented technical research) were assigned to Tekes. Tekes became the key planner and implementer of the new innovation policy.

In terms of funds, Tekes's central instruments to promote industrial R&D have been since its establishment R&D loans and grants awarded directly to firms. They accounted for about two-thirds of Tekes' funds in the 1980s. The principal purpose of Tekes' R&D subsidies has been stimulation of market forces. The subsidies have been distributed on the basis of applications received from firms. The industrial or technological field of a firm's product development project has not been a significant selection criterion. Firms' demands rather than a selective policy approach focused the attention of Tekes on ICT in the 1980s (Lemola, 1994).

National technology programs, which had already proven their worth in countries such as Japan and Sweden, were developed in the beginning of 1980s to serve as a new and important instrument by which Tekes could control research activities. Compared with industrial R&D subsidies the technology programs are an example of a more selective and strategic approach. However, the programs have not been generated by a centralised strategic planning mechanism. Initiatives for new programs have come from universities, research institutes, firms, industry associations, etc., and they are dealt with informally or semi-informally in various co-operation bodies with representatives from the above-mentioned organizations.

The emphasis of the national technology programs in the 1980s was on information technology, not on basic technologies, but rather on generic technologies that could be applied in different branches of the industry. The programs have catalysed technological development in Finland, but perhaps more than that; the national technology programs have been a very important catalyst for national co-operation. An important new feature in these programs has been that the earlier bilateral co-operation has been transformed into multilateral co-operation. Firms, research institutes and universities implement programs together. Co-operation other than that associated with the programs has also been expanded. In particular, this has concerned co-operation between universities and firms.

Tekes also set about creating the pre-requisites for the development of international co-operation. Finland's participation in Eureka co-operation was one of the first steps taken. This program began in 1985, and from the very outset Finland has been one of Eureka's most active members (Ormala et al, 1995). Tekes also played an important role during the period when Finland was preparing for participation in EU's research framework programs. EU research programs were opened up to the Finns, and to other EFTA countries, in 1987.

Due to several factors, but not least due to new initiatives in innovation policy in the early 1980s, economic growth in Finland in the 1980s was more robust than in most other industrialised countries. The paper industry and the metals and engineering industry remained Finland's most important exporters, but the share of high-technology products in industrial exports rose from 4 per cent in the early 1980s to 11 per cent in 1990. Moreover, the growth rate of Finnish patenting in the United States up until the end of the 1980s was one of the fastest in the world. In this respect, Finland was outperformed only by Japan, South Korea and Taiwan (Vartia and Ylä-Anttila, 1996).

4.5 Towards a knowledge based society (1989)

4.5.1 A national innovation system as a policy instrument

The latest transition in Finnish innovation policy occurred in the recession years of the early 1990s. However, this change did not stem directly from the recession. The process of change had already started in the late 1980s. The recession merely accelerated the adoption of new concepts and modes of operation. It is, however, more difficult to show how the 'new' innovation policy helped in conquering the recession. Taking account of the time lags associated with innovative activity, the 'new' innovation policy could not have had any significant impact on development in the first half of that decade. It would be more reasonable to conclude that the innovation policy of the 1980s helped to ensure that the recession, despite its depth, was short-lived.

An important milestone in the formulation of the 'new' innovation policy was the 1990 review by the Science and Technology Policy Council of Finland. The report of this authoritative body, which was led by the Prime Minister of the day, made the concept of a national innovation system an important instrument of Finland's innovation policy. It was a question of fairly direct Finnish application of the observations and conclusions made by evolutionary economists in the late 1980s (Freeman, 1991; Andersen & Lundvall, 1988; OECD, 1991). It should be pointed out that the Finnish application was developed before the publication of Lundvall et al (1992) and Nelson (1993) books.

The following have become key features of the national innovation system in Finland:

- A national innovation system is a whole set of factors influencing the development and utilisation of new knowledge and know-how. The concept allows these factors and their development needs to be examined in aggregate.
- A national research system forms an intrinsic part of a national system of innovation. Education is another important element of the innovation system.
- The general atmosphere prevailing in society also has a profound influence on the production and application of new knowledge. Another characteristic feature of an efficient innovation system is close interaction and co-operation between different actors.
- Internationalisation influences the activities of an innovation system in many ways. But the internationalisation process also emphasises the need to improve conditions for creating innovations nationally.

What kind of effects this approach has had in practice is still an open question. It has largely been a question of rhetoric used at the political level, which has not necessarily had much impact on activity at the grassroots level. However, it can be stated that the concept of a national innovation system has increased awareness of the role of innovations in economic and social development. It has extended the analysis of issues from research activity to other factors influencing research and development, and it has enhanced intergovernmental co-ordination. It has most probably increased national co-operation between different sectors and organizations.

Moreover, it has ensured an increase in the resources for industrial research in particular.

4.5.2 Key production factors: knowledge and expertise

In the mid-1990s, when recovery from the recession was already underway, the concept of knowledge-based society (or information society) began to be integrated into the concept of the national innovation system: the knowledge-based society (Science and Technology Policy Council of Finland, 1996). The new policy places emphasis on globalization, innovations and productivity growth. The central pre-requisite for these is regarded as increased knowledge and expertise through R&D and education. In Finland, particular attention has been paid to the information technology and communications industries and more broadly to the competitiveness of the infrastructure necessary for the application of information technology and for the knowledge-based society.

In 1966, on this basis, the government decided to increase state funding for research so that the GDP-share of R&D expenditure would rise to 2.9 per cent per annum by the year 1999. The funds necessary for these additional appropriations were obtained mainly from the sale of state-owned companies.

As a result of this decision, state funding for research has risen during the years 1997–1999 by a total of FIM 1.5 billion (EUR 250 million), which has meant an increase of about 25 per cent in the state's annual research appropriations from the 1997 level. With private sector R&D expenditure growing even faster than that of the public sector, the GDP share of R&D expenditure has exceeded the 3 per cent level. At the same time the share of the corporate sector in total R&D expenditure has risen to 70 per cent.

Most of these additional public funds have been channelled through Tekes. Tekes's appropriations for R&D loans and grants as well as technology programs have increased significantly in recent years. However, the Academy of Finland was the agency that saw the fastest growth in its research resources in late 1990s: from 1995 to 2000 the Academy's funding volume increased by almost 80 per cent in real terms (The Academy of Finland, 2000). A major part of these resources and part of the resources of Tekes have been allocated to the universities. Consequently, resources of university research have been growing in Finland. On the other hand, universities have become more and more dependent on external financing.

In its latest review the Science and Technology Policy Council of Finland suggests that public funding needs to be increased cumulatively by

EUR 200 million over the 2001–2004 period (Science and Technology Policy Council of Finland, 2000). This means that Finland has decided to follow a different development path from most other OECD countries, in which R&D funding has stagnated or even started to decline. The Council argues that such an increase is justified in relation both to the tasks of the public sector in innovation policies and to the development of private R&D funding and the capacity of state finances. 'The national economy is improved by means of activities which create new knowledge and new operational structures, which in turn also creates better conditions for the operation of the public sector.'

4.5.3 More attention paid to technology diffusion

No significant changes occurred in the basic instruments of innovation policy during the 1990s. The main public-sector actors, besides Tekes, are still VTT and the universities of technology. The activities of the Academy of Finland, which concentrates on funding basic research carried out in universities, have been expanded. Since Finland became a member state of the European Union in 1995, Finland's participation in EU research programs has increased markedly (Luukkonen and Niskanen, 1998; Luukkonen et al, 1999). This has increased the EU's influence on the policy pursued in Finland, but the changes in structures and basic policy directions have been fewer than expected.

The most significant change within national innovation policy has been the creation of new problems and organizations associated with technology transfer, diffusion, and commercialisation. Nation-wide networks of technology parks and centres of expertise have been set up in Finland. The technology parks have initiated spin-off projects and incubators. Different kinds of technology transfer companies have been established to commercialise the results generated in universities and research institutes. Public and private venture capital operations have increased, although the market in Finland is less developed than in many other European countries, not to mention in the United States. Some of these arrangements have been created at the national level, but many have come into being on the basis of local and regional initiatives, albeit with national funding.

4.5.4 Strengthening regional innovation policy

An important factor concerning the strengthening of regional innovation policy has been the EU's regional policy in general and the key instrument of this policy in particular i.e. the EU's structural funds (Lemola, 1998). Regional policy has always been pursued in Finland, and with particular vigour since the end of the Second World War. Up until the mid-1990s, however, the regional dimension of innovation policy was minimal in Finland. According to the innovation policy doctrine of the 1970s and 1980s, regionality would unavoidably lead to the inappropriate and inefficient use of resources. The achievement of critical mass was regarded as a basic pre-requisite for effective and productive research activity. This was seen as requiring that the allocation and use of research resources be examined from a national rather than regional perspective.

This doctrine is still in use, but it is no longer as relevant as earlier. A number of reforms to Finnish regional administration were made in the mid-1990s, and these improved the regions' ability to carry out the tasks associated with innovation policy. Efforts have been made to take advantage of these opportunities, largely with the aid of funding coming through the EU's structural funds. As the role of innovative activity and its funding is strengthened within the structural funds, we can expect to see the strengthening of the regional level continuing in Finland as well. This will mean a new type of situation for national innovation policy, which will face growing pressures from the direction of the EU and from the direction of the regions (with the assistance of the EU). Policy decisions will increasingly be negotiated in multi-level and multi-actor arenas and related actor networks.

4.5.5 Increasing connectivity

As mentioned before, the systemic approach spread to Finnish innovation policy through the writings of evolutionary economists. In addition, Michael Porter and particularly his book 'The Competitive Advantage of Nations', which came out in 1990, has had a strong influence in Finland. In the early 1990s, the Research Institute of the Finnish Economy (ETLA) and the Finnish National Fund for Research and Development (SITRA) started an extensive project on Finnish industries' competitive advantage. It was based on Porter's cluster approach. The project identified and analysed nine specific Finnish industrial clusters (Hernesniemi et al, 1996).

Based on these analyses, the Finnish government made a decision to allocate part of the resources included in the program for increases in government research funding 1997–1999 to the further development of Finland's industrial clusters. The co-ordination of this funding was made by sectoral ministries that started eight national cluster programs. In general terms, the cluster programs have very ambitious aims. They aim to generate growth, improve industries' competitiveness and productivity, increase employment, generate new innovations and improve social welfare. So far, in the real world, the main results of the programs have been improved co-operation between cluster members, increased knowledge flows and spillovers, networking, and deepening co-operation between and within public and private sectors (Pentikäinen, 2000).

4.5.6 Engine of growth: telecommunications equipment

Finland recovered from the last recession almost as quickly and surprisingly as it had plunged into it. This was largely achieved on the back of rapid growth in exports (Pajarinen et al, 1998). Exports have accounted for a larger share of GDP than at any point in Finland's economic history. Traditional industries such as paper, metals and engineering, and chemicals have all increased their exports, but the strongest growth has been in the electronics industry. This has already become a more important exporter than the paper industry.

Finland is rapidly specialising in high-technology fields with global markets. The change of emphasis has been very rapid especially since the recession years. Telecommunications technology has risen to become Finland's area of great strength. Finland and Sweden are more specialised in the exporting of telecommunications equipment than any other country in the world. Telecommunications equipment accounts for a full two-thirds of Finland's hi-tech exports.

Economic development in Finland in recent years, and Finland's innovation policy cannot be examined without considering the Nokia Corporation. At the present time, Nokia is one of the world's leading mobile phone suppliers and it has a strong position as a supplier of mobile and fixed telecom networks, including related customer services. Nokia Corporation's share of Finnish exports was already approaching one-fifth in the late 1990s (Pajarinen et al, 1998). The effect of the company on gross domestic product has been 1–1.5 percentage points. It is difficult to find a comparative situation anywhere else in the world. Nokia is the flagship of Finnish technology, but is it also the flagship of Finnish innovation policy?

Nokia's success is no accident and neither is it a lone star, although it does occupy an exceptionally strong position in the Finnish innovation system (Ali-Yrkkö et al, 2000). Founded over 130 years ago, Nokia Corporation began to diversify into electronics and telecommunications back in the 1960s. At the beginning of the 1980s Nokia was the market leader in the production of mobile telephones among the Nordic countries and, by the end of the decade, was a significant factor in other markets, too. The world's first real GSM phone call was made on a telephone manufactured by Nokia in Finland in March 1991. With the breakthrough of digital telephones in 1993, Nokia was exceptionally well prepared for the growing markets and intensifying competition.

Innovation policy has provided Nokia with good background support. Training and research systems have furnished the company with both knowledge and trained personnel. When the first national technology programs emphasising information technology were launched in Finland in the early 1980s, Nokia Corporation participated actively in the preparation and implementation of these programs. Nokia was also involved in Finland's first Eureka and EU projects. The importance of Finland's innovation system for Nokia is indicated by the fact that 65 per cent of Nokia's R&D work and an even bigger proportion of its strategic research is still performed in Finland.

4.6 Summary

In Finland, science and technology and their economic significance crystallised as a topic of debate and government activities later than in bigger and more advanced OECD countries. The late start was counterbalanced by the fact the development of innovation policy has proceeded quickly in Finland from early 1980s.

In the 1990s, under the conditions of deep economic recession, Finland started to strengthen their orientation towards a knowledge-based society. Innovation policy focuses on the development and utilisation of knowledge and know-how. The long-term development line in Finnish innovation policy has been determined input into R&D, and a strong belief in the potential of ICT for Finland's economic and social development. Even the innovation policy of the future will build on these grounds.

The theoretical roots of the Finnish innovation policy of 1990s originate from three more or less interrelated sources. The first is the concept of the national innovation system developed by Freeman, Lundvall and Nelson. The second is the model developed by Porter for analysis of industrial clusters. The third one is the concept of information society that dates back to the works of several authors from late 1970s. These approaches have offered ideas and justification for policy making.

The concept of national innovation system has emphasised that there is a whole set of factors influencing the development and utilising knowledge and know-how. It has also paid attention to the fact that an efficient innovation system is based on a close interaction and co-operation between different actors. The concept of industrial clusters has increased understanding on the dynamics of industrial development, and the role of the telecommunication cluster in Finnish industrial structure. For its part, the concept of information society has been teaching that the development can be based on high-standard know-how and utilisation of modern information and communications technology.

However, it is worth emphasising that innovation policy in Finland has been a very pragmatic activity. Decision-making has been based to a large extent on the personal knowledge and views of key persons and groups. Closely related to this, the Finnish case demonstrates that the evolution of innovation policy very much reflects path dependence and social relations, which existed at the time of constructing the policy machinery. In Finland, the basic elements and measures of innovation policy were created in the late 1960s, and still today they constitute the core of the machinery.

There are both external and internal factors which may have even dramatic effects on the direction of Finnish innovation policy in the coming years. Of external factors the most important one is the latest phase of globalization, which was initiated in the 1980s by widespread deregulation of financial markets and competition as well as advances in information and communication technology. Foreign direct investments and multinational companies have a central role in this process. Instead of direct intervention, the governments have to pay more attention to improving framework conditions or operational environment of firms (Pajarinen et al, 1998).

Progress of European integration increases pressures on the role of the national level in innovation policy. The room for national manoeuvring will diminish for three reasons. First, the EU is going to take a more active role in the strategic direction of the aggregate and its parts. Secondly, increasing interaction, benchmarking etc. between member countries leads to a natural convergence of national innovation policies. Thirdly, it is most probable that strengthening of regional innovation policy will continue. This is in the interest of the EU, and this development is getting support from global competition. The growing significance of location factors forces regions to take care of their attractiveness or competitiveness.

A central internal factor, shaping Finnish innovation policy, is finding a proper balance between economic and social dimensions in the development and implementation of information and communications technologies. Finland has strongly committed itself to being in the forefront as a developer of an information society. This is a very ambitious aim. Traditionally

Finnish innovation policy has been carried out along the lines of technocratic argumentation. The justification for policy measures has been mainly based on expected economic values in terms of new innovations and firms, productivity gains, employment and economic growth.

In the future, the perspective of Finnish innovation policy has to be widened in the direction of social aspects. One-sided development of information society leads to the exclusion of some population groups and regions. The increasing use of ICT reduces labour needs. Electronic transactions and trade increases inequality between people if the cost of reliable and well-organized information services is too high. The constantly expanding data systems include more and more information about individuals, which, if abused, may compromise people's privacy, and all in all growing dependence on ICT may increase risks in nearly all activities. The Finnish innovation policy has to become more aware of the implications of its activities.

References

Academy of Finland (2000): The State and Quality of Scientific Research in Finland. Publications of the Academy of Finland 7/2000. Helsinki.

Ali-Yrkkö, J./Paija, L./Reilly, C./Ylä-Anttila, P. (2000): NOKIA – A Big Company in a Small Country. ETLA, B:162, Helsinki.

Andersen, E.-S./Lundvall, B.-Å. (1988): Small National Systems of Innovation. Freeman, C./Lundvall, B.-Å. (eds.), Small Countries Facing the Technological Revolution, Pinter Publishers, London.

Freeman, C. (1991): Technology Policy and Economic Performance: Lessons from Japan, Pinter Publishers, London.

Hernesniemi, H./Lammi, M./Ylä-Anttila, P. (1996): Advantage Finland – The Future of Finnish Industries, Taloustieto Oy, Helsinki.

Lemola, T. (1994): Characteristics of Technology Policy in Finland, in: Vuori, S./Vuorinen, P. (eds.), Explaining Technical Change in a Small Country – The Finnish National Innovation System, ETLA, B:84, Helsinki, Published by Physica-Verlag, Heidelberg, pp.184–200.

Lemola, T. (1998): Different Perspectives on the Problems and Challenges Facing the Finnish Innovation System. A paper for an international conference in Helsinki 26.–27.11.1998 'Challenges of the Finnish Innovation System – Transformation Towards a Learning Economy', organised by the Finnish National Fund for Research and Development (Sitra).

Lemola, T./Lovio, R. (1988): Possibilities for a Small Country in High-Technology Production: the Electronics Industry in Finland. Freeman, C./Lundvall, B.-Å. (eds.) Small Countries Facing the Technological Revolution, Pinter Publishers, London, pp.130–155.

Lundvall, B.-Å. (ed.) (1992): National Systems of Innovation, Pinter Publishers, London.

Luukkonen, T./Hälikkä, S./Niskanen, P./Riikka, E. (1999): Finnish Participation in the Fourth Framework Programme, Publication of the Tekes international Co-operation 4/1999.

Nelson, R. (ed.) (1993): National Innovation Systems, Oxford University Press.

OECD (1991): TEP-The Technology Economy Programme: Technology in a Changing World, Paris.

Ormala, E. et al (1993): The Evaluation of the Indusrial and Economic Effects of Eureka.

Pajarinen, M./Rouvinen, P./Ylä-Anttila, P. (1998): Small Country Strategies in Global Competition. Benchmarking the Finnish Case, ETLA B:144, Helsinki.

Pentikäinen, T. (2000): The Economic Evaluation of the Finnish Cluster Programmes. VTT Group for Technology Studies, Working Papers no. 50/2000. Espoo.

Porter, M. (1990): The Competitive Advantage of Nations. New York: The Macmillan Press Ltd.

Science and Technology Policy Council of Finland (1990): Review 1990 – Guidelines for Science and Technology Policy in the 1990s, Government Printing Centre, Helsinki.

Science and Technology Policy Council of Finland (1996), Finland: A Knowledge-based Society, EDITA, Helsinki.

Science and Technology Policy Council of Finland (2000): Review 2000: The Challenge of Knowledge and Know-how. EDITA, Helsinki.

Vartia, P./Ylä-Anttila, P. (1996): Kansantalous 2021 (The Finnish Economy 2021), ETLA B:113, Helsinki (in Finnish).

Vuori, S./Ylä-Anttila, P. (1992): Introduction. Vuori, S./Ylä-Anttila, P. (eds.), Mastering Technology Diffusion – The Finnish Experience, ETLA, B:82, Helsinki, pp.1–38.

Chapter 5

Changes in Danish Innovation Policy – Responses to the Challenges of a Dynamic Business Environment

Jesper Lindgaard Christensen

5.1 Introduction[1]

As in other West-European countries, Danish innovation policies have undergone significant changes during the past couple of decades. Moreover, perhaps one of the most important changes is that innovation has received a great deal more attention and greater priority in overall industrial policy. It is fair to say that even if the importance of technological development has been recognised for a long time, 'innovation' has now become the buzzword of Danish industrial policies to a much larger extent.

Promoting innovation through changing institutional structures and incentives is bounded by the institutional and political set-up in which the policy is to be implemented. In other words, the historical roots of the Danish mode of innovation provide an important trajectory for those policies that could be expected to be effective and efficient.

Policy changes are, however, not only a result of previous developments, because this would require that all past political decisions were made on a completely well-informed basis in a world without different political interests. In practice, governments are unable to operate without failures, political conflicts and public debates, all of which may influence decisions. Furthermore, the knowledge on the nature of the innovation process has improved immensely. Moreover, governments learn from experience about what works and what fails. Likewise, the scope for efficient policy is bounded by the national industrial structure, norms and traditions for collaboration etc.

Therefore, innovation policy is a much more demanding task than simply copying successful schemes from abroad. As a result, political strategies change over time in response to all of these forces.

Following this argument, and in order to understand the development of innovation policy, it is important to define the context in which it is to operate, in other words, the special features of Danish innovation must be explained. This is done in section 2. The main changes in innovation policies are explained in section 3. Next, in section 4, the present challenges for innovation policies are discussed, as is the source of inspiration for these policies, in particular to what extent academic research influences policymaking. Measures to cope with these changes are exemplified in section 5. These examples are not chosen randomly, but illustrate some important principles of policy making. Finally, section 6 summarises the main arguments of the paper and points to possible future policy developments.

5.2 Characteristics of a possible Danish mode of innovation

The headline of this section does, of course, exaggerate how far one can go in defining a uniform mode of innovation, which is characteristic for all Danish firms. In practise, firms differ in their objectives, and in the sources of inspiration for innovation, and in how radical the innovations are, or in how benefits are appropriated etc. Nevertheless, it is possible to point to some general features of innovation in Denmark.

This issue is analysed in a large research project called DISKO (Danish Innovation System in KOmpartive perspective). The overall objective was to map the Danish innovation system and to enhance the understanding of the innovation processes in Danish firms.[2] This research has indeed inspired policy making as will be discussed later. The final report from the project (Lundvall, 1999) summarised the findings and put them in a broader perspective. With respect to a possible specific Danish mode of innovation the following features, among others, were pointed out.

Based on data concerning the specialisation of Danish exports and production, technological development in Denmark may be characterised as being heavily specialised in low-technology products. There are some high technology fields in Danish production, for example, in pharmaceuticals (dominated by NOVO) but generally, the science-based industries make up a small share of the economy.

On the other hand, Denmark is especially successful in the production and export of 'low' and 'low medium' technology goods. This includes food products, furniture, and clothing. In addition, successful niche productions have been established in a number of areas like windmills, health care products, seed production, and environmental technologies. Some of these areas have been stimulated or even started by public regulation and/or the welfare model of Denmark. Firms are generally good at absorbing and using technology including information technology and process optimisation. Incremental product development characterises both the high technology and the low technology firms.

In fact, there was an early recognition by policy-makers about the nature of the Danish technological development along the lines mentioned above. Thus, a 1990 policy document emphasised the following:

> ...for a country like Denmark it is of great importance that new technology is introduced in the production process. Many so-called low-tech industries have survived on skill-full implementation of new technology in all phases of the production process, and this may improve competitiveness significantly. This type of technological development must not be under-estimated (Industri-ministeriet, 1990, p.11).

In spite of this recognition, the same document proceeds immediately after the quoted passage by arguing how vital science-based R&D is, and the policy recommendations derived are without exception targeted at enhancing R&D and the system for appropriation (ibid., p.12). This seems to be a paradox: it is emphasised that technological development is based on a wide range of innovative capabilities, not only science. Nevertheless, R&D-policies are advocated. Apparently, the policy making is subject to a considerable inertia and lack of creativity. Moreover, the political will to make more targeted policies was generally lacking – something which changed shortly after, as we shall see in the next section.

Another feature of the Danish innovation system is the system for vocational and adult training.

In Denmark this may be characterised as heavily targeted towards upgrading general qualifications, at least that part of the training system which is publicly funded. The policy rationale is to improve labour market flexibility by upgrading general skills and avoiding free-rider behaviour of firms if the financing is private. However, the qualifications needed in the new business environment are to a large extent abilities to co-operate, communicate etc., which, it may be argued, are to be learned most efficiently in the specific context in which the persons are expected to co-operate, that is the firm. It is consequently advocated by some observers that the training system should be adjusted towards a more firm specific model (Nyholm et al, 2001 p.264).

Changes in the vocational training system in the direction of a more firm specific model were also called for a decade ago (Industriministeriet, 1990 p.14). Changes in this direction have been small and slow. One of the reasons is probably an internal fight between ministries on what their resort area should be. On the other hand, the collaboration between ministries has generally improved over time as a consequence of pure necessity – innovations are increasingly complex and require different actors to take part.

Still another feature of the innovation system in Denmark is a high propensity to collaborate on innovation. Within firms, there is a growing emphasis on the interaction across departments, between colleagues and between management and workers. Danish manufacturing firms interact with customers and suppliers more frequently than firms in other countries. On the other hand, the interaction with universities is less developed in Denmark than abroad. To a certain degree this reflects a rather well functioning system of technological intermediaries who communicate new technological insights to the firms (Christensen, Schibany, Vinding, 2001).

5.3 Phases of innovation policies

We now move to an overview of the important phases of innovation policies during the past three decades. In some cases, it is difficult to differentiate between the broader industrial policy and innovation policy. We see that policy has changed form being technology oriented to innovation oriented and that different policy principles have been the basis for policies in different periods of time. It is subsequently discussed what the sources of inspiration for the policies pursued are.

5.3.1 The development of innovation policy

Before the 1970s, technology policy was hardly discussed. Only as a part of the general industrial policy and discussions on productivity development was technological development mentioned as a policy issue. During the 1970s, a specific technology policy gradually appeared although it was still not an important part of industrial policy. Instruments used allowed firms tax deductions for R&D-expenditures, and in 1973, the Law on Technological Service was passed through Parliament. This law specified an increased involvement of the Government in the financing and running of the technological assistance to firms. It included the establishment of the Technological Council (Dalum et al, 1991). In addition to this important policy change, a fund was established in 1970 (UdviklingsFondet – the Development Fund), which granted loans to private firms for the development of their product and process innovations and their R&D expenditures. This Fund fulfilled a need in the industry and was administrated in a non-bureaucratic manner. It lived for an unusually long period, since it was not ended until 1990. A complementary Fund was established in 1977 (Statstilskud til produktudvikling – Government subsidy to product development) to fund not only developments of new innovations, but also to fund improvements of existing products in small firms, thus covering more incremental innovations. After a decade in operation, this complementary Fund changed its purpose to that of supporting firms, which were being established. The industrial policy of the 1970s may be characterised as somewhat fragmented and based on firm specific subsidies granted on rather general criteria. The growing number of initiatives in the beginning of the 1970s, were to a large extent a reaction to the economic crises.

In the beginning of the 1980s, a re-orientation of industrial policies started which was more selective rather than general. Some new policy instruments were introduced, under which the collaboration between a firm and a partner with special knowledge was the prerequisite for a grant. Moreover, it was specifically mentioned in the formulation of the policy that socio-economic needs were a valid criterion for granting subsidies. The Technology Council (Teknologirådet) was in particular active in this policy formulation, which did meet some resistance from the Industry Associations (IndustriRådet). Also the government became more active in industrial policy although the role of the government was a both-and. On the one hand, the new, liberal government (which replaced the social democrats in 1982) changed macro-economic policies, including fixed exchange-rate policies. Thus the room for manoeuvre in the economic policy was reduced, as were the available instruments. This made the government look for alternative instruments and consider the possibilities of using industrial policy. On the other hand, the government was reluctant to be too interventionist in its approach.

Even before the change of government, a re-orientation of the design of policies began. In the mid-1980s and to some extent even a couple of years before, there was a rapid increase in the number of different types of subsidies. Moreover, there was an increase in the promotion of business in several ministries. In particular, the Ministry of Environment and Ministry of Foreign Affairs increased their share of industrial policy. In 1983, a policy was introduced which focused upon programs for stimulating specific generic technologies. Thus, as expenditures for technology policy increased gradually and only marginally, the expenditures for this program policy increased steeply. Important examples include the 1983 Teknologisk Udviklings Program (Technological Development Programme), which started the development of this type of policy. It was followed by a bio-tech program, a program for developing and using new materials, a program for Food Technology and a program on Strategic Research in Environmental Technologies (Industriministeriet, 1991; 1992). These programs concentrated on stimulating R&D in selected areas.[3] For example, TUP focused on information technologies.

This new program policy also introduced the incorporation of a wider array of actors in the policy implementation process. Traditionally, the IndustriRådet and Håndværksrådet (two major industry associations) have had an important say in the formulation and implementation of policy. However, they were only marginally included. Instead, the Association of Electronics Manufacturers was an important player in the TUP program.

The new program policy was inspired by, and resembles those of, other countries. For example, programs in Sweden and the UK stimulating IT were much like the Danish TUP-program. However, the Danish program took into account a Danish mode of innovation in that it placed greater emphasis on the diffusion of technology rather than development of basic technologies. It was also broader in the selection of its target industries as it aimed at stimulating the use of IT in traditional industries as well.[4]

After 1989 and a considerable number of years in the 1990s, there was a reduction in the number of subsidies (of which there were more than 40 and were beginning to be complicated for the users). In the beginning of 1990s, there was even a decrease in the amount spent on industrial and technology policy initiatives. A re-orientation had taken place where research policy gained a higher priority relative to industrial policy. This change in policy was inspired by discussions abroad on the inexpedient effects of selective policies by 'picking the winner' or 'supporting the loser'.

In 1992, it was stated that program policies would be continued (Industriministeriet, 1992 p.41). However, it was realised soon afterwards that a re-orientation of policies was needed. Rather than one-sided stimulation of the supply-side, a different perspective was called for, recognising that a top-down direction of technological development was useless. Previously, during the phase of program policy, there was a widespread belief that technological development could be pushed in a planned top-down direction. This perception was abandoned with the shift of policies towards framework conditions. On the initiative of The Danish Business Development Council (EUR), a number of studies were conducted using an approach, which resembles that of earlier Porter studies and similar studies using the cluster approach. These studies were denoted resource area studies meaning studies of not only private firms in a sector or an aggregation of traditional sectors, but rather an array of different firms, public and private knowledge institutions, suppliers etc. The common denominator defining the resource area is to a large extent the demand for the end product.[5] Moreover, the resource areas are defined as sharing roughly the same factor conditions. The latter point is important, because it means that policies may be targeted towards these areas rather than the traditional statistical aggregation of industries or – as in the program policies – towards stimulating the generic technologies.

In addition to studies of these areas, cross-sectional studies were undertaken. Together, they formed the basis for a policy development process. As a follow-up on the analyses it was decided to establish a forum for dialogue with representatives from each of the clusters with the purpose of detecting special framework conditions and needs for targeted policies. A reference group consequently monitors each single resource area with representatives from firms, organizations, and relevant ministries. Discussions in these groups and ad-hoc working sub-groups help policy makers to identify critical framework conditions and possibilities to improve these. Results of these processes are greater cross-ministerial co-ordination as the resource areas are defined in a broader way than traditional industries and because the framework conditions often involves resorts of Ministry of Education, Ministry of Labour and Ministry of Research.[6]

Furthermore, there are concrete results of these processes in the form of policy initiatives. In an early 1997 report (Erhvervsfremme Styrelsen, 1997) on the status of the outcome of the process it was found that 29 ad-hoc working groups have been established, 513 different people from a wide spectrum of organizations, ministries etc. were involved, 152 policy suggestions (both suggestions to completely new initiatives, changes in existing legislation, changes in administration, changes in priorities in fiscal budgets) were developed, of which 66 were actually implemented.

In 1966, when the Ministry, together with other ministries became engaged in analyses and discussions on the broader aspects of innovation – especially in relation to the work in 'Velfærdskommissionen' (Welfare Commission) – focus was extended to the intertwined effects of organizational and technological change and to the importance of development of human resources. Recent surveys show consistently that the role of human resources is still more important for the ability of firms to innovate.

Recently another dialogue was established between representatives from the businesses and The Ministry of Industry. This was initiated as a response to warnings from industry that the long-run competitiveness of businesses was in danger. This was argued to have resulted in a decline in exports (which later showed to be a minor downswing in a long period of increased exports) and should make the Government react, it was argued. As a consequence, a forum for dialogue was established, Industriens Udviklingsgruppe (Industrial Development Group), which included representatives from large businesses and The Ministry of Industry. The purpose was to discuss how long-run competitiveness and productivity growth could be ensured.

Although it may be possible to identify such phases of policy, changes tended to be gradual and some particular instruments existed in more than one period. Moreover, although there may be a certain policy strategy, the actual policy implementation process could considerably modify the original idea.

5.3.2 Inspiration for recent changes in innovation policies

The sources of inspiration for policy development are naturally a multiplicity of types.

The examples above show that the inspiration for innovation policy may be spurred by a downswing, which is what traditional, Keynesian policy principles, should advocate – in recessions, a need for active industrial policy arises. However, the shift is now not to support the loser, rather it is to develop national champions and to let policies follow technological waves rather than economic fluctuations.

It is also clear from the examples above that the Danish policy makers have emphasised a direct dialogue with the businesses, organizations and even single persons with ideas for policy improvements. This direct dialogue is supplemented with various reference groups, which have representatives from industry, either directly from single firms or indirectly from organizations. This dialogue between policy makers and business has persisted in Danish innovation policy for a decade.

Throughout this decade, there has also been a dialogue with academics, and policy makers within The Ministry of Industry have been active in learning what the innovation policy relevant implications of developments in economic theory are. Civil servants from the Ministry of Industry have persistently kept direct contact with academia with the purpose of learning about new developments in the understanding of innovation. There is, however, still room for further development of ways of communication between academia and policy makers as emphasised by Nyholm et al (2001, p.270). Indeed, research in innovation has inspired innovation policy making in Denmark. This goes for various research projects of an applied nature. In addition, policy makers have referred to the general development of economic theory when arguing for changes in innovation policy. In particular, advances in the systems approach to innovation (Edquist et al, 1997) and the evolutionary theory (Metcalfe, 1995a; 1995b) have contributed to a change in the way innovation policy is argued. Some of the policy initiatives and some of the overall formulations of government policies may be characterised as a systems approach. Moreover, the vocabulary is close to that used in the literature concerning the systems approach to innovation policy. However, when it comes to practical policy it is more ad-hoc rather than integrated in an overall strategy. Furthermore, it is most common that the causality is that policy initiatives are decided and arguments for the policy are subsequently found in the literature on innovation and the new economy. The traditional market failure perspective as a rationale for policy making has now been abandoned, at least in The Ministry of Industry.[7] Instead, the focus is upon the coherence of the innovation system.

The direct contact is complemented with the indirect influence of academia stemming from mainly two sources. First, the study of economics has become more oriented towards the introduction of modern innovation theory. At most universities, the students are also introduced to industrial policy, including innovation policy. Consequently, this means greater awareness of innovation theory when these economists eventually become employed in the central administration. This is probably the most important source of long-run change in policy thinking. Secondly, Danish Ministries have used consultants to undertake large evaluations and similar analyses, but it is usually required that the consultants incorporate leading academics either in reference groups or directly in parts of the work. This is an important way of capturing, in a practical setting, the insights gained from developments in economic theory. The evaluations are, of course, themselves an instrument for policy learning, although they are often not used efficiently as such.

Internally, the Ministry of Industry not only keeps contact to academia but also deliberately upgrades the academic skills of policy makers. Thus, civil servants are encouraged to read and write academic papers, and to attend conferences. Recruitment views having had an academic career as an advantage. Furthermore, an internal Center for Research in Industrial Policy (Center for Erhvervspolitisk Forskning) has been established as well as other similar units for applied research on issues relevant for industrial policy.

One strategy for policy learning within this field is to increase the exchange of cross-country experiences. This is already taking place at the level of national civil servants studying innovation policy in other countries. However, the processes are fragmented and to some extent constrained by e.g. language differences. The process could benefit from studies of systematic, research-based foundations. It is currently being considered in the Danish Ministry of Industry how a systematic monitoring of policies in other countries should be organized.

Recent changes in policy are also driven by internal budget constraints. The political system is reluctant to approve permanent expenditures for industrial policy. Therefore, the general change in policy is towards developing more flexible, temporary policy instruments. We shall later get back to this point.

5.4 Challenges for policy posed by the development of the business environment

The above mentioned increased complexity of innovation is probably one of the most important changes in the way the innovation process is perceived. The increased complexity has several dimensions. Firstly, the focus is now on not only new products and new processes. To an increasing extent, it has been recognised that new forms of organizations, augmented services in relation to manufacturing, and development of new after-innovation methods are crucial for economic performance. The way policy makers think about innovation is now broadening from a focus upon manufacturing industry towards innovation in services too.

This is reflected in the intensity and in the way firms collaborate on innovation. Firms tend to innovate in collaboration with other firms and with a broad set of institutions. Moreover, innovations often relate to more than one specific knowledge base. A new food product may for example involve basic knowledge from biotechnology (genetic engineering), chemicals, logistic processes and conservation/packaging. Likewise, the ability to innovate is increasingly dependent upon different types of institutions outside research like labour market institutions, education etc.[8] This constitutes a challenge for policy-making, as it requires collaboration between policy makers from different ministries. Often this is not only a clash of different fields of competencies but also of different cultures and approaches to policy making. Despite the fact that innovation policy in Denmark is viewed in a more holistic manner compared to many other countries,[9] and there is increased collaboration between ministries, there is still a relatively sharp resort-dependent division of policy areas. This is seen a major barrier to a multi-disciplinary innovation policy. To make it even more complicated, the rate and mode of innovation in a nation has been said to be dependent upon social capital, which may be difficult to stimulate by way of traditional innovation policy.

Secondly, innovation is not necessarily based upon glamorous, radical new inventions. A wide range of different firms in different industries innovate, although this is often in an incremental way (Christensen, 2000b). Incremental innovations are often embedded in a firm specific setting, and are based upon tacit knowledge. Tacit knowledge, in turn, is not easily transferable as opposed to the increased flows of codified knowledge. At the same time tacit knowledge becomes still more important. This is also a challenge to innovation policy as it highlights the importance of the regional dimension of policy making. In spite of increasing internationalisation, innovation policy is still important in a national and even regional context (Lundvall & Borras, 1997).

Thirdly, the above mentioned increased tendency to collaborate on innovation makes policies to stimulate collaboration even more central in the future (this is exemplified later). In many countries, special attention is paid to stimulating knowledge transfer from knowledge institutions to private firms. In Denmark, as well as in many other countries, the re-orientation of innovation policy has meant a movement from firm-specific subsidies to supporting institutions collaborating with firms.

Fourthly, the development is characterised by turbulent, fast changes, which in itself makes innovation policy more difficult. This makes it even more necessary to monitor closely the development and to develop flexible, temporary policy instruments. For example, the Danish government has implemented a monitoring exercise, where key indicators on innovation etc. are benchmarked against other countries. Furthermore, through 2001–03 the Government has decided to implement an account on national competence development (Regeringen, 2000 p.24). Official statistical data are, however, often rather old when they are released, and often the data are not focused upon indicators reflecting the new economy. Therefore, dialogue with leading-edge firms and knowledge institutions is essential. Moreover, it is the ambition of the Danish government to develop policies which temporarily stimulate the market forces and then to quickly pull out of the markets as soon as these work properly.

Fifthly, as information is generally available, and as all countries try to set up the best possible general framework conditions, the critical success factor increasingly becomes that of developing specific framework conditions, which may be useful for only a segment of the market and which may be 'softer' factors. Finally, the systems approach to innovation policy advocates focus upon the coherence of the systems and the ability of institutions to upgrade the learning capacity of firms. However, in order for this policy to be successful, it is a prerequisite that competencies of consultants, of investors in new firms, of potential entrepreneurs and managers are sufficient to render fruitful collaboration. In other words, the absorptive ability of firms to incorporate new knowledge is dependent upon the competence of the parties. Therefore, a general increase of competencies will make innovation policy more efficient. This is, however, a difficult policy area, and considerable creativity in policy making is called for. One response to this challenge is the Danish LOK-program (LOK= Management, Organization and Competence),[10] which was heavily inspired by academic research in the Danish innovation system.

5.5 Selected examples of innovation policies – principles for policy making

5.5.1 Policies aimed at improving the risk capital market

It is obvious that the availability of capital is an important part of a well-functioning national innovation system. It has been rightly claimed that financial institutions are the 'glue' in national innovation systems as they bind together different types of agents in the NIS, and are the selection mechanisms of business opportunities. Therefore, it is of paramount importance to have a wide range of institutions within the financial system to perform this selection in a competent and adequate manner.

A number of government initiatives have aimed to fill in the gaps in the financing of firms.[11] The intention behind the design of these initiatives is that they should contribute improving the access to capital in the different stages of the firm's development.

Government initiatives and the private market-driven development have no doubt contributed to a narrowing of the financing gap mentioned earlier.

There are further plans or actions already taken within the government to improve access to finance, including the establishment of a business angels network and changes in the legislative regulation of investments from pension funds.

In general, all initiatives are inspired by similar schemes in other countries. A similar approach is taken in other countries as well: inspiration to policy formulation on risk capital comes to a large extent from abroad,[12] but also through dialogue with suppliers of capital and with academics. Interestingly, ideas within this area have a considerable entry time. For example, a business angel network was proposed in 1992 (Koppel, 1992), a loan guarantee scheme in 1992 (Christensen, 1992), mezzanine capital in 1992 (Christensen, 1992). This is not to say that it was unwise to not implement these schemes earlier. Rather, it shows two things. It shows that the policy process is a balance between interests – in this case the agents on the market have been very conservative and reluctant towards changes that are not purely market driven. In addition, it shows that the timing of government initiatives is crucial. What may be politically feasible and work in practise in one period may function very differently in another period of time. The market may in many cases need certain maturity before private agents adopt policy initiatives.

The above target of policies illustrates two of the general policy principles derived from this case. First, innovation policy is most often targeted towards a specific segment of the industry rather than general, macro policies. It is a very clear picture from government programs that they are primarily targeted towards the seed or early stage segment. Secondly, the need for policy intervention is as dynamic as the development of the business environment. Therefore, the need for innovation policy depends upon the business cycle and structural development in general. Furthermore, the effectiveness of innovation policy may be dependent upon the timing and structural development. In addition to these two principles we may add a third principle, which has guided policy in particular in the risk capital market area but increasingly also other policy areas: the strategy of the policy intervention is to either give the private market forces a spark, then pull out as soon as the private agents have established a sustainable market. The strategy may also be to subsidise costs associated with learning to operate in a segment of the market where learning costs prevent private agents from operating profitably. The very early, seed funding of entrepreneurial businesses is one such market. In pursuing this strategy it is recognized that direct government participation may in some cases lead to government failure: even if the private market is not capable of solving a certain problem, then there is no guarantee that the government is any better. Therefore, the policy strategy is to build upon competencies already existing in the market. In some cases, however, there is no argument why government intervention should not be equally, or more, efficient than private agents.

5.5.2 Policies to stimulate collaboration on innovation

The importance of collaboration, co-operation and networking (ccn) in innovation has been much emphasised in recent economic thinking as well as in empirical work on innovation. For a long period, it has been recognised that firms rely heavily upon external partners in innovation activities. However, it is now widely believed that recent changes in the economy as a whole and more specifically in the way innovations are undertaken, have meant an enhanced role for ccn in innovation as was also pointed out in section 3. It is reasonable to expect this trend to continue and to be reinforced in the future. The arguments for this are several. It should here only be pointed to the fact that production is increasingly dependent upon knowledge, but not just any knowledge. Economists and sociologists alike agree that tacit knowledge is becoming still more important. This is in turn caused partly by the wide, easy access to information in general. When everybody has access to codified knowledge, then a leading edge in the competition must depend upon a unique knowledge not as easily accessible by others; it must depend on tacit knowledge. However, tacit knowledge is rarely produced in isolation and it is above all transferred in an interaction with the user of this information. Therefore, collaboration on developing and transferring useful knowledge for innovation is likely to increase.

Given the fact that ccn is key in tomorrow's industrial development, it becomes interesting to know how ccn is stimulated. In other words, this becomes a major policy issue. Following the argument above an example of Danish policies targeted at stimulating ccn is presented. The case, Centrekontrakter (Centre Contracts) is a scheme designed to enhance collaboration between universities, semi-public research institutions and industry. All three types of parties must take part and it is explicitly formulated that long-term competence building and innovation is one of the major objectives. This scheme may be seen as giving incentives to backward linking with knowledge institutions and it is heavily oriented towards *development* of relatively radical innovations. This scheme is seen as an important, new, instrument in Danish innovation policy.

As was discussed earlier, it has been a general trend in Danish innovation policy to turn focus away from single, isolated elements of the conditions for innovation, and instead enhancing the coherence of the different elements in the innovation system. The Centrecontract-scheme is an important example on such policies as it gives incentives to bring together key actors in the system. Thus, the objective of the Centrecontract-scheme is to intensify the cooperation between universities, private companies and the authorised technological service institutes (Christensen, 2000c). The Centrecontract-scheme was introduced in 1995 and is basically a government co-financing of the costs of Authorised Technological Service Institutes (up to 75 per cent) and research institutions (up to 100 per cent) in participating in a strategic collaboration with private firms on process or product development. The Authorised Technological Service Institutes are not only the key ccn partner and driving force behind establishment of the majority of Centre contracts, but also important intermediaries in the general knowledge transfer in the economy. Generally, the intermediaries are important institutions in Danish innovation system.

The aim with the scheme is that the specific impact should be three-fold: First, an (expected) effect on innovation. Second, the aim with the scheme is to increase competencies, especially in the GTS institutes. The third effect expected from the scheme is a pure network effect. It is explicitly formulated that the scheme is intended to stimulate networking among the partners not only during the centre contract but also on a longer term. One of the sub-objectives of the program is to transfer tacit knowledge.

Generally, the scheme is an adequate measure for bridging different elements in the innovation and knowledge system. It is often a problem to ensure productive collaboration between different types of partners because they have different incentives.[13] Evaluations have shown that the centre-contract scheme is an effective means of ensuring incentive compatibility and facilitating the transfer of knowledge between different parts of the innovation system. The above policy example shows that ccn policy has high priority in Danish innovation policy. The Danish firms tend to collaborate relatively often when developing new products although (due to the institutional structure of the innovation system) not as often directly with universities. Probably, this above average propensity to collaborate is rooted in a historical tradition for informal, trust-based collaboration, perhaps even stemming back to the co-operative movement in the beginning of 20th century. An additional explanation is the tradition for corporatism on the labour market.

5.6 Conclusions

This paper outlined different phases of Danish innovation policies. Although changes have been gradual, there was a clear movement from firm specific subsidies to program policy and subsequently to gearing framework conditions for targeted areas of industry. In recent years, the system approach to innovation policy has been important. Innovation policies now emphasise the coherence of the system, knowledge flows, competence building and ccn.

The inspiration for this change of policy has come from a multiple of sources. The policy formulation has been inspired by a combination of foreign programs, single private firms, organizations and academia. Both international and domestic sources of inspiration for policy change have been important. Thus, on some points, the OECD has inspired policy making as has both the general policy strategies of other countries as well as specific programs. To some extent, economic theory and researchers in other countries have inspired policy making, but probably the domestic sources are more predominant in Denmark than in other countries, even if Denmark is a small country. Moreover, the development of the business environment has resulted in a dynamic pressure on the innovation policy formulation. Specifically, the increased complexity and speed of the innovation process has challenged policy formulation. In addition, a broader perception of what is innovation and an increased collaboration between different actors makes innovation much broader than hitherto perceived. This means in turn involvement of a wider range of policy actors.

Reactions to these trends are necessary because the need for policy intervention is as dynamic as the development of the business environment. Therefore, the need for innovation policy depends upon the business cycle and the structural development in general. There are several policy changes as response to these challenges. One strategy of policy intervention is to support private market forces for a period of time, then pull out as soon as the private agents have established a sustainable market. This is at the same time a means of having flexible instruments and a way of avoiding negotiating for permanent expenditures, which the political system is reluctant to approve. Also among the policy principles is to bind together different elements of the innovation system. This involves giving a high priority to ccn policies as a means of diffusing knowledge throughout the innovation system. An important element in the strategy to increase knowledge flows is to upgrade competencies through interactive learning. With respect to policy learning, the direct dialogue with leading edge firms is important, as is the monitoring of the development.

Recent discussion on Danish innovation policy takes into account the distinction between tacit and codified knowledge as part of developing special framework conditions and selective policies. This debate is inspired by the cluster thinking which has since long been a tradition in Danish innovation policy.[14] Competence building in regional agglomerations is seen as still more important in future industrial development.

Notes

---

1 I am grateful to Jens Nyholm, Mikkel B. Rasmussen, Peter Torstensen and Birgit Kjølbye of The Ministry of Industry for their time to participate in interviews on the issues in this article. The responsibility of the content is solely with the author, and opinions expressed are not necessarily shared by the Ministry of Industry.

2 See further details on the DISKO-project (1996–1999) on http://www.business.auc.dk/disko/

3 These programs were supplemented with a number of other programs of less R&D-orientation.

4 One could add that the Danish economy in some manufacturing areas is ill-suited for public procurement policies compared to other countries. In particular, Denmark has no strong military complex and not a strong aircraft or space technology industry. On the other hand, a strong and advanced service sector is an advantage in the public procurement policy.

5 Examples include Food, Construction and Housing, Medico/Health. See Drejer et al (1998) and www.ressourceomraader.dk for a further description of the resource areas in Denmark.

6 In 1993 The Ministry of Industrial Policy Coordination was established. Even the name signaled a broader approach to industrial policy but it also meant a real policy change.

7 The market failure argument seems to persist in some ministries like The Ministry of Finance and The Ministry of Economic Affairs.

8 Recently The Ministry has attempted to integrate industrial policy with the development of culture. This is reflected in a joint publication from The Ministry of Industry and Ministry of Culture in which it is argued that there is a strong link between industrial development and culture (Erhvervs- og Kulturministeriet, 2000).

9 This is reflected in the strategy for industrial policy published in 2000 (Regeringen, 2000a and 2000b).

10 See further details on this program in Lundvall & Borras (1997, p.98) or http://www.lok-initiativer.dk/

---

11 Among initiatives taken in recent years the following should be mentioned: a guarantee scheme for selected venture capital companies, a fund 'Danish Business Development Finance', a Loan Guarantee Scheme, a specialized institute to provide Mezzanine capital, Tax changes, Establishment of 6 business incubators. See more on these initiatives in Christensen (2000a).

12 See a review of government initiatives to stimulate venture capital in OECD countries in Financial Market Trends, no. 63.

13 These differences are well described in the literature on university-industry collaboration.

14 In the 1980s a number of studies analyzed complexes in the Danish economy such as the agro-food complex (Ministry of Industry, Erhvervsredegørelsen, various years, Ministry of Industry: Ressource area studies).

References

Christensen, J. L. (2000a): 'Effects of Venture Capital on Innovation and Growth', Danish Ministry of Industry, Kbh.

Christensen, J. L. (2000b): 'Innovation i danske industri- og servicevirksomheder – resultater fra den 2. Community Innovation Survey' EUR, Danish Ministry of Industry, Kbh.

Christensen, J. L. (2000c): 'Policies to Stimulate Collaboration on Innovation – Examples from Denmark' Paper for OECD-Workshop on Inter-Firm Collaboration, Rome, 1.–3. Oct, 2000.

Christensen, J. L. (1992): 'Evaluering af udenlandske initiativer med særligt henblik på LINC;MCI,LGS, og udstationering' rapport, Industriministeriet.

Christensen, J. L. (1992): 'The Role of Finance in Industrial Innovation', Aalborg University Press.

Christensen, J. L./Schibany, A./Vinding, A. (2001): 'Collaboration Between Manufacturing Firms and Knowledge Institutions', OECD.

Christensen, J. L./Schibany, A./Vinding, A. L. (2001): 'Collaboration on Product Development Between Manufacturing Firms and Knowledge Institutions – Evidence from Harmonised Surveys in Austria, Denmark, Australia, Norway and Spain', in: OECD 'Innovative Networks – Cooperation in National Innovation Systems', Paris.

Christiansen, P. M. (1992): 'Statslig erhvervsfremme – struktur, beslutninger, koordination', Industri- og Handelsstyrelsen.

Dalum, B. et al (1991): 'Internationalisering og erhvervsudvikling', Industri- og Handelsstyrelsen.

Drejer, I./Kristensen, F./Skov & Laursen, Keld. (1997): 'Studies of Clusters as a Basis for Industrial and Technology Policy in the Danish Economy', DRUID Working Paper 97–14.

Edqvist, C. (ed.) (1997): 'Systems of Innovation – Technologies, Institutions, and Organisations'. Pinter. London.

Erhvervsfremme, Styrelsen (1997): 'Dialogue with the Ressource Areas – Danish Experiences'.

Erhvervs- og Kulturministeriet (2000): 'Danmarks kreative potentiale – erhvervs- og kulturpolitisk redegørelse 2000', kbh.

Erhvervsministeriet/Industri-og Samordningsministeriet: 'Erhvervsredegørelse' various years since 1993.

Industriministeriet (1990): '10 Erhvervspolitiske temaer'.

Industriministeriet (1991): 'Erhvervspolitisk redegørelse'.

Industriministeriet (1992): 'Pejlemærker for fremtidens erhvervspolitik'.

Koppel, P. (1992): 'Pilotforsøg vedr. formidling af privat kapital til særlige projekter', DTI/Innovation.

Lundvall, B.-Å. (1999): 'Det danske innovationssystem', Disko-projektet, sammenfattende rapport nr.9.

Lundvall, B.-Å./Borras, S. (1997): 'The Globalizing Learning Economy: Implications for Innovation Policy', European Commission.

Metcalfe, J. S. (1995a): 'The Economic Foundations of Technology Policy: Equilibrium and Evolutionary Perspectives', in: Stoneman, P. (ed.), Handbook of the Economics of Innovation and Technological Change, Blackwell.

Metcalfe, J. S. (1995b): 'Technology Systems and Technology Policy in an Evolutionary Framework', in: Cambridge Journal of Economics, Vol. 19, 25–46.

Nyholm, J. et al (2001): 'Innovation Policy in the Knowledge-Based Economy – Can Theory Guide Policy Making?', in: Archibugi and Lundvall (eds.): 'The Globalising Learning Economy', Oxford University Press.

Regeringen (2000a): 'Regeringens erhvervsstrategi – kort fortalt'.

Regeringen (2000b): 'Fra strategi til handling'.

Chapter 6

Technology Policy Learning in The Netherlands 1979–1997

Marianne van der Steen

The fear of loss often proves more powerful than the hope of gain
Michael Porter, 1998 p.164

6.1 Introduction

This chapter describes the historical development of technology policy in the Netherlands since the 1980s. Whereas this book as a whole focuses on the transition of technology to innovation policy in the 1990s and beyond, the cumulative and patterned nature of this process in the Netherlands can be better understood if we examine a longer period of time. The historical path leading up to the establishment of the Technological Top Institutes (TTI) policy instrument nicely illustrates this transition process. The establishment of the TTIs[1] can be seen as a typical policy instrument in the light of the Learning Economy.

The main aim of this chapter is to provide a discussion about how the transition from technology to innovation policy has been taking place in the national context of the Netherlands from the 1980s through the 1990s. To structure this discussion, policy development will be perceived *as an evolutionary pattern of change.* Changes often take place in a patterned way, emphasizing on the path dependency of learning – often referred to as 'technological learning trajectories'. In describing this patterned process of change, we are interested to see if it was a radical or incremental process and which factors determined this. In order to do so, *section 6.2–6.4* will discuss so-called '*technology policy mutations*', i.e. the main policy changes along the various policy trajectories.[2] The purpose here is not only to analyze policy development but also to understand the underlying interactive learning processes of the policymaker. In describing the case, technology policy development will be perceived as a process that involves many knowledge-seeking activities where public and private agent's perceptions and actions are translated into practice. The policy changes are the result of interactions among economic agents defined by Lundvall (1992) as interactive learning. These interactions result in an evolutionary pattern of technology policy adjustments. *Section 6.5* will focus explicitly on the interactive learning processes of the technology policy maker[3] in terms of the forces of transition.

The nature and dynamics of the national context of the Netherlands explains, at least partly, why policy transition has been either a gradual or radical transition process.[4] This context determines the ideational basis for a particular policy change, i.e. the economical, administrative and political viability of the new policy ideas. Where necessary, we will refer to the national innovation system and national political context of the Netherlands throughout the chapter.

Finally, *section 6.6* will identify the specific learning patterns of governments observed in the former sections. It will discuss the impact of the institutional structure of an economic system that provides incentives and barriers for the learning pattern of policy-makers. Some final remarks are included on policy issues for the 2010s, focusing on innovation policy in the knowledge-based economy.

6.2 Technology policy trajectory 1980s: 'innovation on the agenda'

In this section we will discuss the technology policy trajectory of the 1980s. It is characterised by a shift in the mental framework of the policymaker, focusing more and more on innovations. The government administration openly embraced the new 'innovation paradigm' and started to redesign the policy instruments and administrative structure accordingly. The policy changes include five relevant shifts in policy (policy mutations) described below.

6.2.1 Innovation paper (1979)

A radical policy change was the *new mental framework of innovation policy* as first presented in the *Innovation Paper* (1979). From this period onwards, innovation performance has been assumed crucial for the economic well being of a nation. As a consequence, innovation and technology policy has become much more important than ever before, replacing the old-style industrial policy of the 1960s and 1970s. This policy paper marked a new vision on innovation processes but it followed developments and ideas primarily developed in business schools and already commonplace in business practice. It is a form of policy borrowing, namely 'borrowed' from another discipline but translated into policy practice.

The Innovation Paper showed a new policy orientation. The policy approach shifted from a linear to an integral vision on innovations in society. It implied that technological development should not be treated any longer in terms of the traditional sequence leading from invention to innovation and diffusion. Instead, technological change was viewed as a much more complex and integrated process; technology was *local*, i.e. *specific* and *tacit* in nature, since it was to a large extent embodied by people and institutions.[5] This new vision resulted in a new type of innovation policy characterized by an integration of industry, science and technology policy.

Until 1979, innovation policy was based on the concept of an 'innovation chain'. The first of this chain is formed by fundamental research usually performed at universities and Research Institutes. The type of public policy involved here is science policy. The policy-maker responsible for knowledge creation in the innovation chain is the Ministry of Science and Education. The next step is applied research. Research and development leads to the application of knowledge in the separate companies. This policy related to private R&D is technology and industry policy, for which the Ministry of Economic Affairs is responsible. The final step is the diffusion of knowledge in the various markets over the various companies and users. The policy trajectories within this mental framework focused mainly on incentives at the beginning of the value chain, namely science policy and subsidies for R&D of (individual) firms.

Clearly, the Innovation Paper marked the new mental framework of the technology policy maker. The current policy directions and policy instruments form the local selection environments of the bounded policy-maker. Selection takes place within a certain (technology policy) trajectory. The trajectory functions as a mental framework; it defines the direction of search of the policy-maker. It also defines what is perceived as important, the sense of potential constraints and not exploited opportunities. This demonstrates the administrative viability of the new innovation approach.

The Innovation Paper basically introduced a new field for attention, namely the relationship between science and applied R&D. We see that the Innovation Paper for the first time detected a mismatch between the demand side for knowledge – firms – and the supply side – research groups and knowledge institutes. In the Innovation Paper several causes of the mismatch between demand and supply were put forward. For example, on the one hand one may observe that firms are often reluctant to ask academic research for assistance in technological questions. On the other hand, individual researchers are often guided by a different incentive structure than purely applied research within firms and enterprises. Often researchers are guided by personal interests, which lead to a research picture that is fragmented and difficult to penetrate.

6.2.2 Technology policy department (1983)

An institutional follow-up of the Innovation paper is the establishment of the Technology Policy Department. A new mental framework such as the discussed 'Innovation Paper' provides new 'software' for the learning activities of the technology policy maker. This 'software', or habits of thought, is often reflected in the 'hardware' of the organization structure. For example, the new mental framework may be reflected in a particular division of labor. Each technology policy maker involved has a certain set of tasks. Often, the distribution of the specific tasks is quite arbitrary, in most cases it could have been organized differently. However, the people involved often consider the division of tasks quasi-sacred, because they have been incorporated into their habits of thought and habits of action.

The new attitude towards technology has 'crystallized' into thinking about new policy trajectories. This straightforwardly led to the establishment of a new technology policy department at the Ministry of Economic Affairs. It mainly involved the transfer of the tasks of the Science Policy Department (OWB) of the Ministry of Education, Culture and Science to the Ministry of Economic Affairs. The establishment of the above-mentioned Technology Directorate (ATB) in the summer of 1983 can be regarded as a direct sign of the new view on innovations. It constitutes the organizational incorporation of the new technology policy regime, and represented a shift from a supply-side-dominated to a market-oriented perception of the technical knowledge infrastructure. Other technology policy mutations followed the more radical policy shifts as discussed before. We may distinguish three new policy routes in the 1980s, based on the new innovation policy framework and the new division of labor as discussed above. The type of policy instruments along these routes, as policy imitations. The type of policy changes can be perceived in terms of the 'technology (policy) race', involving continuous policy imitation among nations. Thus, also the Dutch policy followed an international policy trend (OECD, 1988; 1992; 1995; Sharp and Pavitt, 1993; Mowery, 1994).

6.2.3 From defensive to offensive policy (1984)

The first initiatives towards a more offensive technology policy were expressed in the report of the Zegveld Committee (1984), '*Towards a market-oriented technology policy*' (in Dutch: '*Naar een op de marktsector gericht technologiebeleid*'). The publication of this influential report marked the reorientation of policy within the new policy regime, towards the policy trajectory of the 'Technology policy race' (Roobeek, 1989). In this way, the Netherlands abandoned the path of the defensive industrial policy, which protected individual companies, thus saving companies from bankruptcy to avoid e.g. a new rise in unemployment. The more aggressive technology policies of the 1980s are focused on potentially successful technologies. In this the Netherlands followed the international trend. Organizations such as the OECD have had a direct role in the definition of the new policy instruments with an influencial set of general and country-specific reports on technology and innovation.

6.2.4 Knowledge diffusion policy (1984 onwards)

Secondly, the technology policy route in the period 1984–1990 focused *on knowledge diffusion.* In the meantime, applied research had received more attention. It remained, however, largely the responsibility of large firms, such as Philips. In the Netherlands, the Committee *Dekker (1987)*, 'Matching knowledge and market' (in Dutch: '*Wissel tussen Kennis en Markt*') emphasized the diffusion of knowledge. The committee proposed measures and instruments to spread knowledge. The cabinet Lubbers II adopted several proposals of the committee Dekker.

6.2.5 SME policy (mid 1980s-onwards)

Thirdly, the policy route of increased attention for *small and medium-size companies (SMEs).* It was recognized that SMEs spend much less on research and development. In addition these firms rely, more than large corporations and multinationals, on the *Dutch* knowledge potential. It is recognized that this sector accounts for a large percentage of employment. We should remark that the experience with Silicon Valley had a major impact on the shift of attention towards SMEs (Van Hulst, 1994). In fact, the enormous success of small but very innovative firms in the computer industry changed the focus of many governments. An example are the Innovation centers (1988), which were set up in all parts of the Netherlands in order to stimulate the diffusion of knowledge towards the SMEs. Another instance is the establishment of 'Knowledge Transfer Centres at the Large Technological Institutes (*GTIs*).

6.3 Technology policy trajectory 1990–1994: 'globalization'

Within the new technology policy regime defined in 1979, the core of technology policy in the nineties is epitomized in the policy paper 'Economy with Open Borders' (in Dutch: 'Economie met Open Grenzen', 1990). This paper reflects on the increasing importance of globalization for the performance of the Dutch economy. A new aspect here is that the already mentioned process of restructuring is intertwined with the globalization of technology, competition and finance. The 1980s were dominated by unprecedented flows of foreign direct investments, mergers, acquisitions and strategic alliances, as well as by an ever-fiercer competition from Japanese and South East-Asian firms (Rich, 1991; Thurow, 1993).

In this context, it was a logical consequence that governments found it necessary to rethink technology and industrial policy (Tyson, 1992). The economic recession has a certain impact on the way in which the national governments tackled their policies. Already in the 1980s, technology policies were shifting from merely defensive policies (protecting the existing industrial sectors) towards innovation policy as we have described above. At the time, governments were confronted with the fact that restructuring had an impact on the performance indicators of a national economy, i.e. the employment rate, the Gross Domestic Product, Research and Development performance, the 'investment climate', et cetera. In the 1980s, economic growth lagged behind the EU average, and the costly social welfare system came under pressure. There was increased pressure on the government to implement reforms.

It created pressure to adjust technology and innovation policy as it laid down dissatisfaction about the ability of technology policy of the 1980s to respond effectively to the economic uncertainty. The recession provided clear evidence that the efforts on strategic technologies developed along the previous decade were not enough, as they were not producing the expected results in terms of competitiveness and job-creation.

However, in the same period the Dutch government was confronted with reduced possibilities for control. Particularly, the continued integration at the European level, marked in 1989 by the Maastricht treaty, decreased the amount of policy space for economic steering. Summarizing, there was a clear need for a new policy focus as the old toolbox became more and more obsolete. In this policy climate, we discern two relevant policy mutations in the period 1990–1994. First, the policy paper 'Economy with Open Borders' (in Dutch: 'Economie met Open Grenzen') initiated a new approach to national competitiveness. And subsequently there was the Globalization Debate, which we shall describe as a 'bridging institution'.

6.3.1 Policy paper 'Economy with Open Borders' (1990)

A major policy change in the beginning of the 1990s was *the shift towards a new Porterian policy approach,* or the new 'innovation cluster approach' of the Ministry of Economic Affairs. This vision was laid down in the policy paper 'Economy with Open Borders' (in Dutch: 'Economie met Open Grenzen'). Following the work of Michael Porter (1990), the cluster approach enables a new and coherent vision on national competitiveness. According to Porter, the only way to improve national economic performance is to enhance and improve conditions for the most successful and promising industrial clusters. The innovativeness of industrial clusters determines the welfare of societies in the longer term.

New government tasks emerge, for example, the government as a 'broker', establishing links between the knowledge carriers. Another example is the government acting as 'launching customer' by bringing together various partners to develop new technologies, products or services in areas where the public sector is the main client (e.g., knowledge infrastructure, ICT, defense). Clustering essentially requires public-private collaboration and demands a completely different role from policy-makers compared to the traditional, R&D-oriented innovation policies.

The policy paper 'Economy with Open Borders' (in Dutch: 'Economie met open Grenzen') can be perceived as a *policy innovation, i.e.* new combination of knowledge, which leads to new concepts, organizational settings and policy orientations. A policy innovation differs from 'institutional borrowing' in the sense that the latter requires 'adoption' to allow the concept to fit the existing institutional setting. Instead, the cluster approach systematically changed the core concept of technology and industrial policies. Adaptations in technology policy had been evolving already since the 1980s. The notion of clusters, however, allowed an alternative concept of thinking. This type of policy innovation we may call the *shift in policy orientation*, defined earlier as a new perception of the economy. It is the most fundamental type of change in terms of the toolbox and institutions of technology policy.

This is a policy innovation at the highest level at the Ministry, i.e., the Minister. The policy paper introduced his vision in a comprehensive policy statement and provided the direction for future economic policy. In the terms of Nonaka (1995), the new Minister introduced the 'conceptual umbrella' of competitive advantage; i.e. a definition of the 'domain' or 'field' involved, in order to provide a mental map of the environment of the organization and a general direction of the type of knowledge it should be looking for. To involve the employees, this vision needs to be formulated in a broad and open-ended way which enables employees to independently formulate their own aims. In other words, the new Minister, as an 'outsider', was able to introduce a new way of thinking at the Ministry.

This new era of thinking in terms of industrial clusters was an institutional break with mainstream thinking on the role of government. A good macro-economic climate was not enough to open up completely new policy issues, such as technology and networks, a knowledge production network, impact of globalization and new role of leadership (government/private), new co-operation between private and public, institutional restructuring, and new policy tools.

6.3.2 The globalization platform (1994)

Another major policy change in the mid 1990s was the bridging institution of the Globalization Platform. The increasing awareness of a new international era has forced business, society and government to adopt a more outward-looking vision of the economy. In the Netherlands, this awareness process resulted in the Globalization Debate (1994), with the central question: 'What is the country's position of in the world and, if necessary, how can it improve its performance?'

The Globalization Debate has been a 'bridging institution', an exchange of information between the main economic agents, facilitating institutional renewal. On the one hand, this institution reflected the typical Dutch trait of looking for a 'consensus' and co-operation between all parties involved. On the other hand, this platform (government, business and society at large) broke with the tradition of negotiations and discussion via institutionalized consultative bodies. It also dispensed with some consultative institutional set-ups which had become obsolete.

The Minister at the time, Mr. Andriessen, on the other hand, following the example of Clinton, proposed to organise a discussion about the future of industry. Thus, it was agreed upon to set up a platform where the various players were invited to discuss the topic and together develop the agenda.

The Globalization Debate itself was an important catalyst for new ideas and projects. It set out the idea for the TTIs, mentioning the mutually felt need for 'Technological Meccas' (Report of the International Globalization Platform, March 1994). Because of the commonly felt sense of crisis, it 'was allowed' to question and change the institutional framework that served the Dutch economy in earlier times. The existence of an outdated institutional structure is a common sign of institutional inertia of the economic system. As such, it forms an obstacle for the economy as a whole, and certain sectors in particular, to reap the benefits from new technologies.

The globalization platform is a 'bridging institution', a new interactive ad-hoc institution. This platform has taken up position within the globalization paradigm that has emerged since the policy paper 'Economy with Open Borders' was published. It is an important policy adjustment that has set the agenda for policies in the coming era: The Globalization Debate as a kind of policy borrowing (which refers to the adjustment of an existing concept within the existing institutional setting). It concerns 'borrowing' because this type of institution can be identified (also) in other nations and international organizations. An example here is the 'Employment Debate' organized by President Clinton for the United States. However, the introduction of this new way of organizing the policy-agenda is new in the Netherlands. In addition, it was not pure imitation but 'borrowing' tailored to the specific Dutch setting. That is, it involved the whole set of economic agents in a consensual way, i.e. 'Dutch Model' (in Dutch: 'Polder Model').

The Globalization Debate, as a form of interactive-led policy borrowing, was influenced by pressures for change emanating mainly from the business building block, which met an existing 'entrepreneurial' attitude of the Ministry of Economic Affairs in their role as policy makers. The latter, governmental learning, was inspired and influenced by various sources of change in the policy network, particularly firms, but also by outsiders such as the International Economic Conference and other economic players.

6.4 Policy trajectory 1994–1997: innovation policy and knowledge

In the previous section we have shown that the 'bridging institution' of the Globalization Debate broke with the rusted consultative institutional set-up of the Netherlands and brought together business, universities and government to discuss the agenda for the Netherlands. This unconventional, ad-hoc institution opened up new paths for technology policy. When setting the agenda on the basis of the Globalization platform, knowledge was one of the main priorities. One of the issues that was raised here was the deeply felt need in business for a high-quality knowledge infrastructure in the Netherlands. Firms expressed their concerns about the highly fragmented nature of the research structure and the 'mismatch' between the supply and demand of knowledge. This resulted in the proposal to institute so-called 'Technological Meccas'.

These 'Technological Meccas' were in line with the policy shift of the technology policy maker from the pure 'technology-push' toward the Porterian approach. Particularly at the Ministry of Economic Affairs, knowledge became more and more central to policy-making, as can be seen from the policy papers 'Competing with Knowledge' (in Dutch: 'Concurreren met Kennis', 1993), and 'Knowledge in Action' (in Dutch: 'Kennis in Beweging', 1995).

This period is characterized by a cumulative nature of technology policy making, since this period was clearly based on the preceding period, and on the agenda set during the Globalization Platform. This cumulative tendency was also reinforced by the new Minister of Economic Affairs, Wijers, who strongly believed in entrepreneurship and innovation, and placed the concept of the 'Technological Meccas' high on the policy agenda. From this period onwards, one can clearly speak of innovation policy whereas before it concerned merely incremental changes leading up to innovation policy.

During the term of office of the 'Cabinet Kok I' (1994–1998), the new Minister of Economic Affairs, Wijers, gave priority to the establishment of the 'Technological Meccas', which would eventually become the policy instrument of the Technological Top Institutes (TTIs). As a logical consequence of the new cluster approach, the stimulation of technological co-operation was intensified. The precursor of the TTI instrument fitted in very well with this political trend. However, it was not yet entirely clear what a TTI should involve. This led to a whole range of different policy initiatives (which we shall call 'policy variety'). In the development process leading to this TTI policy instrument various *policy learning paths* can be distinguished.

6.4.1 The science policy vision 'top research schools'

The *scientific path* aimed to improve the technological knowledge infrastructure with regard to the scientific content. The 'Exploration Consultation Committee' (in Dutch: 'Overlegcommissie Verkenningen') played an important role in guiding the direction of policy initiatives. The main idea was to upgrade the quality of science in the Netherlands from a scientific point of view. This scientific path was stimulated by the Ministry of Education, Culture and Science. The relationship between this Ministry and the public Research Institutes and universities was characterized by relatively high level of trust, intensive personal contacts, et cetera. The main initiative of the Science Department of the Ministry of Education, Culture and Science was the instrument of the 'Top Research Schools' (in Dutch: 'Top-onderzoeksscholen').

6.4.2 The economic technology policy vision 'Centres of Excellence'

This policy was stimulated (and steered) by the Directorate for Technology Policy of the Ministry of Economic Affairs. In line with the described business-oriented policy culture of this Ministry, their perception was not only to represent business interests. The culture of this Ministry is relatively more pragmatic, focusing on the question of what is the most efficient way to implement this policy instrument. The relationship between this Ministry (Government building block) and the Business building block can be characterized by a relatively high level of trust, compared to the Ministry of Education, Culture and Science with business. Moreover, the Minister at that time, Wijers, was highly respected in business and industry, and his personal efforts regarding this policy speeded up and improved co-operation between this Ministry and the firms.

The main question for the Ministry was how to enhance the effectiveness of R&D and the use and effectiveness of the knowledge infrastructure. The main policy aim of this paper is formulated as increasing the *knowledge intensity* of the Netherlands, i.e. R&D spending as a percentage of GDP. The government is concerned about this economic indicator, since in the period 1987–1992 knowledge intensity decreased from 1.4 per cent to 1.0 per cent of GDP.

To achieve this goal, three strategic policy paths were chosen: firstly, to increase corporate R&D. Secondly, to improve the *knowledge infrastructure.* In order to increase the knowledge intensity of the economy, the relevant technological knowledge needs to be 'delivered' by the public knowledge infrastructure in order for firms to apply it. There is a weak connection between the public Research Institutes and technical education on the one hand, and the private labs on the other hand.

Therefore, we see here a need to improve the 'fit' between (technical) education, Research Institutes and the needs of firms (systemic failure in the knowledge production system).

6.4.3 Innovation policy in the knowledge-based economy (2000)

From 1997 and onwards the focus has shifted more and more towards non-technological aspects of innovation. Various new instruments have been put in place. The new array of innovation instruments at the various directorates-general (DGs) of the Ministry of Economic Affairs had made the organization structure – based on division of tasks – obsolete. Therefore, a new DG Innovation has been installed since April 2001 to deal with the new innovation policy approach that has been gradually developed since the 1980s.[6] The new DG Innovation clearly has adopted a 'national system of innovation' (NIS) approach (OECD, 2001). This process has been initiated by policy entrepreneurs and gradually adopted by the full administration dealing with innovation policy. The challenge of the 2010s is to fully implement this new array of innovation policy instruments in a new knowledge-based economy context. This requires another way of thinking of the established bureaucracy, including also the art of interactive policy learning which is a new way of working, in particular dealing with flexibility and change.

6.5 Policy learning and pressures for change 1979–1997

In this section we address the learning processes of the technology policy maker in interaction with his policy network from 1979–1990. We will focus on the pressures for change, based on the contigous learning processes, from the various building blocks (or 'populations') in the policy network.

This section discusses the learning processes of the technology policy maker in interaction with his knowledge network and the policy mutations, respectively. Learning activities take place at the *action level* within the broader institutional framework of a nation. The policy mutations are the outcomes, i.e. the 'learning results'.

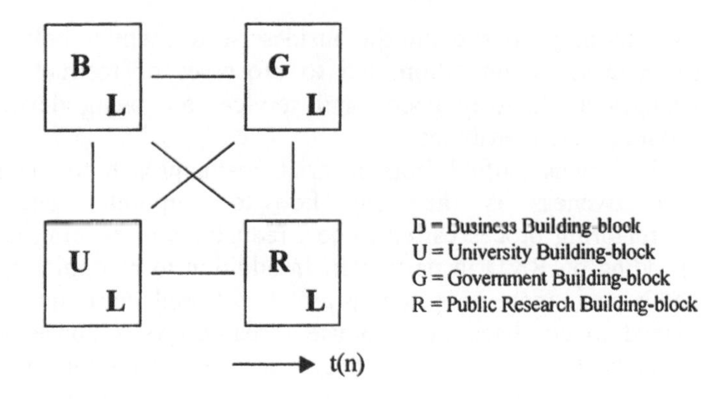

Figure 6.1: Technology policy network and interactive policy learning

In the above figure we observe the *four building blocks.*[7] In our analysis, the government agent is adopted as a separate building block to emphasize the endogenous character of policy development in institutional change processes. Our focus is on the technology policy maker (G). We look at his interactions within the network and the related learning processes. The various economic agents have different knowledge functions which together form the knowledge production system of a nation. Related to this, they have diverse mental frameworks and visions on technology policy. We will take into account the factors for reception of the new ideas in the policy evolution process such as the economic, administrative and political viability.

In general, the 1980s were characterized by market-led institutional change, i.e. by pressures for change that originated from the business building block. Internationally operating firms were among the first to be confronted with increased competition and were forced to engage in major industrial restructuring processes. In other words, economic viability has been an important pressure for change accelerating the adoption of the new innovation concepts and modes of operation in the policy arena.

6.5.1 Pressures for change; the business building-block

The learning processes in the business sector, which took place in response to increased competition, led to processes of restructuring. That is, to changes in the way goods and services are being developed, designed, produced and distributed.

The focus shifted from a strict cost-approach to the recognition that innovativeness is the only key to corporate success. Small-scale restructuring processes led to cost reductions in general, and a decrease in spending on R&D in particular. In addition to recognizing that knowledge had become more important as a factor of production, international business tended to cut back on in-house research. As a consequence, the R&D intensity decreased. In response to the new technological possibilities and increased competition, the 'big players' in the Dutch economy began to consider reallocating various parts of the production system to lower-cost regions in the world. In addition, they complained about the economic rigidities of the Dutch economic system: labor market, research, knowledge infrastructure, regulation, and so on.

The above-mentioned developments were, and are, being strongly felt in the Dutch business sector. The reasons seem to be clear: first of all, the Netherlands is a small, open economy sensitive to developments in the world economy. Second, the Dutch structure is vulnerable, since its specialization patterns are found mainly in cost-sensitive sectors such as the agro-business, petro-chemical natural resources, and microelectronics. The increased competition from emerging economies is felt strongly.

At the same time, given that innovations are central to gaining a competitive advantage, new issues become imperative: flexibility, new (combinations of) knowledge, a skilled work force, networks, co-operation and firm environment. In addition to increased competition, business agents felt hampered by the institutional rigidity of the Dutch economy; the institutional environment was perceived as a static, 'old-fashioned' framework that impeded economic recovery. In line with this, more and more firms and companies began to complain about factors such as the high tax burden, and the low quality of the technological infrastructure. A strong sense of urgency was felt in the market sector towards the government for institutional change (NRC 12/2/94).[8]

These developments led to new business demands. Basically, these demands were bottom-up forces that aimed at adjusting the institutional structure of the economy. Many firms felt that the Netherlands offered a far from good environment for entrepreneurial activity. In some cost-focused industries such as basic chemicals, the agro-business, and the energy and transport sectors, the high financial burden of the Dutch system was felt strongly. Other sectors, such as biotechnology, the commercial sectors, and information and communication technology were suffering from the poorly developed knowledge infrastructure and the poor correspondence between demand and the supply of knowledge. At the same time many businesses were faced with the short-term need to reduce costs, and to become more flexible to survive the increased competition. And last but not least, because of the protection that many Dutch industries had for a long time, the increased level of European competition was difficult for many firms.

Clearly, the restructuring of business also led to new demands regarding the technological knowledge infrastructure. If in-house research declines and at the same time innovations are an important property for business, new knowledge production relations need to emerge to neutralize the decline in in-house knowledge production. The government was blamed for the often seen institutional inertia. In response to the restructuring processes in the business sector in the late 1980s and the early 1990s, certain governmental actions were carried out. Particularly the Ministry closest to the business sector, i.e. the Ministry of Economic Affairs, played a prominent role in undertaking these actions, which also involved significant bottom-up institutional change at higher levels of the subsystems within the system of innovation hierarchy.

To sum up, the national loss of competitiveness in a rapidly changing economic context has served as a powerful driving force in the process of technology policy evolution in the Netherlands.

6.5.2 Pressures for change; the government building-block

The main policy-makers in this process each have a different focus and a different policy network. The Ministry of Education, Culture and Science is also responsible for education policy with its many implications. The Ministry of Economic Affairs is more focused on the interests of business. These Ministries have different mental frameworks in determining the most promising and desirable policy routes. In addition, they have different knowledge networks; for instance, the network of the Ministry of Education, Culture and Science is dominated by the public research sector and universities, while that of the Ministry of Economic Affairs more focused on business interests.

In the government building block, two main pressures for change can be identified. First, international policy competition. Since around 1988 there exists a broad political support for innovation policy. Innovation policy is often judged to be neutral; that is, it appears as if this type of policy doesn't need fundamental political choices. The idea of perceived 'neutrality' of technology policy is reflected in the lack of political differences between the various political factions in parliament during the period considered. Technology policy-making has a rather technocratic character.[9] There is an increased governmental attention for staying ahead in the technology policy race. Policy competition becomes the dominant pressure for institutional change.

This can partly be explained from the new technology-push, which many authors interpret as an international technology race. The idea of policy competition is also reflected in comparative studies among OECD countries. All of these countries pursue a comparable technology policy, while at the same time differing (sometimes substantially) in their institutional, economic and political structures (OECD, 1987; 1992; 1995). The innovation policies of most countries look alike. The Netherlands, as a small open economy, shows a tendency to follow the leading economies like Germany and the United States (see for instance Roobeek, 1989 p.247).

A significant budgetary expansion may be discerned. Since 1979, many new technology policy instruments have been introduced, increasing the number of instruments from about fifteen in 1980 to some sixty in 1993 (Van Hulst, 1994 p.133). The total available array of policy instruments was differentiated further by the introduction of a number of specific instruments. In the 1980, these technology policy instruments developed more and more from generic to specific instruments, targeting specific groups or technologies.

The early 1990s was the era of the aftermath of the technology policy race among nations in order not to fall behind, particularly in the high-tech sectors. Also later policy competition remained the dominant pressure for change in the government building block. Although at the beginning of the 1990s the technology-push strategy shifted towards what we have called a 'Porterian approach', innovation policy retained its technocratic character, i.e. a 'neutral' attitude which did not require any political choices to be made. However, a new dimension was added to the policy competition discussion. The need for institutional reforms became more and more apparent. An increasing number of Dutch firms were considering outsourcing economic activities, i.e. relocating them outside the Netherlands, mainly because of the institutional rigidities and costs of the Dutch economic system. The background of the new Minister of Economic Affairs, being a businessman himself, reinforced the demand from business and industry for institutional change. This resulted in various adaptation processes in the policy sphere, which eventually led to the 'bridging institution' of the Globalization Debate. The political and policy intrapreneurs have played an important role in the policy transition process, accelerating the administrative viability for new innovation concepts.

We also observe that the Dutch administration has been influenced by the developments of ideas on innovation by the OECD, the general and country-specific reports but in particular also the national innovation system approach. This influenced the thinking of the policy intrapreneurs in the Netherlands and eased the way of the national policy transition.

By the mid 1990s, we can clearly see how the views of the various policy-makers are influenced by their respective interactions with their knowledge networks. For instance, the business perception of the Ministry of Economic Affairs results from its interaction with its business-dominated knowledge network, its own mental framework, and its focus on the needs of business. This is clearly reflected in their vision of a TTI. Subsequently, we see a process of interactive decision-making between the various policy-makers, intended to arrive at a single vision to be placed on the agenda for the knowledge economy. This phase involved internal interactive learning processes within the government building block. It required the building of new routines by the technology policy maker, who was forced to combine a research-oriented with a business-oriented perspective. Since there was no script available to develop such a policy instrument, technology policy makers were forced to co-operate within a technology policy structure that was fragmented as well. Combining policy skills with the ideas developed by the various technology policy makers with different policy networks, is a process of trail and error.

6.5.3 Pressures for change; the university building-block

In the mid 1990s, universities were subjected to an increased pressure for change by the government, society and industry: they were called upon to add to the competitiveness of nations, and as such were given increased importance in the general drive towards the acquisition and 'production' of knowledge. In view of this pressure, the universities were forced to make a move, but because of the relatively limited competition among universities, the compulsion to improve was less strongly felt here than in business. Various interests played a role, and the universities tried to limit the impact of change by presenting a new policy vision of a 'Technological Mecca'. Particularly the Ministry of Education, Culture and Science, which mainly communicated the views of the established research community, operated within this policy network, wishing to concentrate only on the existing knowledge infrastructure.

6.6 Summary and conclusions

This chapter discussed the transition of technology to innovation policy in the Netherlands for the period 1979–1997. We described what we have called the cumulative path leading up to a technology policy instrument of the Technological Top Institutes (TTIs).

In this chapter we have employed the concept of technology policy learning as a tool to map a number of examples of government learning in the period 1979–1997. In this set of examples, we identified cases of patterned, cumulative learning. Many initiatives of the 1980s and 1990s date back to the Innovation Paper presented in 1979. Clearly, this paper marked a new mental framework of the technology policy maker. Such a mental framework defines the direction of search of the technology policy maker, what is perceived as important, his possibilities, constraints, and unexploited opportunities.

In this chapter we have also given examples of the embeddedness of policy learning in the Dutch institutional framework. We argued that the Dutch model can be characterized as a 'Consultation Economy', closely related to a social market economy. The combination of a liberal market, a fairly dominant role of the government and a co-operative relationship between public and private agents, have led to learning paths characterized by a commitment to incremental change and an interactive style of policy-making. Incremental change was explained from the type of institutions that have been built since the Second World War to enhance solidarity, co-operation and commitment within the economy and hence also in technology policy making. The latter, i.e. the interactive style of policy-making, is closely related to the co-operative exchange between the policy-maker and his knowledge network. Namely, the policy-maker has a market focus and, more importantly, is relatively open to the knowledge carriers in society in at least some of his roles.

The policy learning process can be seen as a 'patterned', cumulative process of continuous adaptation. We referred to it as 'institutional borrowing', since this was the case most of the time; at least regarding the policy mutations that we highlighted in our study, which was adapted to the Dutch institutional framework. Instead of blaming a lack of creativity, process simulation shows that consultation processes in the then rather rigid knowledge infrastructure of the Netherlands did not stimulate any really innovative policy-making.

Our policy examples have confirmed our conjecture regarding the relationship between the evolutionary institutional framework and the type of technology policy learning. On the one hand, we presumed that the characteristics of the consultation social-market economy were rather dominant, while at the same time the government played a major role in the way the TTI policy instrument was formulated, as we have seen. Here we are of course referring to the various initiatives from the Ministry of Economic Affairs, the Ministry of Education and Agriculture, Nature and Fisheries, in close co-operation and consultation with their associated knowledge networks. These policy examples also served to show the openness of the (economic) policy-maker towards the outside world in his desire not to miss out on any policy instruments (policy competition).

In conclusion, this chapter has made clear that there is a need for systematic, ongoing technology policy learning. In a dynamic world of constant technical and institutional change, a sustainable knowledge-based economy requires constant renewal. Sometimes top-down (exogenous) trends demand adjustments, but also endogenous (bottom-up) may evoke unintentional responses to incentives within an economic system. These changes often only become apparent to a bounded rational policy-maker after some time. Therefore, experimentation by entrepreneurs may help to uncover what works and what does not.

In addition, our illustrations have shown that a broad, coherent strategy is often the most optimal one for a bounded policy-maker. A single solution addressing the various trends is not available, and may even be dangerous because of bounded rationality. Governments are thus advised to rely on a broad range of instruments. Policies are often complementary, in the sense that the effect of each policy is greater when it is implemented together with other policies than when it is introduced in isolation. Taking action on several fronts diversifies the risks. Indeed, the process of social and institutional innovation is a process of trial and error, in the face of current problems and newly emerging trends.

Notes

1 The TTIs constitute a policy instrument designed to strengthen co-operation between business and industry on the one hand, and centres of knowledge such as universities and Research Institutes on the other hand. The main policy goal is to stimulate excellent research, particularly in the R&D-intensive sectors of the Dutch economy ('Knowledge in Action' – Kennis in Beweging, 1995). The TTIs have been established in 1997.

2 This concept is based on the evolutionary notion of the '*generation of novelty*'. This functions as a mechanism that creates diversity. Randomness is an aspect, but the process may also produce predictable novelties, such as purpose-oriented development work. For a further discussion on the ontological basis of the concept, see Van der Steen (2000).

3 We include the behavioural assumptions of the 'adaptive learning policy-maker' (Simon, 1959). In our analysis this term refers to the bounded rational policy-maker who has the intention to improve his policy measures while building on his accumulated experience, knowledge, or knowledge network.

4 In the evolutionary literature, *social selection* is a mechanism that determines the direction of technology policy learning, i.e. social embeddedness in the institutional environment. Selection takes place among the entities present in the system. In the literature, selection mechanisms include both market and non-market selection. Selection processes tend to reduce diversity. The selection process has been explicitly defined as social, i.e. the creation of a social environment. In our study, the selection environment is defined as the broader institutional framework of the economy. For an indepth discussion on the national institutional framework of the Netherlands see further van der Steen (1999).

5 Fundamental research is still the main concern in science policy. Applied research takes place in the Research Institutes and companies. Before, it was a concern of traditional industry policy to stimulate (semi) public Research Institutes such as TNO and the GTI's. The chain between applied research and the exploitation of knowledge is R&D. This type of R&D is supported by the government since 1954, namely for instance through the Technical Development instrument, in Dutch: 'Generieke Technische Ontwikkelingskredieten'.

6 Another example of this mental shift of the policy maker forced by the new innovation paradigm is the report 'Naar een Nieuwe Maatschap' (Towards a New Economic Partnership, 2001). The report is the result of the rethinking of the policymaker together with business on the economic principles of doing business and policymaking in the economy of the 21st century. Innovation performance is the new guiding principle.

7 In the literature, these building blocks are also referred to as 'knowledge populations'. The term 'building block' is more commonly used in the system of innovation literature, while 'knowledge populations' is more common in evolutionary economics (see for instance Carlsson 1995). Here both these terms are interchangeable.

8 In fact, based on newspapers from around that period, one out of every five corporations were considering to relocate part of their activities to foreign countries (NRC 15/3/98).

9 Other criticism concerns the lack of attention of the administration and public servants for the social relevance of the new technologies (viz. e.g. Roobeek, 1989).

References

Carlsson, B. (ed.) (1995): Technological Systems and Economic Performance: The Case of the Factory Automation, Dordrecht: Kluwer.

Commissie van Wijzen (1996): 'Op Weg naar de Technologische Topinstituten', Commissie van Wijzen, rapportage fase 1, 25 september 1996.

Commissie van Wijzen (1997): 'Technologische Topinstituten van Start', eindrapport van de commissie van Wijzen aan de Ministers van Economische Zaken, Onderwijs, Cultuur en Wetenschap, Landbouw, Natuurbeheer en Visserij, 5 maart 1997.

Dekker Committee (1987): 'Matching Knowledge and market' (Wissel tussen kennis en Markt'), The Hague, Ministry of Economic Affairs.

Edquist, C. (ed.) (1997): Systems of Innovation – Technologies, Institutions and Organizations, London: Pinter Publishers.

EZ (1990): 'Economie met Open Grenzen', Second Chamber 1989–1990, no. 21670, Ministry of Economic Affairs, The Hague: SDU Publishers.

EZ (1992): 'Economie met Open Grenzen, vervolgrapportage', Second Chamber 1991–1992, no.21670.

EZ (1992): 'Publiek-private samenwerking in de kennisinfrastructuur', Minstry of Economic Affairs, 'Kadernotitie PPS/3', december 1992, The Hague.

EZ (1993): 'Concurreren met Kennis; Beleidsvisie Technologie', Second Chamber 1992–1993, no. 23 206 – 1.

EZ (1994): 'Nationaal Platform Globalisering, 24 maart 1994', Ministry of Economic Affairs, The Hague March 1994.

EZ (1994): 'Nationaal Platform Globalisering, verslag van de Slotmanifestatie', Ministry of Economic Affairs, The Hague March 1994.

EZ (1995): Competitiveness Indicators, Dutch Ministry of Economic Affairs, The Hague.

EZ (1996): 'Business Plan Framework for Leading Technological Institutes', 18/10/1996, Framework LTI Business Plan, Ministry of Economic Affairs, The Hague.

EZ (1996): Rijksbegroting 1997, Economische Zaken, Second Chamber 1996–1997, 25000 chapter XIII, no. 1.

EZ (1997): Benchmarking the Netherlands, Prepared for the Future?, October 1997, Ministry of Economic Affairs, The Hague.

EZ (1997): Enabling the Information Society; Supporting Market-led Developments, Informal Council of Industry Ministers 31 January – 2 February 1997, The Hague, The Netherlands.

EZ (1997): EZ-begroting, Ministry of Economic Affairs 12 September 1997.

EZ (1997): Verzamelde knipsels over TTIs; periode 10 maart 1997 t/m mei 1997, Ministry of Economic Affairs, The Hague.

EZ (1998): Technology Radar; Global Views on Strategic Technologies, Ministry of Economic Affairs, March 1998, Drukkery Plantijn: Capelle a/d IJssel.

EZ/OCW/LNV (1995): Kennis in Beweging: over Kennis en Kunde in de Nederlandse Economie, Dutch Ministry of Economic Affairs, Dutch Ministry of Education, Culture and Science and the Dutch ministry of Agriculture and Fisheries.

Lundvall, B.-A. (ed.) (1992): National Systems of Innovation – Towards a Theory of Innovation and Interactive Learning, London: Pinter Publishers.

Lundvall, B.-A./Borras, S. (1998): Innovation Policy in the Globalising Learning Economy, Paper Presented at Séminaire Interdisciplinaire du 21 au 24 Janvier 1998, Université de Technologie de Compiègne.

Malerba, F./Orsenigo, L. (1997): 'Technological Regimes and Sectoral Patterns of Innovative Activities', Industrial corporate Change, Vol. 6, pp.83–117.

Mowery, D. C. (1994): 'Survey of Technology Policy', Science and Technology Policy in Interdependent Economies, pp.7–55.

Nelson, R. R. (1995): 'Recent Evolutionary Theorizing About Economic Change', Journal of Economic Literature, Vol. XXXIII, March 1995, pp.48–90.

Nonaka, I./Takeuchi, H. (1995): The knowledge-creating company; How Japanese companies create the dynamics of innovation, Oxford: Oxford University Press.

NSTB (1996): National Science and Technology Plan. Towards 2000 and Beyond, National Science and Technology Board, Singapore.

OCW (1991): Wetenschapsbudget 1992, Dutch Ministry of Education, Culture and Science, Zoetermeer.

OCW (1992a): Wetenschapsbudget 1993, Dutch Ministry of Education, Culture and Science, Zoetermeer.

OCW (1992b): Research and Development in the Netherlands: Policy, Sources of Funding and Sectors of Performance, Ministry of Education, Culture and Science, Zoetermeer.

OCW (1993): Onderwijs en Onderzoek in Cijfers, Dutch Ministry of Education, Culture and Science, Zoetermeer.

OCW (1993): Wetenschapsbudget 1994, Dutch Ministry of Education, Culture and Science, Zoetermeer.

OCW (1994): Wetenschapsbudget 1995, Dutch Ministry of Education, Culture and Science, Zoetermeer.

OCW (1995): Wetenschapsbudget 1996, Dutch Ministry of Education, Culture and Science, Zoetermeer.

OCW (1996): A Vital Knowledge System: Dutch Research with a View to the Future, Foresight Steering Committee, Amsterdam.

OCW (1996): Report on of the NWO Evaluation Committee, Dutch Ministry of Education, Culture and Science, Zoetermeer.

OECD (1987): Structural Adjustment and Economic Performance, Paris: OECD Publications Service.

OECD (1988): New Technologies in the 1990s. A Socio-economic Strategy (The Sundqvist Report), Paris.

OECD (1992): Privatization, Regulatory Reform and Competition Policy, Paris: OECD Publications.

OECD (1992): Technology and the Economy – The Key Relationships, Paris: OECD Publications.

OECD (1993): Economic Surveys, the Netherlands, Paris: OECD Publications.

OECD (1995): Competition Policies in the OECD Countries, 1992–1993, Paris: OECD Publications.

OECD (2001): Dynamising National Innovation Systems, draft.

Porter, M. E. (1990): The Competitive Advantage of Nations, London: Macmillan Press Ltd.

Reich, R. (1991): The Work of Nations: Preparing Ourselves for the 21st Century Capitalism, New York: Alfred Knopf.

Roelandt, Th. J. A./den Hertog, P. (1999): Cluster Analysis and Cluster-Based Policy; New perspectives and rationale in innovation policy-making, OECD National Innovation Systems Project, Focus Group on Cluster Analysis & Cluster-based Policy, Paris: OECD Publications.

Roobeek, A. (1989): Een race zonder finish (A finish-less race), PhD Thesis, Amsterdam: Free University.

Roobeek, A. (1990): Beyond the Technology Race; an Analysis of Technology Policy in Seven Industrial Countries, Amsterdam: Elsevier Science Publishers.

Sharp, M./Pavitt, K. (1993): 'Technology Policy in the 1990s: Old Trends and New Realities', Journal of Common Market Studies, Vol. 31, no. 2, June 1993, pp.129–149.

Simon, H. A. (1959): 'Theories of decision-making in economics and behavioral science', American Economic Review 49: pp.129–138.

Steen, M. van der (1999): Evolutionary Systems of Innovation; A Veblian-oriented study into the role of the government factor, Van Gorcum Publishers.

Steen, M. van der (2000): Technology Policy Learning: new implications for policy, paper presented at the International Schumpeter Society Conference, Manchester June 2000; to be published in Research Policy.

Thurow, L. (1992): Head to head: the coming economic battle among Japan, Europe and America, New York, William Morrow.

Thurow, L. (1996): The Future of capitalism; how today's economic forces shape tomorrow's world, London: N. Brealey Publishing.

Tyson, L. (1992): Who's Bashing Whom? Trade Conflict in High Technology Industries, Washington DC: Institute for International Economics.

Van Dijk, J.W.A. and N. van Hulst (1988): Grondslagen van het technologiebeleid, Den Haag, Ministerie van Economische Zaken.

Winsemius, P. L./van Driel, F./Leijnse and K. Vuursteen (2001): 'Towards an New Economic Partnership', Den Haag, Ministerie van Economische Zaken.

Zegveld Committee (1984): 'Towards a market-oriented technology policy' (Naar een marktsector gericht technologiebeleid), The Hague, Ministry of Economic Affairs.

Chapter 7

The Internationalization of Science and Technology Policy: Malta Case Study 1988–1996

Jennifer Cassingena Harper

7.1 Introduction

In the late 1980s, Malta embarked on a 'new paradigm' path of S&T policy development, drawing on an innovative blend of national and international policy learning processes. These efforts were, however, dogged by a number of constraints arising from the national context: a small island state with a weak S&T infrastructure, low levels of R&D spending in the public and private sectors, and poor networking of local researchers at the national and international levels. The limited resources made available to the Malta Council for Science and Technology (MCST), the body set up to spearhead the process, in practice produced limited long-term results in S&T policy development.

This paper addresses the following questions:

- To what extent has the rapid development of Malta's S&T policy since the late 1980s followed new paradigm thinking?
- Has Malta's national S&T policy been the product of an internationalized form of policy learning and strategy?

7.2 The stimulus for Malta's national S&T policy

Whilst UNESCO's S&T policy advice Mission to Malta in March 1985 served as an important international stimulus, the first tangible steps to develop a National S&T Policy were taken by the Nationalist Government when elected to power in 1987. The Nationalist Party's Electoral Program stressed 'the importance of the establishment of a National Board of Technology to help stimulate Malta's technological progress.'[1] Thus, the impetus for a National S&T Policy was primarily a political one. In July 1988, the Prime Minister of Malta, the Hon Dr Eddie Fenech Adami, appointed two bodies to advise the Government on S&T Policy: the National (Malta) Council for Science and Technology and an ad hoc panel of international advisors. The two bodies were made answerable to the Cabinet Committee responsible for the implementation of Government's objectives in the field of S&T. As recommended by UNESCO, the MCST Board was composed of leading personalities from the public and private sectors and academia.

However, the Board was not set up within the Office of the Prime Minister, as recommended by UNESCO, but under the auspices of the Parliamentary Secretariat for Industry. Indeed in the first three years of operation, MCST worked from the offices of the Foundation for International Studies (a public foundation). This resulted in certain disadvantages in the short/medium-term, as MCST was not able to command sufficient resources or high level profile to carry out its functions. Thus, in its first years, MCST functioned under a considerable handicap, as a result of the non-appointment of staff, the 'lack of an official Charter or other instrument clearly establishing its status and role in the public mind and consequent bureaucratic problems in running its day-to-day affairs.'[2]

In the short-term, MCST would have been better placed within the Office of the Prime Minister, where it could benefit more directly from the more extensive resources, policy networks, and the authority and prestige this Office afforded. MCST would also have been in a more strategic position to develop co-ordinated, inter-Ministerial S&T policy approaches. In practice, a direct link between MCST and the Office of the Prime Minister did exist, as the MCST Chairman (1989–1996), Professor Peter Serracino Inglott, was also the science advisor to the Prime Minister. In the long-term, MCST's location outside Government proved an advantage, as it was able to operate outside formal government structures and was therefore less prone to 'bureaucratic capture'. This coupled with the fact that in 1995 MCST was also set up as a public foundation, meant that MCST was able to develop innovative policy approaches, so crucial in the formulation of policies to bring about innovation and change. Other long-term advantages resulted from the fact that as MCST operated over time under different Ministries (Economic Services, 1989–91; Education, 1992–4 and Transport,

Communications and Technology, 1995–6), it was able to learn about and influence the latter's internal policy-making processes and exercise an important S&T awareness-raising function.

The mandate given to MCST by the Prime Minister in 1988, stipulated that national S&T policy should be developed within the framework of an updated national development strategy and was 'expected to serve as a means for improving the efficiency and international competitiveness of the Maltese economy and of meeting the social development needs and aspirations of the Maltese community.'[3] This emphasis, which was not drawn from UNESCO's Mission Report (although the Report did recommend mission-oriented research related to socio-economic priorities), is highly significant as it provided a key policy orientation: *the linking of national S&T policy to the country's development strategy.* The functions and objectives assigned to MCST were equally significant, including:

a) 'To submit proposals and recommendations to the Government concerning a national policy for science and technology, research and development that will take account of the specific situation and requirements of the Maltese Islands;
b) To participate in the national socio-economic planning process;
c) To assess the national science and technology potential…;
d) To prepare short, medium and long-term plans for science and technology activities…;
e) To undertake periodic reviews of existing educational programs and structures for the training of scientists and technologists…;
f) To manage the national budgetary allocation for the development of science and technology…;
g) To identify developments overseas in science and technology …of direct interest and relevance to the Maltese situation.'[4]

Other functions related to the development of indigenous technologies, the promotion of effective University-industry links, and the coordination of efforts to promote technology transfer and innovation. MCST was thus assigned a remit, far broader than the one envisaged by UNESCO, leaning more towards the new 'learning-oriented' paradigm, as indicated in the mandate's implicit reference to national context in (a), policy learning in (g), and international networking in (g). However, UNESCO's recommendations regarding the training of policy analysts and managers, a key priority in developing policy learning capacities, is not included in the list of functions.

This oversight hindered the development of S&T policy-making skills both within MCST and the country as a whole.

7.3 Analyzing MCST's efforts in orienting the national S&T policy process

In this section, we explore the extent to which the concepts guiding the evolution of Malta's S&T Policy between 1988–1996 reflect an orientation towards new paradigm thinking. MCST's policy focus on networking and the development of integrated policy visions is particularly relevant to our analysis (see table 7.1).

7.3.1 Networking and priority-setting

As indicated in the previous section, MCST was entrusted with a range of functions but was forced to operate under a substantial number of handicaps, not least among them, an institutional vacuum. Not only did Malta have no previous track record or experience in S&T policy, but there existed no support structures to assist MCST in its work, in terms of scientific societies, policy research institutes or S&T-related lobby groups. Moreover, the level of public awareness on S&T and related issues was low. UNESCO in its Mission Report had provided no specific advice or guidelines for overcoming this institutional vacuum. Despite institutional constraints, MCST was able to consult national and foreign experts, working within the University, and the public and private sectors, in Malta and abroad. A number of *inter-sectoral policy networks*, were set up, tasked with drawing up policy recommendations on a core set of national priorities, including laboratories, industrial applications, information technology, marine sciences, energy and water. The networks were tasked to develop:

- an inventory of current resources and capabilities;
- a sectoral profile of projected S&T development;
- educational programs;
- international links.

Table 7.1: Changing S&T policy paradigms in the globalizing learning economy

Old Paradigm	**New Paradigm**
Neoclassical economics.	Evolutionary economics.
Production-based economy.	Globalizing 'learning' economy.
Linear approaches:	Non-linear, iterative approaches:
Basic science → technological development.	Learning and innovation.
Focus on *what* decisions are made.	Focus on *how* decisions are made.
'Market' failures.	Network failures & systemic lock-ins.
Technology = information = codified knowledge.	Tacit knowledge (know how).
Equal access to information.	Uneven access to skills & expertise.
Production of knowledge.	Interactive learning through networking.
Universally applicable.	National context very important.
Static approach.	Dynamic approach (global change).
Main policy focus	**Main policy focus**
Providing incentives.	Networking and interactive learning.
Investing in:	*Investing in:*
– basic science, – technological development, – IPR to encourage industry-led R&D, – policy watching and copying.	– learning organizations, – access to relevant international networks, – integrated policy visions, – policy watching and policy learning.

The *networking* approach proved an important innovation in policy-making, bringing together multidisciplinary teams of scientists and policy-makers from the University, public and private sector triad. The networks generated important processes of interactive policy learning and consensus-building, as the conflicting interests of different institutions were aired and in the majority of cases, resolved. It is significant that in a number of areas, the networks extended to include representatives of non-governmental organizations, local councils and schools. The importance of developing *policy networks* as a basic building block of sustainable national S&T Policy was recognized in the S&T Policy Document approved by Cabinet in December 1994, as 'deserving priority in the perspective of holistic national development.'[5] The MCST Biennial Report (1994–95) further notes that 'MCST has adopted a policy of intensive networking on a national scale in an effort to pool national resources and efforts to promote effective science and technology policies.'[6] Thus, while at the start, networking was adopted intuitively rather than as part of a rationalized policy approach, as the benefits in terms of collaborative learning became apparent, it emerged as a core component of MCST's policy formulation process.

A major drawback of the networking approach was that in certain sectors, it was perceived as an important process per se, rather than as the means towards implementing policy. Thus, the policy networks progressed through phases of policy formulation, submission of proposals and implementation with varying levels of success. The constraints ranged from a lack of financial and human resources, in particular policy and management skills, to bureaucratic capture. Policy implementation proved particularly problematic and in 1991, MCST embarked on a process of S&T institution-building. In a number of policy areas, the need emerged to set up other institutions to take over responsibility from MCST, for developing and implementing policies on an ongoing basis. MCST formulated proposals on the setting up of the National Laboratories Corporation, the Science and Technology Museum, the Marine Science Centre and the National Information Technology Unit, among others. Similar financial, human and bureaucratic constraints affected the implementation of these projects.

7.3.2 Policy visions and consensus conferences

The reallocation of Ministerial portfolios in 1992, shifting the responsibility for S&T Policy to the Minister of Education and Human Resources, marked the launch of a program of S&T awareness-raising and consensus-building on a national scale, to promote more open participatory processes of policy-making. MCST launched the first in a series of high profile national conferences, on the theme '*Vision 2000: Developing Malta as a Regional*

Hub through Communications Technology'. The conference, responding to an emerging awareness nation-wide of Malta's potentially important role as a Euro-Mediterranean hub, was 'primarily aimed at creating a convergence of corporate strategies nation-wide towards this common vision'.[7] The conference resulted in the appointment of a Vision 2000 Strategy Task Force, chaired by the Minister for Transport and Communications, and the launch of the National Strategy for Information Technology (NSIT) Project, commissioned by the Government through MCST, which in turn generated extensive networking and policy learning processes. 'Since it was set up in October 1993, it has become apparent that the NSIT has developed into a highly interactive process which has generated a dynamic of its own. The number of persons working on this exercise, on a temporary basis, has extended to approximately one hundred and it has given rise to increased networking between all sectors of the economy.'[8]

Apart from these tangible results, the Vision 2000 Conference helped to launch MCST's work on a nation-wide scale, bringing it to the attention of key decision-makers in the public and private sectors. For a small country like Malta with limited resources, nation-wide networking is not only feasible, but also constitutes an important key to national competitiveness. The Conference extended MCST's networking processes from the expert level to a broader scale, capturing political, private and public interest. This approach was similar to the large consensus conferences held in Denmark, where experts and social groups met to debate strategies, thereby generating a more informed public debate and a wider awareness and acceptance of new technologies by society. Lundvall and Borras note that

> (O)pening up more real social participation at all levels of policy-making (European, national and sub-national) could be a way of stimulating the emergence of a collective vision on technological development alternatives, a positive input into long- and medium-term policy strategies.[9]

Indeed, the development of an integrated and coherent vision through nation-wide social and political participation is a core component of the new policy paradigm.

MCST recognizing this approach as a strategic policy tool in its work, decided to organize consensus-building conferences on a regular biennial basis. Significantly the theme of the second biennial conference in 1994, *'Integrated Resource Management: A Follow-up to the National Information Technology Strategy'*[10] reflected the new paradigm focus on integrated policy visions. By making accessible comprehensive, real-time information on the country's resources and their interdependencies and use, integrated resource management (IRM) is aimed at enabling policy-makers to make more informed decisions on sustainable resource development over long time spans, by exploring alternative policy scenarios, and making more rational decisions based on foresight. A high profile event, the IRM Conference had several important outcomes, including the setting up of an IRM National Task Force. and a pilot project on the integrated management of energy and water resources (given the high percentage of energy resources required for desalinating the country's water supply). In highlighting the constraints of current systems of government in managing separately resources, which are interdependent, IRM provides the tools for the holistic management of resources, based on an evolution from individualistic to more collaborative modes of working. The IRM concept is thus particularly attuned to the new policy paradigm for the globalizing learning economy. In practice, overriding concern with guarding and preserving control over individual areas of responsibility, has prevented the IRM concept from taking root.

7.3.3 Consensus-building

In 1994, the Government published the National S&T Policy Document, drawing on the policy recommendations and strategies developed by MCST to date. The Document identified two key national policy objectives, sustainable development in recognition of the Rio Summit (1992) and Agenda 21; and the development of the IRM concept. The National S&T Policy was thus not oriented primarily at developing S&T per se, but as a means to an end, i.e. supporting the country's sustainable development. The Document notes

> To secure our future prosperity we cannot wait for a natural organic growth in our scientific awareness and proficiency; we have to spearhead a rapid and strategic Science and Technology penetration in all areas (institutional, educational, industrial). This process would require initially a considerable *stimulus from above* to combine with a diffused bottom-up approach.[11]

This highlights an important orientation for National S&T policy, through open processes of social participation and not through exclusively top-down approaches. The S&T Policy Document also features a number of innovative concepts, including S&T prospecting for the anticipation of emerging technologies and related niches, strategic long-term technology planning; S&T audits of public and private sector institutions to replace obsolete practices; and public-private sector partnerships (a concept introduced to Malta by the CPTM).

7.3.4 Summary of the findings

The development of National S&T Policy in Malta evolved along a more creative 'learning-oriented' path than the one envisaged by UNESCO, although the latter's emphasis on industry-university links and priority-setting linked to national context and socio-economic development, did feature in MCST's mandate and activities. UNESCO's important recommendations on R&D planning and budgeting, and the surveying of S&T potential were included in MCST's mandate, but MCST's prime focus on sectoral priorities, meant that this important aspect was not sufficiently addressed. UNESCO's recommendation on investments in policy and management training at all levels and sectors, was not included in MCST's mandate and as a result, an S&T policy competence was not developed.

The main findings from the analysis have been summarized below in table 7.2. Despite the 'teaching-oriented' policy advice provided by UNESCO and the fact that the initial impetus to develop National S&T Policy was political, the general orientation of Malta's S&T Policy reflects new paradigm thinking. However, the implementation of these policy strategies has proved problematic in practice.

The setting up of MCST as a public foundation took six years to accomplish and whilst, as a public foundation, MCST was able to evolve more as a learning organization, less prone to bureaucratic capture, its impact on government structures was limited as a result. Both MCST's mandate and the National S&T Policy Document reflect new paradigm thinking, however, the lack of sufficient investment in relevant policy and management skills, and the informal nature of the periodic assessments on the effectiveness of S&T Policy, meant that in practice a number of the policy recommendations were not carried to completion. The implementation of integrated policy visions and IRM were thwarted by problems of policy lock-ins, constraining the emergence of new policy approaches.

Table 7.2: Summary of the findings on MCST's efforts to promote new paradigm policies

Strengths	Weaknesses
The setting up of MCST and its constitution in 1995 as a public foundation.	Insufficient resources; poor support framework; time lag.
Policy networking.	Implementation problems.
Policy visions and nation-wide consensus-building.	Difficult to sustain.
Combined 'top-down', 'bottom-up' policy approaches.	
Integrated policy approaches – IRM.	Problems of implementation.
Informal policy learning processes.	No formal policy learning capacity.
S&T Policy Document.	Limited implementation.

In general, the S&T policy development process was hindered by a number of constraints, including, the insufficient resources available to MCST to fulfill its mandate; the time lag in the legal constitution of MCST; and the lack of a support framework, in terms of a parliamentary group on S&T, scientific associations and societies, research policy institutes, and other independent bodies or NGOs. This meant that MCST had to act as a pioneer in developing the S&T policy framework and related processes single-handedly. MCST developed these innovative approaches on the basis of intuition and ongoing policy learning rather than as part of a previously drawn up plan or strategy. By identifying those policy approaches which worked well and building on them, MCST developed over time its own policy paradigm, based on innovative policy approaches and informal policy learning processes.

In the next section, we explore the level of internationalization of National S&T Policy, i.e. how and which international sources of policy learning were tapped and their contribution to the development of innovative policy approaches.

7.4 The internationalization of Malta's S&T policy: MCST's international relations strategy

Both UNESCO's Mission Report to Malta and the list of functions assigned to MCST by the Prime Minister in 1989 stressed the importance of nurturing international links. The UNESCO Report focused more on the development of bilateral and multilateral links to promote and support mission-oriented research in Malta. The functions assigned to MCST by the Prime Minister were more wide-ranging, including:

- monitoring developments overseas in S&T of direct interest to the Maltese situation;
- identifying bilateral and multilateral sources of training in relevant fields; and,
- coordinating efforts related to technology transfer and innovation.

The Charter establishing the Foundation for Science and Technology (1995) added a number of other functions, including:

- 'to assist Government in the formulation and negotiation of educational, cultural, scientific and technology transfer agreements with foreign Governments or international bodies;
- to set up databases and obtain access to international databases in the fields of science and technology; ….
- to act as a focal point with respect to various regional, interregional and international organizations.'[12]

These functions, with their emphasis on obtaining access to worldwide sources of knowledge and training, are oriented more towards the new paradigm for the globalizing learning economy. They also assign MCST an important role in the conduct of the country's international relations in S&T, reflecting an implicit linking of national S&T and foreign policies. In the early years, MCST's international remit was largely undertaken by the Networks, which independently and proactively developed their own international links, although a degree of cross-fertilization did occur between the Networks. Over time, MCST realized that the Networks' dissipated activity in developing international links and initiatives, would be better promoted as part of a single, coherent strategy, where limited resources and efforts could be pooled. MCST thus decided to rationalize the diverse links and projects that had been developed by the individual

Networks on an ad hoc basis, into a comprehensive framework, by setting up at the end of 1991 an International Relations Unit.

The International Relations Unit was given the remit of developing a more integrated approach to MCST's and Malta's conduct of international relations in S&T, by reviewing and rationalizing the international links established to date, and acting as the focal point for MCST's links with the Ministry of Foreign Affairs, and other bodies responsible for Malta's international relations in S&T, in particular the University of Malta's International Office.

The rationale for setting up the Unit related to the fact that:

- Potential areas of cooperation may have been overlooked and these may form part of a more systematic approach to the effective pursuit of certain key priorities as determined by MCST and the Government of Malta.
- Information on S&T and related activities should be centralized to allow 'the 'piecing together' of a more comprehensive picture of national S&T endeavor and progress. This should facilitate the strategic management of Malta's international links to promote technological innovation and technology transfer and the development of indigenous technologies. Central to this strategy is the factor of timeliness, i.e. the ability to react immediately and effectively to international developments in S&T.'[13]

The Unit's key functions included:

- Acting as a proactive channel for MCST's international S&T links and initiatives, by working in close liaison with the Ministry of Foreign Affairs, particularly with regard to intergovernmental links;
- working closely with the Networks to support their needs and priorities;
- providing relevant information from overseas to the Networks and other interested institutions in the public and private sectors and University;
- co-ordinating MCST's participation in international events and follow-up action; and,
- responding to requests from abroad for information on S&T in Malta.

7.4.1 Policy networking and coordination

The Unit's work between 1992–93 focused on promoting a better coordination of Malta's international links in S&T and a core network of senior policy-makers from the Ministry of Foreign Affairs, University of Malta, Foundation for International Studies and the Mediterranean Academy for Diplomatic Studies was set up. The network addressed a dire need for sharing information on the various S&T-related activities being undertaken independently by these organizations, and the pooling of efforts to reinforce Malta's various international S&T initiatives. Whilst all the organizations involved agreed on the importance of addressing this need, it proved difficult to put it into practice, partly because the network was not able to meet frequently, and therefore the information was not timely. Organizations were also reluctant to fully share information, particularly in relation to initiatives where other organizations might have an interest. Thus, whilst the rationale was excellent, the Unit's networking function was limited, largely due to the fact that no formal (ICT-based) system was established for the sharing of information in a timely manner.

Another network supported by the International Relations Unit was the National Agenda 21 Group, set up by MCST in 1993, to co-ordinate Malta's response to Agenda 21 at the local, national, regional and international levels. The Group brought together a wide spectrum of interests and expertise, including the Ministries of Foreign Affairs, Agriculture and the Environment, the University of Malta and the Planning Authority. Despite the cross-sectoral policy networking which it facilitated, the Agenda 21 Group stopped functioning at the end of 1994, reflecting the difficulties of putting into practice and sustaining cross-sectoral policy-making.

Between 1994/95, the remit of the International Relations Unit broadened considerably with the growing number and diversity of international links, including:

- MCST and the University of Malta developed closer links with COST (European Cooperation in the field of Scientific and Technical Cooperation) and began to participate in COST projects.

- In 1995, with Malta's prospective membership of the *European Union,* MCST was entrusted with the task of promoting participation in the EU's Fourth Framework Program for Research and Technological Development. A National Coordinating Unit (NCU) was set up within MCST's international relations unit, with the task of facilitating

Malta's participation in the Program. National focal points were appointed for each of the areas of the Program to ensure more effective participation. As Malta's participation in the Program was on a self-funded project-by-project basis, a National Steering Committee was set up to evaluate projects and determine the allocation of funding. The system of focal points also served as an important network for circulating program-specific information on the Program, and developing contacts with relevant research groups in EU member states and Mediterranean partner countries. However, as the focal points were mainly drawn from the University of Malta, the main benefits of networking were felt at the University and less in the public and private sectors. Malta was successful in joining six FPIV main Activity projects, despite the fact that the allocated national funds were cut drastically at the end of 1996.[14]

- In 1995, MCST was nominated as Malta's representative on the *Euro-Mediterranean Monitoring Committee for Research and Technological Development*, set up to promote and coordinate S&T cooperation within the Euro-Mediterranean Partnership. The Committee brings together high level representatives from the national organizations responsible for international S&T policy, of the 15 EU member states and the 12 Mediterranean partner countries. The main objectives of the Committee are to promote an open exchange on national S&T policies between the member countries and discussions on the development of collaborative projects under MEDA and INCO-MED. One of the Committee's main achievements has been its initiative to promote Mediterranean-specific S&T priorities within the FPIV's International Cooperation component, i.e. information technologies and preservation of cultural heritage. Moreover, the Joint Research Centre's Institute for Prospective Technology Studies which participates in the Committee meetings, has also compiled S&T profiles of the Mediterranean partner countries and published them on its website. This updated information is very useful for both the EU and Mediterranean partner countries, both in terms of establishing direct bilateral and multilateral links between research organizations and for developing collaborative projects. An obstacle hindering Euro-Mediterranean S&T cooperation is the lack of updated information on the countries' national S&T policies and research systems, including specific contact points.

Participation in COST, the EU's Framework Program and the Euro-Mediterranean Monitoring Committee for RTD expanded MCST's learning curve, by providing its international initiatives with a clear and effective strategy. This was largely based on the fact that this cooperation built on Malta's historical links with Europe and the Mediterranean and the emerging Euro-Mediterranean Partnership. Unfortunately, MCST's limited resources prevented it from playing a more proactive role in this emerging scenario.

7.4.2 Policy learning

Although MCST's international relations did generate a considerable level of policy learning, the links with the Commonwealth Science Council, ComManSat (CSC team of senior science managers) and the Commonwealth Consultative Group on Technology Management (CCGTM) were particularly significant, as they addressed more strategic S&T policy concerns, related to the development of innovative approaches to S&T management. A number of important activities were co-organized in Malta, including:

- The ComManSat meeting (May 1990) had a number of key objectives, including advising MCST on the implementation of S&T priorities and the development of more long-term strategies for improving current and proposed links with Government bodies, in order to render MCST's work more effective.
- The first-ever meeting of Commonwealth Ministers responsible for Science and Technology (November 1990), was designed to promote an exchange of experiences in using and generating S&T, and the sharing of policy approaches in addressing national needs through the application of S&T. 'Among the key issues discussed, was the role of governments in supporting science and creating an environment favorable to scientific activity.... (and) ways of utilizing Commonwealth cooperation to assist member countries, particularly the smaller ones, with the transition towards economies with a significant science and technology element.'[15] These two events were significant in promoting international policy learning, particularly in relation to the specific needs of small states and islands.
- The CCGTM meeting on the theme 'New Perspectives on Network

Development for the 21st Century – The Case of CCGTM' (1992) attracted a multidisciplinary group of experts from Malta and overseas. The meeting focused on the concept of self-organizing networks. A Think-Action Forum (TAF) was set up to review CCGTM's operations and long-term plans. The activity provided useful insights into how networking processes could evolve more effectively through self-organized networks and this constituted an important policy learning process. The links with CCGTM were strengthened, and the Government of Malta became a founder member of CCGTM's successor, CPTM that was set up as a public-private sector partnership.

- CPTM Meeting (1994) to discuss the development of Malta as a node for cooperative networking, responsible for compiling CCGTM/CPTM experiences in providing S&T policy advice to Commonwealth countries. It was envisaged that the experiences, made up of reports, images and videos, would be compiled into multimedia form, so that they could be used as part of training modules in co-operative networking. This initiative was aimed at tapping the policy learning experiences generated by CPTM through the innovative approaches it promoted. It was recognized that MCST and Malta would gain from being associated with such initiatives in terms of the policy learning processes and knowledge generated.

MCST's links with these Commonwealth organizations thus generated an important policy learning curve. However, MCST did not institutionalize these policy learning processes by developing an internal policy learning capacity. As a result, it did not fulfill an important function assigned to it by Government, i.e. to carry out regular reviews of the effectiveness of S&T Policy. As a result MCST's policy learning experiences were not captured or rationalized in a formal way, thus preventing it from identifying possible policy lock-ins.

7.4.3 Summary of the findings

This brief overview of MCST's international relations strategy has focused on the effectiveness of the following policy approaches:

These policy approaches extended beyond UNESCO's advice, and are oriented more to the new paradigm of the globalizing learning economy. However, implementation was thwarted by a number of factors, in particular a lack of resources, the inability to formalize and sustain policy networking processes, the difficulties of introducing and sustaining teamwork and integrated cross-sectoral policy approaches; and the non-institutionalization of MCST's policy learning processes. In general, the international relations strategy reflects innovative policy approaches but suffers from the same symptoms as MCST's experience in implementing S&T Policy.

Table 7.3: Summary of the findings on the internationalization of Malta's S&T policy

Strengths	Weaknesses
Strategic linking of S&T and foreign policies.	Not formalized.
Policy networking and coordination.	Not supported by an IT-based network.
Extending links to international organizations.	Constrained because of limited resources.
Policy learning initiatives.	Not formalized, limited implementation.

7.5 Conclusions

The analysis has shown that UNESCO's advice to Malta provided some initial direction, reflected in a number of the functions assigned to MCST by the Government. In practice, MCST adopted over time new paradigm policy approaches, based on networking at the national and international levels and the development of integrated policy visions through consensus-building conferences and integrated resources management. These approaches emulated the success of other small island states like Singapore, but Malta's particular socio-cultural context meant that combined top-down and bottom-up processes of policy formulation and implementation based on sectoral and inter-sectoral networking would prove more effective. MCST's policy approaches were also informed through links developed with international 'learning' organizations, such as the EU and CPTM. Indeed, MCST's International Relations strategy was oriented intuitively at developing strategic links with learning organizations to enhance policy learning experiences. These approaches, adopted as part of an informal strategy to link S&T and foreign policies, were oriented more towards the new paradigm of the globalizing learning economy. However, the process of implementing and sustaining these policy approaches proved, in the majority of cases, problematic. The development of an effective, visible and co-ordinated S&T policy was impaired by a number of factors related to national context, in particular an inability to translate Government's formal commitment to a National S&T Policy into a tangible commitment of resources to implement the policy. It is difficult to determine whether this was due to a failure on the part of MCST or Government, or the fact that there were other more pressing demands on those resources.

An important conclusion that may be drawn with the benefit of hindsight, is that in a small country with limited resources, clear strategies on how to mobilize the necessary resources (human, financial, technical) to implement the policy, must form an integral part of S&T policy proposals. Such advice should take the form of a complete and integrated package of recommendations, including strategies to generate extra-Government funding or to re-orient Government's spending patterns. These insights highlight the need for evaluating the effectiveness of S&T Policy strategies on an ongoing basis, to identify immediately obstacles and constraints, as well as the success factors or best practice in S&T policy-making. The knowledge base of individual, institutional and network learning, thus harnessed, should be captured through the development of formal policy learning processes. This analysis has shown that successful policy approaches are rooted in national capacity-building in policy-making and networking coupled with access to relevant international knowledge networks.

This case study has shown that Malta's decision in 1988 to embark on a S&T policy development process was radical and driven by a combination of stimuli: international 'ideas' and national political 'interests'. Given Malta's small size, limited resources, colonial heritage and traditionally low investments in research, it was inevitable that the S&T policy development would evolve as a product of internationalized and national processes of policy learning. The policy was to evolve primarily along an *inspired* path of new paradigm thinking explained largely by the fact that the catalyst agency (MCST) escaped bureaucratic capture. However, MCST could not escape the particular circumstances of national context, which restricted the implementation of these new paradigm policies and their long-term sustainability.

Notes

1 MCST (1989), 2.
2 P. Serracino-Inglott, Letter to the Prime Minister published as a foreword in the MCST Biennial Report 1990/91, 3.
3 The Hon. E. Fenech Adami, Letter to Prof. Serracino Inglott, published in the MCST Annual Report 1989, 2.
4 MCST (1989), op. cit. 5.
5 A Science and Technology Policy Document, printed by the Government of Malta (1994), 3.
6 MCST Biennial Report 1994/95 (Malta 1995), 3.
7 MCST Vision 2000: Developing Malta as a Regional Hub through Communications Technology, Proceedings of the first MCST National Conference (Malta 1992).
8 ibid. 20.
9 Lundvall, B.-A. and Borras, S. (1997): op. cit. 67–68.
10 MCST Proceedings of the Biennial Conference on Integrated Resource Management (held between 17–18 May 1994) (Malta 1994).
11 A Science and Technology Policy Document (1994): op. cit. 2.
12 'Charter and Deed establishing the Foundation for Science and Technology' (1995): 4–5.
13 MCST (1991): op. cit. 36.
14 A change of government lead to the freezing of Malta's application for EU membership.
15 ibid. 32.

References

Cassingena, J. (1994/5): A Report on Current R&D Activities in Malta (internal MCST Report, unpublished).

Cassingena, J. (1996): National Science and Technology Profile of Malta (report prepared as part of an EU-sponsored study on the Third Mediterranean countries).

Kwiatkowski, S. (1985): Malta – National Policy for Science and Technology, Paris: UNESCO.

Lundvall, B.-A./Borras, S. (1997): The Globalizing Learning Economy: Implications for Innovation Policy, Directorate General Science Research and Development (Brussels: CEC).

Malta Government (1995): 'Charter of the Foundation for Science and Technology'.

MCST(1989), Malta Council for Science and Technology Annual Report 1989 (Malta: Poulton Ltd).

MCST (1991): MCST Biennial Report 1990/91 (Malta: Poulton Ltd).

MCST (1992): Vision 2000: Developing Malta as a Regional Hub Through Communications Technology (Malta: Poulton's Ltd).

MCST (1993): MCST Biennial Report 1992/93 (Malta: Gutenberg Press).

MCST (1994): Proceedings of the Biennial Conference on Integrated Resource Management (held between 17–18 May 1994) (Malta: Gutenberg Press).

MCST (1995): MCST Biennial Report 1994/95 (Malta: Gutenberg Press).

M'Pherson, P.K. (1992): 'Malta and the Future Information Economy' (paper presented at the 1992 MCST Annual Conference on Vision 2000).

Sanz-Menendez, L. (1995): 'Policy Choices, Institutional Constraints and Policy Learning: The Spanish Science and Technology Policy in the Eighties,' International Journal of Technology Management, Special Issue on the Evaluation of Research and Innovation, x, 4/5/6, 622–641.

Chapter 8

Running After the International Trend: Keynesian Power Balances and the Sustainable Repulsion of the Innovation Paradigm in Austria[1]

Kurt Mayer

8.1 Introduction

Austria seems to deviate from the general trend in the OECD where in many countries a principal approach to a learning economy based on the innovation paradigm could be observed during the 1990. Until recently, the Austrian mode of development has rejected the new paradigm to a large extent. The main reason for this can be found in the strong implementation and the success story of the bureaucratic-corporative Keynesian welfare state[2] along with the corresponding power balances and institutional set-ups. The deep institutionalization of these arrangements embodied in the state bureaucracy, in the social partners' organizations as well as in many businesses, especially in the Austrian SMEs, has reproduced traditional policy strategies for longer than in other countries. Consequently, until the mid 1990s, the patterns of change in economic policy as well as in RTD policies mainly took place within the Keynesian-Fordist framework. The evolutionary trajectory established by the 'Fordist class compromise' (Hirsch 1991, p.67) has – to a large extent – enabled a co-operative and more or less smooth strategy of adjustment to new economic and social conditions, keeping at bay a full-fledged realization of neoliberal policies implemented by some other countries in the 1980s. On the other hand, the Austrian trajectory with 'an affinity towards corporatist decision structures, along with compensatory interventions by welfare-state measures to absorb the effects of the high exposure on the world market' (Aichholzer et al, 1994 p.376) can be seen as a barrier to the introduction of a new innovation paradigm. Consequently it was not until the mid-1990s – with a major impact from the countries' accession to the European Union in 1995 – that a gradual change of paradigms could be observed.[3]

The first part of the article will briefly explain our theoretical framework based on the concepts of Fordism and the Keynesian welfare state, which were developed by the French Regulation Theory. In a second step, we will discuss some major structural features, bottlenecks and strong points characterizing recent Austrian innovation performance and the Austrian trajectory of innovation in the second half of the 20th century. In a third step, we will investigate the contribution of technology and innovation policy to the development of the Austrian innovation trajectory. How did technology policy develop in correspondence to the main deficiencies and bottlenecks? Which phases of technology policy can be determined and what are the main characteristics of these phases? What are the major approaches, strategies and problems of innovation policies in the 1990s? Given that background, we will finally try to reveal the interplay between actors, institutions and economic ideas in correspondence to the Austrian innovation trajectory. In this respect, we will especially refer to the Austrian system of social partnership, and the Austrian way of compromise-based decision-making in the formulation of industrial and innovation policies. This system had major advantages in the Fordist period and was a basic feature of the impressive catching-up process of the Austrian post-war economy till the 1980s. Nevertheless, the strong institutionalization of that system in interest associations and in rules, norms and traditions also became a barrier for the new innovation paradigm in the 1990s.

8.2 Theoretical framework

The conceptual framework of Fordism was pioneered by the French Regulation Approach in the late 1970s and refined in the 1980s (see Aglietá, 1979 p.117ff.; Boyer, 1992 p.55ff.; Jessop, 1986 p.12ff.; Lipietz, 1985 p.124ff.). Since then it has made a huge international impact and has emerged as a major theorization of the patterns of post-war economic growth and the predominant mode of development in the OECD countries until the mid-1970s and of its crisis thereafter (Amin, 1994 p.7). As a theoretical concept, Fordism is applied at separate levels of analysis (industrial paradigm, regime of accumulation, mode of regulation, general pattern of social organization; see box 1). Nevertheless, the concept points to the internal systemic coherence of the separate levels synthesizing a stable and relatively predictable macrosystem of change during the Fordist period from the end of the Second World War to the 1970s.

Box 1: Institutional forms of Fordism

At the level of the industrial paradigm, Fordism[4] involves mass production based on assembly line techniques as the main source of industrial dynamism. These technologies are mainly applied by semi-skilled workers in a Taylorist concept of division of labor.

As a regime of accumulation, Fordism points to a virtuous cycle of growth based on mass production for national markets, rising productivity based on economies of scale, rising incomes linked to productivity, increased mass demand due to rising wages, increased profits based on a full utilization of capacity, and increased investment in improved mass production equipment and techniques.

As a mode of regulation, Fordism is based on the performance of a Keynesian welfare state and national monetary, fiscal and demand policies.

At the level of a general pattern of social organization, the Fordist mode of development involves the consumption of standardized, mass commodities in nuclear family households and the provision of standardized collective goods and services by state bureaucracy.

The 'Keynesian welfare state' marked the political structure of the developed capitalist countries in the period of Fordism – certainly to varying degrees, but nonetheless as the determining tendency (Hirsch, 1991 p.67). The Keynesian welfare state played a key role in managing the conflicts between capital and labor over both the individual and social wage. Its institutional design involved union recognition and collective bargaining, wages indexed to productivity growth and retail price inflation, as well as the acceptance of the hierarchical division of labor and the privileges of management and skilled labor by the unions ('Fordist class compromise'). The material foundation of the Keynesian welfare state was a state-sponsored full employment policy, mass consumption and increasingly bureaucratically articulated state-reformist redistributive policies. These state policies have been linked to income policies based on social partnership and other corporative arrangements. Consequently, as a continuously reproduced relation the Keynesian welfare state made compatible the material demands of workers with the reproduction requirements of the overall economic system (Hirsch, 1991 p.68; Jessop, 1986).

8.3 Approaching the trajectory of the Austrian innovation system

8.3.1 Innovation performance

In the course of the transition from an industrial economy to a knowledge-based economy (OECD, 1996) or a learning economy (Lundvall/Johnson, 1994; Lundvall/Archibugi, 2001) the total amount of R&D expenditures, and especially the R&D expenditures of businesses, are still important performance indicators. Furthermore, the relations between science and industry and the integration of firms, research institutes and knowledge-intensive business services (consultancy services, patent bureaux, market research, etc.) into high-level learning networks become important characteristics for the adoption of the innovation paradigm (OECD, 1999 and 2000). As box 2 below indicates, Austria is lagging behind in terms of these innovation indicators.

Box 2: Selected performance indicators of the Austrian innovation system

R&D expenditures are rather low and include a high share of public budgets.
The Austrian R&D quota, which amounts to 1.63 per cent in 1999, does not indicate any substantial forward progress in the 1990s and remains below the international average – EU (1997: 1.83 per cent) and OECD (1997: 2.21 per cent)[5] (Polt et al, 1999, p.9).

Whereas in comparison with the OECD average, the majority of R&D activities are mainly found in business (EU average 63 per cent; OECD average 69 per cent), a mere 56 per cent of Austrian R&D activities are carried out in the business sector. Therefore the share of R&D activities in Austrian universities is correspondingly high. At 35 per cent, Austrian universities are at the top of the list in international comparison. The financing of R&D activities of the Austrian business sector is just below EU average, whereas the percentage of public financing in Austria is above average, surpassed only by Italy (Polt et al, 1999 pp.10f.).

Furthermore, the *linkages and interaction of the higher education sector in Austria with the business enterprise sector* or with other establishments abroad are weak with regard to flows and funds. As a mere 2 per cent of university R&D in Austria is financed by the business sector, the country remains well below the 6 per cent average in the EU. During the last two decades, there has been no structural change in the financing of university research in Austria, hence the total public share of 97.1 per cent in higher education expenditure on research and development (HERD) is tremendously high. Compared to that, the share of industry and foreign entities supporting university R&D is quite limited and therefore represents no viable source of financing for Austrian universities (Schartinger et al, 2000 p.2f.; Polt et al, 1999 p.78f.). One more indicator for a rather modest interaction between the business enterprise sector and other sectors is the share of externally performed R&D in total R&D funded by business enterprises, which in Austria is the lowest of all OECD countries.

The *analysis of sources of information in the innovation process* is coherent with these results of weak co-operation between industry and the science system. Customers are clearly the most important source of information for Austrian businesses when it comes to innovation. The second most important source is the business itself, as well as related companies, fairs and exhibitions, followed by competition, industry specific conferences and seminars, and finally the suppliers. Less important are management consultants, computer networks, universities, upper secondary vocational and technical schools, patent specifications, and non-profit research institutions (Polt et al, 1999 p.23f.).

These innovation performance indicators are deeply interrelated with the industrial structure and the corresponding development of the (H)ERS ((higher) education and research system) of the country.

8.3.2 Industrial structure

In respect of its industrial structure, Austria is first and foremost a country of small and medium-sized companies: Almost 99 per cent of all firms have less than 100 employees and only 0.2 per cent of the firms (i.e. merely a total of 49 companies) have 500 or more employees.[6] As a consequence, there is a lack of large domestic corporations operating on a worldwide basis, serving as 'flag-ships' that could breach and thus open up foreign markets. In addition to that, several research-intensive industries, such as airplane construction and especially IT hardware (office machinery and computers), are more or less absent. Hence the sectors with a gross domestic product clearly above the OECD average are rather settled in low-tech areas like stone products or glass, mechanical engineering, electrical engineering, iron production, textiles/clothing/leather, and rail transportation manufacturing. Altogether, one may conclude that Austrian manufacturing is mainly engaged in rather traditional industrial sectors with a rather outdated production structure – characterized by being 'raw material heavy'[7] – and shows major deficiencies in the sectors of the new knowledge-based economy (especially IT and biotechnology) and in traditional 'high-tech' sectors. Moreover, a lack in R&D can also be observed in some of its strong sectors like mechanical and electrical engineering (Polt et al, 1999).

8.3.3 The system of skill and competence supply

In a process of co-evolution private entrepreneurs as well as public companies have been reinforcing that pathway by pursuing a recruiting strategy giving preference to graduates from higher secondary vocational/technical schools over graduates from universities.[8] This kind of engineer has been cheaper in terms of labor costs on the one hand and presented less of a challenge to the leading management role of the private entrepreneur on the other hand (who typically did not have an academic degree either) (see Lassnigg, 1998 p.85ff.).

As a consequence, the supply of vocational skills has developed the following characteristics: The highly formalized IVTS (initial vocational training system) clearly shows the highest level of development. Compared to most EU and OECD countries, the Austrian IVTS mainly focuses on the provision of medium-level vocational qualifications to a high proportion of the population. At the upper secondary level, the Austrian IVTS has both a strong apprenticeship sector (40 per cent of young people at the 10th year of their educational career) and a strong system of vocational and technical schooling.[9] The success of the system is to a large extent explained by the fact that the production of unskilled or semi-skilled labor, without any education at the upper secondary level, is avoided. On the other hand, the system also largely neglects the development of competences at the higher education level (Mayer, 2001).

8.3.4 The Austrian innovation trajectory

Altogether, the Austrian innovation trajectory, which was established during the post war period, has been drawing on a risk-averse but nevertheless very successful strategy of modernizing the domestic economy by a combination of purchasing and imitating foreign know-how[10] (Aichholzer et al, 1994 p.380) *and* a concentration on '*the continuing improvement of their products and processes and therefore on incremental innovation*' (Polt et al, 1999 p.20). Austrian businesses typically executed innovation projects of low volume and projects necessitating limited financial expenditure (Polt et al, 1999). The knowledge involved in this innovation trajectory can be characterized as 'work process knowledge'[11] based on widespread medium-level qualifications produced by the apprenticeship system and by upper secondary vocational and technical schools. Research and academic knowledge did not play a significant role.[12]

In this specific form of innovative environment, the major part of the Austrian population did not develop a high interest in issues of science and technology. On the contrary: As the field of genetic engineering shows, a large part of the Austrian population combines a critical attitude with modest levels of knowledge in terms of the technological background and the chances and risks of that technology (Wagner et al, 1998).

This innovation trajectory corresponds to a weak presence of private capital, a traditional sloppy attitude towards market capitalism (Tálos, 1996; Lauber, 1996), and a principal strong position of the state in economic affairs. From a historical point of view the Austrian economy is characterized by long-lasting phases of protectionist and regulated markets.[13] This excessive amount of regulation, mainly in the war and post-war periods, is supposed to have been a sustainable barrier for the development of an uncompromising attitude towards a market economy among politicians as well as among entrepreneurs (Goldmann, 1998 p.213).

Nevertheless, despite its obvious contradictions to modern innovation theory the Austrian model of innovation was very successful. The Austrian economy has clearly succeeded in catching up and Austria now ranks among the highly developed welfare states of the Western world.[14] We will come back to this 'paradox' in section 4.

8.4 Technology policy in Austria

After the Second World War industrial policy in Austria was – for the present – distinguished by a combination of high direct and indirect subsidies of investments in physical assets on the one hand (especially with regard to the large nationalized sector) and of high protective tariffs to enable competitiveness of Austrian goods on the other hand. In terms of technological development the general goal was to support, favor, and shelter Austrian companies so that they would be able to import technology from outside. Nevertheless, in the long run this strategy, driven by imitation, had negative consequences: qualified researchers went abroad, licenses had to be purchased from competing nations, and the country was dependent on the purchase of technology-intensive pre-products (see Goldmann, 1985 p.194f.; Steindl, 1977). In the course of these problems in the mid-1960s an analysis of the Federal Economic Chamber brought to the fore that Austrian R&D expenses only amounted to 0.3 per cent of the GDP, while they ranged between 1.5 per cent and 2.5 per cent in the rest of Western Europe (Goldmann, 1985 p.196). In the context of these deficiencies the *Research Promotion Act in 1967* was initiated as a first step towards a purposive R&D policy (Goldmann, 1985 p.196).

8.4.1 The 1970s: Initial phase of technology policy

The subsequent first 'naive' phase of Austrian R&D policy lasted until the end of the 1970s and was based on the idea that R&D as such would contribute to higher economic growth and a higher standard of living (Aichholzer, 1994 p.381; Zaruba, 1985 p.499).[15] However, in time this idea was increasingly questioned since no 'automatic structure' took care of the transfer of new knowledge into technologies and its incorporation in the production process. Consequently, it turned out that applied research and the transfer to production require a special infrastructure (separate research institutions) and policies of coordination and strategic planning including new financial instruments (see Goldmann, 1985 p.206; Detter, 1985 p.440ff.). Hence in a second phase, starting at the beginning of the 1980s (see Aichholzer et al, 1994 p.382ff.), new efforts have been made to establish a more integrated technology policy based on intensified conceptual considerations.

8.4.2 The 1980s: The awareness phase

Throughout the 1980s, it became increasingly evident for policy makers that innovation – as a much wider concept than just technology adoption – has a variety of important dimensions such as design, business models, as well as issues of regulation and financing. Within a proclaimed 'technology offensive' the Austrian R&D policy was reoriented towards a new framework, aiming at:

- Propelling not only general but increasingly *selected focal programs*;[16]
- searching for new types of cooperation between the state, economy,

and science;[17]

– applying instruments of general economic policy (investment policies and tax incentives) to *support and facilitate the industrial exploitation of R&D results.* This was especially the case with the Research Organization Act of 1981, which introduced tax privileges for R&D expenses and promotion measures.

In the coalition agreement of 1987 the new government[18] envisaged the elaboration of a technology policy concept that would introduce an 'efficient innovation and technology policy' as an 'important prerequisite for the renewed modernization of Austrian economy' (BMWF, 1989 p.11). As a first step, the *ITF* (*Innovation Technology Fund*) was established to strengthen the diffusion orientation of technology policy, especially to finance application-oriented R&D and to promote the transfer of research results into products and production processes.

Using the 1989 Technology Policy Concept,[19] the Austrian government claimed to have for the first time a comprehensive technology policy concept, defined as an 'essential element of the overall economic, structural, environmental, and industrial policy' (BMWF, 1989a p.12). Despite these high-flying ambitions the concept can be assessed as a collection of ideas and potential measures rather than a strategic orientation for technology policy.

8.4.3 The 1990s: Innovative concepts and sluggish policies

In terms of technology and innovation policy, the 1990s exhibit a peculiar contradiction: On the one hand, the decade is characterized by an increasing amount of innovative and progressive innovation policy consulting programs, technology reports, and technology policy concepts. Important research reports, conceptual papers and programs commissioned by the Federal government are based on theories of institutional and evolutionary economics, applying and adapting the NSI approach and the innovation paradigm to analyze the Austrian innovation performance. On the other hand, despite the high acceptance of theoretical analyses among the government coalition parties and despite several initiatives only few proposals of the theoretical concepts have been implemented. Nevertheless, towards the end of the decade – and reinforced by the membership in the EU since 1995 – a certain dynamism concerning the adoption of the innovation paradigm in the realm of policy can be observed.

8.4.3.1 Innovative concepts

At the level of research-based policy consulting, the TIP (technology – information – policy consulting) program, the technology reports of 1997 and 1999, the OECD Conference in 1997, and the Technology Delphi Report of 1998 (see box 3) can be quoted as projects and documents based on the innovation paradigm. These projects/documents indicate that in the area of science-based policy consulting the concerned research institutes have intensively discussed the innovation paradigm since the early 1990s and adopted it as the main scientific approach. Furthermore, these institutes have been closely interlinked with the science and technology policy departments in the concerned ministries, which in most cases have been the customers of the projects and reports. Vice-versa one can argue that the science and technology authorities have obviously been interested in the new paradigm; otherwise they would not have provided the research institutes with such extensive resources.

Box 3: Research-based policy consulting initiatives inspired by the innovation paradigm

The Austrian 'tip' (technology – information – policy consulting) research program

'Tip' was launched in 1993 as an innovation research and consulting program based on an initiative by the Austrian Federal Ministry of Science and Transport and the Austrian Federal Ministry of Economic Affairs. The overall goal of the program – which is carried out by two major research institutes (Austrian Institute of Economic Research (WIFO), Austrian Research Center Seibersdorf (ARCS)) – is to produce information and recommendations relevant to Austrian technology policy, based on analyses of technological change and its impact on the national system of innovation at the macro level (enterprises, public and private institutions and their interactions), the meso level (structural analyses of the Austrian economy), and the micro level (analyses of firm behavior). During the first period from 1993 to 1995, strong emphasis was placed on cluster analyses of various kinds. Based on the experience gained from the first phase of the program, the core theme of the second phase (1996–99) was: 'Ways into the Knowledge-Based and Information Society – Technology Policy in Complex Systems' (Peneder, 1999 p.340; http://www.wifo.ac.at/projekte/tip/ 15.08.01).

The technology report (1997/1999)

The 1997 technology report (updated and revised in 1999) used the concept of a knowledge-based economy to describe certain important developments of the Austrian innovation system. The report for the first time provided a survey of facts and linkages within the Austrian innovation system and was designed to serve as a source of information for the definition of positions and the promotion of a debate on technology policy issues (Hutschenreiter et al, 1998 p.153).

OECD conference: 'New rationale and approaches in technology and innovation policy' (1997)

Jointly organized with the TIP program and supported by the Austrian Ministries for Science and Transport and for Economic Affairs, the OECD conference discussed technological change as a phenomenon influenced by a range of conditions, including the properties of product and factor markets, and the extent to which technical change is accompanied by organizational change and human capital development. The analytical contributions discussed the limits of the 'market failure' approach and proposed to widen the policy rationale to take account of 'systemic failure', arguing that market forces, government institutions, regulations and other policies influence the preconditions for technological change, often with different components strengthening or interfering with each other (OECD, 1998 pp.3–5).

The technology delphi report (1998)

Entrusted by the Ministry for Science and Transport, the Institute of Technology Assessment at the Austrian Academy of Sciences applied a bottom-up research approach to investigate sustainable technology fields for the Austrian industrial location beyond short-term market and technology trends. The study largely focused on the problems and needs of society in relation to Austrian research and innovation capacities (http://www.bmv.gv.at/tech/delphi/index.htm#Downl, 15.08.01).

To what extent has the intensive work in the area of science and technology policy consulting been reflected in the actual technology policy concepts? To address this issue we will briefly discuss the Technology Policy Concept of 1996, the Hochleitner/Schmidt concept of 1997, and the Green Book for Austrian Research Policy in 1999 (see box 4 below). The first concept was supposed to 'give a consistent idea of a new Technology Policy' (BMWV,

1996 p.1) and to be a first step in a consensus-oriented process for a following development of institutional reorganization and policy measures. Taking up the 1996 Technology Policy Concept, the Hochleitner/Schmidt paper proposed an institutional reorganization at the level of funds and instruments. The Green Book for Austrian Research Policy aimed at a co-ordination and strategic reorientation of a variety of traditional sectoral concepts in the area of science and research. All three documents point out that not only the realm of research-based policy consulting, but also the realm of technology policy concepts of the Federal government extensively exhibit the increasing influence of the innovation paradigm throughout the 1990s. We can observe a far-reaching interaction-based transfer from the area of economic and social research to the area of policy concepts. Now we need to find out to what extent these innovative efforts at the research and conceptual level are actually reflected in implemented policies.

Box 4: Science and technology policy concepts inspired by the innovation paradigm

The technology policy concept of 1996

In spring 1994, the Austrian government entrusted three major research institutes (two of them involved in the above mentioned 'tip' program) to rework the 1989 Technology Policy Concept and to include representatives of the respective ministries, of the major research funds, of the social partners, and of other actors and experts of the field in this process of redesigning. After an intensive discussion process the Technology Policy Concept was issued in 1996. Since the major actors of the 'tip' program have also been the major actors in the design of the 1996 Technology Policy Concept the innovation paradigm was extensively expressed in the program. As a consequence, the NSI (National Systems of Innovations) approach, which focuses on knowledge flows, learning activities, and on the connectivity and interaction between the different actors in the innovation system, is explicitly mentioned as a framework of the concept. In addition to economic intentions, the concept also follows ecological and social goals (BMWV, 1996).

The concept is divided into 5 key strategies[20] which reflect the main pillars of the innovation paradigm. Especially the promotion of a diffusion orientation – in contrast to the formerly preferred mission orientation – was a major step towards leaving the old linear model.

The Hochleitner/Schmidt concept (1997)

In February 1997 the new Federal Chancellor Klima appointed the CEO of Siemens Austria, Albert Hochleitner, and the President of the Austrian Science Fund, Arnold Schmidt, as government representatives in charge of developing a concept for the institutional reorganization of funds and instruments on the basis of the principal orientation of the 1996 Technology Policy Concept. In June 1997 the two experts presented their concept, which is well known as the Hochleitner/Schmidt paper in the Austrian debate (Hochleitner/Schmidt, 1997).

Among many others, one core point focused on the establishment of two independent bodies responsible for strategic development, coordination and implementation of research and technology. These two bodies (the 'Council for Research and Technology' and the 'Office for Research and Technology') were intended to replace all the fragmented competences in the ministries, other federal bodies and regional promotion schemes. Another core point promoted the establishment of a new fund for promoting competence centers (to strengthen industry-science relationships, see below), stimulation activities (to stimulate the development of industrial clusters) and government initiatives (to enforce RTD with respect to other social goals like environment and transport).

The basic intentions of the Hochleitner/Schmidt concept can, once more, be regarded as saliently driven by the innovation paradigm, since major attention is directed towards the creation of a positive normative environment for innovation (pointing out that research and technology policy has to correspond to infrastructure, an appropriate diffusion system, a developed venture capital market and new high-tech start-ups, an innovation-fostering regulation system and a general friendly climate for RTD), the coordination of policy initiatives, developing measures under the umbrella of strategic goals, strengthening the appropriability and the diffusion of scientific knowledge production, and encouraging SME's participation in collaborative research. Accordingly, this concept was widely acclaimed in both the political as well as the scientific debate.[21]

Green book for Austrian research policy (1999)

This medium-term policy concept – which also includes a variety of concrete proposals for the implementation of the envisaged research policy – relies, to a large extent, directly on the innovation paradigm and promotes ideas like strengthening the co-operation between different actors and networking, the evaluation of programrs, the interplay of research policy with technology policy in particular, the co-ordination of both policies with other policy areas, as well as research that interacts with the needs and problems of society. The history of the origins of this concept also mirrors the spirit of the innovation paradigm: The public discussion process in this context involved the experience and the knowledge of more than 500 experts and researchers from science, industry and the administration.

However, since the grand coalition, which promoted the Green Book, dropped out of government only two months after its announcement – and the new right-wing government did not attach any value to it – it was never taken into account in any policy measures.

8.4.3.2 Sluggish policies

The establishment of polytechniques ('Fachhochschulen'[22]) in 1993, the liberalization of the telecommunications market in 1997, and the establishment of K+ competence centers to interlink and cluster industry and science in 1998 (see box 4) have been major milestones in approaching an innovation paradigm in Austria. These rather big reforms have been accompanied by a variety of measures and tools, which correspond to the innovation paradigm at different levels (e.g. the promotion of seed financing, technology transfer, innovation management or technology consulting).[23]

Box 5: The K+ competence center program

Without any doubt, the most ambitious policy plan inspired by the innovation approach is the 'K+ Competence Center Program', which was publicly announced by the Federal government in December 1997. This initiative aims to improve the interaction between academic research and private industrial R&D by establishing collaborative research institutions, the so-called 'competence centers'. Set up as independent legal entities, they are selected by competitive tender based on the double criteria of scientific excellence and economic relevance. Funding provided by federal and other public bodies can cover up to 60 per cent of the budget, while a minimum of five strategic private partners must cover at least 40 per cent of the total expenses. In December 1998, five competence centers (3 in the area of ICT and two in the area of metal research) have started to work in a pilot scheme, in January 2000 five more centers have been established, and a new call was foreseen to be issued in December 2000. By December 1999, 160 companies of all sizes are participating in one of the 10 competence centers.[24]

In spite of this undoubted progress the issue of realization and implementation of technology and innovation polices throughout the 1990s also exhibits major deficiencies and omissions.

One of the most urgent problems, the fragmentation of competences for technology policy and the lack of a comprehensive policy guided by strategic goals – which was pointed out in most of the aforementioned concepts – could not be improved.[25] Although this is perceived as an undisputed deficiency by the public debate, triggering double-tracked measures and contradictory policies, several policy attempts failed to come up with a generally accepted strategy. Hence one of the most important weaknesses is still embedded in the institutions of technology policy themselves and in their ability to formulate and execute policy.

More weaknesses – especially criticized by the OECD – can be found in the current situation of the 'culture of evaluation' in Austria (frequency, level of development of methodical approaches, execution of the results of evaluation in policy) and in powerless policies directed toward the promotion of the founding of technologically oriented businesses. Criticism is also related to the slow progress regarding the university reform throughout the 1990s and – due to weak incentives – to the poor industry-science relationships (even though the K+ competence center program is unanimously benchmarked as a major innovation in this area). Furthermore, the policies regarding the use of the Internet are either seen as pronounced weaknesses or at best as average. Despite the recent liberalization of the telecom market in 1997, the political support of the new field of growth – the Internet – is supposed to be unsatisfactory (Polt et al, 1999 p.103ff.). And in the area of education and training – in spite of several reforms in the second half of the 1990s – the education and training system is still very much related to initial education and only very loosely focused on further training and life-long learning.

Altogether, the policy is rather ambiguous, rich concepts are hollowed out when they cross the border to implementation. For the most part, it consists of announcements, the implementation of single instruments and measures. A comprehensive innovation-orientated technology policy initiative like in the Nordic countries or in Bavaria has never been started. At the level of policy implementation, the transition towards an innovation paradigm has remained sluggish. The question about the barriers *for* and the institutional roots *of* change in the 1990s remains to be answered.

8.5 Actors, institutions and ideas: Keynesian power balances and a sustainable repulsion of the innovation paradigm

Since World War II, economic and social policy in Austria has been based on two pillars: The democratic institutions (government, parliament) as defined by the constitution, and the social partners.[26] Since the late 1950s, the social partners' involvement in the policy process has not been restricted to issues of wage and price negotiations but covered a broad range of policy fields, based on a high degree of responsibility for the whole economy. Until the beginning of the 1980s, the government left most of the issues related to economic and social policies to the interest associations, to resolve conflicting points before submitting a draft proposal to the parliament. Policy-making in these areas has been the prerogative of the social partners, the cooperation of which was based on the protection of social peace by raising the standard of living of all wage and salary earners on the one hand and on the promotion of the competitiveness of the Austrian economy on the other hand (Mayer, 1994; Mayer et al, 2000).

Austrian social partners could be found in a huge number of committees, boards, task forces, networks and steering processes in the wide fields of economy and society. The Austrian neocorporatist model has by far not been restricted to interest intermediation between the large representative associations of interest. Instead it was expanded to a system of cooperation between the social partners, the public authorities and the political parties striving for economic growth, full employment and social stability. In sum, the Austrian trajectory of corporatism represented a very strong institutionalization of the Fordist compromise in the Austrian post-war society.

But did the neocorporatist actor network also take the responsibility for technology policy? We will address this issue by approaching two different observations:

> *Observation 1*: 'The comprehensive system of cooperation ***is above all relevant for technology policy***, due to its role as a political control pattern in balancing interests and its privileged position in the implementation of public and, in particular, economic and social policies' (Aichholzer et al, 1994 p.378).

> *Observation 2*: Despite the far-reaching activities of the social partners in Austria, the relevant social research concerning social partnership in Austria (Gerlich et al, 1985; Tálos, 1993; Bischof and Pelinka, 1996; Karlhofer and Tálos, 1999) did not perceive S&T policy as a field of remarkable involvement

> for the social partners. On the contrary, the general assumption was that *'the interest associations are not very involved in the fields of justice, education, arts, science and research'* (Tálos, 1996 p.114).

The two statements on the role of the social partners in the field of RTD policy may at a first glance be contradictory. In reality, however, they approach the same phenomenon, albeit from opposite perspectives. Observation one reflects an analysis of technology policy in Austria, concluding that the social partners are major actors in the field of technology policy. Observation two reflects an analysis of the social partners' involvement in the process of overall policy development in Austria, concluding that in comparison to macro-economic policies (e.g. wage and price policies) technology policy was only a field of inferior priority and activity. In view of this, we will develop our basic argument – the sustainable repulsion of the innovation paradigm in Austria corresponding to the strong institutionalization of a 'Fordist class compromise' (see section 2) – along the following seven steps.

1. When – as it was mentioned in section 3 – the Austrian catching-up strategy of 'progress without research' (Marin, 1986), which was driven by the imitation and adoption of technologies developed abroad, came to its limits in the mid-1960s, it was regarded as a matter of course that – besides the numerous other activities in the economic and social policy field – the social partners also became responsible for the area of research and technology policy. On the one hand, the public administration and especially the new Ministry of Science simply did not have the resources and the strategic capacities to establish a department for technology policy. The social partners' organizations, on the other hand, had big think tanks and some leeway to take on the new agendas. Hence the establishment of the *Research Promotion Act in 1967* as a first step towards a purposive R&D policy can be seen as a result of the social partners' commitment. And in the 1970s and 1980 the most important changes in the area of technology and innovation policies came from the social partners' initiatives (e.g. the establishment of the *Innovation Agency* in 1984 and the setting-up of the *Innovation Technology Fund (ITF)* in 1987).
   As a consequence, the Austrian social partners have been linked to most of the important research and technology policy organizations.[27] Furthermore, the social partners' Advisory Council for Economic and Social Affairs both in the narrower sphere of technology policy (e.g.

industrial policy) and in their ambient fields (e.g. structural, capital-market, educational, and environmental policies, and the internationalization of the economy) has continued to give strong policy impulses, in particular through scientific studies and related policy concepts.[28] Concurrently with this 'agenda-setting' function, the contents of public policy were also influenced to a certain degree (see Aichholzer et al, 1994 p.384f. and p.396ff.).

2. Nevertheless – despite the social partners' substantial engagement and even due to their substantial involvement – since the late 1980s the trajectory of the Austrian neocorporatist actor network was considerably characterized by sluggish activities and a certain conservatism of established Fordist-Keynesian routines, institutional structures and distribution patterns:

   - The social partners' common basis of interest mainly consisted of **a growth and productivity coalition,** hence collective bargaining with respect to income policy via wage and labor market regulation on the one hand and price regulation on the other hand has been the core activity of the social partners. This focus on interest intermediation in terms of wage policy and labor market regulation had no original relations to issues of technology and innovation.
     Given the social partners as the main actors in the Austrian system of economic policy, it is evident that the focus of their agenda-setting – guided by issues of income policy, wage regulation and stable and secure jobs – gained a certain predominance in the system of political economy as well as in society in general.
     However, when in the mid-1960s, the deficiencies of the Austrian innovation adaptation strategy became obvious (see section 2), the social partners – due to a lack of other professional actors in the field, as the Austrian bureaucracy in the 1950s and 1960s had not built up such capacities – also started to take care of technology and innovation issues.
     But for the social partners matters of technology and innovation never became issues of priority, since their most challenging job had been interest intermediation in terms of wages, income and labor regulations. Thus, within the social partners' rationale technology policy took on the role of a stepchild.
   - On account of the principle of consensus, the typical pattern of decision-making is characterized by incremental changes (as a

consequence to the need of compromise) and concomitant high legitimacy (see Pelinka, 1981 p.84f.). From a procedural point of view, decisions on the institutionalization of promotion programs were the result of an internal balance of interests of competing groups in science, economy, and central administration. (Aichholzer et al, 1994 p.384). This commitment to a certain balance of interests can also be interpreted as a major barrier for radical policy change and basic innovation, since the principles of compromise and interest intermediation overrule the principles of excellence and (sometimes risky) decision-making towards fundamental change. Moreover, the decisions in the area of technology policy were hardly public and hence not intensively discussed or promoted. In technology policy, the formulation of objectives usually took place without the participation of the parliament, the parties or the political public (Aichholzer et al, 1994 p.384).

3. Since the late 1980s, the social partners' influence on the shaping of technology policy has also decreased due to the following phenomena:

   - Like in most other industrialized countries throughout the 1980s and more especially in the 1990s, the Austrian traditional socio-economic system was increasingly challenged by pressures of globalization, increased market competition, and new information and communication technologies (ICT). The loss of autonomy in general economic policy, in monetary policy and in finance policy as a consequence of these developments was inseparably related to a loss of significance of the social partners in terms of policy shaping.[29]
   - In the second half of the 1980s and especially in the 1990s, a changed competitive environment for Austrian businesses[30] further diminished the leeway for traditional policy intervention.

4. In this situation of pressure and change the social partners exhibited tendencies of "'*oversteering*' *and major difficulties in regaining the balance*" (Karlhofer, 1996 p.132; see also Traxler, 1995 p.271ff.; similar Schienstock, 1993 p.63f.) and proved to be '*too bureaucratic*,' perpetuating '*sluggishness and lack of innovation*' (Tálos, 1996 p.118) as well as technocratic rigidity and a tendency to conserve traditional structures (Nowotny, 1989). Consequently, there was little leeway for constructive initiatives in the field of technology and innovation.

5. In terms of the context of actors and institutions, the period of 'innovative concepts and sluggish policies' (see section 3) is consequently characterized by an interplay of the social partners being forced back and actively retreating from the whole area of wider economic policy as well as from technology and innovation policy. But in spite of the fact that the social partners have been the main actors in the field of technology policy the gradual loss of their constructive engagement in technology and innovation policy throughout the 1990s to some extent reinforced the slow transition of the Austrian system to a broader innovation perspective. A lack of initiative in the field was mainly observed in the first half of the 1990s.

6. In view of the aforesaid pressures of change the area of economic and social research has been the first one to perceive, discuss and adopt the innovation paradigm and to stimulate a transfer into the area of policy concepts (see section 3). This process was reinforced by the more or less intense co-operation of these research organizations with international organizations like the OECD. On the other hand, a public administration, which increasingly took responsibility for technology and innovation policy, was interested in basic concepts and promoted interaction with the area of economic and social research.

7. Nevertheless, the process of implementation of the new paradigm was not easy and had to face several bottlenecks: The aforementioned fragmentation of competences and dispersed power structures, the traditional mentality of interest intermediation and satisfying vested interests, a low-developed management tradition in the area of public administration, little interest among the broad public in issues of technology, a sluggish demand for a new technology policy by the Austrian SMEs, and last but not least the success of the traditional Austrian pathway of innovation are found to be remarkable barriers on Austria's way towards a comprehensive innovation policy.

8.6 Concluding remarks

In the post-war development of the Austrian innovation performance some parts of the institutional set-up of the bureaucratic-corporative Keynesian welfare state have been more deeply incorporated in the norms and organizations of society than in other countries. On the one hand, this has caused the magnificent success – with regard to growth and low unemployment rates – of the Austrian model until the 1980s. On the other hand, the deep corporatist-Keynesian roots also presented a strong barrier for the new innovation paradigm in the 1990s, since the issues of technology and innovation have not been sufficiently focused on by the Austrian neocorporatist actor network. As a consequence, the main innovation indicators still performed below the European average at the end of the 1990s.

Nevertheless, some major steps towards the adoption of the innovation paradigm were taken in the second half of the 1990s. The aforementioned barriers were overcome to a certain extent by innovative policy measures, such as the K+ program (see section 3) at the federal level and – probably due to the lack of initiative at a central level – by an increasing amount of initiatives and innovative regional development projects on a decentralized level,[31] maintained by regional and local governments, regional and local companies and regional and local interest associations and other bodies. Again, the social partners play an important role in the initiation and development of a lot of these bottom-up projects, although it seems to be very different from the traditional mode of intermediation in the Fordist paradigm. Future research will show whether this new role of the social partners is favorable to the organizational changes in the transition from Fordism to a knowledge-based economy.

Notes

1 Apart from a literature study the contribution is based on four in-depth expert interviews in December 2000 and January 2001 (*Dr. Doz. Josef Fröhlich,* Head, Division Systems Research, Austrian Research Centers Seibersdorf; *Dr. Caspar Einem*, Minister for Science and Transport 1997 – 2000; *Univ. Prof. Dr. Arnold Schmidt*, President of the Austrian Science Fund; *Univ. Prof. Dkfm. Dr. Werner Teufelsbauer*, Head of Department, Austrian Economic Chamber) and a focus group discussion in October 2000.

2 The bureaucratic-corporative Keynesian welfare state denotes the political form of the Fordist mode of development. The concept of Fordism characterizes the specific patterns of post-war economic growth and the predominating mode of development in the OECD countries until the mid-1970s (Amin, 1994 p.7). In the Fordist period the Keynesian welfare state based on national monetary, fiscal and demand policies played a key role in managing the conflicts between capital and labor over both the individual and social wage. Both concepts are further developed in section 1.

3 This contribution largely focuses on the decade from 1990 to 2000, nevertheless – as we will argue – a brief discussion of the Austrian innovation trajectory and the respective policies in the 1970 and 1980s is necessary to understand the developments regarding the innovation paradigm in the 1990s. The analysis stops in February 2000, when a new right-wing government coalition removed the great coalition between the Social Democrats and the Austrian Peoples Party from power – after 13 years of government. Hence this paper does not touch changes and new policy approaches reinforced by the new right-wing government.

4 The following arguments concerning the different conceptual levels of Fordism are mainly based on Jessop, 1991 p.136f.

5 The technological advancements in Finland, which started in the 1980s at the same level as Austria, yet has reached an R&D quota of 2.92 per cent by 1998, are of particular interest in this respect (Polt et al, 1999 p.8).

6 Data from 1998, source: HVSH, WKÖ.

7 Correspondingly, Austria's sectoral specialization in terms of outstanding success in R&D shows some particular characteristics: the emphasis of Austria's patent applications at the European Patent Office is on technologies relating to 'construction' (due to innovative enterprises which frequently occupy a significant position in the global market within their respective market niches). By international comparison, core areas of high technology, such as instrument engineering, electronics and communication, are clearly underrepresented.

8 Just two indicators: In 1991 the rate of graduates in total employment (5.2 per cent) was rather low compared to other European countries. However, 56 per cent of these graduates were employed by the state and only 44 per cent by the business sector. Hence the number of people with a university degree working in the business sector amounted to less than 2.5 per cent in 1991 (Kellermann/Lassnigg, 1996).

9 This system has a strong inclusive and a strong exclusive effect: On the one hand, among 18-to-24-year-olds the proportion of persons having completed no more than the lower secondary level is only about 12 per cent (WIFO/IHS, 2000 p.93). But on the other hand, the permeability of the system is rather low. In spite of various pronounced statements in favor of strengthening the permeability, which have been made since the 1970s, that aim has only been met to a rather limited degree (exclusive effect; 'lock-in' in apprenticeship).

---

10 According to Steindl (1997, p.211) '... *a process of catching up with other countries took place and this largely explains why product per man in manufacturing rose in Austria by 5 per cent per annum and in the United States by 2,7 per cent per annum in the period from 1950-1952 to 1967-1969. We have absorbed technology faster than it can be currently produced, drawing it, as it were, from a stock of accumulated knowledge.*'

11 According to Fischer (1999, p.12) 'work process knowledge' '... *is different from construction and planning knowledge of engineers, however it does exceed the mere operational knowledge of semi-skilled workers. It is not only knowledge about single operations, but also knowledge about how different work processes are integrated into the overall factory context. Therefore work process knowledge is not a secondary knowledge, deducted from scientific (academic) knowledge, but it has its own quality. It conveys the relationship between the conceptual models of work organization and the culture of interaction in the company, between the artefacts constructed by engineers and their actual characteristics in the production process (...). Practical, rational and aesthetic moments of work operations form a unity in the knowledge of how to do something (...), i.e. of how one carries out a task practically. For this it is necessary to realize (...), and to understand respectively the relationship between things.*'

12 The president of the Austrian Science Fund – who was in 1997 entrusted by the Federal chancellor to develop a technology policy concept (see also section 3) – commented the relations between industry and knowledge from the higher education system in the following way: "*The discussions with business people in the course of the development of that concept totally convinced me that from the point of view of the need, of manpower and new ideas, the Austrian companies are happy with the upper secondary vocational and technical colleges and the newly established 'Fachhochschulen'. If you lock up the universities today no one will care less about them. They are not locked up since it is not usual in a rich and civilized country to lock them up, but industry does not need them*" (Interview by the author).

13 One of the characteristics of the Austrian industry after World War II was the overwhelming concentration of state property due to various attempts to rescue industrial assets from Soviet reparation claims. These state industries were concentrated in the basic sector and were used as a tool for economic and social policy (Kittel, 2000 p.3).

14 Two figures will illustrate the process: In 1954, Austria's domestic gross product per capita (valued at 1990 prices in US dollars) was only 55 per cent of the US figure, but by 1995 it had already reached 90 per cent. In the mid-1950s, Austria's national product per capita (at current exchange rates) at 17 per cent still lagged behind that of today's EU members, but in 1996 Austria had surpassed this figure by 24 per cent (Mayer et al, 2000 p.4).

15 This phase was characterized by (see Aichholzer et al, 1994 p.380f., Goldmann, 1985 p.196ff.): 1) *a general expansion of science and research* (the share of R&D expenditures in the GDP rose from around 0.85 per cent to 1.17 per cent, although this was still below

the OECD average; the number of persons employed in research grew from 7,665 to 18,599); 2) *the implementation of a centralist research organization structure* (with the establishment of two funds – the Austrian Science Fund and the Research Fund for Austrian Business – as the main top-down instruments in 1967, and the establishment of a Ministry for Science and Research coordinating the development of further concepts in 1970); 3) *a constant 50:50 sharing* of research expenses between the state and the partially state-owned industrial sector over this time period (see Aichholzer et al, 1994 p.381).

16 Since 1985 – and therefore 20 years later than in France or the UK – the federal government has approved and implemented a number of different technology programs to make promotion more focused. The focus on 'microelectronics and information processing' was followed by the promotional focus on 'biotechnology and gene technology', and by corresponding programs in the areas of 'new materials', 'environmental technology', 'space technology', 'laser technology', and 'flexible computer-integrated production for small and medium-sized firms.' It has to be stated that this focusing rather reflects the running after the international trend than the implementation of an autonomous technology policy; hence these strategies also deprived Austria of the chance to benefit from competitive advantages (see Glatz, 1992 p.61).

17 To promote the transfer of knowledge to the industrial sector several intermediary institutions and projects have been established in the 1980s: *technology and innovation centers*, the *innovation agency* conceived as an interface between research and industrial commercial practice, the *Federation of Austrian Technology Centers* serving as an executive body of the so-called seed financing program promoting management planning and the establishment of firms and accompanying advice, the *Christian Doppler Laboratories* to establish close cooperation between the national industry and university research, the model projects 'Scientists for Industry' and 'Scientists Found Companies' with the intention of transferring knowledge by transferring staff. Moreover, the universities' partial legal capacities have been expanded, which also facilitated the use of funds from third parties for solicited research (see Aichholzer et al, 1994 p.386ff.).

18 While from 1970 to 1983 the Social Democratic Party was the only party responsible for government and from 1983 to 1986 a small coalition (with the Freedom Party) was dominated by the Social Democrats in 1987, a grand coalition between the Social Democrats and the Austrian Peoples Party took up responsibility for Federal government and held it till February 2000.

19 The four strategic goals in the concept comprised (BMWF, 1989 p.8f.): 1) strengthening and modernizing applied R&D by appropriate funding and the development of key programs; 2) strengthening the international competitiveness of the Austrian industry by targeted direct and indirect subsidies; 3) intensifying the co-operation between industry and science; 4) improving the strategic position of public authorities in the process of planning and implementing long-term and large-scale projects; reforming federally

owned R&D institutions, and planning the medium- and long-term assessment of the consequences of technology.

20 1) *Diffusion orientation*: Increasing knowledge transfer by means of improved mobility between university and industry, with special regard to the specific problems of small and medium-sized enterprises. New, suitably presented knowledge is made available to the economy in order to increase competitiveness on a broad basis. 2) *Research orientation:* Supporting knowledge-based enterprises by combining the strengths of Austrian industry and Austrian science. Industry-related RTD establishments are set up and enlarged to form innovative co-operation models. 3) *Infrastructure orientation*: Supporting material (telecommunication, transport, energy) and immaterial (human capital) infrastructure for sustained high-quality education and highly efficient research facilities. 4) *Task orientation:* Special subject-related targets in research and technology programs, promotion of 'clusters' instead of an undifferentiated promotion of individual projects. 5) *Guaranteeing high-quality education* at universities and 'Fachhochschulen' is a general precondition for implementing the technology policy concept (BMWA, 1996a).

21 Hutschenreiter G./Leo H. in: Der Standard, 29.7.1997, p.23.

22 'Fachhochschul' courses – lasting six to eight semesters including work placement periods – provide high-quality professional and academic training for specific occupations. In contrast to traditional higher education this system is more concretely oriented towards the creation of vocational competences.

23 Some selected measures: 1) The *Christian Doppler Association* was reorganized in 1995 and continually expanded since. The association promotes joint research laboratories for science and industry in the area of basic research. SMEs receive higher funding if they participate. 2) Industrial competence centers were established in 1999 to promote the clustering of applied research activities. 3) The programs AUSTRO-BUNT and MINT, which were established in 1995, support the reorganization of SMEs, especially in terms of the implementation of ICTs. 4) The program 'Technokontakte', which was initiated in 1996, promotes the diffusion of technological and management knowledge by 'learning from the best'. 5) Seed financing activities have been widely extended over the last decade, and a business angels stock exchange was established in 1997 (for further activities see: Zwerenz, 2000 p.7ff.; BMWF, 1999 p.113ff.).

24 For detailed information see: http://www.tig.or.at/

25 Besides the Federal Ministry for Science and Transport and the Federal Ministry of Economic Affairs, which have been the main actors in Austrian technology policy throughout the 1990s, each federal ministry was also responsible for matters of R&D connected with the respective ministry's assignments. In the second half of the 1990s the participation of 7 ministries, 33 federal bodies and 133 different regional promotion schemes in R&D competences mirrored the striking non-presence of any strategy very well (a representative of the Federal Association of Industry in: Der Standard, 14.07.1999, p.22f.).

26 The Austrian model of social partnership has for a long time been *'widely regarded as the 'paradigm case' of corporatism'* (Ljiphart/Crepaz, 1991 p.241) and, in spite of all the changes until the mid-1990s, it is still supposed to be *'the most stable form of European corporatism'* (Tálos, 1996 p.103). Social partnership in Austria includes the different chambers, as public corporations with compulsory membership established by law, the trade unions, business associations, and the government (Tálos, 1996 p.103). This institutional set-up mirrors the predomination of *'highly concentrated, centrally organized and quasi-monopolistic interest organizations'*, which are a salient part of the political decision-making structure. Their activities are primarily determined by a spirit of co-operation and the desire to establish a balance of interests (ibid.).

27 At the end of the 1980s, the social partners were represented in the two major research promotion funds (*FFF*, *FWF*, see above), in equal number in the 'Finanzierungsgarantie-Gesellschaft' (*FGG*; a financial organization providing venture capital) established in 1969, and they also had shares in the *Innovation Agency*. Moreover, the social partners were also prominently represented in the bodies of the ITF (Innovation Technology Fund), they had observer status in the *Departmental Committee on Technology Promotion,* and they were represented in the *Advisory Board on Technology Development* established in 1989 (see Aichholzer et al, 1994 p.384f.).

28 For example, the *Advisory Council* founded the *Working Committee on Innovation* in 1984. This committee drafted programs and elaborated research and technology policy suggestions, which were incorporated in the *Federal Governments' Technology Policy Concept 1989.*

29 In more concrete terms the following economic, political and socio-cultural developments and trends have affected the political role of the social partnership:

- In the course of the general political tendencies of the 1980s towards deregulation, flexibilization, rising unemployment and the move away from the state-driven demand management (see Tálos, 1987 p.118ff.) the employees' side lost power and consequently the incentives for the employers to co-operate were decreasing (Unger, 1999 p.173f., Tálos, 1991 p.407f., Tálos, 1999 p.280ff., Kittel/Tálos, 1999 p.105f., Biffl ,1999 p.208, especially Karlhofer, 1999 p.39ff.).
- Changes in the economic climate and the political options (budget consolidation, departure from Keynesian demand management, prioritization of supply) have made collaboration between associations and the harmonization of interests within associations more difficult (Unger, 1999 p.173f., Tálos, 1991 p.407f.,Tálos, 1999 p.280ff., Kittel/Tálos, 1999 p.105f., Biffl , 1999 p.208).
- The increasing emergence of new occupations and jobs spreading beyond the traditional schemes of employees and employers (new self-employed, portfolio workers, under-employed, unemployed) challenged the social partners' emphasis on stable and traditional occupations (Kittel/Tálos, 1999 p.102).

- In the political system the voting behavior of Austrian voters has changed dramatically (increasing 'issue voting', increasing 'late deciders', increasing changing voters, increasing amount of voters voting for a certain personality rather than a certain party). Moreover, new parties have emerged and the strength of the opposition parties has risen (Plasser, 1990; Plasser, 1999), and NGOs (Non-Governmental Organizations) have increasingly started to play a role in the policy process (Lauber, 1996).
- These processes of decentralization and emergence of a multitude of actors have reinforced the decomposition of the ideological camps by loosening the relationships between the associations and the respective parties they are affiliated with (Pelinka, 1993 p.69ff.).
- Furthermore, since the late 1970s the values of economic growth and full employment have been complemented by 'new' values like quality of life, healthy environment, etc. (Brand, 1982).

30 At the same time, this change has been indicated and triggered by the following points:

- The crisis of state-owned industries in 1985 led to the adoption of a new law on state-owned industry, which has diminished the possibilities of government intervention and triggered a far-reaching process of privatisation (Kittel, 2000 p.4-6).
- The fall of the iron curtain in 1989 has stimulated trade and co-operation with partners from Eastern Europe as well as competition especially in low-tech areas. Since competition with the Eastern countries was not possible in terms of labor costs, Austrian companies in the low-tech areas (construction, textiles) were forced to adopt new strategies.
- In 1989 Austria applied for membership in the EU, in 1994 Austria joined the European Economic Area and in 1995 it was admitted as a full member to the EU. The biggest economic impact of EU membership was expected to be the strong transformation pressures on the sheltered sector due to increasing competition (Lauber, 1996 p.143). This process forced Austria to revoke the sheltered sectors and to adopt the European rules for market competition. With respect to competition Austria had adjusted to the European average by the end of the 1990s.

The principal transition towards a knowledge-based economy also changed the structure of the Austrian businesses, their strategies, as well as the strategies of policies.

31 The *'Styria Automobile Cluster'* – initiated in 1994 by the Federation of Austrian Industry in Styria and various Styrian senior experts and subsequently supported by the government of the province of Styria – is a particularly instructive example in this regard. Building on high-performing local enterprises in motor technology and gear units, a successful agglomeration of related companies (covering assembling as well as the production of special automotive components) has been achieved in this southeastern province of Austria. The cluster currently includes more than 120 individual enterprises, research institutes and technical colleges (see e.g. Peneder, 1999 p.354ff.).

References

Agliettá, M. (1979): A Theory of Capitalist Regulation: The US-Experience, London.

Aichholzer, G./Martinsen, R./Melchior, J. (1994): Technology Policy under Conditions of Social Partnership: Development and Problems of an Integrated Strategy in Austria, in: Aichholzer, G./Schienstock, G. (eds.): Technology Policy. Towards an Integration of Social and Ecological Concerns, Walter de Gruyter, Berlin-NewYork, pp.375–404.

Amin, A. (1994): Post-Fordism: Models, Fantasies and Phantoms of Transition, in: Amin, A. (ed.), Post-Fordism. A Reader, Oxford (UK)/Cambridge (USA), pp.1–39.

Biffl, G. (1999): Der Arbeitsmarkt der Zukunft – Implikationen für die Sozialpartnerschaft, in: Karlhofer, F./Tálos, E. (Hg.), Zukunft der Sozialpartnerschaft. Veränderungsdynamik und Reformbedarf, S. 191–214.

Bischof, G./Pelinka, A. (eds.) (1996): Austro-Corporatism. Past-Present-Future, New Brunswick-New Jersey.

BMWF Bundesministerium für Wissenschaft und Forschung (1989), Technologiepolitisches Konzept der Bundesregierung, Vienna.

BMWF Bundesministerium für Wissenschaft und Forschung (1999): Grünbuch zur österreichischen Forschungspolitik, Wien.

BMWV Bundesministerium für Wissenschaft und Verkehr (1996): The 1996 Technology Policy Concept of the Federal Government. Expert Proposal (Abridged Version), Vienna.

BMWV Bundesministerium für Wissenschaft und Verkehr (1996a): Technologiepolitisches Konzept der österreichischen Bundesregierung 1996 (Langfassung), Wien.

Boyer, R. (1992): Neue Richtungen von Managementpraktiken und Arbeitsorganisation. Allgemeine Prinzipien und nationale Entwicklungspfade, in: Demirovic, A./Krebs, H.-P./Sablowski, T. (Hg.), Hegemonie und Staat. Kapitalistische Regulation als Projekt und Prozess, Münster, S. 55–103.

Brand, K.W. (1982): Neue soziale Bewegungen: Entstehung, Funktion und Perspektive neuer Protespotentiale, Opladen.

Detter, H. (1995): Strategische Planung von Forschungs- und Technologieschwerpunkten und ihre Umsetzung in die industrielle Praxis, in: Fischer, H. (1985), Forschungspolitik für die 90er Jahre, S. 434–455.

Fischer, H. (Hg.) (1985): Forschungspolitik für die 90er Jahre, Springer, Wien-New York.

Fischer, M. (1999): Knowledge in the Learning Company, Paper presented at the European Conference on Educational Research (ECER), Lahti, Finland, 22–25 September 1999.

Gerlich, P. et al (Hg.) (1985): Sozialpartnerschaft in der Krise. Leistungen und Grenzen des Neokorporatismus in Österreich, Wien-Köln-Graz.

Glatz, H. (1992): Die Industrie-, und Technologiepolitik kleiner Länder im Vergleich, in: Wirtschaft und Gesellschaft 1, S.47–74.

Goldmann, W. (1985): Forschung, Innovation und Technologie in Österreich, in: Fischer H., Forschungspolitik für die 90er Jahre, S.187–210.

Goldmann, W. (1992): Österreichische Industrie-, und Technologiepolitik, in: Wirtschaftspolitische Blätter 4, S.461–468.

Goldmann, W. (1998): Für eine fortschrittliche Industriepolitik, in: Zukunfts- und Kulturwerkstätte Hg.), Re-Engineering der österreichischen Industriepolitik, S. 213–225.

Gottweis, H./Latzer, M. (1991): Technologiepolitik, in: Dachs et al (Hg.), Handbuch des Politischen Systems Österreichs, Manz, Wien, S. 601–624.

Hirsch, J. (1991): From the Fordist to the Post-Fordist State, in: Jessop, B./Kastendiek, H./ Nielsen, K./Pedersen, O. (eds.), The Politics of Flexibility. Aldershot, Edward Elgar, pp.67–81.

Hochleitner, A./Schmidt, A. (1997): Technologieoffensive für das 21. Jahrhundert, unpublished paper, Siemens, Vienna.

Hutschenreiter, G./Knoll, N./Ohler, F./Paier, M. (1998): Austria's Innovation System in an International Comparison. The Austrian Report on Technology 1997, in: WIFO, Austrian Economic Quarterly 3/1998.

Jessop, B. (1986): Der Wohlfahrtsstaat im Übergang vom Fordismus zum Postfordismus, in: Prokla 65/Dezember; S. 4–33.

Jessop, B. (1991): The Welfare State in the Transition from Fordism to Post-Fordism, in: Jessop, B./Kastendiek, H. /Nielsen, K./ Pedersen, O. (eds.): The Politics of Flexibility. Aldershot, Edward Elgar, pp.82–105.

Karlhofer, F. (1996): The Present and Future State of Social Partnership, in: Bischof G./Pelinka A. (eds.): Austro-Corporatism. Past-Present-Future, pp.119–146.

Karlhofer, F. (1999): Verbände: Organisation, Mitgliederintegration, Regierbarkeit, in: Karlhofer und Tálos (Hg.), Zukunft der Sozialpartnerschaft. Veränderungsdynamik und Reformbedarf, S. 15–46.

Karlhofer, F./Tálos, E. (Hg.) (1999): Zukunft der Sozialpartnerschaft. Veränderungsdynamik und Reformbedarf, Wien.

Kellermann, P./Lassnigg, L. (1996): HochschulabsolventInnen und Beschäftigung '96. Forschungsbericht an das BMWV. Klagenfurt.

Kittel, B. (2000): Deaustrification? The Policy-Area-Specific Evolution of Austrian Social Partnership, forthcoming, in: West European Politics, January 2000.

Kittel, B./Tálos, E. (1999): Interessenvermittlung und politischer Entscheidungsprozeß: Sozialpartnerschaft in den 1990er Jahren, in: Karlhofer, F./Tálos, E., Zukunft der Sozialpartnerschaft. Veränderungsdynamik und Reformbedarf, S. 95–136.

Lassnigg, L. (1998): Qualifizierungspolitik, Innovationssystem und Beschäftigung – Herkömmliche und neue Perspektiven, in: Zukunfts- und Kulturwerkstätte (Hg.), Re-engineering der österreichischen Industriepolitik, Zukunfts- und Kulturwerkstätte, Wien, S. 76–132.

Lauber, V. (1996): Conclusions and Outlook, in: Lauber, V., Contemporary Austrian Politics, pp.253–263.

Lauber, V. (1996): Contemporary Austrian Politics, Boulder-Oxford.

Lipietz, A. (1985): Akkumulation, Krisen und Auswege aus der Krise: Einige methodische Überlegungen zum Begriff Regulation, in: Prokla 58/März, S. 109–137.

Ljipard, A./Crepaz, L. (1991): Corporatism and Consensus Democracy in Eighteen Countries – Conceptual and Empirical Linkages, in: British Journal of Political Science, Vol. 21, No. 2, pp.235–246.

Lundvall, B.-Å./Johnson, B. (1994): The Learning Economy, Journal of Industrial Studies, Vol. 1N. 2, pp.23–42.

Lundvall, B.-Å./Archibugi, D. (2001): The Globalizing Learning Economy, Oxford University Press, New York.

Marko, J. (1992): Verbände und Sozialpartnerschaft, in: Mantl, W. (Hg.), Politik in Österreich. Die Zweite Republik: Bestand und Wandel, Wien, S. 429–478.

Mayer, K. (1994): Die Theorie der Regulation und ihr analytisches Potential zur Erklärung gegenwärtiger Veränderungsprozesse in Politik und Staat, Diplomarbeit an der Universität Wien.

Mayer, K. (2001): Industry-Science Relationships in the Austrian ICT Industry. Sector Report Austria, Contribution to the SESI Project (Contract: SOE1-CT97-1074; Project: 1297), European Commission Targeted Socio-Economic Research Program, 4th Framework Program.

Mayer, K./Lassnigg, L./Unger, M. (2000): Social Dialogue on Training. Case Study Austria, Project Report by the Institute for Advanced Studies (IHS) commissioned by CEDEFOP.

Nowotny, E. (1989): Institutionelle Grundlagen, Akteure und Entscheidungsverhältnisse in der österreichischen Wirtschaftspolitik, in: Abele, H. et al (Hg.), Handbuch der österreichischen Wirtschaftspolitik, S. 125–148.

OECD (1996): The Knowledge Based Economy, OECD, Paris.

OECD (1998): Special Issue on 'New Rationale and Approaches in Technology and Innovation Policy', STI Review No. 22, Paris.

OECD (1999): Managing National Innovation Systems, OECD, Paris.

OECD (1999a): Boosting Innovation: The Cluster Approach, Paris.

OECD (2000): A New Economy? The Changing Role of Innovation and Information Technology in Growth, OECD, Paris.

Pelinka, A. (1981): Modellfall Österreich? Möglichkeiten und Grenzen der Sozialpartnerschaft, Vienna.

Pelinka, A. (1993): Parteien und Verbände, in: Tálos, E. (Hg.), Sozialpartnerschaft. Kontinuität und Wandel eines Modells, S. 69–78.

Peneder, M. (1999): Creating a Coherent Design for Cluster Analysis and Related Policies: The Austrian 'Tip'Experience, in: OECD (1999a), Boosting Innovation: The Cluster Approach, Paris, pp.339–359.

Plasser, F. (1990): Die Auffächerung des Wahlverhaltens in westeuropäischen Demokratien. Neue Strukuren – Alte Muster? Arbeitspapier des Vortrages zur ÖGPW-Tagung „Politik unter Druck', Wien.

Plasser, F. (1999): Das österreichische Wahlverhalten am Ende der 90er Jahre, Thesenpapier zur ÖGPW Tagung: Das Superwahljahr 1999. Die repräsentative Demokratie in Österreich auf dem politikwissenschaftlichen Prüfstand, 26. Oktober 1999, Wien.

Polt, W./Paier, M./Schibany, A./Gassler, H./Hutschenreiter, G./Peneder, M./Knoll, N./Leo, H. (1999): Austrian Report on Technology 1999, Study by the Austrian Institute of Economic Research (WIFO) and the Austrian Research Centers Seibersdorf (ARCS).

Schartinger, D./Rammer, Ch. (2000): Knowledge Interactions between Universities and Firms in Austria, Paper prepared for the workshop on Innovation, Entrepreneurship and Regional Economic Development, Pécs, July 3–4, 2000.

Schienstock, G. (1993): Neue Produktions- und Arbeitskonzepte als Herausforderung an die Sozialpartnerschaft, in: Tálos, E. (Hg.), Sozialpartnerschaft. Kontinuität und Wandel eines Modells, S. 51–68.

Steindl, J. (1977): Import and Production of Know-how in a Small Country: The Case of Austria, in: Industrial Policies and Technology Transfers between East and West, Vol. 3, Wien-New York.

Tálos, E. (1987): Arbeitslosigkeit und beschäftigungspolitische Steuerung: Problemwahrnehmung/Problemartikulation, Zielsetzungen, Strategien und Maßnahmen in Österreich seit Mitte der 70er Jahre, in: Tálos, E./Wiederschwinger, M. (Hg.), Arbeitslosigkeit. Österreichs Vollbeschäftigungspolitik am Ende, Wien, S. 91–166.

Tálos, E. (1991): Sozialpartnerschaft. Kooperation – Konzertierung – politische Regulierung, in: Dachs, H. et al (Hg.), Handbuch des politischen System Österreichs, Wien, S. 390–409.

Tálos, E. (Hg.) (1993): Sozialpartnerschaft. Kontinuität und Wandel eines Modells, Verlag für Gesellschaftskritik, Wien.

Tálos, E. (1996): Corporatism – The Austrian Model, in: Lauber, V. (ed.), Contemporary Austrian Politics, pp.103–124.

Tálos, E. (1999): Sozialpartnerschaft: Zwischen Entmystifizierung und Anpassungsherausforderungen. Ein Resümee, in: Karlhofer, F./Tálos, E. (Hg.), Zukunft der Sozialpartnerschaft. Veränderungsdynamik und Reformbedarf, S. 277–298.

Tálos, E./Kittel, B. (1996): Roots of Austro-Corporatism: Institutional Preconditions and Cooperation Before and After 1945, in: Bischof, G./Pelinka, A. (eds.), Austro-Corporatism. Past-Present-Future, pp.21–52.

Traxler, F. (1995): From Demand-Side to Supply-Side Corporatism? Austria's Labor Relations and Public Policy, in: Crouch, C./Traxler, F. (eds.), Organized Industrial Relations in Europe, Avebury, pp.271–286.

Unger, B. (1999): Österreichs Wirtschaftspolitik: Vom Austro-Keynesianismus zum Austro-Neoliberalismus?, in: Karlhofer, F./Tálos, E. (Hg.), Zukunft der Sozialpartnerschaft. Veränderungsdynamik und Reformbedarf, S. 165–191.

Wagner, W./Torgersen, H./Seifert, F./Grabner, P./Lehner, S. (1998): Austria, in: Durant, J./Bauer, M.W./Gaskell, G. (eds.), Biotechnology in the Public Sphere. A European Sourcebook, Science Museum, London, pp.15–28.

WIFO/IHS (2000): Begleitende Bewertung der Umsetzung des Nationalen Aktionsplanes für Beschäftigung im Jahr 1999. Research Report, Wien.

Zaruba, E. (1985): Überlegungen zur Forschungskoordination und Forschungskooperation, in: Fischer H. (Hg.), Forschungspolitik für die 90er Jahre, Springer, Wien-New York, S.499–508.

Zukunfts- und Kulturwerkstätte (1998): Re-Engineering der österreichischen Industriepolitik, REMAprint, Wien.

Zwerenz, G. (2000): Technologie- und Innovationspoltik für die österreichische Industrie, in: Wirtschaftspolitische Blätter 2, Wien.

Chapter 9

Evolution and Revolution in Policy-Making: Hungarian Industry, Science and Technology Policy-Making

Peter S. Biegelbauer

9.1 Introduction

Social scientists are trained to identify similarities. In the case of time-series policy studies, they quickly come up with periods in which certain elements of policies look more alike than others. That by itself is hardly surprising. It would be more interesting to see if there are periods in which similarities between policies are clearly more marked than the differences and which are ended by periods of rather rapid policy change instead of the incremental policy changes we are used to in day-to-day politics. One could look if these proposed times of rapid policy change either show a certain regularity and/or can be found in several different cases. Accordingly, in this paper an effort will be made to identify such cases, in which the political, social and economic structures involved vary to some degree, so that one can make assumptions on the impact of factors such as economic growth, political stability, or, more broadly, the institutional set-up of a country or system on the change of policies. This paper aims at providing greater insight into the processes of, and the reasons for policy change by focusing on a nowadays small and semiperipheral country in Central and Eastern Europe. It is to deal with industrial, science and technology policy-making in Hungary since World War II (WW II), with an emphasis on the 1990s.[1] The case promises interesting data as Hungary has featured two distinctly different political regimes during these decades, one state-socialist and the other pluralist-democratic. In addition, the four decades of state-socialism can be differentiated into the time of orthodox state-socialism of the 1940s and

1950s, with the uprising of 1956 as an intermission and the time of reform-socialism, from the 1960s to the 1980s.

9.2 Three periods of industry, science and technology policy-making

When following the procedures suggested before, one can identify three periods of policy-making since WW II. Although this paper shall focus on the developments of the 1990s, the changes in the last decade of the outgoing 20th century cannot be explained without a look at the earlier decades. Since World War II, Hungary has gone through three transitions. All of these had effects on the science and technology system. During the late 1940s and early 1950s the science and technology system, especially the part responsible for industrial research and development, was transformed from a market-based system to a centrally planned one. During this process the whole science and technology system was compartmentalized and confronted with a centralization and bureaucratization of its control functions. It was the goal of this transformation to create a 1:1 copy of the Soviet science and technology system, which was strongly influenced by a paradigmatic notion about the innovation process, which shall be referred to as the 'science push' policy paradigm.[2] During the 1960s and 1970s large parts of the national economy, and with them the science and technology system, went through a transition from a centrally planned and bureaucratically controlled to an indirectly bureaucratically controlled structure with integrated market elements. As early as in the 1960s, in Hungary ideas were utilized, which stemmed from a paradigmatic notion, here referred to as the 'demand pull paradigm' – a notion seriously discussed in the rest of Europe only after the Rothschild report induced reforms of the British science and technology system in the early 1970s.

The comparatively small Hungarian military-industrial complex was largely exempted from this development. The third transition has led the country from the reform socialist economy to a market based capitalist economy during the 1990s. The reforms of the years since 1989 have brought the country ever closer to a West European model. Indeed, the policy makers have introduced new and more complex notions underlying science and technology policies, based on the 'innovation process paradigm'. For a schematic comparison of the three time periods, the predominant science and technology policy paradigms and typical policy instruments, see table 9.1.

Table 9.1: Science and technology policy paradigms in Hungary, 1870s–1990s

Time	Predominant S&T Policy Paradigm	Typical Policy Instruments
1950s – 1960s	science push: S&T as the motor of progress and of military strength.	block funding of S&T by the state.
1970s – 1980s	demand pull: S&T as a problem solver targeting societal and economic problems.	partially peer reviewed funding systems through intermediary organizations.
1990s –	innovation process: S&T as a source of strategic opportunity, particularly for national and regional economies (both in the short and long term).	public tender systems by national intermediary and supranational organizations and programs.

9.3 Policy paradigms

The term 'policy paradigm' has been introduced. Why not speak about waves or periods, when signifying similarities of policies? Why evoke an ideational picture in the tradition of Thomas Kuhn (1970), when speaking about 'paradigms'?

For the sake of clarifying what is at stake, one might say in somewhat simplifying terms that political science and economics have obtained quite a clear vision of the 'know-why' and of the 'know-how', but much less of the 'know-what' of the political and economic processes. In other words, the reasoning behind the entrance of individuals and groups into politics and the economy as well as the governance of the two areas are comparatively well-understood, but the cognitive basis upon which individuals and groups in politics and the economy form their decisions, leading to policies, management strategies and the like are often left out in the dark.

This said, it is important to mention a strand of literature concerned with the role of the 'know-what', primarily in political economy, policy studies and international relations, which has been growing throughout the 1990s. Several books have been published, which are part of neo-institutionalism in both its historic (Hall, 1993; Rein and Schön, 1995) and rationalist (Goldstein/Keohane, 1993) variants (for overviews, see Jacobsen, 1995 and Blyth, 1997; on neo-institutionalism see Peters, 1998; 2000). In addition, in Germany, Hofmann (1993) and Braun (1997) have analyzed the roles of ideas with regards to the steering problems modern states face in societies of growing complexity. Moreover, a small strand of literature exists, which analyses the topic from the angle of discourse theory (compare with Gottweis, 1998; Radaelli, 2000).

The term 'policy paradigm', which is used here, has been introduced by Peter Hall (1993) and is applied to traditions in (here science and technology) policies that are paradigmatic in the sense of distinct cognitive frameworks, which form the basis of a new tradition in a policy field, including new overarching goals, new instruments and new instrument settings. It is important to notice that a set of policies here are not understood by themselves as a paradigm – different from Beatriz Ruivo's (1994) understanding of the notion. Here a policy paradigm is a network of underlying assumptions about a set of science and technology policies, which are then shared and used by an increasing number of decision-makers in a specific policy-field (compare with the notion of 'epistemic communities' of Haas, 1993). Policy paradigms provide knowledge on how to structure the world, interpret phenomena related to a specific problem-set and policy-field. Thereby, policy paradigms pre-select possibilities of political action, primarily with regards to the ends, but partially also the means to reach these ends. Policy paradigms are specific, small-scale views of the world. However, they do not address the whole world as does a 'Weltanschauung' in the Weberian sense, but rather a limited part of the world such as the innovation process in the case of science and technology policies or the nature and function of the market in economic policies. Thereby policy paradigms are also important for the actual policy-making process, as they create inter-subjective meaning for persons and groups.

This understanding of the term policy paradigm is an adaptation of Peter Hall's definition of the concept. As Hall's notion was created to account for the impact of economic theories on economic policy-making, with France and Great Britain as his prime cases illustrating the changes from Keynesian to Monetarist macroeconomic policies, a few differences in scope and nature of the terms seem to apply. First, Hall's notion of policy paradigms as 'ideologies', defined as 'well developed networks of ideas, which prescribe a course of economic action' (1986, p.278) may overextend the usage of the term for our purposes. Indeed, one of the goals of the concept of policy paradigms is to make the concept independent of classical ideologies such as

Marxism-Leninism or Liberalism.

A particularly helpful aspect of Hall's work is his elaborate distinction between the three different orders of change (see especially Hall, 1993). First order changes signify changes in policy setting, second order changes are changes of policy instruments and setting and third order changes apply to changes of the former two and the overarching goals of policies. For this paper only third-order changes are of interest with respect to a policy paradigm's effects. These, however, are understood as consisting of two levels, the first of which pertain to changes in policy paradigms, such as the science-push to the demand-pull paradigm (a more thorough discussion of the specific paradigms is to follow). The second level pertains to changes in the notions on which the paradigms themselves are based, i.e. the models of technological change. These form the basis, but are not congruent with, the policy paradigms. Extending the terminology of Peter Hall, these might be termed fourth order changes.

Another important facet is that actual science and technology policies might be partially outside the currently dominant policy paradigm. This is also a clear difference to Kuhn's notion of a paradigm that did not entail the parallel existence of paradigms for prolonged periods of time. In the case of policy paradigms in the science and technology policy field, the demand pull paradigm never was able to eliminate block funding as a significant source of income for research institutions in any economically developed country, including Hungary.

'Science push' and 'demand pull' refer to the 'pipeline model', in which innovation is seen as consisting of a chain of events from basic research, to applied research, to development, to engineering and finally to production. In the science push paradigm basic research is the leading force responsible for progress, in the demand pull paradigm it is the demand of the market, which pulls the research with it. The third, more complex paradigm, tries to circumvent this oversimplification. This paradigm is still developing, but lacks at the moment a singular unifying notion comparable to the role the pipeline model had for the two preceding paradigms. Here, it is referred to as the 'innovation process' paradigm, which itself is based on the complex holistic model, whose name is a reference to the more complex nature of the model, overcoming linear thinking and including feed-back loops (Kline/Rosenberg, 1986).

9.4 Reasons for change: external shocks, internal crises

A problem the notion of policy paradigms shares with many concepts based on historical neo-institutionalism is that it appears a bit static (Peters, 1998, 2000) and that it has difficulties in explaining why and how paradigms, once in place, should and could change. Once a clear majority of the policy-making elites shares a view on a central problem in the policy field, it should be difficult to change these views.

Let us consider an example: once the opinion that science and technology are important for progress in general, and national defense in specific, was established as a majority opinion amongst policy-making elites after World War II, this view of the world found its expression in the establishment of a number of institutions such as science funds, offices, agencies and later ministries for research and so forth.

To be sure, the institutional set-up of the science and technology systems differed from country to country according to national specificities accountable to the national historical development (national post-World War II geopolitical situations translated into the relative importance of defense technologies, which demanded a specific kind of organization of science and technology – compare the situation in Germany with that one in the US) and societal structures (the relations of the state, business and labor translated, amongst other factors, into more centralized or federalized institutional set-ups, in turn influencing general qualities of policies such as mission or diffusion-orientation; compare with Ergas 1987, Diederen et al 1999, Foray in this book). Nevertheless, in most countries of the First and the Second World, including Hungary, a certain understanding of the roles of science and technology policies was dominating discussions, which again fostered a certain set of institutions planning, regulating and carrying out science and technology and led to a typical set of policy instruments.

Because of the understanding of current systems as evolved through gradual historical processes and ensuing path-dependencies, it is difficult to see how these paths of development should be broken. The easiest way to imagine change in such a situation would be a strong external shock impacting on the political and/or economic system and forcing the system to change the very premises upon which the policies addressing a specific policy-field rest.[3]

A possible explanation for changes of science and technology policies during the 1970s may be the oil crisis, which certainly qualify for pronounced external shocks, impacting on budgetary priorities of most industrialized countries. Yet, in the case of Hungary, the change from one policy paradigm to another came already in 1968, years before the first oil crises, with the implementation of a general economic reform, impacting also on the science and technology system.

On May 7, 1966, the Central Committee of the Communist Party produced a resolution that led to a basic economic reform – the New Economic Mechanism – finally launched in 1968. The principle of central planning was to be replaced by what came to be called an indirect bureaucratic system. Free market elements were introduced to the economy of Hungary for the first time in two decades. Management and workers took part in a profit-sharing system, prices reflected to a certain extent the valuation of the products by the market (Balassa, 1982).

The document most aptly describing the reasoning behind the reforms targeting the science and technology system is the same document, which was the very basis for the reforms: the 'Science Policy Guidelines of the Central Committee of the Hungarian Socialist Workers Party'. The 'Science Policy Guidelines' give an overview over the condition of science in the country. The interrelations between societal and economic goals and research and development are described: science, according to the document, not only affects the social consciousness, but also enhances the skills of people and forms a basis for the management and organization of production: 'The achievements of science are utilized in the interests of the entire society'.[4] The document sees science as a problem solver, which is typical for the time and for the demand pull policy paradigm.

Two obvious effects of the Science Policy Guidelines are the reform of the Hungarian Academy of Sciences in 1970 and the 'rehabilitation' of the universities, which were henceforth granted more possibilities of income (especially with regards to industrial research and development) and autarchy. In general the science and technology system was liberalized, the degree of freedom was enlarged[5] and the structures and to some degree also the functions of the system moved into the direction of the organization of science and technology in capitalist economies.

Industrial research institutes were, at least in theory, to operate as profit-oriented businesses. Incentives were provided for corporations to contract research and development work out instead of carrying it out in-house. Furthermore the companies were pressed to increase the quality of their products and to adopt innovations more quickly. The policy makers wanted to foster exports to market economies in order to be able to import technology in the form of capital goods such as machinery.

In this case, not only the policy instrument setting and the policy instruments themselves changed in the field of science and technology policy, but also the very goals of science and technology policy. These were first seen as fostering societal progress, but later had to solve specific problems society had to face. According to the definition of a policy paradigm, these changes qualify as the full-scale change from one policy-paradigm to another, here from the science-push to the demand-pull paradigm.

When accounting for the reasons of change through an external shock, the problem of course is that in 1966 no external shock of political, economic or whatever nature can be discerned that could be somehow relevant for Hungary and therefore qualify as a reason for the change in policy paradigms. Yet even if there was no external shock, there certainly was a crisis discernable in Hungary during the 1960s: it was a crisis of trust of policy-makers in the available policies. Indeed an important precondition for the change of policy paradigms seems to have been the prolonged impression of non-suitability of the existing policy paradigm for the problems the policies were supposed to tackle in the specific field.

On a general level this might at first glance seem to be a quite trivial statement, but actually it is not. It entails that a dominating policy paradigm has already gone through a number of small and medium scale changes, which, at least in the last few years, have not led to satisfactory results. This means that in all likelihood a number of politicians have already tried new solutions to problems they could not cope with, in some instances ending their careers. It means also that a number of persons and institutions, which have stakes in existing policies and which therefore in all likelihood have tried to resist change, have been overruled and are under the danger of being replaced or at least revamped. In other words, the uneasiness about the existing paradigm and its inability to cope with a set of existing problems has grown large enough to overcome the inertia, which is, to varying degrees, inherent to all institutions and societal structures (compare with notions of institutional inertia in neo-institutional concepts as the social systems of production concept, see Hollingsworth/Streeck, 1994; Hage, 1998; Hollingsworth, 1998).

In the concrete case of Hungarian industry, science and technology policies both cases of complete policy paradigm change under discussion here were preceded by such an inability to cope with existing sets of problems. A case in point is the New Economic Mechanism, the above mentioned economic reform program of the late 1960s. During the first half of the 1960s, labor and capital, both drawn from agriculture, were becoming scarce resources. The labor reserves of the agricultural sector were diminishing and a large share of women was already included in the labor force (Marer, 1986 p.65). Capital was missing, too, as the Hungarian exports to the capitalist countries were shrinking – which was amongst other things a result of the weak technological basis.

Technology had been a scarce resource right from the start of the economic program furthered by Stalinist policies. As a result the quality of products was lower than in capitalist Western Europe and could be sold only on Council for Mutual Economic Assistance (COMECON) markets.

In the early 1960s, it became increasingly clear for the Hungarian science and technology planners that the old institutional structure of the system was inadequate. This observation led to a series of innovations regarding functions and structures of the science and technology system. Already in 1959 each company was required to set up a Technical Development Fund, out of which its research and development expenses were to be paid. Other institutions followed, such as the first National Long Range Plan for Scientific Research in 1960 (Müller 1985) and the State Committee for Technical Development (OMFB) in 1961 (Tolnai/Quittner/ Darvas, 1985).

Only when all of these reforms, of which the here mentioned are only exemplary, had found their counterparts in educational, industrial and economic policies, had failed, did a complete revision of the existing policy paradigm become possible. This paradigm change then came with the New Economic Mechanism in the late 1960s described above.

An example for an external shock, that could be expected to be large enough to cause an immediate change of policy paradigms, is the political transition from realsocialism to pluralism in the late 1980s, which went hand in hand with a transition of the economic system from central planning to a market based system. And although the relation between shock and policy change is much clearer in this case, it is difficult to explain the change in policy paradigms without mediating factors. Most importantly a time delay has to be explained between the external shock in 1989 and the paradigmatic change in policies in the mid-1990s.

In an analysis of the policies implemented since the Hungarian elections in 1990, three phases can be distinguished.[6] The first months of 1990 and 1991 were marked by the same euphoria that flooded Europe, East and West, immediately after the fall of the iron curtain. The expectations of policy makers and the general public was that the market forces, once unleashed, would generate an order of their own.[7]

During this 'phase of euphoria' the Hungarian government reacted to the problems of the science and technology system primarily by initiating changes in the structure of the system. As was the case in other Central and Eastern European Countries, too, the science and technology system was granted representation on the highest levels of government: two new ministers were established, one for science, one for technological development.[8] The largely uninfluential 'Science Policy Council' of the Antall/Boross governments, replacing the 'Science Policy Committee' in 1990, was headed by a chairman who was at the same time Minister of Science without portfolio.

In stark contrast to the new representation of science and technology at the highest levels of government stood the funding for the science and technology system, which decreased. On the one hand, science and technology were not the first priority of governmental action. On the other hand, the government seemed to expect the invisible hand of the market powers to bring about a balance of supply and demand for research and development, a manifestation of the demand-pull model's influence.

The next phase was characterized by the realization that the obstacles on the road to a market economy were bigger than expected. In this 'phase of frustration', which took place from 1991 to 1993, the decline in levels of production, which was due to the political upheaval in the area of the (former) USSR, the subsequent loss of markets, the rising unemployment levels and various interlocked economic, social and political problems led to a widespread frustration about the prospects of the immediate future, not only in Hungary, but in the whole region.

The science and technology policies of the Hungarian government during the phase of frustration changed only marginally. During this time, policy-makers saw their main task in (short-term) crises management. Because of the weakness of industry and its inability to fund research and development, the government was forced to step in. The National Committee for Technological Development, at that time a ministry responsible for technology, began to implement a policy of allocating the Central Technological Development Fund's capital primarily to near-market innovations. The third phase may be called the 'phase of realism'. Since the mid-1990s on, East and West European governments[9] and the general public alike had learned from the experience made in the transition period. Expectations in most cases were not unrealistically optimistic or pessimistic anymore. Medium and long-term strategies of governments now had been formed.

During the first years of the transition from realsocialism to capitalism the Hungarian science and technology organizations all were subject to a huge pressure to reorient their structures and functions according to the needs of the new capitalist system. The Hungarian governmental agency responsible for technology policy, the National Committee for Technological Development (OMFB), with a staff of 170, is a good example for an organization reacting relatively flexibly to the changing environment. During the transition period OMFB showed clear indications of learning.

Beginning with modestly structured programs in 1990, the organization has applied a competitive funding scheme primarily for industrial research and development since 1991. In addition to this, the organization has regularly used outside expertise, as for example an evaluation of the applied research and development system by Swedish NUTEK (the Swedish Agency for Industry and Technological Development) and the Academy of Sciences Research Institute on Industry and Enterprise Economics during 1995 and 1996, for the restructuring and evaluation of its programs. Moreover, the official publications of OMFB mirror the increasing 'realism' of the organization. Whereas, in a text from the institution's phase of euphoria, in 1991, buzz-words such as 'artificial intelligence', 'biotechnological processes' and 'robotics' were used for the description of the organization's priorities, in 1994 a similar text more modestly uses 'infrastructure development' (in 1991 the last item in the list, in 1994 the first), 'agriculture and food processing' or 'promotion of small and medium sized enterprises', which is a reflection of the organization's entering into the phase of realism (OMFB, 1991 p.4 and OMFB, 1994 p.6). Yet, it is also an indication of the organization's beginning acceptance of a new policy paradigm, which has a strong emphasis on infrastructure upgrading and the fostering of small and medium-sized enterprises.

An indication for the partial acceptance of the new policy paradigm on the side of the then government (under prime ministers Antall and Boross) is the issuance of innovation policy guidelines in 1993, which were the result of a lengthy discussion process between the three most important ministries in the field (OMFB/Ministry for Industry/Ministry of Finance 1993). In addition, after an even longer discussion process full of conflict, a long-term technology concept was worked out by OMFB in 1995 – already during the next government (prime minister Horn). The document was blocked by the Prime Minister's Office and was supplanted by a government action plan in early 1996. The next government (prime minister Orban) had in 1999 a new OMFB strategy paper developed, but then decided to downgrade the agency and put it into the Ministry for Education. Shortly thereafter, government adopted a more science and less innovation oriented document, which was produced by the Science and Technology Policy Council (compare with Havas, 1999; 2001). None of these papers had long-lasting effects on the Hungarian science and technology policy.

It is interesting to note that since the mid-1990s government publications and statements of policy makers acknowledged the necessity to intervene in cases of market failure,[10] which in Western Europe, Japan and the USA in fact is a typical rhetorical figure for the 'demand-pull' paradigm. In the case of the countries in transition the market failure reference had won a special quality, however, which was linked to the rejection of the realsocialist past and the role the state played then in the economy.

This is all the more likely as at the same time Hungary began to make first steps to change its science and technology policies into the direction of what since the early 1990s came to be recognized as innovation policies. These included such elements as efforts towards strengthened coordination of different policy-fields such as industry, transport, technology, science and education, which at least during some time-periods seemed to be visible and the fostering of international cooperation and coordination efforts in these areas. Therefore, at least some Hungarian policy-makers can be seen to have acknowledged the difference between the older science and technology and the new innovation policies. Regrettably, the effects of this acknowledgement are incoherent and in general rather meagre, mainly due to the low priority science and technology enjoy in Hungarian policy-making since 1989.[11]

Nevertheless, it could be argued that first steps have been taken to a change from one to another policy paradigm, however incoherent and halty the process might be. And indeed, not only the setting of and the instruments themselves, but also the overarching goals of science and technology policy changed (at least during some of the post-1989 administrations). These were first seen to solve specific problems of society, yet later were even more instrumentalized, this time as a source of strategic opportunity in the global competition for economic development. At the same time, they acquired a systemic quality through the inclusion of factors as infrastructure policy into innovation policy, leading – at least in policy documents and single initiatives – to a stronger interdependency of several policy fields.

9.5 Sources of change: exogenous alternatives?

After examining the reasons for policy paradigm change, which were identified as a combination of crisis situations with internal and external causes and the resulting pressure on policy-makers due to policy-failure, another question comes into mind: Where do the policy paradigms themselves come from? In the case of Hungary, and again Hungary might stand here exemplary for more cases of small and medium sized countries, the answer seems to be quite clear: from abroad.

More concretely, Hungarian policy-makers imported policies, instruments and paradigmatic notions underlying the policies from large countries, which during the respective time periods were hegemonial powers (not necessarily in the power political sense; this notion obtains here a sense of intellectual hegemonialism as in Gramsci's thinking) and had a concrete intellectual influence on the policy-making elites. Examples can be found for all three time-periods analyzed.

The first example took place in the late 1940s, although this transition had a forced character: After the Hungarian Communist's successful struggle for power, the declaration of the People's Republic of Hungary and the passing of the new constitution in 1949, the country's science and technology system was reformed. As has been pointed out, the reform consisted first of all in copying the Soviet system as it has just been laid out.

And indeed, just like in the Soviet Union, the universities lost most of their research functions, the Academy of Sciences was rapidly enlarged and gained most of the basic research and, later, also some applied research, whereas industrial research and development was to be carried out in the ministerial research institutes.

Until the early 1960s, the science and technology system remained unchanged. Then, in the second policy-change, after a phase of small-scale policy experimentation, which was described earlier on, the New Economic Mechanism was to reform the set-up of the economy and the science and technology system.

The ideas behind these reforms are based on the demand-pull model. The New Economic Mechanism should create a 'simulated market', with the goal of arriving at a 'regulated market economy' (Marer, 1986 p.18) or a 'market socialism'.[12] The price mechanisms of the simulated market were supposed to have a regulative function, steering supply and demand, but were at the same time held under control by the state bureaucracy. Analogous to the workings of a market economy, the demand of the market for new products should in turn lead to a demand for innovation, which would be met by the industrial research and development system.[13] The research and development institutes now could choose from a variety of incomes: the shrinking en bloc funding by the state, government procurement, national technical development programs administered by OMFB and, finally, the technical development funds of the companies, which provided an increasing source of income.

Without ever having been stated explicitly, it can be inferred from the reform measures that the model for the reform of the science and technology condensing of research potential in large universities on the other hand was envisioned by policy makers after the transition had begun (Melchior/Bessenyei, 1996 p.49). However, the process of reorganization of higher education units with the goal of creating universities, colleges and 'Höhere Technische Lehrschulen'[14] in the Western sense is slow and still in progress.

For the rationalization of peer-review and project evaluation procedures institutions such as the Deutsche Forschungsgemeinschaft (DFG) or the US National Science Foundation (NSF) have been models. Yet another example for foreign institutional models is the applied science oriented Bay Zoltán institutes, which have been formed after the German Fraunhofer Gesellschaft institutes. The three institutes are to work closely together with industry, utilizing Ph.D. students from universities. According to the institutes, already by the end of the 1990s, clearly more than half of the organizations' income was generated through contract research (Griessler/Biegelbauer, 2001). Summing up the information about the four time periods of industry, science and technology policy-making in Hungary, one clearly can link these periods with certain predominant policy paradigms, which were taken from major powers at that time (see table 9.2).

9.6 Change: evolution or revolution?

Coming back to the remarks at the beginning of this paper, here it was possible to identify a number of similarities of policies over several clearly definable time periods. These periods were ended by periods of rapid policy change. Does this now mean that policy changes come primarily as revolutions? Certainly not, as has been shown, policy changes are much more likely to come as incremental changes in policy instrument settings and instruments, and only in a comparatively small number of cases they come as revolutionary changes in the sense that not only settings and instruments, but also the overarching goals of policies change. In even fewer cases, the underlying premises on which the policies and indeed the whole process of policy-making rest, are being changed – one such case could be identified.

Table 9.2: Models of technological change, science and technology (S&T) policy paradigms, international historic setting and major powers, 1940s–1990s

Time	Leading model of technical change	Predominant S&T policy paradigm	International historic setting	Major powers
1950s – 1960s	linear model.	science push: S&T as the motor of progress and of military strength;	bipolarism, Cold War;	USSR
1970s – 1980s	linear model.	demand pull: S&T as a problem solver targeting societal and economic problems;	intermittent weakening of bipolarism, Vietnam and Afghanistan Wars, oil and debt crises;	USA
1990s –	complex holistic model (including feed-backs and loops).	innovation process: S&T as a source of strategic opportunity, particularly for national and regional economies (both in the short and long term).	(economic) trilateralism, fall of the iron curtain, economic confrontation gradually replaces military confrontation.	Germany (USA)

With regards to the regularities of these periods of change under the condition of varying political and economic regimes and concomitant structures, which have been called for in the beginning, some have been identified. It has been found that crises, regardless if stemming from external economic and political shocks or primarily internal factors, when accompanied by a critical opinion of elites regarding the chances of success of a certain measure, are a major factor in large-scale policy change. Indeed, it seems to be very important how the policy-making elites view the possibilities of active policies to cope with societal problems. Only when these policies, for a prolonged period of time, are seen as not being able to satisfactorily deal with an important set of problems and several policies have already been tried out, is the complete policy paradigm likely to be exchanged – potentially disturbing power balances and hurting entrenched interests. In this view, factors such as economic growth and political stability have less of an immediate impact on policies, but are mediated through the institutional set-up of a system. This intermediation through institutions would appear to lead to a time-delay in response insofar as the entrenched interests of institutions and persons, which have learned to cope with a certain policy of a certain policy paradigm, will have to be overcome and the interest conflicts of the different players will have to be settled.

Yet there is another factor, which is important in the explanation of rapid in-depth policy changes: the availability of an alternative. In our cases these were identified as consisting of policy paradigms, which had already been established in other countries. These countries were defined as ideational hegemons, i.e. countries, which could serve as successful examples for the Hungarian elites.

Whilst this finding is consistent with the data presented before, this second precondition for policy change certainly is not a satisfying one. After all, an important element of change is exogenized and therefore only cursorily dealt with. Moreover, the question if the most recent policy paradigm change in Hungary has been influenced by institutional (Hollingsworth 1998) or evolutionary (Nelson/Winter, 1982) economics cannot be answered before the genesis of the policy paradigms in the hegemonial countries and relevant international organizations as the OECD or the European Commission (compare with Edler in this volume) has been clarified.

Notes

1 I should like to thank Attila Havas from UNU/INTECH in Maastricht, himself a specialist on Central and Eastern European innovation systems, for critical input on my work on Hungary.

2 Science and technology 'policy paradigms' are understood as the paradigmatic notions of and ideas underlying the science and technology policies in the time period studied. The next section is to deal with this term in more detail.

---

3 This is also a major variable Hall and others found for change in economic policy-making (Hall, 1989).

4 Az MSZMP Tudománypolitikai Irányelvei (Science Policy Guidelines of the Central Committee of the Hungarian Socialist Worker's Party), Kossuth Könyvkiadó, 1969, cited in: Vas-Zoltán, P. 1985 p.283.

5 As a number of interview partners have pointed out, with the exception of a few taboos such as the presence of the Red Army in Hungary, research topics could be chosen freely by the end of the 1960s. Despite this development, during the roll-back of the New Economic Mechanism's reforms the freedom of expression was also limited again. For instance, a number of social scientists who, at the beginning of the 1970s, attempted to reinterpret scientific Marxism were subsequently excluded from Party membership and faced with disciplinary measures.

6 Compare the three phases considered here with the three time periods distinguished in: Wedel, 1994 p.14. Jozsef Imre similarly finds three stages of transition, 'fragmentation – stabilization – reintegration'; see Imre, 1998.

7 This misbelieve was fostered by the policies of different international agencies, which assumed a spontaneous resurrection of the market from the ashes of the realsocialist planned economies. A detailed analysis of the problems arising in the transition economies from laissez faire politics has been given by Kregel/Matzner/Grabher, 1992 see especially p.112.

8 Of course, the organizational structures were already existing. OMFB, from 1990–94 the 'technology ministry', was a governmental agency before, supervising the National Office of Measures, the National Patent Office and the National Bureau of Standards. The 'science ministry', that existed from 1990–94, consisted of a small office and the restructured Science Policy Committee, headed by a minister without portfolio.

9 As can be inferred from the funding strategies of the Western European governments as well as international institutions, with respect to the prospects of reform the West was on the same emotional roler-coaster as the East of Europe (Biegelbauer/Giorgi/Pohoryles, 1998). This becomes especially clear in the case of the reunification of the two Germanies, which has been led by unrealistic expectations on both Western and Eastern sides. People, who cautioned the high hopes of Germans, were disregarded as being indecisive 'Zauderer'.

10 Which, after all, is consistent with neoclassical economics, too. For example OMFB/IKM/Ministry of Finance 1993, especially p.58.

11 A fact reflected in the notoriously low funding level of science and technology both by private and public sources, in 1999 about 0,68% of GDP were spent on research and development, see http://www1.oecd.org/publications/e-book/ retrieved at 21–02–2002.

12 See the discussion of the 'third path' between capitalism and communism in the introduction and the chapter 'The Hungarian Reform Process: Visions, Hopes and Reality', in: Kornai, 1990.

13 For a discussion of the original intentions of the policy makers and what reality looked like in the Hungarian post-NEM S&T system of the 1980s, see Balázs, 1993.

14 Schools in German speaking countries with a curriculum concentrating on a specific technical field, as communication technologies or electrical engineering, attended by students at ages 14–19. These schools aim at enabling students to be mid-level engineers with the title of 'Ingenieur'.

References

Balassa, B. (1982): The Hungarian Economic Reform, World Bank Staff Working Paper No. 506, 2/82.

Balázs, K. (1994): Transition Crisis in Hungary's R & D Sector, Institute of Economics of the MTA, Budapest, Typescript.

Bay Zoltán Foundation (1998): Bay Zoltán Foundation for Applied Research, Budapest.

Bessenyei, I./Melchior, J. (1996): Die Hochschulpolitik in Österreich und Ungarn 1945–1995, Peter Lang.

Biegelbauer, P. (2000): 130 Years of Catching Up With the West: A Comparative Perspective on Hungarian Industry, Science and Technology Policy-Making Since Industrialization. Aldershot, Ashgate.

Biegelbauer, P./Giorgi, L./Pohoryles, R. (1998): 'Research and Technological Development Cooperation Activities of the EU/EEA Countries with the Central and Eastern European and Baltic States in the Field of Scientific and Technological Research', Working Paper Series of the ICCR, Vienna, Austria.

Borras, S./Lundvall, B.-A. (1999): The Globalising Learning Economy: Implications for Innovation Policy. European Commission.

Braun, D. (1997): Die politische Steuerung der Wissenschaft: Ein Beitrag zum kooperativen Staat. Frankfurt/Main. Campus.

Darvas, G. (ed.) (1988): Science and Technology in Eastern Europe, Longman.

Darvas, G. (ed.) (1995): 'Transformation of the Science and Technological Development System in Hungary', in: Mayntz, R. (ed.), Transformation Mittel- und Osteuropäischer Wissenschaftssysteme – Länderberichte, Leske + Budrich, pp.853–977.

Didieren, P. et al (1999): Innovation and Research Policies – An International Comparative Analysis, Edward Elgar.

Donner, K.O./Pál, L. (eds): Science and Technology Policies in Finland and Hungary – A Comparative Study, Akadémiai Kiadó.

Ergas, H. (1987): 'Does Technology Policy Matter?', in: Technology and Global Industry, National Academy Press.

Fischer, H./Szabadváry, F. (1995): Technologietransfer und Wissensaustausch zwischen Ungarn und Deutschland, R. Oldenbourg Verlag.

Füzeséri, A. (1992): Über die Ungarn, in der Geschichte der Naturwissenschaft und Technik, OMFB, Budapest.

Goldstein, J./Keohane, R. (1993): Ideas and Foreign Policy, Ithaca, NY, Cornell University Press.

Gottweis, H. (1998): Governing Molecules: The Discursive Politics of Genetic Engineering in Europe and the United States. Cambridge, Massachusetts. MIT Press.

Grabher, G. (ed.) (1993): The Embedded Firm: On the Socioeconomics of Industrial Networks, Routledge.

Graham, L. (1993): Science in Russia and the Soviet Union – A Short History, Cambridge University Press.

Griessler, E./Biegelbauer, P. (2001): 'The Bay Zoltàn Foundation as an Example for the Transfer of German Institutional Models to Hungary in the Field of Applied Research', mimeo.

Haas, P. (1992): 'Introduction: Epistemic Communities and International Policy Coordination', in: International Organization, 46 (1), 1–35.

Hage, J. (1998): Organizational Innovation and Organizational Change, Typescript.

Hall, P. (1986): Governing the Economy: The Politics of State Intervention in Britain and France, Oxford University Press.

Hall, P. (ed.) (1989): The Political Power of Economic Ideas: Keynesianism Across Nations, Princeton, Princeton University Press.

Hall, P. (1993): 'Policy Paradigms, Social Learning, and the State', Comparative Politics, April, pp.275–296.

Havas, A. (1999): 'A Long Way To Go: The Hungarian Science and Technology Policy in Transition', in: Laki, M. et al (eds), Institutional Change and Industrial Development in Central and Eastern Europe, Aldershot, Ashgate.

Havas, A. (2001): 'Innovation Policy Profile: Hungary', in: 'Innovation Policy in Six Candidate Countries: The Challenges', Project Report for DG Enterprise, Contract: INNO-99–02, ADE.

Hofmann, J. (1993): Implizite Theorien in der Politik – Interpretationsprobleme regionaler Technologiepolitik, Opladen, Westdeutscher Verlag.

Hollingsworth, J. R. (1998): Doing Institutional Analysis: Implications for the Study of Innovations, Mimeo.

Hollingsworth, J. R./Streeck, W. (1994): Governance of Capitalist Economies, Oxford University Press.

Imre, J. (1998): 'S&T in Hungary', in: Meske, W. et al, Transforming Science and Technology Systems – The Endless Transition? IOS Press.

Jacobsen, J. K. (1995): 'Much Ado about Ideas. The Cognitive Factor in Economic Policy', in: World Politics, 47/95, pp.283–310.

Keck, O. (1993): 'The National System for Technical Innovation in Germany', in: Nelson, R. (ed.), National Innovation Systems, Oxford University Press, p.122.

Kline, S./Rosenberg, N. (1986): 'An Overview of Innovation: The Positive Sum Strategy', in: Landau, R./Rosenberg, N. (eds), Harnessing Technology for Economic Growth, Washington, DC., National Academy Press.

Kornai, J. (1990): Vision and Reality, Market and State, Harvester Wheatsheaf.

Kregel, J./Matzner, E./Grabher, G. (1992): The Market Shock – An Agenda for the Economic and Social Reconstruction of Central and Eastern Europe, Austrian Academy of Sciences (Research Unit for Socio-Economics).

Kuhn, T. (1970, 1.ed 1962): The Structure of Scientific Revolutions, Chicago, Chicago University Press.

Marer, P. (1986): East-West Technology Transfer, Study of Hungary 1968–1984, OECD, Paris.

Meske, W. et al (1998). Transforming Science and Technology Systems – The Endless Transition? IOS Press.

Müller, L. (1985): 'Planning and Coordination in Science and Technology', in: Donner, K.O. /Pál, L. (eds), Science and Technology Policies in Finland and Hungary – A Comparative Study, Akadémiai Kiadó, p.225.

Nelson, R./Winter, S. (1982): An Evolutionary Theory of Economic Change, Cambridge, Harvard University Press.

OECD (1998): "Special Issue on 'New Rationale and Approaches in Technology and Innovation Policy'", in: STI Review 22.

OMFB (1991): The National Committee for Technological Development of the Republic of Hungary, Budapest.

OMFB (1994): OMFB – National Committee for Technological Development, Budapest.

OMFB (1995): OMFB – National Committee for Technological Development, Budapest.

OMFB (1995): The Government's Technical Development Concept, Proposal to the Government, September, Budapest.

OMFB (1996): OMFB – National Committee for Technological Development, Budapest.

OMFB (1998): Research and Technological Development in Hungary, Budapest.

OMFB/IKM/Ministry of Finance (1993): Innovation Policy of the Hungarian Government, Budapest.

Péteri, G. (1994): On the Legacy of State-Socialism in Academia, Paper presented at the 4th Conference of the International Society for the Study of European Ideas, The European Legacy: Towards New Paradigms, August 22–27, Graz, Austria.

Peters, G. (1998): Institutional Theory in Political Science, Pinter, London.

Peters, G. (2000): Institutional Theory: Problems and Prospects, Working Paper No.69 of the Political Science Series of the Institute for Advanced Studies, Vienna.

Radaelli, C. (2000): 'Policy Transfer in the European Union: Instituitional Isomorphism as a Source of Legitimacy', In: Governance 13(1), January 2000, pp.25–45.

Rein, M. and Schön, D. (1995): Frame Reflection: Toward the Resolution of Intractable Policy Controversies, Ingram.

Rothschild, (1971): The Organization and Management of Government Research and Development: A Framework for Government Resarch and Development, London.

Ruivo, B. (1994): 'Phases or Paradigms of Science Policy'?, Science and Public Policy, 3/94, p.157.

Tolnai, M./Quittner, J./Darvas, G. (1985): 'The Organizational Framework of Science and Technology Policy', in: Donner, K.O./Pál, L., (eds), Science and Technology Policies in Finland and Hungary – A Comparative Study, Akadémiai Kiadó.

Vámos, É. (1995): 'Deutsch-Ungarische Beziehungen auf dem Gebiet der Chemie', in: Fischer, H./Szabadváry, F., Technologietransfer und Wissensaustausch zwischen Ungarn und Deutschland, R. Oldenbourg Verlag, p.217.

Vas-Zoltán, P. (1985): 'Methods of Evaluation of R&D Achievements', in: Donner, K.O/Pál, L. (eds), Science and Technology Policies in Finland and Hungary – A Comparative Study, Akadémiai Kiadó, p.239.

Wedel, J. (1994): 'Lessons of Western Technical Aid to Central and Eastern Europe', in: Transition – The Newsletter about Reforming Economies, Vol. 5, July/August, p.14.

Chapter 10

Socio-Economic Transition and New Challenges for the Science and Technology Policy in Slovenia[1]

Franc Mali

10.1 Introduction

Slovenia is a young state, but it has a rich history. The latter also applies to the field of science and technology (S&T). Only since 1991, when Slovenia became a sovereign state, can we speak of the national science and technology policy (STP) as a state institutional process, guiding research and development. It does not mean that Slovenia, before that time, did not start to establish a parallel and complementary concept of STP in spite of its being restricted by the multinational Yugoslav concept of managing S&T and introducing socialist ideology into science. Hence, it can be stated that even before the constitution of the Slovenian state, the national scientific community was being formed with all its essential sociological characteristics. In particular, we saw a division of the roles in research activities among the institutes, the two universities, and research units in enterprises. The relationship between the basic, applied, and industrial research work had also been established. It was very significant for the development of science in Slovenia before the changes in 1991 that the Soviet model of the organization of science, which had been known in most of the other East and Central European countries, had never been introduced in full. For example, in the Soviet model universities were essentially confined to education, while basic research was performed by the science academy institutes and the industrial research by the so-called branch institutes. This was not the case in Slovenia. Here, universities emerged and remained important centres of basic research. Moreover, research-development units of industrial companies had a lot of organizational similarities to industrial research in the West.

Notwithstanding this, in the 1990s the transition of the science and technology system in Slovenia suffered from many similar structural problems as S&T systems in most of the other East and Central European countries. A communist heritage and the process of transition account for the common characteristics. Of course, there are, as in the past, some important differences. One of these differences is that some elements of the new concept of STP which had been introduced in the 1990s had already been started in the 1980s.

10.2 Preparing for the nineties

The political act of establishing the nation-state of Slovenia, in the beginning of the 1990s, did not change the concept of STP in any revolutionary manner, but it deepened and speeded up the processes of professionalization, integration and, especially, the differentiation of the scientific community, which had already been formed. The empirical analyses, which have been made in the 1980s, pointed out that some aspects of science were rather well developed in Slovenia at that time. This is in particular with regard to its participation in the current international science, while, in contrast, incorporation into the social and economic environment was very minimal. The direct influence of social and economic actors on the creation of scientific and technological cognition was insignificant or non-existent. The STP of that time did not consider the fact that the crucial problem of scientific development in Slovenia was not at the intellectual level or in the degree of the scientific excellence in global terms. Rather the problem was one of the lack of basic infrastructure, even of staff, and of adequate managerial and organizational models, which would link the academic scientific and economic spheres.

During that period, STP was able to open the system development issues only in the context of the debate about the role of science and the effects of the intellectual elite on economic and social development. Characteristic for that period were political and ideologically motivated campaigns aimed at integrating scientific capacities into the economic growth programs. The situation in Slovenia at that time was not much different from the situation described very well by authors David Dyker (Dyker, 1996), Henry Etzkowitz (Etzkowitz, 1996) and others. They pointed out that official ideology in all old socialist regimes favoured a chain of linkages in the research and productive sectors; however, despite them, in practice, the links in the innovation chain were completely broken even when the quality part of the research would be a good starting-point for the transfer of knowledge.

In the second half of the 1980s, Slovene companies showed an increasing interest in co-operation with the researchers only when such co-operation was connected with strictly specified tasks and did not imply any market risks related to the new product. However, the more the researchers' activities were likely to interfere with the social and economic environment, the less was the readiness for co-operation with them.

In the middle of the 1980s, Slovenian STP intervened in the researchers' labor market by almost doubling the state budget funds for research activity – this money was earmarked for the planned post-graduate studies in research groups. The new post-graduates were expected to create the core of the innovation potential in the economy. The program was set up in 1985. The objective of this postgraduate doctor's program, which was wholly funded by the government, was not only to revitalize the ageing research groups, but also to support non-research organizations. Although the young academics were expected to bridge the gap between scientific and industrial sectors, this type of postgraduate education had been all the time, not only in the 1980s, but also in the 1990s, too closely linked with basic research support facilities. The data which shows that most young Ph.D.s stay within the science sector after the completion of their studies confirms this conclusion.[2]

10.3 Slovenian science and technology policy in the nineties

The transition towards a market economy after the establishment of a new state has stimulated changes throughout society. The broad socio-political circumstances confronted by the S&T system in the 1990s were quite different from those which prevailed in the 1980s. It would be wrong to say that all difficulties were the heritage of the past. The deficiencies now faced by Slovenia regarding a more effective regulation of science, technology and innovation have resulted from the incompetence of the actual politicians as well. Namely, although Slovenia, as a post-socialist country in transition, is considered to be successful in establishing new democratic, political, institutions and holds, in all regional economic analyses, a clear lead over the other countries of Central and Eastern Europe. It has been less successful regarding the shaping of a new type of 'social contract' between functionally differentiated parts of society (see more: Bukowski, 1999; Filipović, 2000). During the last ten years, the inability of governmental STP, to connect the scientific and economic subsystems is one of the practical cases which proves that the model of new, social and economic effective corporativism has not been realized in Slovenia. In the emerging processes of globalization, it is very important to break down social barriers which occur in the transfer of academic knowledge from the research sector to industry. James Gow and Cathie Carmichel, external observers of the current situation in Slovenia and the authors of a recent book about it, have written: 'What the period of transition made clear was that, like other small economies, Slovenia would need to find its place in the international economic setting through openness, if it were to realize its potential' (Gow and Carmichael, 2000 p.112).

Economic globalization and the intensification of international industrial competition required Slovenia to develop a smart strategy to organize effectively the weak national innovation system. Expectations can be interfaced and communicated across the boundaries of different social subsystems or, as B.A. Lundvall and S. Borras wrote: 'National systems of innovation orient the attention of policy-makers to linkages and interactions within and between different sub-systems. For instance, it is now unthinkable to optimize university systems without taking into account connections and interactions with industry and other major users of research and higher education' (Lundvall and Borras, 1997 p.61).

Slovenian STP of the 1990s is marked by the tension between tradition and modernity, as well as between ambition and inoperativity. This reflects a discrepancy between its declared goals and its actual actions. At the empirical level, we have actually noticed the constant decrease of state budget funds for R&D in the 1990s. During the process of transition, the government (most importantly the Ministry of Science and Technology) became the primary source of finance for the majority of R&D activities in Slovenia. This could probably be considered one of the important characteristics of the transitional STP in the 1990s, the state's macro level role in the marginalization of the development of S&T. Although, during the last ten years, there has been a constant decline in the funding of science, from our point of view an even greater (long-term) problem is how to make this system better connected with the economic sector and on this way more 'efficient' and 'accountable'.

The so-called National research program (prepared by the government as the first constitutional document of STP in Slovenia and adopted by Slovene Parliament in 1994), foresaw that 30 per cent of state funds for R&D should be distributed to the experimental phases of technological projects. The support for the experimental phases of R&D projects should include subsidies for pre-competitive research, for salaries of researchers employed in R&D departments of the business sector, and for technology parks and information centers. In practice, there was no advancement in the planned technological upgrading of industry. In the period from 1994 to 1998, technological support schemes had been decreasing from year to year. In the same period, the state budget for R&D in terms of percentage of GNP had decreased as well, from 0,74 per cent to 0,69 per cent.

The guidelines for the National Research Program, clearly state that the 'Promotion of science and education is the most certain path to fast economic and social development, because the quality of science and higher education is decisive for the quality of production factors' (National Research Program, 1995, p.4). Such a conceptual starting-point has clearly defined the role of the STP in society. But, neither the National Research Program nor any other STP document from the 1990s prepared by the government contains the guidelines for researchers with respect to the social and economic aspects which should be given priority in research, nor as to the deepening and transferring of knowledge into practice.

In spite of the fact that Slovenia is small – indeed its size may be considered as an argument in favor rather than against a priority system – the government did not define the problem oriented research priorities. Therefore, the scientific community remained, during the 1990s, mainly disciplinary and not problem-orientated. That is the opposite of the situation in a lot of small countries in the European Union. These countries do not leave the matters of scientific and technological development just to the 'invisible hands' of the scientific market. They drive publicly financed R&D in the direction of strategic research programs, which is entirely clear, because'...it might not be possible to have all S&T fields represented in the higher education system of a small country, but for sure it is not possible to harbor more than only a few of the most important industrial sectors, which are necessary for the creation of successful knowledge based economies' (Biegelbauer, 1998 p.30).

As numerous authors warn, in current STP the term 'strategic' revolves around the reorientation of national S&T potentials to be engaged in the realization of long-term socio-economic goals (see for example: Irvin and Martin 1984; Zimman, 1994). To set priorities in S&T means to demand socio-economic relevance from science. It might be expected that Slovenian STP should put all its effort into dealing with the problems of specifying and carrying out long-term strategic R&D program in accordance with the main socio-economic targets. Reality is not in accordance with these expectations. The majority of scientists are engaged in the development of 'knowledge for its own sake' without any reference to a more specified socio-economic orientation.

The above data show that in Slovenia, if we attempt a comparison with some small countries in the EU at the end of the 1990s, there was still, ineffectiveness in links between the activities of scientists and applications of their work to broader socio-economic needs. State STP was not bound to ensure a better 'fit' between the scientific programs and economic objectives. There are lot of reasons for this deficiency. One of them is that the industrial sector was never sufficiently involved in the development of national research programs. The other reason for such a negative state of affairs could be sought in the prevalence of the traditional concept of scientific autonomy among academic scientists. This is based on the idea that scientists alone should identify scientifically and technologically promising fields, make priorities between them, and implement actions to promote chosen areas. This may have been justified in the pre-transition period, but not today, at the beginning of the new century. At that time, the concept of emphasized scientific autonomy had represented a strong defense strategy against the irruption of politics and ideology into scientific research. The syntagm, constantly repeated by the key actors of the scientific community, stating that 'the basic research work is the basis of application and industrial development', was the means for ensuring a relative scientific autonomy, political peace and resulted in the sufficient amount of state funds for untroubled research. In the 1990s, the proven syntagm aimed at the survival of science was applied again; this time not only by the scientific community but also by the STP.

One of the negative features of Slovene STP is too small a differentiation between the scientific community and policy decision-making. The lack of transparency in the decision-making processes and the role of informal lobby groups in STP increases this feeling. To explain the weak socio-economic problem orientation of S&T system in Slovenia, it is necessary to examine the background and to ask which part of the small S&T system in Slovenia has the most influence on decision-making in STP.

Table 10.1: Breakdown of government R&D appropriations in some countries of EU and in Slovenia (year: 1997–% of total)

Strategic goal / Country	BEL	DK	IRL	NL	FIN	SLO
Earth: exploration /exploitation	0,7	1,4	0,4	0,4	1,2	0,8
General planning of land use	0,9	1,5	2,5	4,0	2,9	0,7
Environment: control/care	2,2	2,9	1,5	2,9	2,3	1,8
Human health: protection	1,3	1,6	3,5	2,0	7,9	2,1
Energy: production/utilisation	2,8	2,6	0,2	3,3	4,1	1,3
Agricultural production	3,1	8,8	20,5	4,0	6,4	3,2
Industrial production/technology	17,8	10,4	34,4	12,1	27,3	13,8
Social structures and relationships	2,8	7,7	6,0	2,1	5,4	2,7
Space: exploration /exploitation	12,1	2,9	2,9	3,6	2,5	0,0
General university funds	30,8	36,2	21,4	46,1	26,4	2,9
Non-oriented research	20,9	23,5	6,9	11,2	12,1	69,7
Other civil research	4,4	0,0	0,0	5,0	0,0	0,9
Defense	0,5	0,5	0,1	3,2	1,5	0,1
Total	100,0	100,0	100,0	100,0	100,0	100,0

Source: Statistical Yearbook 1999. Research & Development, Science and Technology 1997. Rapid Reports, No.292. Ljubljana: Statistical Office of the Republic of Slovenia and Eurostat Yearbook 2000 – A statistical eye on Europe. Data 1987–1997. Luxembourg: Office for Official Publications of the European Communities.

Science lobbies in Slovenia, which mostly are linked with the big state institutes, follow a more 'defensive conservative' than 'offensive innovative' strategy concerning the socio-economic orientation of science (Weingart, 1998). In that sense we could speak about one of the negative legacies which Slovenia shares with other transitional countries. David A. Dyker and Jacques Perrin wrote that the prestigious institutes of the academies of science in post-socialist countries survive through a combination of ingenous improvization and persistent lobbying (see more: Dyker and Perrin, 1997). State institutes in Slovenia were themselves never identified with the former Soviet type of academic institutes. Notwithstanding, their decision power concerning science-policy questions was high in previous times and is still too strong today. In a sense, the situation seems more rigid than in other post-socialist countries, where big academic institutes were confronted, in the 1990s, with a '...massive legitimation crisis' (Sztompka, 1997 p.84). Large state institutes' negative consequences on STP decision-making can be seen when analysing the existing system of S&T evaluation. This evaluation system is defines the 'rules of the game' of the Slovene S&T system. As has been noticed by several authors (e.g. Frankel and Cave, 1997) – these rules are not oriented towards socio-economic problems.

As we have already said, the Slovenian scientific community of the 1990s was mainly disciplinary and not problem-orientated. Consequently, the basic instruments of STP were not the social and economic research priorities that asserted themselves, but the system of peer review. The lack of this regime of scientific control is that it does not include different agents in the evaluation practice. To use Helga Nowotny's terms, the control of science is still not exercised indirectly and from 'inside', but directly and from 'outside' (Nowotny et al, 2001 p.114).

The system of the peer review of individual researchers and groups as a basis for decisions about projects and provision of funds from the public budget was often the only policy instrument regarding S&T strategy in Slovenia in the 1990s. The proposed system of internal evaluation should introduce a positive selection among scientists and should act as a long-term stimulus for acquiring and increasing research capabilities, as well as for greater research achievements. The positive effect of such a concept for STP at the beginning of the 1990s was the abolition of the previous larger state research programs and introduction of the grant system. This had to stand the positive evaluation selection of the national, and partly of the international, scientific market as well. The grant system in the financing of R&D has brought various other advantages. After a long period of bureaucratic and ideologically controlled administration of science in the former socialist regime, the new condition of financing fosters the motivation of researchers for competition. It was an important step in the processes of S&T system reform at the beginning of the 1990s.

Unfortunately, the absolute dominance of the grant system in governmental financing of ST has abolished any form of co-operation between different research teams. The increased disintegration of larger research groups led at the end to an absurd situation, when the average amount of financing for a research project was equal to the funds required for one full-time researcher. This would mean one project for one researcher. To be awarded and to have a research project became not only a matter of existence, but mostly a matter of prestige and status. Such disintegration was strongly criticized by some external observers (see for example: Witschel, 1995). They were also critical of the very complicated formal structure of the expert system of Ministry of Science and Technology, which has been formed to ensure the objective evaluation of scientific quality by means of the peer review system.

In the prevailing grant system without any balance between the different models of financing, the scientists must have a new research theme and title every three years. Besides, proving and confirming the importance, originality and uniqueness in the struggle for financing could thus be even greater. It was successful only if a researcher, regardless of his/her scientific quality, managed to obtain sufficient allies with the monopolists of scientific research and decision-making in the form of a strong scientific coalition, which would enable him/her to fight his/her competitors, which – in the social and scientific sense – were unable to make winning coalitions.

The power attributed to the researchers was especially strengthened through the already mentioned complicated structure of the existent expert system at the Ministry of Science and Technology. Thus the breakthrough of the new, different and innovative was almost impossible, except under the patronage of recognized researchers. According to Thomas Kuhn, only by breaking with traditions, not only the scientific ones, but especially the social ones, is the development of science possible. Thus the positively conceived scientific competition, instead of stimulating greater research creativity, started to strengthen the existing scientific monopolies and to stabilize the existing state of affairs, simultaneously locking the scientific community more and more into the ivory tower.

10.4 Industrial managers' and academic scientists' lack of interest in cooperation

As we can see, there is a significant discrepancy between government declarations and the actual realization of the declared STP. Namely, in the 1990s Slovene researchers were continuously facing, not only in written documents, but also in everyday statements of high state officials, the official rhetoric on the importance of finding new legal and institutional forms of cooperation between the main actors of the national innovation system: science, politics and economy. Notwithstanding this, at the same time even some elementary action has been lacking. The changes in STP were introduced very slowly during the whole period of the 1990s.

One of the reasons lies in the slow modernization of the industrial sector. The industry in Slovenia is still not oriented enough towards development, modernization and innovation. The industrial firms in Slovenia are still unable, or are not motivated, to articulate their strategic development demands. They express an even smaller desire to work with researchers at academic research institutions in solving urgent development and innovation problems. This is in spite of the fact that a survey of the development plans of industrial enterprises has shown that only 25 per cent of them estimate that they are capable of solving development problems on their own (see more: Bucar and Stanovnik, 1999). Industrial managers could not deal with tasks concerning effective management, innovation and development problems of the enterprises. It seems that at the end of the 1990s, the situation had not improved much. The private initiatives based on innovation, knowledge, new forms of management, are not yet fully developed. The new type of industrial managers who rely on the new role of S&T are still rare. The results of empirical studies performed in different periods of the 1990s showed that the application of research results in industry were not perceived by most leaders of Slovenian firms to be the core problem (Mali, 1998a).

The main shortcoming is the lack of a broad industrial R&D base which should be developed, and put to practical and commercial use in a wide array of industrial sectors. On the one hand, only 20 per cent of the big companies (1,000 or more employees) in Slovenia have in-house S&T facilities. Additionally, the educational level of researchers employed in the industrial sector is quite low. According to official statistical data only 2 per cent of researchers employed in the business enterprise sector have Ph.Ds. (Statistical Yearbook, 1999). Additionally, those employed in the business enterprise sector have in many cases been absorbed into the everyday operation of running and maintaining technological equipment and have suffered serious financial cuts. Regarding the existing level of R&D in big companies, the biggest differences can be observed between different industries rather than within a certain industry.

On the other hand, the activities of small and medium-sized enterprises (SMEs) have little to do with high technology and innovative activity. The big companies, which have succeeded in maintaining their own R&D units during the transitional period, have been able to keep some form of contact with research groups from the academic sphere. For example, according to M. Kos' analyses, firms with more than 1,000 employees plan twice as much cooperation with government institutes and universities than enterprises with less than 50 employees (see more: Kos, 1998). They are mostly big and very successful companies with organized development orientation, especially in the areas of pharmacy, electronic components and technologies and polymer materials production. 88,5 per cent of all expenditure for S&T in Slovenian industry is concentrated in the above-mentioned industrial branches.

Although SMEs are an important field of economic activity in Slovenia (they have increased lately to more than 80 per cent of all firms), their major deficiency is a lack of development orientation.[3] They are usually small family companies. Their typical characteristic is that they express unwillingness to employ high professional (non-family) managers.

One of the arguments often heard in the 1990s as to why industrial managers did not pay more attention to innovation and the application of knowledge at academic research institutions, was their preoccupation with the problems of privatization. This argument was acceptable to some degree in the first half of the 1990s when the private economic sector was still in its infancy, but not at the present time, when the privatization process is practically at the end. By 1999, less than two percent of companies were not formally privatized and this was mostly because of unresolved claims for denationalization of part of their assets or because they have started bankruptcy procedures.

Generally, the technological level of manufacturing and service industries, especially in SMEs, lags substantially behind the Western European economies. For Slovenia, as a small economy with limited resources and insufficient domestic industrial competition, it would be necessary to create new innovative links between academic science and the economic sector.

If cooperation between academic research and industry exists at all, it is based mostly on short-range contacts remaining from the past. Various surveys performed during the 1990s have shown that most Slovenian companies use academic scientific institutions, especially universities, to obtain singular consultations, as opposed to long-term forms of formal and informal cooperation (see more: Phare Report, 1995; Mali, 1998). What is most lacking here is a well established link between public R&D and industrial requirements, which might be created in the so-called intermediary sphere. As noted, there are different reasons which prevent the links between the academic research and the industrial sector, and many of them could certainly be found on the scientific sector side.

Complaints from the industrial sector, that academic research is too characterised by 'l'art pour l'art' research, are often justified. Academic researchers do not know the problems of industry well enough, or cannot solve them. One of the reasons is that the direct influence of industry and other potential users of research results in society, by definition of the national research program and strategy, remained small during the 1990s. As we have already said, the Slovenian scientific community is mainly disciplinary and not problem-orientated. The majority of academic scientists are engaged in the development of 'knowledge for its own sake'. The investigation of academic research group activities in Slovenia in the middle of the 1990s showed that in 80 per cent of all cases, the research project content had been proposed by the heads of research groups themselves, and only in 20 per cent of all cases was this done by potential users of results (Mali and Sorcan, 1995).

To increase cooperation between science and industry, it is very important to introduce the concept of the diversification of functions of academic science institutions to the system. Today, experts agree that diversification is a most welcome trend in academic science in modern societies which should be supported. Here, it is necessary to mention that Slovenia, concerning institutional proliferation of the university system is very undeveloped, even if we compare it with other small European countries. For example, Slovenia has only two universities: The University of Ljubljana and the University of Maribor. The third university, on the coast of Adria is still being established. In Finland, the European country with a similar population to Slovenia, there are 20 universities, mostly multifaculty universities and some specialised in technical and commercial sciences. As we know, Finland is one of these EU countries, where in the 1990s the aims of technology policy have deeply penetrated into university policy (see more: Hayrinen-Alestalo, 1999).

The concept of the capitalization of academic knowledge at the universities in Slovenia still lacks social legitimation.[4]

Attempts to evaluate academic knowledge as an economic commodity with market value, rather than as an intellectual pursuit for its own sake, are challenging the concept of the university as a highly hierarchical organized institution. In that sense, how the university system is managed and governed is important. The university system in Slovenia has, until now, not responded to the challenges presented by the changing economic-political circumstances. Its main feature is a strong institutional fragmentation, dispersion of intellectual efforts and hierarchical-bureaucratic organization of academic 'life'. All these factors result in the absence of meaningful strategic thinking, especially about a true policy for industrial contacts. In particular, the university management pays too little attention to the question of assigning the ownership of knowledge to higher education institutions in which a certain innovation has been made. We are still at the beginning in regard to the establishment of some mechanisms which have proved efficient in transferring research results from the university into industrial application. The absence of an organized university policy is quite different from the situation in some EU countries, where higher education legislation led university institutions to experiment with a variety of arrangements to develop fruitful relations with industry and to encourage academic staff to include commercial activities in their roles.

It would be wrong to say that there are, in Slovenia, no positive examples of cooperation between the academic research institutions and industry, but there are still few cases of academic spin-offs and scientific-technological parks.[5]

After providing the legal framework, two technological parks were established in Slovenia in 1994. The main objective of the parks, the first in Ljubljana and the second in Maribor, was to create a favorable infrastructure for SMEs which makes commercial use of innovation from the research sphere, to market services and products of new technologies and stimulates the mobility of researchers to entrepreneurship.[6]

For the transfer of knowledge from academic research institutions to industry, the mobility of young research staff from universities to industrial corporations is very important. Not only because, in Slovenia, there is a lack of highly educated and trained staff within the industry, but also because the most effective vehicle of knowledge transfer is the transfer of highly educated personnel. Today, not only in the post-communist countries in transition, but all around the world, universities still remain the most important place for the training of competent experts in the business-economic sector (see for example: Nowotny et al, 2001 p.80).

The social distribution of scientific knowledge is, above all, performed by people and their ways of interacting in a socially organized form. The emphasis is on the tacit components of knowledge. As we have already said, the program of junior researchers (so-called 'Young Scientists Programme'), which started in 1985, did not meet the expectations of increasing the mobility of young research staff into industry. The majority of young doctors, after completing their studies, stayed within the R&D sector. In that sense, the Slovenian 'Young Scientists Program' did not succeed in following the more known TCS (Teaching Company Scheme) which was used at a time in England. The Teaching Company Scheme was a governmental program which linked universities and industry through the placement of young doctors in firms and whose work was jointly supervised by members of the academic staff and members of the companies. Even if a good institutional framework for the transfer of academic knowledge into industry would exist, a number of other external conditions for its success should be fulfilled. Every process of transformation is multidimensional and its final shape depends on the interaction between the organizational-institutional level on the one hand and the mental-cultural level on the other hand, and not on the shape of each of these levels taken separately.

In that sense, the idea of the capitalization of academic knowledge as conditio sine qua non for the transfer of knowledge from university to industry cannot be solved by a single program. It has to become a value of the academic community. It must give rise to entrepreneurial behaviour of the university staff, without any fear of universities becoming a bad imitation of industrial corporations. On the other hand, industrial sectors must adopt some norms of academic culture. In general, it must come to 'the mixing of norms and values in different segments of society' (Gibbons et al, 1994 p.37), but the differences between universities and businesses should never be forgotten.

10.5 Challenges for Slovenian STP at the end of the nineties

We can find two general and remarkable statements about weaknesses of Slovenian STP in the 1990s regarding:

1. the rationalisation of the S&T system, especially to the inter-sectorial, inter-institutional and inter-disciplinary cooperation and
2. the non-industrial orientation of research actitivities.

It seems that, on the policy level, the main social actors in Slovenia with significant political power (government, parliament, political parties) are not aware of the challenges arising with the changing forms of scientific knowledge production. For example, politicians are still looking at R&D sectorially, as something that should be socially isolated, and not connected, even in the phase of knowledge production, with other parts of society. For them, science is often rather an idle bottleneck in the social system than a strategic factor for the economic recovery and growth of society. Again, the major issue in Slovenia is how to arrive at a more efficient R&D system based on stronger cooperation between academic science and industry.

We are faced continuously with statements made by the government about how its primary task is to revitalise the R&D potential in industry. However, the key institutional changes, which could – if I use the categories of Mode 2 (Gibbons et al, 1994) – lead to heterogeneity and organizational diversity, have not been executed in practice. Let us mention, at the end, the example of scientific agencies.

In the beginings of the 1990s, the foreign experts who reviewed the institutional organization of R&D in Slovenia, warned about the low level of interconnections between the academic scientific community and the external social environment (Phare Report, 1995; Walter, 1997). They suggested a reorganization of the existing academic sciences under the umbrella of the Slovenian Ministry of Science and Technology into new independent national research agencies. This reorganization should be accompanied by transferring a part of the scientific management from the state to these agencies. The emergence of new scientific agencies could be treated as the first and the most important step in the establishment of contemporary intermediary structures in the management of science. And indeed, the intermediary institutions in parliamentary democracy have a relative autonomy from the state, which is especially important in the negotiation processes between the interests of different parts of society (see more: Braun, 1997; Guston, 1996).

Looking at the actual situation in Slovenia, it seems that the political establishment still does not understand the new role of scientific (research) councils and agencies in a parliamentary democracy. The new law on the organization and financing of R&D in Slovenia, which should introduce into the processes of social regulation of science a European dimension, has not yet been passed by parliament and put into force. The reason is a clash of interests between different social and political actors, the issue being whether the proposed definition of agency's responsibilities meets the required institutional changes of public funds of R&D. The Slovenian R&D

policy has become highly politicised. Processes of state regulation of R&D demand continuity and strategic orientation, but have been disturbed by frequent changes of ministers of science during the last few years. In a short space of time (less than 10 years) there have been 5 different ministers, each of them from a different political party. Each of them endeavoured, with a small team, to change the strategic policy orientation of the preceeding minister. Daily politics has too great an influence on the work of ministerial bodies. Greater depolitication of decision-making in this bodies would allow for greater responsiveness to the scientific community without loss of modernized forms of state control over the spending of public money.

For Slovenia, in the future, it will be important that the bodies of the new agencies should comprise representatives of different parts of society. It is clear that the election of the majority of agency council members from the scientific community, and not from other parts of society, would lead to an unacceptable isolation of science. Indeed, even in many West European countries, which have the long tradition of scientific agencies and councils, there have appeared recently dramatic changes in their functions, aims and objectives. They are all stressing the role of strategic research, priority areas or targeted research and more entrepreneurial behavior of all sort of buffer institutions. But, what is from our point of view most important, '...research councils and agencies are now key institutions, linking the academic community to the research interests of government and industry' (Nowotny et al, 2001 p.77).

We can only hope that the governmental R&D policy in Slovenia will shift as soon as possible to new research agencies. The new phase in the cooperation between academic science, industry and government will not commence before the establishment of new scientific agencies, which will take over part of the state's management in the science field. It is very important that in these new agencies the voice of the business sector will be heard as well. Until now the representatives of the business world and industry in Slovenia did not have many opportunities to participate in the defining of research programs and projects performed at academic institutions. Their role in the selection of criteria and in the appraisal of program and project proposals is negligible as well. Moreover, under the existing circumstances, where the STP is too concentrated in the narrow frames of one ministry, the economic sector in general (although there are positive exceptions of single firms) does not have a sufficient overview of the relevant research programs and projects at research institutes and universities. A prompt establishment of new scientific agences, as well as a more active role of other already existing intermediate bodies (chambers of commerce, regional entrepreneurs' associations), is necessary to improve the situation concerning the cooperation between academic institutions and industry.

10.6 Conclusion

The Slovenian association process to the European Union might very well be the right moment to rethink and reshape the Slovene STP in the direction of a new innovation policy. For Slovenia, as a small post-communist country in transition, it is very important to follow the positive experiences of the countries of European Union. Many regions throughout Europe have formed productive collaborative relationships between firms, laboratories, universities and governments. The possibility which has been given to Slovenian S&T groups to participate in EU framework programs has even greater importance for the country's STP. The involvement of Slovenian research groups in EU science and technology programs is not important only for the increasing demand for the internationalization of the S&T system in Slovenia. Of even greater importance is the opportunity of scientists in Slovenia to learn to cooperate with the business sector. The EU R&D programs foster research partnerships between scientists of different countries, focus their efforts on interdisciplinary, practically relevant and applicable issues, give attention to civilian, instead of military research, etc. (see more: Biegelbauer, 1998; Haller, 2000). From our point of view, it is significant that the EU framework programs are highly successful in establishing closer links of co-operation between the academic research sector and industry. For example, industrialists count among the most influential advisers to the Fifth Framework Program of the European Union. Moreover, they play a prominent role in most technology foresight exercises. For that reason, Slovenian scientists and STP in general can only benefit from these forms of co-operation. One of these benefits could be knowing how to create a framework for a multi-sectorial approach in science. Innovating is not a random process. The co-operation between science, industry and government is nurtured by a wide range of societal, cultural, political and economic arrangements. Of course, full integration of Slovenia into the European Union should be another important step to S&T system and S&T policy in Slovenia, in spite of the fact that the EU programs can only be considered as a supplement to the national S&T policies. In that sense, even small steps are sometimes very important. One such small step of harmonization with the European Union could be an institutional scheme for public funding of research activities. The biggest task for Slovenian STP is to adjust the financing of science in similar proportions as in the developed European countries. Introducing long-to-medium term funding of programs is one of the important structural changes in Slovenian STP in the last two years. Instead of 1,200 research projects, there are now 300 research programs, which represent 80 per cent of all public S&T funding. The division of the current project funding into three parts (long-term institutional funding, long-to-medium funding of programs and short-term project funding) should improve the transparency of S&T activities, in terms of the budget as well as for its users and, at the same time, steps up the accountability of contractors of Ministry for Science and Technology. To conclude, the real question is not whether STP will be transformed (the need for a new mode of knowledge production will become even more pressing in post-communist countries in transition), but rather who will take over the initiative and social responsibility to speed up the changes.

Notes

1 The author would like to thank Stojan Sorcan for valuable suggestions and comments in preparing the article.

2 Let us take a look at the program's first ten years, from 1985 to 1995: during that period, 3,386 junior researchers were admitted for qualification. Of those, 74 per cent stayed at academic research institutions or in government. Only 26 per cent have continued their professional career in industry (Bertoncelj, 1998).

3 According to the standard classification of activities in manufacturing used in statistical surveys in Slovenia, the size of enterprises (small, medium, large) is defined by the number of persons in paid employment. Small enterprises employ 1–50 persons, medium enterprises employ 50–250 persons and large enterprises employ over 250 persons (Statistical Yearbook, 1999).

4 The concept of the capitalization of academic knowledge here is understood as explained by Henry Etzkowitz and Andrew Webster (Etzkowitz and Webster, 1995). The authors use this concept to characterize the transformation of academic knowledge into economic activity on the grounds of three main steps: the first step in the capitalization of academic knowledge is to secure this knowledge as private property, the second step is to accrue and the third step is to renew and increase its value.

5 The spin-off is usually defined as a new organization set up by the parent organization in order to resolve its organizational incoherence by developing and commercializing activities which are not part of its current core but which may become so in the future, or remain as independent activities. As numerous authors notice, in transitional countries the

privatization, crisis conditions and slow restructuring of R&D institutes create very specific, post-socialist forms of spin-offs which are better described as quasi-spin-offs (see more: Radošević, 1999).

6 Within the technological park in Ljubljana there are at the moment 32 small companies, with about 300 employees (Lesjak, 2000). These small companies are included in the following high technological programs: industrial automation, information technology, biotechnology, optoelectronics, new materials and environmental technologies. The companies in the technological parks cooperate mainly with individual research groups from the University of Ljubljana, first of all with the Faculty of Engineering, the Faculty for Chemistry and the Faculty for Mathematics and Physical Science. At present, the Steir Technology Park, which is located in Maribor, a traditional industrial city in the north-east of Slovenia, is even more renowned, although only about 20 small companies operate under his umbrella (Knez, 2000). Namely, at present it has succeeded in establishing not only strong connections with the 'big brother' in Ljubljana, but also with the technological parks and technological centers in Graz, a very developed industrial and university city in Austria, situated only about 50 km from Maribor.

References

Bertoncelj, M. (1998): 'Mladi raziskovalci' (Junior researchers), Raziskovalec, 27 (5): 32–35.

Biegelbauer, P. S. (1998):'Mission Impossible: The Governance of European Science and Technology.' Science Studies, 11(2), pp.20–39.

Braun, D. (1997): Die politische Steuerung der Wissenschaft. Frankfurt: Campus Verlag.

Bucar, M./Stanovnik, P. (1999): 'Some Implications for the Science and Technology System in a Transition Economy. The Case of Slovenia,' pp.97–126, in: Brundenius (ed.), Reconstruction or Destruction? Science and Technology at Stake in Transition Economies. Hyderguda: Universities Press.

Bukowski, C. (1999): 'Slovenia's Transition to Democracy: Theory and Practice.' East European Quarterly, 23 (1), pp.69–96.

Dyker, D. (1996): 'Technology and economic transformation,' pp.175–191, in: Kuklinski (ed.), Production of Knowledge and the Dignity of Science. Warsaw: European Institute for Regional and Local Development.

Dyker, D.A./Perrin, J. (1997): 'Technology policy and industrial objectives in the context of economic transition,' pp.3–20, in: Dyker, D. A. (ed.), The Technology of Transition – Science and Technology Policies for Transition Countries. Budapest: Central European University Press.

Etzkowitz, H. (1996): 'Losing our Bearings: The Science Policy Crisis in Post-Cold War Eastern Europe, Former Soviet Union and USA'. Science and Public Policy, 23 (1), pp.13–26.

Etzkowitz, H./Webster, A. (1995): 'Science as Intellectual Property,' pp.480–506 in: Jasanoff, S. et al (ed.) Handbook of Science and Technology Studies. London: SAGE Publications.

Eurostat Yearbook (2000): A statistical eye on Europe. Data 1987–1997. Luxembourg: Office for Official Publications of the European Communities.

Filipović, N. (2000): 'Slovenia – Small is Successful', pp.150–175, in: Kozminski, A.K/Yip, G. S. (ed.), Startegies for Central and Eastern Europe. London: Macmillian Press Ltd.

Frankel, M./Cave, J. (ed.) (1997): Evaluating Science and Scientists. An East-West Dialogue on Research Evaluation in Post-Communist Europe. Budapest: Central European University Press.

Gibbons, M. et al (1994): The New Production of Knowledge. The Dynamics of Science and Research in Contemporary Societies. London: SAGE Publications.

Gow, J./Carmichael, C. (2001): Slovenia and the Slovenes. A Small State and the New Europe. London: C. Hurst & Co (Publishers) Ltd.

Guston, D. (1996): Principal-Agent Theory and the Structure of Science Policy.' Science and Public Policy, 24 (4), pp.229–240.

Haller, M. (2000): 'The Model of Science and Research Policy of the European Union in Perspective,' pp.363–393, in: M. Haller (ed.), The Making of the European Union – Contributions of the Social Sciences. Berlin –Heidelberg – New York: Springer Verlag.

Hayrinen-Alestalo, M. (1999): 'The University Under the Pressure of Innovation Policy – Reflecting on European and Finnish Experiences.' Science Studies, 12 (1), pp.44–69.

Irvine, J./Martin, B. R. (1984): Foresight in Science. Picking the Winners. London: Frances Pinter.

Knez, L. (2000): 'Stajerski tehnoloski park' (Steyer Technological Park). Raziskovalec, 30(1), pp.24–26.

Kos, M. (1998): Trends in Development of Transition Countries: Characteristics and Possibilities of Slovenia in Comparison with Other Post-Communist Countries and the European Union, London: Center for Research in Post-Communist Economies.

Lesjak, I. (2001): 'Pomen tehnoloskega parka v Ljubljani' (The relevance of technological park in Ljubljana). Raziskovalec, 30(1), pp.18–24.

Lundvall, B.-A./Borras, S. (1997): 'The globalising learning economy: implications for innovation policy'. European Commission. Brussels: Science Research Development. EUR 18307 EN.

Mali, F. (1997): 'The Eastern European transition.' Industry & Higher Education 12 (6), pp.347–357.

Mali, F. (1998): 'Application of Science and Knowledge Transfer to Industry.' Researcher – Journal for Research and Innovation Policy in Slovenia, 28 (3), pp.35–38.

Mali, F./Sorcan, S. (1995): 'Znanstvena skupnost na Slovenskem' (Scientific community in Slovenia). Research report. Ljubljana: Faculty of Social Sciences.

National Research Programme (1995): Science and Technology in Slovenia. Ljubljana: Ministry of Science and Technology of Slovenia.

Nowotny, H. et al (2001): Re-Thinking Science – Knowledge and the Public in an Age of Uncertainty. Cambridge: Blackwell Publishers Ltd.

Phare Report (1995): A Science and Technology Strategy for Slovenia. Phare Report. Ljubljana: Ministry for Science and Technology of the Republic of Slovenia.

Radosevic, S. (1997): Science, technology and growth: issue for Central and Eastern Europe. Brighton: SPRU – University of Sussex.

Statistical Yearbook (1999): Research. & Development, Science and Technology in Year 1997. Rapid Reports, No. 292. Ljubljana: Statistical Office of the Republic of Slovenia.

Sztompka, P. (1997): 'University and society: between autonomy and engagment' pp.25–37 in: Syzmonski, M/Guzik, I. (ed.), Research at Central and East European Universities. Krakow: Jagiellonian University Press.

Walter, H.G. (1997): 'Slovenian – German Co-operation in the Field of Technology Policy. Lectures on Technology Transfer, Innovation, Financing, Evaluation 1993–97'. Research Report. Karlsruhe: Frauenhofer Institute for Systems and Innovation Research.

Weingart, P. (1998): 'Self-Conception, Strategies of Transformation, and Moods in Coping' pp.141–51, in: Mayntz, R. et al (ed.), East European Academies in Transition. Dordrecht: Kluwer Academic Publishers.

Witschel, G. (1995): 'Slowenians Wissenschaft im Umbruch.' Südosteuropa Zeitung, 5(1–2), pp.280–89.

Ziman, J. (1994): Prometheus Bound. Cambridge: University Press.

Chapter 11

The Italian System of Innovation: The Gradual Transition from a Weak 'Mission-Oriented' System to a Regionalized Learning System

Fiorenza Belussi

11.1 Introduction

The various studies conducted on the performance of the Italian innovation system have almost inevitably underlined the weakness of the Italian R&D systems. Its salient feature is that of the poorly performing, insufficiently developed, and scarcely organized block of activities related to Scientific and Technological Research (STR).

The failure of the Italian system to promote basic science and technological development in high-tech sectors is not just 'institutional' and it does not only involve the public sphere. In fact, it cannot be limited to the issue of the structural inefficacy of the complex of public institutions which have been delegated to support STR programs (Universities, centralized authorities at ministerial level, and government funded public centers). On the contrary, it also involves the business sector, namely, the private system of R&D in-house laboratories.

As an inevitable result, Italy is still very backward in high-tech sectors. It has failed to develop any sustainable capability in high-tech sectors such as aerospace, nuclear energy, computer technologies and superconductors, telecommunication and bio-technologies, all of which require strong cooperation of the various actors of the 'national innovation system' (Nelson, 1993). The Italian system lacked a high level of government support, technology transferring institutions, top frontier universities and institutions involved in basic science, and leading Schumpeterian entrepreneurs that are able to launch new products onto the market. Home-based firms in high-tech sectors are now on the margin of the international scene (Piccaluga, 1996). During the restructuring of the 1980s and 1990s, many closed down, or were acquired by foreign multinationals. In high-tech sectors, the Italian contribution to global developments is marginal, and the international competitiveness of the few existing firms is declining (Guerrieri and Sasson, 1990; Amendola and Perrucci, 1995).

11.2 The dualistic structure of the Italian innovation system

As discussed by many authors, Italy is characterized by the presence of two innovation systems. One has been discussed above, and it is related to the R&D core in high-tech sectors,[1] the second is represented by various local networks of small firms with a local base and strong export orientation.

11.2.1 The R&D core system and the organization of public research

Even after the reform of the 1990s, the public research system is very fragmented (nearly 50 centers with about 24,000 employees). It is organized by eight Ministries, of which the most important is the Ministry of University and Scientific Research. This is a newly established institution, which was created at the beginning of the 1990s in order to increase R&D expenditure. The two biggest public organizations remain the Italian CNR, with about 6,400 employees (and about 289 centers), and Enea with nearly 3,600 employees (Murst, 1997). About 100,000 people are employed in Italian universities, half of which are administrative staff. This system has been quite weak in the generation of endogenous capabilities, because of organizational failures and limited resources, as was stated in the previous sections. In Italy there is insufficient osmosis between academic research and the world of industry and services (Colombo, 1990). This situation is perhaps changing now (Gambardella and Malerba, 1999), because there is more awareness of the importance of knowledge as a strategic factor in economic development at the political level. Italian researchers and scientists participate frequently in numerous EU programs (Gambardella and Garcia-Fontés, 1994).

11.2.2 The industrial district model and its innovation performance

Despite their low rating in terms of R&D indicators, small firms and large networks located within industrial districts (and local production systems) are often innovative, especially with respect to the conceptualization of new products. The dominance of the industrial district model is particularly visible in Italy in both traditional sectors, and niches of industrial machinery (for instance: machine tools, medical instruments, and machinery for packaging).

In the first cluster, the strength of the innovative performance of the Italian firms lies essentially in the firm's design capability (this includes the ability to integrate innovative parts and components into products). In the latter, Italian firms are sophisticated specialized suppliers and are able to provide specific applications to demanding customers (large multinationals, health institutions, mass-production oriented producers) in a segment of the market characterized by high quality performance. Also in relatively low-tech sectors, the accumulation of firm-specific competencies has implied a transformation of these firms into quite modern organizations, very different from the analogous firms existing in many developing and backward countries.

Small and medium size firms operating in traditional Italian industries have often been described as 'highly dynamic atomistic learning networks ...characterized by advanced capabilities of absorbing, adapting, improving, and tailoring new technologies (developed externally) to specific market needs... innovation originates not from formal R&D, but from informal learning by doing, by using and interacting.' In this group of firms, engineering skills, product know-how, and understanding customers' requirements, are the major sources of incremental innovations and product customization (Malerba, 1993 p.234). This description leaves out three main elements.

Firstly, small firms typically do not compete alone in international markets, they are grouped in the so-called 'industrial districts' where they form quite stable co-operation networks (Becattini, 1989).

Secondly, one could infer that innovation activity performed by these firms is marginal, not deliberate, and a rare phenomenon. On the contrary, these localized systems of firm networks, in relation with their products and processes, not only produce incremental innovation (Bellandi, 1992; 1993), but also radical changes (what is marginal or radical must, clearly, be related to the type of the product and sector we are referring to). Moreover, often innovations are not just acquired by firms outside the local area (Becattini and Rullani, 1996), they are developed *locally*, combining various resources and competencies of existing local specialized firms and suppliers.

A third point of disagreement lies in the evaluation of the policies that have guided these systems into reaching a high level of international competitiveness. A picture of the Italian innovation system is sketched in Figure 11.1.

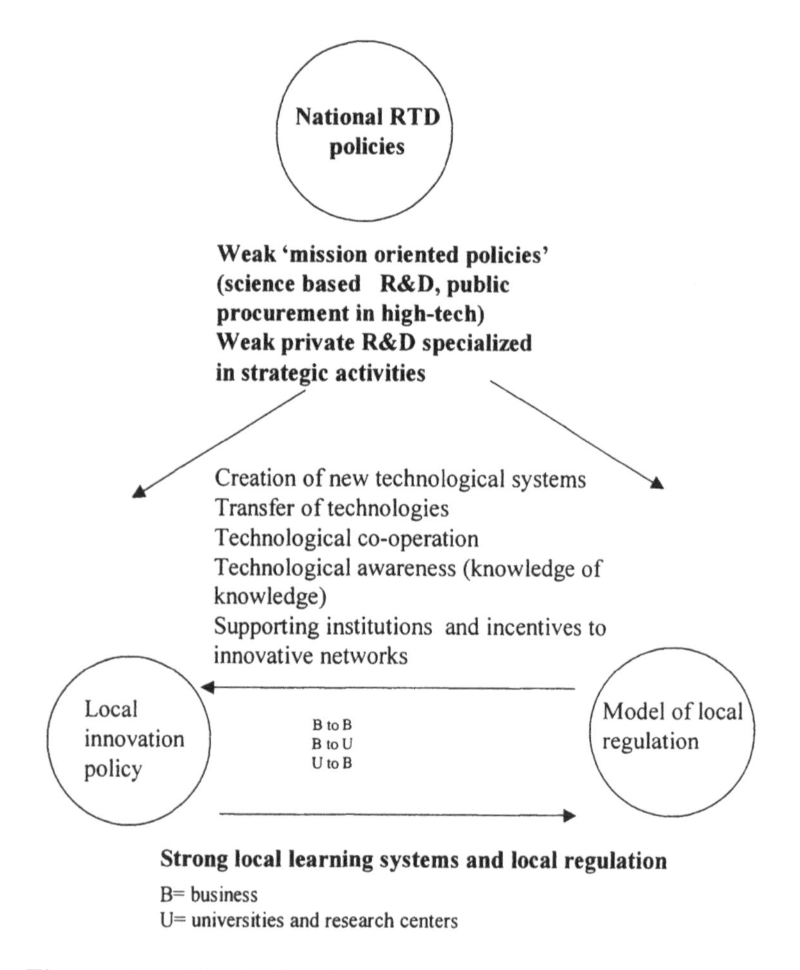

Figure 11.1: The Italian innovation system

For reasons too complex to be dealt with here, top-down diffusion policies at the central level have always been very weak. On the contrary, local innovation policies were developed in interaction with the institutional framework existing at the local level. This has been a clear tendency, since the beginning of the 1970s, when, at local level, we find the first cases of regional legislation in favor of small firms. And, again, during the 1980s, under the pivotal efforts of the local associations of entrepreneurs, some initiatives take place, sometimes in conjunction with local private and public institutions (chambers of commerce, regions and local authorities, etc.).

It is commonly asserted that in France and Germany, the régie of the State in innovation and technology policies was quite effective (Chesnais, 1993; Keck, 1993). In the case of Italy, most of the legislation adopted was fragmented, submitted to a very inefficient state bureaucracy, and political patronage. In contrast to Malerba's claim (Malerba, 1993 pp.241–2), policies launched by the central government aimed at fostering the adoption of new capital equipment (and policies for developing local technological infrastructures) did not have much impact on the whole structure of Italian districts.[2] The important feature of the Italian system is *not* a well-developed set of interventions regarding innovation-diffusion policies, organized by the central state, to overcome 'market failures' with the allocation of public funds (Gerybadze, 1992). Its central characteristic, as depicted in Figure 11.1, is the fact that both direct and indirect innovation policies were supported by the slowly emerging model of local regulation in which firms, collective actors, and institutions worked together (Leoni and Mazzini, 1993; Messina, Riccamboni and Solari, 1999). The following sections will deal with these three main lines of discussion respectively.

11.3 A picture of the technological dynamics of industrial districts in the presence of synergies and network externalities

In this section we will try, at a very abstract level, to describe the feature of the innovative model of the typical Italian districts/local production systems, where geographical proximity matters (Bellet, 1993). Because traditional indicators of innovative activity (R&D and patents) score very low, external observers may infer the existence of few activities devoted by firms to technical change.

In order to understand the increasing returns mechanism at work, we will contrast the standard innovation model with the prevailing district/local production system model of innovation generation and diffusion (Belussi and Gottardi, 2000). A complex frame may be envisaged characterized by localized network externalities created by agents' interactions.

Table 11.1 The industrial district model of innovation

Standard model	A model of localized interactive chains without elevated levels of intramural R&D activities.
University R&D laboratory Innovations/patent	*Innovations are developed in firms by Schumpeterian entrepreneurs. Innovations and improvements* are embodied in the *design* of new products and new machinery (Universities do not play a major role). *The engineering departments* of firms are the source of continuous improvements (incremental innovations) in firms. New solutions are also suggested by sophisticated and technically demanding *clients: client-suppliers (interacting learning).* *Vicarious learning* in firms is decisive (new technical information is acquired through exhibitions, fairs, and technical meetings organized by the local associations); the district is characterized by a high density of information channels. *Tacit knowledge* is developed in *firms,* where an accumulation of know-how occurs (learning by doing activities). Tacit knowledge spill over: with new firm start-ups, with inter-firm mobility, and through professionals. Local technical schools are the main source of *codified knowledge.* New external scientific knowledge is tested in advance (innovation watchers), simplified and adapted to the linguistic codes used and socialized by local firms.
Knowledge as artefact	Accumulated knowledge.
All knowledge is abstract and codified	Knowledge is partially tacit and non-codifiable.
Knowledge is a free good	Knowledge is localized and embedded in people and organizations. Knowledge is costly to transfer outside the local industrial structure.

The creation of new knowledge appears to be the output of localized agents' interactions. However, this is more the result of search strategies and random interactions, rather than a planned and deliberate effort in which R&D activities are involved as described in the standard model (Gibbons and Johnston, 1974). Dynamic feed-back and positive interactions are created along the productive *filière* and the various networks existing in each district/local production system, where firms co-operate in the manufacturing of the various components and sub-components. The generation of new knowledge (innovation) occurs via numerous sources: design and engineering activity, learning processes coming from the production departments, interactions with clients and suppliers, re-use and re-working of existing external knowledge (Arora and Gambardella, 1994). In table 11.1, we have sketched a localized model of innovation, which re-elaborates the seminal contribution of Kline and Rosenberg (1986). We have defined it a model of localized 'interactive chains'. It envisages the innovative process as a circular process with feedback and information links between market needs, design, production and search processes. It recognizes that to create innovation many forces are at work: design and product development departments, production engineering departments, machinery producers, and customer suggestions. While standard economics treats the creation of new knowledge as a 'one-shot' process (Arrow, 1994), in industrial districts it is a type of continuous process. From time to time, the existing pool of knowledge is re-used, and re-combined with new knowledge, for contingent problem-solving goals, or for implementing new entrepreneurial ideas. Our model points out the importance of innovation as a collective and historical process of accumulation of know-how.

The standard model can be accurate for measuring the innovative process in high-technology sectors, but it fails to represent the innovative process in medium or low-technological sectors.

Firms belonging to industrial districts are often not only innovative leaders but also fast adopters. What are the economic incentives to accelerate the process of adoption of innovations? To begin with, let us discuss the case where the innovation is freely available on the market. The original innovation, during its diffusion within industrial districts and local systems, is typically improved, and it changes considerably (in the cost of adoption, or in performance, or, again in other important intrinsic characteristics). The higher is the population of potential adopters, the higher is the generation of variety (Di Bernardo, 1991), and the higher is the probability that some modifications are introduced along the diffusion cycle. This appears to be the first advantage that firms enjoy. A second advantage is the existence of an ample range of firms endowed with differentiated capabilities and resources. This preserves the versatility of the local structure. A third advantage is the inter-firm linkages with the suppliers of machinery localized very often in close proximity. Porter (1990) has also noted this element. A fourth advantage relies on informal channels of information and knowledge sharing and transmission. They may be considered a collective sunk investment in immaterial capital.

In some cases, within the Italian districts/local production systems, innovation diffusion is also a 'sponsored' process. In order to control costs, compatibility and standardization, producers typically press their subcontractors to adopt the more advanced models of new machinery just launched on the market. In any case, spatial proximity activates imitative behavior ('learning by watching'). The dense net of social relationships acts as a means for accelerating the natural rate of adoption and for absorbing the inevitable spill over of knowledge. If innovation (and invention) is less protected, innovative firms have only a single chance to maintain their technological leadership (Robertson and Langlois, 1995). They must accelerate their rate of introduction of technical change. As in other cases discussed in the literature on innovation economics, competition is managed moving down along the learning curve or maintaining the lead time (Levin et al, 1987). Among rival firms the 'innovative' pressures become stronger. This accelerates the rate of adoption of technical change and, as a consequence, the international competitiveness of firms.

While intra-district diffusion may be accelerated, extra-district diffusion remains blocked by the existence of elements of tacit knowledge and by cultural barriers.

Thus, bandwagon effects and production network externalities emerge, thanks to market-driven or voluntary and involuntary strategies of co-operation and 'forced' quick adoption.

Another advantage may be seen in the cost of capital. The agglomeration of activities facilitates the development of a market for second-hand machinery. This can reduce entry barriers and increase market contestability where high rates of new firm start-ups occur (the founders of which are very often skilled senior blue-collar workers of existing firms). Within the Italian districts/local production systems, the market shares of the dominant firms are continuously attacked by new local competitors.

11.4 The formation of an endogenous growth mechanism

Some characteristics of the diffusion of technical change and know-how can be described as an endogenous growth mechanism (Belussi and Pilotti,

2000). The Marshallian theorists discuss the 'laws' of motion of districts mainly in terms of external economies, 'industrial atmosphere' and reduction of transaction costs. This tends to differentiate the 'pure' Marshallian School of Florence (Becattini, Dei Ottati, Sforzi and Bellandi) from the 'Northeast' approach (Rullani, Pilotti, Gottardi, Grandinetti, Corò, and Belussi). Elsewhere (Belussi, 1996; 1999), we have emphasized the dynamic aspects related to the various learning models existing within the local production systems focusing on three factors. Firstly, the processes of inter firm 'cognitive' division of labor, which is related to the intra-district division of innovative labor (where only few agents, and sometimes large firms belonging to the local context, are truly Schumpeterian). This is more than a generic capability to imitate existing practices, as argued by Bellandi (1992). Secondly, there is a related specialization of knowledge, which guides the mode of resource co-ordination of the local systems, whose knowledge connections are very often external to the local system. So, in many cases, local production systems are not self-sufficient 'knowledge communities' (as implied by Loasby (1998) who has a more traditional Marshallian perspective), but they are able to build up innovation using the international circuit of knowledge (Lombardi, 2000). Thirdly, we must focus our attention on the process of accumulation of embedded 'contextual knowledge' among local agents. In our interpretation, the process of accumulation of contextual knowledge refers to technical capabilities and know-how that stem from both tacit (difficult to transfer) knowledge and the absorption of available codified knowledge (Cowan and Foray, 1997). This gives rise to the growth, during time, of 'knowledgeable' agents (individuals, firms and institutions) and, relating to this, to a stock of 'contextual knowledge'. It is important to stress that, contrary to what Marshall thought, 'contextual knowledge' is not 'in the air', (external observers crossing the systems do not have access to this type of knowledge, rather is it ingrained in knowledgeable agents). Therefore, we must also assume that it is difficult to transfer, or to imitate. Within the Italian local production systems contextual knowledge has been spread mainly in two ways: a) through a diffused social system of birth of new firms, founded by the employees of the most technologically dynamic firms, and b) within the matrix of the inter-firm relations of subcontracting. The existence of this form of social capital, which we have called 'contextual knowledge', bears important consequences for economic analysis. In turn, it is precisely the existence of this distinctive character of embedded capital (Antonelli, 1999; Maskell and Malmberg, 1999) that brings about the competitiveness of most of the Italian local production systems and that contributes to explaining the phenomenon of the territorial agglomeration. Contextual knowledge is not simply to be copied from outside. Spatial differences are not washed away by the formation of global markets. Agents, therefore, possess specific long-lasting competencies that influence their level of competitiveness.

A recursive sequence of a cumulative growth-inducing mechanism can be described, and the various stages of growth of a typical local production system can be modeled. Typically, each system starts with a small group of firms endowed with some artisan skills. At the beginning, a distinctive competence appears (Carlsson and Eliasson, 1994) which can be mobilized by local productive forces. Initially, firms are characterized by being 'phase-enterprises'. The governance of the local production cycle is highly decentralized among small entrepreneurs. Cost competitiveness (and self-exploitation by self-employed small entrepreneurs) is typically the principal attribute of the start-up. Once the local system is able to capture a specific segment of demand, the growth-mechanism starts. The first earnings are invested in the modernization of production processes. This tends to maintain at a minimum level all the production costs. So, the shares of the national or international market initially acquired tend to expand. Demand growth increases the returns from the further division of labor among firms that has now been made possible. Specialization increases economies of scale and may induce the generation of new knowledge (with the introduction of incremental innovations). In turn, this renders the local production system more competitive. The proximity of agents forms an integrated system where interactions are fluid. Over time many channels (both informal and institutionalized) are created through which information and knowledge circulate quickly within the productive matrix of subcontracting and specialized firms. The capability of combining 'dispersed pieces of knowledge' (Hayek, 1945), within these channels, is intensified when the proximity of agents allows for repeated interactions. Here starts the evolutionary pattern of diversification among the various local production systems, depending on the type of learning they are able to develop. In one case, it may be a simple type of learning by doing or using, that mainly influence costs. In another, a more complex form of learning might be envisaged, which has an intrinsic technological content, via the interactions built with suppliers, providers of machinery, technical consultants, demanding clients, and suppliers of intermediate components, that may radically change the product or its performance. Using their absorptive capability, firms change and continuously improve their performance in products and processes (Cohen and Levinthal, 1989 and 1990). If the cumulated effect of changes is radical, the competitiveness of the local systems may be affected and its (national or international) market shares will grow again. A higher volume of production allows a greater division of labor among enterprises, and the sequence recursively starts over.

In order to grow, industrial districts require favorable economic conditions, as were available in Italy in the post-war period when the Common Market was created. This enabled the industrial district model to take-off. Knowledge creation and propagation (Vicari, 1998) occurred as a consequence of the development of local firms.

The evolutionary path of growth that originates within the districts started with the growth of a few firms: the founders of the district. Knowledge propagation was achieved *via* the entrepreneurialization of technical and professional people within the founder firms. Their level of professionalism allowed them to leave their employer and become small independent entrepreneurs themselves. The industrial structure expanded through a process of firms' scission. Subsequently, new waves of spin-offs occurred, populating the district with small innovative producers. This process, thus, is highly path-dependent, and built up upon a nucleus of original local skills and competencies.

During this time, Italian districts have proved to be quite stable structures, and not footloose organizations. They have indeed deepened their roots in their territory. The process of globalization has passed over them: yet during the 1980s local production systems were already global in their market outlets. At the end of the 1990s, recent empirical research shows the deepening of a globalization process through the activation of international supply chains of subcontracting. Even in recent times (Quadrio Curzio and Fortis, 2000) they are characterized by still quite high export flows (typically 40–50 per cent of total firms sales), and some remarkable peaks.[3]

11.5 Does the success of Italian local production systems depend on local innovation policies or on a partially spontaneous market-driven process of collective learning?

Some general remarks about the Italian case deserve to be addressed in relation to innovation policies.

Firstly, in the Italian case the general philosophy with which RTD policies are transformed into innovation policies is more related to the weakness of the core R&D system than to any consciously planned action. In general, Italy lacked an articulated set of inter-connected tools, and policy devices that, starting from existing technological systems (Carlsson et al, 1996), could be deployed also at local level (Justman and Teubal, 1995). For instance, the interest of Enea (the institute for atomic energy) for innovation policies started only after the victory of the referendum against the use of nuclear energy as a result of which it was obliged to find a new mission. It is also difficult to judge the overall efficacy of its efforts. For instance, the main Enea project for the diffusion of ICT technologies in the Prato district took place during the 1980s and resulted in a quasi-failure: it was too advanced for that type of local firm, and the firms did not want to share much of their information with competitors. It was necessary to wait twenty years to find advanced experimental applications of new technologies in the district, thanks to a guided project for the building of an electronic market place by the local association of entrepreneurs.[4]

Secondly, the emergence of rationalized learning systems occurred quite separately from any reform in RTD policies. It was the result of an atomistic institutional change of local regulation rather than a deliberate introduction of new ideas and policy instruments (Bellon, 1994).

Thirdly, the model of local regulation we have described can be interpreted as a reasonable match between resources, objectives, and appropriate tools, rather than as the maximization of a well-defined set of objective functions. So, Italian local policies were implemented as a series of experiments, which local government agencies and collective actors undertook in order to solve local needs.[5] Therefore, innovation policy emerged at local level within intermediary institutions that were neither business enterprises nor government agencies, but which formed an integral part of the local/regional system of innovation.[6]

In the framework that we have represented for the Italian case, the system mainly involved a bottom-up strategy, loosely (or not at all) linked with national RTD policies. A mobilization of 'local' knowledge and collective learning took place, where local policies, generally speaking, have only played an important, but not an exclusive, role. In the case of Italy, the influence of policy in determining the performance of local production systems has been mainly indirect. This is not to say that on the local level policy actors have not taken any action. What must be stressed here is that they have not tried to substitute the spontaneous work of the market[7] (with *ad hoc* 'market failure' measures of strong direct 'intervention'). They have 'accompanied' the market, with the slow but constant growth of local productive systems, by choosing, from time to time, a type of intervention that was regulatory, or adjunctive, but not a substitute to the way in which market was allocating the productive resources. So, at least in part, institutional inefficiency or institutional failure was avoided (Wolf, 1993). The model of local innovation system worked at local/regional level as a regionalized learning system where some local innovation policies (diffusion policies) were activated to transfer technologies, to enforce technological cooperation, and to provide support and incentive innovative networks (Figure 11.1). However, they were inserted in a very dynamic model of local regulation, where there was an interaction between firms, collective agents, and institutions.

The operations of Italian institutions[8] and the focus of local policy was typically set in a context in which they were supporting the firms' technological dynamics, through:

- specific regional legislation (such as easier credit for small firms),
- the encouragement of co-operation among firms (directly involved in the creation of positive externalities), and sometimes,
- by providing quasi-public goods directly to the industrial environment, a policy known as *servizi reali alle imprese* (real services to firms).

Freschi (1994), using a comparative methodology, has described the adoption of local policies in the regions of Tuscany, Emilia Romagna and Veneto. In the Emilia case the policy of *servizi reali alle imprese* was usually chosen (i.e., the creation of these centres was organized by Ervet, an independent institution for regional policy), while this type of intervention was rare in Tuscany and totally absent in Veneto. In other words, the three most important regions of the Third Italy model, containing many 'industrial districts' and 'local production systems', have been doing things quite differently. The planning of industrial sites has been, very, systematically pursued in Emilia Romagna (Bartolozzi and Garibaldo, 1995), while, in Veneto, intervention has concentrated on providing credit facilities for small firms.[9] In Lombardy, the policy of building up sector-specific infrastructures for the assistance of small and medium firms was pursued during the 1980s, following the model of Steinbeis Stiftung Foundation of Baden-Württemberg (Sironi, 1995). In the South, the planning of industrial sites has been largely unsuccessful.

The existence of a local regulative model in Italy did not imply one unified set of innovation strategies. Within the Veneto region, the main actors that developed local innovation policies were mainly private or collective organizations (Chambers of Commerce and entrepreneurial associations). Emilia Romagna policy-makers directly promoted some institutions for tackling the innovation, supporting the market dynamics.

Recently the policy adopted by Emilia Romagna, as described by Amin (1999), was that of 'agenda setting', of stimulating new ideas on local development (enforcing the linkages with R&D centers, forming new venture capital, developing new projects for young entrepreneurship, promoting export projects, developing information networks).

There is contradictory evidence on the causal relationship between the policies adopted by institutions and local performance.

However, the essential lesson from the Italian case is that the real influence of policies related to the provision of 'real services' has probably been exaggerated (Nomisma, 1991). In Italy a wide array of local intermediate institutions[10] like trade associations, chambers of commerce and professional associations have worked in a less planned task, playing the role of learning laboratories for their respective firms and members. It can also be said that the positive impact of vocational training, based on the needs of local economies, has been largely underestimated. It is important to note that many local initiatives resulted from the 'cultural evolution' of economic agents interacting in a specific context. This was not an ex-ante policy but a clear mechanism of co-evolution between markets and institutions (Grandinetti, 1999).

In the experience of Italian local policies, either more market-led policies (Veneto and Friuli Venezia Giulia) or state-driven policies (Emilia Romagna) worked. However, this arrangement was supported by a coherent regulative setting of institutions, collective actors and firms.

The Italian success of many industrial districts or local systems can be viewed as a 'social experiment', where the spontaneous working of the market has been channelled, and promoted, by the role of institutions.

So, pure market outcomes have been regulated by institutional (extra-economic) factors, and the market has limited co-ordination failures.

Competition as 'a discovery process' remains the driving force behind the operation of the Italian local system. So there are no general recipes for local innovation policies that can be applied in less developed countries to transfer the 'beauty' of the Italian model. Policy and institutions cannot substitute the market (in Arrow's sense). In addition, what has been successful, under certain conditions in one context, may not work in others. The essential claim is that institutions cannot recreate or develop 'markets' if they lack productive capability.

11.6 Conclusions

In this chapter, we have tried to schematically present the Italian transition from a model of RTD policies toward a model of innovation policies as a gradual shift and a spontaneous 'adjustment' of an institutional failure in the development of a strong, centrally governed, core R&D system, public and/or privately financed in high-tech sectors. The development of an institutional frame of local regulations went in accordance with the strengthening of Italian industrial districts, and its international leadership in traditional sectors ('made in Italy' sectors).

In Italy, local institutions have played an important role in the establishment of a model of local innovation policies, and in the implementation of general rules incorporated in the local context. This has favoured creative co-operation among firms and has generated the spontaneous aggregation of firms into systems. Another important aspect has been the accumulation and mobilization of knowledge, a process in which both markets and institutions have played a crucial role.

However, is the Italian case a clear demonstration that good innovation policies must only be articulated at local level? Innovation policy, both at national and local level, needs to be properly evaluated and inserted in the institutional setting of each specific context, and within the institutional features of each innovation system. Here it must be said that Italy failed to orchestrate with efficacy a complete set of innovation policies at the central level. However, the Italian case must not be interpreted as an ideal model. Innovation policies, at national and local (regional) level must be evaluated, in relation to the state-of-art of the specific economic and institutional system to which they are addressed (Lundvall and Borras, 1997; Metcalfe and Georghiou, 1998). The fact that at local level the Italian system was able to create a quite successful bottom-up approach, in which a localized process of innovation took place, especially within specific industrial districts or local production systems, does not undermine the importance of a 'good set' of national (or super-national) innovation policies. Clearly, the Italian system in specific sectors performed quite well in innovation diffusion issues. But perhaps it would also have benefited a great deal from good 'traditional' R&D or from innovation policies organized at central level for the promotion of a selective cluster of R&D intensive sectors.

Notes

1 The weakness of the Italian R&D system does not only depend on the small amount of resources involved (Istat (1999) reported a net value of about 23,000 billion lira, of which 13,000 billion lira was spent by public source). The Italian system has been criticized (De Benedetti, 1990) for having a restricted number of oligopolistic firms, poor use of public procurements, an unsuccessful mechanism of industry-university co-operation, and the poor co-ordination of public interventions.

2 Let us take the case of the laws supporting the acquisition of new technologies embodied in machinery (L. 696), or innovative projects (L.36 and L.399). It has been calculated by Bartolozzi and Garibaldo (1995, p.218) that during the 1980s, nearly half of the funds provided for the so-called 'diffusion policies' was absorbed by the limited group of the largest Italian firms. Moreover, the specific law for industrial districts voted in 1991 (L.317), remained largely inapplicable.

3 See, for instance, the packaging machinery district in Bologna (Capecchi, 1990), where about 95 per cent of the total output is exported, or the Montebelluna district specialized in ski boots (Pilotti, 1998), which supplies 75 per cent of the international markets.

4 Personal communication with A. Balestri, Club dei Distretti director.

5 This process is very similar to the one described by Teubal (1997). OECD (1999) also recently discussed local innovation policies.

6 The role of intermediary organizations has been discussed recently for the Japanese case by Best and Forrant (1996).

7 At the theoretical level, the approach chosen was analogous to the one described by Aoki et al (1997) for the Japanese case.

8 The use of the word institutions has two meanings. First, we refer to institutions as public bodies and local authorities. Second, we refer to the emergence of a spontaneous order of rules that allow a certain type of interaction among the agents operating in the local context (co-operative behaviours, codes of conduct, knowledge sharing practices, etc.).

9 The policy of the Veneto region changed during the mid-1990s. Specific legislation fostering innovation was promoted, and a virtual net of scientific parks was created (Nest, 1999).

10 The Italian model is 'spontaneous' and is quite different from other cases like that of the Welsh Development Agency described by Morgan (1995).

References

Amendola, G./Perrucci, A. (1995): L'Italia nella competizione tecnologica internazionale, Angeli, Milan.

Amin, A. (1999): Il modello emiliano. Sfide istituzionali, Paper IPL (Istituto per il Lavoro, Bologna.

Antonelli, C. (1999a): The Microdynamics of Technological Change, Routledge, London.

Aoki, M./Kim, M/Okuno-Fujiwara, M. (1997): Beyond the East Asian Miracle: Introducing the Market-Enhancing View, in: Aoki, M./Kim, M./Okuno-Fujiwara, M. (eds.), The Role of Government in East Asian Economic Development, a Comparative Institutional Analysis, Clarendon Press, Oxford.

Arora, A./Gambardella, A. (1994): The Changing Technology of Technological Change: General and Abstract Knowledge and the Division of Innovative Labour, Research Policy, 23.

Arrow, K. (1994): The production and distribution of knowledge, in: Silverberg, G./Soete, L. (eds.), The Economics of Growth and Technical Change, Edward Elgar, Aldershot.

Bartolozzi, P./Garibaldo, F. (eds.), (1995): Lavoro creativo e impresa efficiente. Ricerca sulle piccole e medie imprese, Rome, Esi.

Becattini, G. (1989): Modelli locali di sviluppo, Bologna, Il Mulino.

Becattini, G./Rullani E. (1996): Local Systems and Global Connections: the Role of Knowledge, in: Cossentino, F./Pyke, F./Sengenberger, W., (eds.), Local Regional Response to Global Pressure: the Case of Italy, Ilo,Geneva.

Bellandi, M. (1992): The Incentives to Decentralized Industrial Creativity in Local Systems of Small Firms, Revue D'economie Industrielle, n. 59.

Bellandi, M. (1993): Structure and Change in the Industrial District, Studi e Discussioni, n. 85, Department of Economic Science, University of Florence.

Bellet, M. (1993): Evolution de la Politique Technologique, et Role de la Proximité. REPÉRES sur le Cas Francais. Revue d'Economie Régionale et Urbaine, n.3.

Bellon, B. (1994): L'etat et L'enterprise, in: Bellon B. et al (eds.), L'Etat et le Marché, Economica, Paris.

Belussi, F. (1996): Local Systems, Industrial Districts and Institutional Networks: Towards a New Evolutionary Paradigm of Industrial Economics?, European Planning Studies, Vol. 4, n. 3.

Belussi F. (1999): Policies for the Development of Knowledge-Intensive Local Production Systems, Cambridge Journal of Economics, Vol. 23, n. 6.

Belussi, F. and Gottardi G. (2000): Model of localized technological change, in, Belussi F. and Gottardi G. (eds.), Evolutionary Patterns of Local Industrial Systems, Ashgate, Aldershot.

Belussi F./Pilotti, L. (2000): Knowledge Creation and Collective Learning in the Italian Local Production Systems, Working Paper Dipartimento di Scienze Economiche Marco Fanno, University of Padua.

Best, H. B./Forrant, R. (1996): Creating Industrial Capacity: Pentagon-Led Versus Product-Led Industrial Policies, in, Michie, J./Grieve Smith, J. (eds.), Creating Industrial Capacity, Cambridge University Press, Cambridge.

Capecchi, V. (1990): A History of Flexible Specialisation of Industrial Districts in Emilia Romagna, in: Pyke, F./Becattini, G./Sengenberger, W. Industrial Distinct and Inter-Firm Co-Operation in Italy, Ilo, Geneva.

Carlsson, B./Eliasson, G. (1994): The Nature and Importance of Economic Competence, Industry and Corporate Change, Vol. 3, n. 3.

Carlsson, B./Jacobsson, S. (1996): Technological Systems and Industrial Dynamics: Implications for Firms and Governments, in: Helmstädter, E./Perlman, M. (eds.), Behavioral Norms, Technological Progress, and Economics Dynamics, University of Michigan, Ann Arbor.

Chesnais, F. (1993): The French National System of Innovation, in: Nelson, R., (ed.), National Systems of Innovations, Oxford University Press, Oxford.

Cohen, W./Levinthal, D. (1989): Innovation and Learning: the Two Faces of R&D, Economic Journal, Vol. 99.

Cohen, W./Levinthal, D. (1990): Absorptive Capacity: a New Perspective on Learning and Innovation, Administrative Science Quarterly, Vol. 35.

Colombo, U. (1990): L'Europa nelle politiche dell'innovazione e la posizione dell'Italia, in: Guerrieri, P./Sasson, E., (eds.), La sfida high-tech, IL Sole 24 Ore, Milano.

Cowan, R./Foray, D. (1997): The Economics of Codification and the Diffusion of Knowledge. Industrial and Corporate Change, Vol. 6, n. 3, pp.595–622.

De Benedetti (1990): Preface, in: Guerrieri, P./Sasson, E. (eds.), La sfida high-tech, Il Sole 24 Ore, Milano.

Di Bernardo, B. (1991): La dimensione di impresa: scala, scopo, varietà, Angeli, Milan.

Freschi, A.C. (1994): Istituzioni politiche e sviluppo locale nella Terza Italia, Sviluppo Locale, a. 1., n. 1.

Gambardella, A./Garcia-Fontes, W. (1994): Regional Linkages Through European Research Funding, Paper presented at the conference 'New Research Findings: the Economics of Scientific and Technological Research In Europe', Urbino, 24–5 February.

Gambardella, A-/Malerba, F. (1999): The Organisation of Innovative Activity in Europe, Cambridge University Press, Cambridge.

Georghiou, L. et al (1986): Post Innovative Performance, Macmillan, London.

Gerybadze, A. (1992): The Implementation of Industrial Policy in an Evolutionary Perspective, in: Explaining Process and Change, Witt, U. (ed.), The University of Michigan Press, Ann Arbor.

Gibbons, M./Johnston, R. (1974): The Role of Science in Technological Innovation, Research Policy, Vol. 3.

Grandinetti, R. (1999): Il seggiolaio e l'economa globale, La transizione evolutiva del distretto friulano della sedia attraverso i risultati di un'indagine di campo, Cedam, Padua.

Guerrieri, P./Sasson, E. (eds.), (1990): La sfida high-tech, Il Sole 24 Ore, Milano.

Hayek, F. (1945): The Use of Knowledge in Society, American Economic Review, Vol. 35, pp.519–30.

Justman, M./Teubal, M. (1995): Technological Infrastructure Policy (TIP): Creating Capabilities and Building Markets, Research Policy, Vol. 24, pp.259–281.

Keck, O. (1993): The National System for Technical Innovation in Germany, in: Nelson, R., (ed.), National Systems of Innovations, Oxford University Press, Oxford.

Kline, S./Rosenberg, N. (1986): An Overview of Innovation, in: Landau, R./Rosenberg, N. (eds.), The Positive Sum Strategy, National Academic Press, Washington.

Leoni; R./Mazzini; M. (1993): Processi di innovazione tecnologica e istituzioni di sostegno a livello locale, Quaderni del dipartimento di scienze Economiche, n. 14.

Levin, R./Klevorick, A./Nelson, R./Winter, S. (1987): Appropriating the Returns From Industrial Research and Development, Brooking Papers on Economic Activity, Vol. 3.

Loasby, B. (1998): Industrial Districts as Knowledge Communities, in: Bellet, M./L'Harmet, C. (eds.), Industry, Space and Competition, Edward Elgar, Cheltenham.

Lombardi, M. (2000): Learning and Organisational Structures, paper presented at the Padua Seminar, 'Evolution, complexity, and institutions', 7th December.

Lundvall, B./Borrás, S. (1997): The Globalising Learning Economy. Implication for Innovation Policies, DGXII, Brussel.

Malerba, F. (1993): The National System of Innovation: Italy, in: Nelson, R. (ed.), National Systems of Innovations, Oxford University Press, Oxford.

Maskell, P./Malmberg, A. (1999): Localized Learning and Industrial Competitiveness, Cambridge Journal of Economics, Vol. 23, pp.167–185.

Messina, P./Riccamboni, G./Solari, S. (1999): Sviluppo economico e regolazione politica nelle regioni di piccola e media impresa: un'analsi comparata tra Veneto ed Emilia Romagna, Sviluppo Locale, IV, pp.44–78.

Metcalfe, S./Georghiou, L. (1998): Equilibrium and Evolutionary Foundation of Technology Policy, STI- Science Technology Industry Review (no. 22), pp.75–100.

Morgan, K. (1995): The Learning Region. Institutions, Innovation and Regional Renewal, Mimeo, Cardiff University.

MURST (1997): Linee per il riordino del sistema nazionale della ricerca scientifica e tecnologica. Relazione alle Camere del Ministro dell'Università e della Ricerca Scientifica e Tecnologica –Murst (Rome, 31st July 1997).

Nelson, R. (1993): (ed.), National Systems of Innovations, Oxford University Press, Oxford.

Nest (1999): Network for science and technology. Parco scientifico e tecnologici, Rapporto finale, Veneto Innovazione, Marghera.

Nomisma (1991): Strategie e valutazione nella politica industriale, Milan, Franco Angeli.

OECD (1999): Boosting Innovation: The Cluster Approach. OECD Proceeding, Paris.

Piccaluga, A. (1996): Impresa e sistema dell'innovazione in Italia, Guerrini scientifica, Milan.

Pilotti, L. (1998): I distretti innovativi del nord, Sviluppo e Organizzazione, n. 187, pp.15–32.

Porter, M. (1990): Competitive Advantage of Nations, The Free Press, New York.

Quadrio Curzio, A./Fortis, M. (eds.) (2000): Il made in Italy oltre il 2000, Il Mulino, Bologna.

Robertson, P./Langlois, R. (1995): Innovation, Networks and Integration, Research Policy, Vol. 24.

Sironi, M. (1995): Sistemi innovativi regionali: Lombardia e Rhône-Alpes, unpublished thesis, Università Bocconi.

Teubal, M. (1997): A Catalytic and Evolutionary Approach to Horizontal Technology Policies, Research Policy, Vol. 25, pp.1161–1188.

Vicari, S. (1998): L'impresa creativa, Etas, Milan.

Wolf, C. (1993): Markets or Governments. Choosing Between Imperfect Alternatives, The MIT Press, Cambridge, Massachusetts.

Chapter 12

How Do Economic Ideas Become Relevant in RTD Policy Making? Lessons From a European Case Study

Jakob Edler

12.1 Introduction

The underlying premise of this volume is a general, almost consensual perception that RTD-policy has considerably changed in the 1990s, and taken on the shape of systemic innovation policy.[1] This change is not bound to individual nation states but can be observed throughout the OECD. It is a question of increasing interest as to what have been the driving forces which cause national policies to move in the same direction. To answer this question, analysts increasingly turn towards a school of thought which takes the scientific ideas underlying the ongoing change into consideration. The premise of this cognitive line of analysis is that new scientific ideas in economics, rooted in evolutionary and institutional economics, exert their influence on policy-makers and that the ideational coalition of experts and policy-makers circumvent barriers established by interest groups and coalitions (Biegelbauer, 2000; Borrás, 2000). Indeed, analysing policy concepts in various OECD countries brings to the fore a set of scientific ideas. To explain this, therefore, one must trace back the construction of policy concepts, i.e. to identify the origin and especially the venues of the scientific ideas. To lay open the impact of scientific ideas on the policy concepts and on the outcome is, no doubt, a central task of the analysis of innovation policy.

A change of reference in RTD policy-making has been a constant feature in the history of RTD policy making. For some decades now, the basic rational always has been, one way or another, to support the actors of the respective innovation system thereby securing and enhancing individual and general wealth and thus contributing to human progress. Nevertheless, the history of national RTD policies shows that to reach this overall goal, very different policy recipes have been used. RTD policy-making is a process of constant trial and error, of many attempts to set up appropriate regulations and suitable incentives for the various stakeholder groups involved. In addition, new analytical ideas concerning the innovation process and normative ideas about policy-making justify policy changes in the first place.

Consequently, to analyse the whole policy-making process, it is not sufficient to detect internationally converging policy concepts or a correlation between scientific ideas and policy-concepts. From a political science perspective, the question of *how* the dominant ideas acquired their dominance is at least equally important. The political struggle for influence and resources cannot be separated from the question as to which kind of conceptual ideas are perceived as being legitimate and are accepted as being valid. What are these underlying theoretical ideas that determine the interpretation of the policy problem at stake and suitable strategies to solve it, and therefore, at the same time, shape the strategies of all stakeholders involved?

The purpose of this paper is threefold:

- Empirically, the paper presents a detailed *case study* of the genesis of a new policy concept in the eighties and analyses its realisation in the *European RTD-program BRITE* (Basic Research in Industrial Technologies for Europe).
- In doing so, it sheds some light on *the beginning of the current move towards innovation policy*. It is argued that BRITE for the first time consequently pursued an integrative approach that was, at least partly, based on early evolutionary thinking and took into consideration the meaning of vertical and horizontal co-operation in the innovation system. Although BRITE was far from being an all-embracing innovation policy approach in its current sense, all of these features make BRITE appear like an important milestone towards the breakthrough of the new innovation paradigm.
- The basic assumption of this volume is that the transnational success of the innovation paradigm rests on a dominant cognitive reference. Therefore, the article should present some insights into the *general conditions of this international consensus building* between experts, policy-makers and interest groups from academia and industry. To do

so, the paper presents a general theoretical framework to make sense of the fascinating processes in which causal and normative ideas shape an internationally accepted, almost consensual cognitive frame of reference under the conditions of heterogeneity. This framework follows a constructivist understanding of the political process. It rests on the premise that realities – and therefore actor's interests – are constantly reconstructed and that ideas and their processing over time shape this process of reconstruction, with all the consequences for the political process.

12.2 BRITE and the beginning of a new era in European RTD policy making

To understand the power of a new policy concept, one has to take a short look at its historical context. Since a Council decision in 1974, the mission of the Commission and the General Directorate for Research GD XII,[2] was twofold: to co-ordinate national policies and to formulate and design a European RTD policy. However, until the 1980s, not much had happened (e.g. Kalka, 1984; Schneider/Welsch, 1990; Guzzetti, 1995):

1. National policies had not been co-ordinated. On the contrary, until the mid 1980s, the catchword for the approach in the Member States of the EC had been the strategy of 'national champions'.
2. A genuine European RTD policy, with a relevant budget and a clear-cut added value, had not been developed. There was no explicit legal basis for European RTD policy.[3]

In addition, especially in Europe, private actors in traditional industries had not yet discovered trans-border co-operation in RTD as a strategic means of speeding up innovation, the number of technological co-operation before the mid-1980s is negligible (Meyer-Krahmer/Kuntze, 1982; Narula, 2000).

However, from the mid-1980s, a new trend of technological co-operation in traditional industries emerged. In 1985, BRITE was agreed upon in the Research Council. This program had a couple of new features, which are taken for granted nowadays as core elements of modern innovation policy-making. In the mid-eighties, however, they marked a paradigm change:

- obligatory co-operation across country borders;
- trans-sectoral and inter-disciplinary co-operation;

- co-operation between industrial companies, even competitors, and between industry and research institutes;
- co-operation across disciplines and industrial sectors.

The last feature is especially important. Unlike ESPRIT, which was set up just a few months before BRITE and concentrated on the Information Technology sector,[4] this program was geared towards *all* industries. It essentially urged not only high-tech providers but also high-tech users across all sectors to change their minds and adopt co-operative and international RTD strategies.

BRITE, which for reasons of efficiency was soon merged with the related Materials Programme (EURAM[5]) to become BRITE-EURAM, was continued several times and the core of BRITE-EURAM essentially forms the core of the 'growth' program of Framework Programme 5 (FP5). It started with a small budget of 125 million ECU, but this budget was constantly increased to reach 1.617 million ECU for BRITE-EURAM III of FP4. Although BRITE-EURAM is widely believed to be especially important for the cohesion countries, internal statistics of the former GD XII indicate that the program, unlike some other specific programs of the EC, gained relevance in each Member State.[6] It is obvious that BRITE has had a decisive impact in the sense that nationally closed innovation systems have opened up and thousands of private actors turned towards international partners to improve their research efforts.

It is not argued here that the relatively small program BRITE was instrumental in the sweeping re-orientation of industrial RTD strategies or national RTD policy design. The numbers of international collaborations increased in the second half of the 1980s even without the incentive of European co-financing. In Japan, Great Britain and Germany national attempts using co-operative research funding were under way. But given the political stalemate in European RTD policy and the reluctance to join forces in RTD across companies and across country borders at the end of the 1970s, it is interesting to analyse why BRITE was agreed upon at a time when international co-operation was *not* a common practise. So the questions remain: why was it possible to set up a policy that was built on the understanding that (1) co-operation in RTD was necessary and feasible, (2) this co-operation had to span across borders and (3) to be managed on a supranational level, thus finally providing the European Commission with an autonomy it had sought for more than a decade? In answering these questions, some light shall be shed on the pre-conditions to redefine RTD policy and to establish a new policy concept.

12.3 A theoretical model for grasping the relevance of ideas

To understand the driving mechanisms of change, and especially the importance of economic ideas for this change, an appropriate theoretical understanding is necessary. The claim of the following analysis is based on specific understanding of the political process; these cannot be elaborated in full within the framework of this paper.[7] It rests basically on three pillars, first on the importance of *ideas* for the political process, second on the importance of *interaction* for the diffusion and processing of political ideas and third on the importance of a *central actor*, who to some extent shapes these interactions.

The main theoretical premise is the constructivist claim that all politics rests upon the interpretation of reality and that all definitions of interest are dependent upon the construction of what is perceived as being real (Berger/Luckmann, 1967). Political decisions are based on an interpretation of problems and concepts derived from a supply of causal and normative ideas. Thus, interests – and even identities (Wendt, 1992) – are, in principle, open to change that is triggered off by complex cognitive processes of coming to grips with the constant flow of information. Therefore, the conditions and processes of the exchange of ideas and information determine the political process. To avoid a misunderstanding, conflicts over the right policy recipe are always conflicts of interest, but a constructivist view looks for the underlying rationales that define conflicting interests and the forces and processes that change the very perception of actor's interests.

The most obvious and influential way to process ideas is through social interaction, thereby, one way or the other, constructing social reality. To understand the mechanism by which social interaction results in political action and decision, one must keep in mind what, in turn, determines interaction. To do so, our constructivist understanding of the political process must be complemented by a social concept of political institutions as, for example, laid out by March and Olsen (March/Olsen 1984, 1989, 1994). Very generally speaking, political institutions are social regulations guiding political action. However, political institutions are not only constitutionally defined or derived organizations and rules of the game that determine who is to do what. They also comprise social norms, rules, and shared beliefs.

This representation of norms and beliefs through institutions can be well illustrated by looking at the EC itself. The EC is shaped by the causal and normative ideas explicitly and implicitly laid down in the treaties. Most importantly, the normative goals for the first four decades of the EC were aimed at furthering economic integration, based on the cognitive understanding that further economic integration serves the common welfare and security of European people. This is the institutional rationale of the EC, and the Member States have to actively comply with it. Therefore, every political concept discussed within the framework of the EC must comply with this normative and cognitive framework, and every concept decided upon entails – if only implicitly – this norm.[8] Thus, the stronger the *causal* basis of a concept is linked to the *normative* core of an institution, the more powerful it will become for the actors that belong to the respective organization or institution.

What is important now is that institutionally inscribed and processed social norms, rules, and beliefs are not fix, but evolve dynamically, they are constantly reproduced through *social interaction* within political institutions. Repeated or continuous interaction to exchange ideas and worldviews has the potential to generate a new-shared understanding and interpretation of reality over time. Ephrem Lau has called this mechanism 'vertical institutionalisation' (Lau, 1978). New ideas can be defined as 'institutionalized' as soon as they are perceived as valid, guide the interpretation of the participants of the repeated interaction, determine their interest definition and thus finally their future action. The more ideas are taken for granted, the more they are institutionalized.

To understand the very mechanism of political change within this framework, it is important to note that institutions on the one hand and ideas and interactions on the other show a *reflexive relation*. Interactions process normative and causal ideas, potentially transform traditional understandings and build up new, common understandings, in short: they institutionalize ideas. At the same time, however, the institutional setting of these interactions normatively filters the ideational discourse provided by social interactions. It predetermines what is perceived as being legitimate. The more interactions which process ideas are linked to specific accepted institutions, the more these institutions determine the legitimacy of new ideas. The less an ideational discourse is linked to specific institutions, the more open its outcome and the more important the convincing power of new ideas and of their promoters will be. Interaction and ideas, discourse and construction of shared understanding are the driving forces of the social process of political change, and they are reflexively linked to institutions.

Finally, in order to comprehend fully these mechanisms of political change, one has to look at the *origin of ideas* and at the driving forces behind interactions to process ideas. The origin of ideas is an empirical question: once the analyst knows what idea he/she wants to analyse, he/she has to go back and look, who has spread the word first? The scope and composition of the relevant interactions, however, strongly influences the ideational input, the *a priori* expectations, and the distribution of the resources to influence interactions and so on. Generally speaking, there is a scale ranging from entirely *spontaneous and self-dynamic* interactions only driven by the power of the ideas themselves at the one end and an *instrumental* interaction entirely dominated by a powerful interaction moderator at the other. We shall call an actor, who is willing and able to shape ideational interaction, the process manager or the *central actor* of the institutionalization process. Every analysis of the power of new ideas must look at the degree of spontaneity – or instrumentality respectively – of the ideational interaction.

With this abstract theoretical framework in mind, we now can re-formulate the main argument of the paper with a set of theoretically based theses:

1. The genesis of a new RTD-policy paradigm – as manifested in BRITE – was a processing of new *ideas* about the innovation process. This process took place in complex transnational *interactions* at various levels and among very differently motivated actors.

2. Multi-stage interaction overcame heterogeneity and led to a sufficient level of consensus in Europe. The pre-political ideational discourse pre-determined political decisions.

3. The European Commission was the *central actor* which succeeded in turning the spontaneous interaction into a 'European' discourse by linking the causal innovation concepts to the normative idea of European integration.

4. This new policy concept turned out to be immune to various criticisms because of two sources of legitimacy, (1) the legitimacy of the *European norm* to which it was attached, and (2) the legitimacy of the *underlying causal beliefs* originating from a mostly de-politicised, scientific environment.

12.4 The genesis of BRITE: A transnational multi-stage process of institutionalization

12.4.1 The set of underlying ideas

In the late 1970s, new theoretical paradigms in the area of innovation and technology policy emerged in the transnational arena. Based on a bulk of empirical studies and conceptual thinking innovation experts started to come up with a new understanding of the very nature of industrial and public RTD, of their potential benefit and the way to influence industrial progress. From the enormous amount of literature on the innovation process, three lines of reasoning can be analytically identified, the first rooted in an intensive macro- and techno-economic discourse, the second and third emerging from innovation theory.

1. *RTD as the basic driving force of economic growth within supply-side economics.* The 1970s saw a new type of macroeconomic crisis labelled stagflation – the combination of stagnation and inflation – and low productivity was perceived as being its major cause. Higher productivity was needed, and this was tightly linked to innovation and to efficient and effective RTD processes. However, as studies showed, the reaction of private actors towards the crises was counter-productive, since the expenses for RTD in almost all industries decreased (Boyer, 1979; IFO, 1980; OECD, 1980; Freeman, Clark, Soete, 1982). Therefore, RTD became a central pillar of economic policy and gradually turned into the key triggering innovation and growth as directly and as widely as possible (BCG, 1978; Science Council of Canada, 1979; Royal Swedish Academy of Engineering Science, 1979; IFO, 1980).[9]

2. *Interdependent, recursive understanding of the innovation process.* A new model of technological progress emerged, replacing the old linear model of succession of different stages (Pavitt, 1976) by a model of feedback loops and recursion between the different stages of the innovation process. In this understanding,[10] basic science cannot be separated from applied science and development, not even from marketing and procurement (von Hippel, 1978). Effective and efficient innovation requires intensive interaction, first between the actors of the various stages of the innovation process, second between producers,

clients and suppliers (EIRMA, 1982a; von Hippel, 1978; Keck, 1986; Kline/Rosenberg, 1986; OECD, 1991). This thinking was confirmed and sharpened by analyses within the framework of the so-called 'evolutionary economics'. This school of thought analysed the complex socio-institutional arrangements needed for innovation and concluded that the most important condition for innovation was a high degree of exchange and interaction to trigger mutation and selection leading to technological progress (Nelson/Winter, 1977; 1982; Freeman, 1982; Nelson, 1982).

3. *Generic technologies*. Related to the first line of ideas, the growing importance of a few key technologies, most of all microelectronics, were recognised. These so-called generic technologies were identified as being influential for innovation and growth, not only in one core industrial sector, but also across a range of sectors. This made integration of the RTD process instrumental, for both the generic technology and the technologies applied in a whole range of industrial sectors. Moreover, since formerly separate industrial sectors had similar applications for the same technologies, co-operation across sectors suddenly became sensible.[11]

In combination, these three lines of reasoning led to a paradigm shift in RTD and innovation policy-making. It was shaped by experts from both sides of the Atlantic and step by step established new innovation and RTD policy rationales:

- Innovation was seen as being crucial for competitiveness for companies and national economies, therefore, the concept was innovation-led competition and growth, speed and cost-effectiveness gained importance.
- The message for industrialists and policy-makers alike was: Enhanced productivity is the key to growth, RTD is the key to enhanced productivity, open innovation systems with increased co-operation across RTD stages, disciplines and sectors is the key to effective RTD and fast and broad diffusion of technologies.
- The state has to provide incentives and the best environment possible to enable actors to interact and co-operate, exploring synergy effects, building up critical mass, accelerating the diffusion of technologies.
- Last but not least, since the potential for effective co-operation grows with the number of potential co-operators,[12] this concept set the stage for action on a transnational (European) level.

12.4.2 Functional interaction

12.4.2.1 Transnational discourse of experts

The new problem definition and the new understanding of the role of RTD and RTD policy emerged gradually, with input from different corners of the globe. The first level of interaction suggesting these ideas was not bound to the EC, but rather was transnational. A remarkable number of transnational conferences and studies undertaken between 1976 and 1984 dealt with new ideas in innovation and RTD policy. The annex of this paper gives a list of relevant conferences. These conferences not only brought together the most recognized experts in the field, thus spreading new problem definitions and conceptual ideas among the scientific and administrative community, but also led to publications and conference reports that spread these ideas even further.[13]

These kinds of interaction were to some extent spontaneous and not mediated centrally. However, facing stagflation and the need to find new policy concepts, the OECD started to bundle and promote the discourse in the second half of the 1970s. It thus helped to build up common ground and transnational momentum for transnational discussion, since

> ...statistics of R & D became generally available and were put on an internationally comparable basis, largely through the efforts of the OECD. This organization also initiated a series of national science policy 'Reviews' in each of the member countries, which *heightened awareness and understanding of the problem* (Freeman, 1982 p.199. J.E.).

In 1977, the OECD called together a trans-Atlantic group of first-rate experts to produce a study on the link between 'Technical Change and Economic Policy'. The OECD picked experts who were most recognised in the field of innovation and RTD policy, they were the core of the relevant trans-Atlantic 'epistemic community' (Haas, 1993).[14] First of all, this linked the discussion in the USA to the European context and introduced the 'technology gap' discussion. The ad hoc experts within the OECD themselves perceived their role as being providers of data and ideas, without the ambition and responsibility to represent national interests (Delapalme, 1980). Moreover, the analysis of the experts was accompanied by a series of conferences linking the expert group to a wider scientific and administrative community.[15] The experts were highly active in other contexts and involved in various other forums, on national level and – more importantly – on the European level.[16]

The OECD report mainly laid down the new thinking as described above (OECD 1980). The influence of the report and the interaction around it cannot be overestimated. The report was clearly the most often cited source in the discussion in the early 1980s, and among many policy-makers influenced those members of GD XII who had to work on new concepts for European RTD policy.[17] Moreover, it became the basis of a resolution within the Council of Ministers in the OECD and the core of its argument was put forward by some of the members of the expert group at the world economic summits in Versailles (1982) and Williamsburg (1983).

The transnational expert discourse put forward by the OECD had various consequences:

1. A new problem was defined and put on the agenda of political decision-makers; problem definitions and concepts to solve them converged trans-nationally.

2. The new ideas discussed internationally, once they were formulated within the institutional context of the OECD, were attributed high legitimacy, which is mainly due to the technical, non-political character of the organization and the top-level reputation of its experts.

3. Since the institutional rationale of the OECD is to foster *economic development*, the discourse within the OECD helped to frame RTD policy as *industrial*, thus fostering growth very directly. This, however, fitted well into the institutional logic of the European Commission in general, since the most important leverage of the 'promoter of integration' is the economic efficiency attributed to its proposals.

4. Since the level of analysis and deliberation had been transnational, the conclusion to react beyond a national level seemed logical. The supra-national setting looked like a perfect arena to give it a try.

Why was it that the OECD deliberation became so relevant? The reason lies in its institutional shape, which is very well suited to ideational discourse. The organization does not have operational leverage and authoritative decision-making powers, neither 'carrot nor sticks' to make its members follow the deliberation coming out of the OECD discourse (Bayne 1987). To promote its ideas it rather has to convince by the power of its arguments, which most importantly rest on the reputation of the experts involved and the enormous amounts of comparative data gathered. The technical character of its expertise de-politises and legitimises its deliberations. In addition, the OECD has a standing committee for RTD policy that on a *regular and permanent* basis serves as a forum for national RTD policy-makers and experts alike, thus building a *common* understanding on the administrative level (Henderson, 1993; BMFT, 1984).

12.4.2.2 Functional interaction on the European level

Although the OECD was not the only organization shaping the international discourse, it was clearly the most influential international body to put forward and legitimise new thinking in RTD policy-making. However, it was a complex, multi-lateral interaction on the European level that resulted in the formulation of a European approach to RTD policy-making.

First of all, there was an *industrial European discourse* mostly organized and fed by the European Commission and centred on a newly established Committee. In parallel to the epistemic discourse at the OECD level, the Commission had turned to a more industry-focused approach in its RTD policy. In the second half of the 1970s, a new form of interaction within industry emerged, starting with conferences and informal contacts moderated by GD XII and the European industrial federation UNICE (Union des Confédérations de l'Industrie et des Employeurs d'Europe). UNICE already had a permanent committee to discuss technology policy matters that consisted of representatives from national federations responsible for RTD in their respective organizations. In 1978, the Commission established the Industrial Committee CORDI (Comité Consultative pour la Recherche et le Développement Industriel) which was to become the source of the industrial RTD program BRITE. It consisted of representatives of European industrial federations, a majority of which came from UNICE. In addition, the European Industrial Research Management Association (EIRMA) was included. This is important, since EIRMA had been a forum for European industrial discussion on RTD matters since 1966 and in the late 1970s and early 1980s one can find industrial co-operation in RTD as a prime topic in the documentation of EIRMA conferences and in EIRMA studies (EIRMA, 1978; 1982b; 1983a; 1983b). Finally, CORDI also included three observers from CERD[18] who had also been attached to the OECD discourse. Thus, CORDI was a forum for a specialised and broadened discourse on the new RTD ideas. The body, which in 1984 became IRDAC,[19] is regarded even today as the most influential body for the formulation of BRITE,[20] most importantly because of its functional structure. As one of the responsible members of GD XII put it:

> CORDI committee was a *framework*, all the subgroups and so on, were very effective when we brought people together, because it enabled us to invite people to Brussels We had working groups, subgroups, specialist groups and studies and gradually this thing [BRITE] evolved.

One of the working groups ('Basic Technological Research') had the explicit task of formulating an industry-oriented policy concept. Like all working parties, it was very flexible, enabled a very wide discussion with hundreds of experts involved, and provided the transfer of the transnational ideas onto the European level and back to the national interest groups participating in the European discourse.[21]

In addition to the standing committee CORDI and the flexible and permanent interaction it provided, the Commission organized a number of big conferences, and through high level representatives, played an outstanding part in international conferences organized by universities, business federations and the OECD expert group. According to interviews and to the documentation of participants and contributions, two key conferences were held in Paris and Strasbourg (Fusfeld/Haklisch, 1982a; 1982b; 1982c; Com, 1982). Both conferences intensively discussed the necessities for European industry to co-operate in RTD. The first linked the US discourse to the European context, the second – organized by the Commission – explicitly discussed the OECD deliberations and gave shape to a concrete European concept (Colombo/ Zegveld/Tuininga, 1982).[22] Strasbourg was especially a breakthrough, it indicated the direction for the GD XII and it gave the discussions within its advisory body CORDI a new momentum and new analytical basis. It is interesting to note that after the Strasbourg conference, the statements coming out of the CORDI and GD XII (COM, 1980; 1981a; 1981b) and out of UNICE (UNICE Monthly Report, 11/1980) had literally taken up the expertise of the OECD expert group and thus the common understanding of the epistemic community.

After the outline of a new program for industrial RTD was elaborated, GD XII started a new discourse with the *scientific experts in the technological fields* the new program was supposed to support (especially materials technologies and advanced production technologies). In several countries and for several disciplines, GD XII commissioned central, widely acknowledged nationally based scientific institutions to conduct studies

(European surveys and interviews) on the need for a European program.[23] These studies identified and specified the scientific and industrial priority areas for the program.

To sum up, the various interactions at European level triggered a virtuous circle of interaction and conceptualization. Interaction between GD XII and industry, loosely started in the mid 1970s, was institutionalized in CORDI, was linked to scientific expertise ranging across country borders, was accompanied by intensified industrial discussion on RTD matters and finally – once the concept of BRITE was formulated – made industrialists not formerly involved in the discourse turned to the GD XII. In this process, GD XII had been developing a sense of what was feasible with European industrialists and how far it could go in demanding a certain change in industrial RTD strategies. More importantly, as GD for Science and Research, the interaction with industry opened up new needs and possibilities to incorporate 'industrial thinking' into its own institutional rationale. It is fair to say that the processing of new paradigmatic ideas and the interaction with experts and industrialists alike let the institutional identity of GD XII develop from being dominantly oriented towards research and research institutions towards including industry and its RTD needs more thoroughly.

The industrialists involved in the interaction, in turn, developed a new understanding of their own interests. The first internal UNICE reports of the CORDI discussions clearly indicated that industry started out with demands for indirect support through tax incentives, the demolition of obstacles for 'technologically sensitive' goods, the co-ordination and harmonization of national policies and so on.[24] However, after several years of intensive discussion industrial experts at CORDI had finally learned about the potential of co-operating in industrial RTD, and – obviously – of the potential financial support via a European approach. In 1983, BRITE was formulated and agreed upon by representatives of potential participants from each member state.

12.4.2.3 Inter-administrative interactions

Only *after* the processes of mutual learning and common conceptualization that Commission, industrialists and scientists had developed; this concept was lifted to the national political and administrative level, mostly by bi-lateral consultations. Here, the consultations had the character of marketing, of selling the new program approach, of convincing. There were essentially two leverages:

1. *first*, of course, that the concept was accepted in industrial and scientific circles throughout Europe through the previous interactive construction with nationally based industry and science;
2. *second*, the match to several national attempts for new concepts in innovation policy, since the new thinking had reached nation states as well.

Thus, national ministries, although reflexively defending their own national room for manoeuvre, did not have a very high level of resistance. Not just in the small countries, but not even in the big ones with programs of their own.

The German administration, however, was a special case, and this case illustrates the power of consensus already reached in European interaction. In Germany, two different kinds of ministries had to be convinced, the Ministry of Research and Technology (BMFT) and the Ministry of Economics (BMWi).[25] Only the BMFT was involved in the international flow of conceptual ideas and showed a similar policy rationale to the GD XII. By and large it shared the logic of what by now was called the 'Technology Community'. The Research Ministry quite easily acknowledged the Commission's approach.

The Ministry of Economics, on the other hand, could not be convinced. This is due to its deeply rooted ordo-liberal, non-interventionist institutional philosophy. Moreover, actors of this ministry were not integrated into the specific transnational discourse. For them, the European program was a central, industrial interventionist policy to be opposed. This attitude could not be reconciled with the interventionist approach of the Commission, but the new consensus was too broad and too pervasive, the BMWi remained the odd man out.

12.4.2.4 A European approach: the normative uplift of economic ideas

The combination of various causal ideas into a feasible and acceptable concept of governance for industrial RTD in Europe is a necessary condition for a new European policy, but it is not sufficient. As the current debate on the European Research Area shows, in order to successfully turn a new concept into a new European policy, it is necessary to demonstrate that its causality and logic *serve the norms* of the European treaty, most of all European integration and economic growth. The more conclusive this normative match, the more convincing a new *European* policy concept. The last open question therefore is, how and why did the ideas processed and formulated with administrators, industrialists and scientists turn into a *European* policy?

The documents produced by the heads of state of the European Community and the integration discourse by foreign secretaries indicate that the broad debate about industrial productivity, technological gap and appropriate RTD concepts slowly reached top level politics in Europe. Initial momentum was built up after the Commission launched the results of the Strasbourg conference of October 1980 – which connected the 'neutral' causal ideas with the European level as locus of governance (see above) – into the Council. In December 1980, the European Council accepted this paper and for the first time (!) the heads of state and governments officially made a comprehensive statement on innovation (European Council 1980: 138). They basically instructed the Commission to examine further how the fragmentation of the European Market could be overcome and the incentives for innovation and diffusion of results throughout Europe could be improved. From now on, the European Council repeatedly included technological matters in its summit talks.

Several impulses led the heads of state finally to turn towards explicitly embracing the concept of co-operation of European companies. First, the leaders of the 12 leading information technology companies in Europe approached the national governments and demonstrated their willingness to co-operate throughout Europe. This active lobbying, although concentrated in one sector with clearly defined interests, once again heightened awareness for technological co-operation and, more importantly, for the first time gave the debate on 'Eurosclerosis' (Dahrendorf, 1981; Kaiser et al, 1983; Moravczik, 1991) an optimistic twist. Secondly, in March 1982, the European Council shortly after the resolution of the OECD research ministers who had adopted a resolution based on the report by the OECD expert group (OECD 1980) for the first time linked the European dimension to the development of an industrial strategy and a technology and innovation policy (European Council, 1982 p.150). Thirdly, in April 1983 the expert group 'Technology, Growth and Employment TGE)' of the economic world summit in Williamsburg – which included some members of the OECD group and of GD XII – stressed the issue of technology-driven growth and RTD co-operation and linked it to the issue of employment (Working Party TGE, 1983). Three months after the official adoption of this document in Williamsburg, the European Council followed this approach and – again for the first time – stressed the need for European companies to co-operate in RTD (European Council, 1983a p.170). Fourth, the European Council formally recognized the effective and instrumental interaction between industrialists and European institutions (European Council, 1984 p.175). Therefore, not only the content and scope of the new concept, but also the processes by which it had been constructed, were agreed upon at the highest European level.

This development indicates the integrative appeal of the concept elaborated in a complex European discourse that was increasingly organized and shaped by the Commission. This integrative appeal can be well illustrated by the argumentation put forward by the German Foreign Ministry (AA, Auswärtiges Amt). Traditionally, this ministry has been pushing for further European integration and been eager to embrace policy concepts which serve European integration (Kohler-Koch, 1998). In the years leading up to the adoption of BRITE (1985) and the article for European Technology policy in the Single European Act, there were a number of statements coming out of the AA that emphatically welcomed the Commission's approach (Genscher, 1984; Grewlich, 1981; 1984; 1985; Seitz, 1985[26]) and elevated the question of technological development in Europe to a 'matter of survival for the EC'. Most importantly for the genesis of BRITE, the German Foreign Ministry stressed the potential value for integration in a concept including all industries and not only IT industries (Genscher, 1984 p.5 ff; Grewlich, 1984 p.231). It is interesting to note that the AA was very much aware of the underlying theoretical ideas of the new concept for a European RTD policy. Even more telling, the AA had realised the complex web of interactions of industrial and scientific actors as well as the Commission and welcomed this consensus building as a prerequisite for effective RTD policy-making.[27]

The dynamic with which RTD policy gained relevance in the integration discourse is impressive. The re-launch of the integration dynamic was started by Genscher and his Italian colleague Colombo in 1981. In their common paper, however, there is no single sign for RTD policy at all. But when the transnational discourse of experts, mostly through the moderation of the Commission, was tailored towards the European level, advocates of integration captured the concept and normatively lifted it up, demanding the establishing of a 'Technology Community' (Dooge Committee, 1985). RTD policy, not on the agenda at the beginning of the 1980s, was one of the least controversial articles of the Single European Act (de Ruyt, 1989 p.71). This is an indication of the power growing out of continuous, broad interaction to produce consensus on new ideas.

12.4.3 The agent of change: the commission as central actor

The analysis has shown that only one actor has actively participated in the interactions at all levels and in all stages: the European Commission, more exactly, the GD XII. However, this does not automatically give it the role of central actor – a political entrepreneur – throughout the whole process. The GD XII did not have the intellectual, financial and institutional resources in the 1970s to act as a political entrepreneur. The process of the institutionalization of the new ideas began slowly and was not influenced by GD XII. Rather it was initiated and driven by a somewhat heterogeneous epistemic community, which came to complementary conclusions. The GD XII, on the other hand, closely watched this process and accompanied it with its scientific and industrial committees, always waiting for ideas to adopt for its institutional interests.

However, during this process of observing, influencing, and interacting with experts and hundreds of industrialists, the GD XII itself adjusted to the new ideas it to which it was exposed. Founded as a science-oriented GD in the early 1970s, GD XII became a more focused and industry-oriented administrative body. The final norm of the BRITE concept, to support application-oriented RTD in order to foster economic growth, did not really fit the initial institutional rationale of GD XII. Only after a gradual shift in its identity, did the GD XII succeed in linking the scientific ideas to its institutional interest. After this adaptation, the Commission more and more developed into an entrepreneur; the more clearly the new thinking emerged, the more the Commission became its 'advocate' (Kingdon, 1984).

The functionality of the GD XII in the genesis of BRITE can be explained by its institutional features. Since the Commission lacks certain hierarchical powers of a national government (Wallace, 1983; Cram, 1994; Mayntz/Scharpf, 1995), it has to concentrate on the function of a 'process-manager' (Eichener, 1996) of European policy-making. All the specific powers and tactics needed to manage a complex process were applied to create a new RTD policy. It used all its specific 'strategies of inclusion' (Kohler-Koch, 1998) and built up, quite typically, a web of inter-related forums (Wallace, 1996). It mobilized its exclusive power to set the agenda by utilizing expertise (Peterson, 1995) in largely non-political environments. Finally, the Commission is very well suited to absorb and transfer ideas internationally; it participates in the most relevant international organizations. However, unlike most of these organizations, this international integration goes along with a certain degree of autonomous room for manoeuvre, giving the processing of ideas an operative leverage.

12.5 Conclusions

Looking back, the causal and normative policy concept of BRITE seems simple and self-evident: technological progress and industrial innovation should be fostered through co-operation between industrial companies and between companies and research institutes throughout Europe, thereby both increasing the competitiveness of European industry and the process of European integration. This basic idea is still valid and has been integrated in the more embracing innovation policy concepts nowadays. The discussion leading to BRITE must be seen as a first milestone towards more integrative RTD policy in Europe.

The genesis of this normative policy concept was characterized by a complex and broad interaction to process and transfer ideas, this went along with the perception of a new kind of crisis that seemed to be resistant against traditional policy approaches. This genesis can be characterized as the institutionalization of techno-economic and normative ideas that became the guidepost for RTD actors throughout the Community, surviving several re-formulations of the framework program. Its basic logic has been broadened, but has not been opposed in principle ever since.

The case study of BRITE highlights the necessity of an appropriate discourse in order to make sweeping policy change happen. This is especially true in a complicated and interdependent arena which characterises RTD policy, the more so at European level. As we have seen, the genesis of BRITE unfolded on five different discourse levels:

- Transnational discourse of experts in innovation and economic theory;
- European industrial discourse combined with a European discourse on innovation theories;
- European scientific and technical discourse to formulate the specific needs for the program;
- interadministrative discourse in bi-lateral negotiations between the Commission and national administrations;
- integration discourse which normatively uplifted the policy concept.

Empirical evidence clearly indicates that these various levels of discourse heavily influenced each other by various means such as multiple memberships in organizations, committees and working groups, conferences, studies, 'marketing' exercises and so on. The analytical separation presented in this paper was due to heuristic purposes. Moreover, the ideas did not diffuse through the various levels and arenas according to a sequential, linear model of policy innovation. In contrast, feedback loops and spontaneous linkages between the various levels pushed the process. From the de-construction of this process, several conclusions can be drawn.

12.5.1 Form has to fit function: the conditioned functionality of interaction

Policy related interaction is functional if it succeeds in producing a widely accepted, consensual policy concept. The case study discussed here identified some major reason for successful interaction. These pre-conditions for successful policy discourse might be generalized to all kinds of complex policy change at the European level and thus provide some lessons for the current discussions on a European Research Area triggered by the turn to the innovation policy paradigm at European level.

First, representatives of all stakeholders were included in the process of transferring more or less abstract scientific economic ideas into a practical political concept. Thus, the organization of the discourse matched the requirements of the very concept that was discussed: the discourse was transnational and interdisciplinary. Experts and industrialists alike were brought together at the European level, they discussed the conceptual elements in many different forums for several years, in standing committees and ad hoc working groups. The ideas 'infected' divergent practical backgrounds, could, slowly, and not without frictions, be reconciled with different perceptions. In a policy area like RTD policy, which in the long run cannot succeed by extrinsic incentives alone but by nature requires intrinsic readiness to follow; this early integration is crucial.

Secondly, the discourse for the concept was established at the appropriate levels. The broad interaction of stakeholders was detached from the traditional discourses that were mostly very much shaped by the clash of national interests. Concepts for European RTD policy since 1974 most often had been formulated and negotiated within the international administrative body CREST (Comité de Recherche Scientifique et Technique), thus new ideas had to pass through the filter of 'national interest'. In the case of BRITE, the guardians of national interests had been involved at a stage when industrialists and scientists alike had already realized and welcomed the potential benefit of a European program, following the logic of a larger market for co-operation.

Moreover, the organization of the discourse not only belittled the danger of competing national interests, it also belittled the danger of sectoral interests competing for budgets. Through most of the process – especially in the early stages – the representatives from national horizontal industrial federations or individual companies who participated in the discourse had already been active on European level before through their UNICE function or through EIRMA. Therefore, strong clashes of sectoral interest was prevented, at least in the stage of conceptualisation.

An interactive process organized along these lines and kept up as an enduring, timely mechanism, has the potential to reduce complexity and to build up a common purpose and a common frame of reference. The different theoretical sources of the BRITE concept should have added up to a complex web of academic argumentation and should have lead to severe interest conflicts between sectors and between nations alike. Nevertheless, in the end, the interactions between theorists and practitioners, between industrialists and administration, had reduced this theoretical web to the final norm as a rather simple and commonly accepted message. This timely process is exactly what has been labelled 'vertical institutionalization' (Lau, 1978).

12.5.2 Lessons from history?

The integrative and all-embracing innovation policy paradigm that drives the current debates in Europe and elsewhere is a patchwork of a whole bunch of theoretical ideas. It seems that this concept is even more complicated than the RTD paradigm of the early eighties. Most likely it is also much more complex, since the arena of actors is even more crowded and heterogeneous. Consequently, challenges for consensus building are numerous.

This might have implications for the very identity of the actors involved. The historical case study on BRITE provides – among others – one simple message: new ideas have to fit the persistent institutional logic within the respective policy arena. In the long run, if there is no match between what the institutional bodies involved normatively and intrinsically seek on the one hand and the policy concept they come up with on the other, political success will not be enduring. In this case, there will either be an adjustment of ideas or of the institutional identity of the entity taking them up. The case study has given two examples. The idea of transnational co-operation to foster economic growth perfectly fitted the OECD as an international forum with this very purpose. On the other hand, the idea to concentrate research efforts on industrial innovation did not fully fit the rationale of the Commission, and the build up of interaction forums with industry was instrumental for the breakthrough of the ideas, most importantly because of the gradual changes in the Commission analyzed above. Moreover, only after the causal concept was closely connected to the normative framework of the overarching institutional setting – the EC treaty – did it gain momentum in high politics. This points to a crucial pre-condition of all RTD paradigm change: a new scientifically sound paradigm has to be reconciled with the normative foundations of the different administrations and stakeholders involved. It might very well be that the crucial challenge for modern national innovation policy with its claim to integrate very different policies and administrations is exactly this reconciliation of very divergent policy rationales even within one country. In this perspective, a European approach seems to meet severe obstacles: first, the European concept is still in the stage of collecting, adapting and reformulating *ideas* and struggles with the European dimension of innovation policy; second, given the structure of the Commission, the *central actor* for innovation policy consists of two somewhat competing GD (enterprise and research) with very different institutional rationales rather than one strong moderator; third, the multitude of current – and future – member states, to a large extent even with blurred internal administrative responsibilities for innovation policy (research, economic, education ministries etc.) makes *appropriate interaction* – as defined in this paper – a Sisyphean task. An all-embracing innovation policy approach at European level might take much longer than somewhat optimistic discussion papers out of the Commission suggest.

Annex: International conferences on technology and RTD policy

Overview of international conferences dealing with a new definition of the RTD process and new concepts for RTD policy between 1976 and 1983 (brackets indicate the organiser)[28]

1976: 05–09 April, Bonn (BMFT, National Science Foundation NSF (USA)): 'Technologische Innovation' (Wirtschaftlicher Wandel und Technologiepolitik), representatives from European and US administrations and the scientific community.

1976: 24–26 May, Milan (EG): Über die sich abzeichnenden Ziele, Prioritäten und Einzelheiten einer gemeinsamen F&T-Politik.

1977: 31 May – 02 June, Brüssel (EG): 'The Crisis of Science in European Society'.

1978: 19–20 October, Compiègne (EG): 'European Science and Technology and the Challenges of Contemporary Society'.

1978: 15–17 March, Paris (EIRMA (European Industrial Research Management Association)): 'Technology 88' (EIRMA 1978).

1979: 27–28 March (New York University/National Science Foundation): 'International Conference on Science and Technology Policy' (Fusfeld/Haklisch 1979).

1979/1980: Conferences to compile the OECD Report: – 'Policies for the Stimulation of Innovation in the United States' (National Science Foundation, Washington) 'Links between Technological Progress and Economic Growth' (Science Policy Research Unit of the University of Sussex); 'The Need for and the Possibilities of Social Technologies' (FhG ISI, Karlsruhe).

1980: 17–18 June 1980, Paris (OECD Conference): 'Innovationspolitik'; with top level government representatives responsible for innovation policy from research and/or industry ministries (OECD 1981a).

1980: 20–22 October 1980, Strasbourg (EG-Konferenz): 'A New Development on the European Scientific Policy' (KOM 1982a), representatives from national and EG Commission, EG consulting committees, European industry and science.

1980:	20–21 November, Paris (Center for Science and Technology Policy, New York University): 'Industrial Productivity and International Technical Cooperation'; participants from the scientific community, politics (national, EG, OECD) and industry from USA, Europe and Japan (Fusfeld/Haklisch 1982a).
1981:	March 1981, Paris (OECD, Ministerebene): 'Science, Technology and Innovation in the 1980s – National and International Perspectives', discussion of four reports on technology policy, passing of a declaration on future science and technology policy (OECD 1981a).
1981:	24–26 June, Kiel (Institute für Weltwirtschaft, Symposium 1981 together with the Directorate for Science, Technology and Industry of the OECD, patronised by the OECD Council): 'Emerging Technologies: Consequences for Economic Growth, Structural Change and Employment', scientific community and government representatives as well as RDT institutions (Giersch 1982).
1983:	18–20 May 1983, Interlaken (EIRMA): 'The Role of Industrial RTD in the 1980s (EIRMA 1983a), discussion of the new context (innovation theory, framework conditions, new approaches for RTD in enterprises), contributions by GD XII-General Director Fasella and EG/OECD expert Delapalme and OECD dept. Head of Science and Technology Salomon, as well as the later chairmen of the EG committee IRDAC, Beckers (Shell) and FAST chief Petrella (Petrella 1983) (EIRMA 1983a). Relation of a 'European crisis context' with the new paradigms and with the profit interests of the participating enterprises.
1983:	22–23 September.1983, Brüssel (EIRMA, special conference): 'Technological Challenges to European Industry Today'. Director General of GD XII, Fasella, reports on the EG dimension and EG offensive (ESPRIT and BRITE) and their consistency in the new R&T context in Europe. Beckers (Shell, later IRDAC) chaired the meeting (EIRMA 1983b).

Source: Own compilation from conference proceedings, in some cases supplemented by summaries of secondary literature.

Notes

1. Since this paper discusses policy-processes in the 1990s, the term RTD policy will be used instead of the more recent concept of innovation policy. RTD policy-making is defined as all public policy measures and activities that aim to influence the action of public and/or private actors in research, technology and development. Therefore, RTD policy is one core element of innovation policy (IP), the latter being defined as all policy systematically influencing and governing the innovation system of the respective polity, therefore comprising fields like tax policy, regulation, and education policy.
2. GD XII is now labeled GD Research, however, this article deals with 'historical' developments and therefore will stick to the old numerical label.
3. The few minor programs that had been implemented until the early 1980s had been decided upon under the general clause of article 235 of the EEC treaty.
4. The genesis of ESPRIT is well documented (Schneider, 1986; Sandholtz, 1992; Grande, 1994). In contrast to BRITE, ESPRIT was proposed by a power coalition of the Commission (Commissioner Davignon) and the big twelve IT companies in Europe that represented imprint potential in the various Member States. The number of relevant players in the beginning was very limited, the problem in one sector was more easily defined, new concepts more easily agreed upon and linked to personal commitment by the company leaders. Thus, in a co-ordinated effort, the coalition succeeded in putting direct pressure on Member State governments. It will be seen that the genesis of BRITE followed a very different logic that was characterized by slow but powerful transnational ideational scientific and political policy discourse.
5. European Research for Advanced Materials.
6. In Germany, for example, despite a strong research base and strong national programs, BRITE and BRITE-EURAM have become the most extensively used programs in relation to the budgets of all specific programs.
7. For a detailed conceptualization see Edler, 2000 pp.46–64.
8. The institutional rationale of the OECD, as a second important example of an international organization, is that the organized economic co-operation through the mutual exchange of information and economic co-operation is a suitable means for economic development in the Member States. This is the institutional rationale of the OECD, and while the organization is not empowered with autonomous and operative authority, it can be shown that this rationale is indeed powerful mostly through the shared belief in its very norm.
9. This development fit to the overall shift in economic (and political) paradigm towards supply-side economics, which replaced Keynesianism and concentrated on the build up of favorable conditions for growth (Edler, 1993).

10 There have been different labels for this recursive model of the innovation process, e.g. 'concomittance model' (EIRMA 1982a) 'Kopplungsmodell' (Keck, 1985), 'chain-linked model' (Kline/Rosenberg, 1986).

11 For the meaning of microelectronics see OECD 1980; Perez 1983; Freeman/Soete, 1985; Hohn u.a., 1985.

12 This of course only holds true within the limits set by rising transactions costs.

13 The annex cites the relevant publications.

14 The US experts were the main representatives of the systematic, evolutionary innovation theory Nelson (USA) and well-known analyst of the RTD process and its economic effects (Rosenberg, Fusfeld, Hirschmann, Gilpin, Rothschild); from Europe the group had nine renowned specialists, who all had published in the field, some of them were still active in industrial research management (Caracciolo di Forino (I), Colombo (I), Delapalme (Fr), Freeman (GB), Gruson (Fr), Krupp (D), Lagermalm (S), Pavitt (GB), Rathenau (Nl).

15 See annex.

16 Umberto Columbo and Bernard Delapalme, for example, had been members of CERD and of the EIRMA (European Industrial Research Management Association, see below).

17 This information is based on various interviews with (former) members of the GD XII.

18 Comité Européen pour la Recherche et le Développement, a European scientific advisory body of the 1970s and 1980s.

19 Industrial Research Advisory Committee.

20 This assessment is again based on several interviews with CORDI members from the Commission and from industry.

21 Interviews with German representatives indicate that the link between CORDI and EIRMA was important for industrialists, in order to learn at a very early stage what conceptual ideas were processed and what their basic rationale was.

22 Colombo had been member of the expert group of the European scientific committee CERD, president of EIRMA and contributed to the work in CORDI (Colombo, 1982). He is one important example of several high level experts linking the transnational and European academic and industrial discourse.

23 In Germany, for example, the Commission chose the Federal Agency for Materials Research and Testing (BAM, Bundesanstalt für Materialforschung und -prüfung), which to a large extent is paid for by the federal government and is the focal point for materials research in Germany. Its final report (BAM, 1982) can to a large extent be found in the first proposal for BRITE by the Commission (COM, 1983).

24 Based on analysis of various years of UNICE's 'Monthly Report' and other documents analyzed at the archive of UNICE, Brussels.

25 Both ministries have meanwhile changed their names, BMFT now is BMBF and BMWi now is BMWT.

26 Grewlich and Seitz both were senior members of Genscher's working staff in the Foreign Ministry.
27 Grewlich gives a very concise and informed summary of the complex set of causal ideas making up BRITE (Grewlich, 1984 p.255ff), and Genscher himself put forward this understanding (Genscher, 1984; 1985).
28 Unfortunately, it is not possible to quote the conference proceedings each time, as there is no existing documentation in some cases.

References

BAM (Bundesanstalt für Materialforschung und -prüfung) (1982): Technische Materialforschung und –prüfung. Entwicklungstendenzen und Rahmenvorschläge für ein EG-Programm 'Basic Technological Research; Berlin.

Bayne, N. (1987): Making Sense of Western Economic Policies: The Role of the OECD, in: The World Today (2); pp.27–30.

BCG (Boston Consulting Group) (1978): A Framework for Swedish Industrial Policy; Boston.

Berger, P. L./Luckmann, T. (1967): The Social Construction of Reality. A Treatise in the Sociology of Knowledge, New York.

Biegelbauer, P. (2000): Searching for an Ideational Framework of Innovation Policies; paper delivered at the EASST conference 2000, Vienna, September 2000.

BMFT (Bundesministerium für Forschung und Technologie) (1984): Bundesforschungsbericht 1984. Bonn.

Borrás, S. (2000): From Technology to Innovation Policy in the 1990s: a Silent Transition?; paper delivered at the EASST conference 2000, Vienna, September 2000.

Boyer, R. (1979): Déterminants d'Evolution Probable de la Productivité et de l'Emploi; Paris.

Colombo, U./Lanzavecchia, G. (1982): Plan by Objective: R, D & D to Promote European Industry Competitiveness; Rom (commissioned by GD XII).

Colombo, U./Zegveld, W./Tuininga, E. J. (1982): The European Community and Innovation Opportunities. Constraints and Recommendations; in: KOM (Kommission der Europäischen Gemeinschaften) (1982a): 1980–1990: A New Development on [sic] the European Scientific Policy. Proceedings on a Conference held in Strasbourg (20–22 October); EUR 1721; Brussels, Luxemburg; pp.271–386.

COM (Commission of the European Communities) (1980): Industrielle Entwicklung und Innovation. Mitteilung der Kommission an den Europäischen Rat in Luxemburg am 1. und 2. Dezember 1980, Brüssel, 27.11.1980.

COM (Commission of the European Communities) (1981a): Discussion Paper. Basic Technologic Research. Preliminary Ideas and Suggestions for Actions; internal manuscript; Brussels.

COM (Commission of the European Communities) (1981b): Zur Entwicklung der Industrie in Europa: Eine Strategie der Gemeinschaft; KOM (81) 639 endg., 12.11.1981.

COM (Commission of the European Communities) (1982): 1980–1990: A New Development on [sic] the European Scientific Policy. Proceedings of the Conference held at Straßbourg, 20–22 October (EUR 7121); Brussels, Luxemburg.

COM (Commission of the European Communities) (1983): Proposal for a Council Decision Adopting a Multiannual Programme of the European Community in the Field of Basic Technological Research, COM (83)350; Brussels.

COM (Commission of the European Communities) (1984): The Research and Technology Policy of the EC: Developments until 1984. Office for official publications, Brussels/Luxembourg.

Cram, L. (1994): The European Commission as a Multi-Organization: Social Policy and IT Policy in the EU; in: Journal of European Public Policy 1 (2); pp.194–217.

Dahrendorf, R. (Hg.) (1981): Zeitenwende. Europas Wirtschaft in der Krise; Wien u.a.

Delapalme, B. (1980): Letter of Transmittel; in: OECD (Organization for Economic Cooperation and Development) (Hg.), Technical Change and Economic Policy; Paris; pp.109–110.

Dooge-Ausschuß (Ad-hoc-Ausschuß für institutionelle Fragen) (1985): Bericht des Ad-hoc-Ausschuss für institutionelle Fragen an den Europäischen Rat in Brüssel am 29. und 30. März 1985; abgedruckt in: Weidenfeld, W./Wessels, W. (Hg.), Wege zur Europäischen Union. Vom Vertrag zur Verfassung; Bonn; S. 130–145.

Edler, J. (1993): Die Bedeutung von Ideen, Interessen und Institutionen bei der Herausbildung wirtschaftspolitischer Strategiewechsel. Diplomarbeit, Universität Mannheim; Mannheim.

Edler, J. (2000): Institutionalisierung europäischer Politik. Die Genese des Forschungsprogramms BRITE als reflexiver sozialer Prozeß; Baden-Baden.

Eichener, V. (1996): Die Rückwirkung der europäischen Integration auf nationale Politikmuster; in: Jachtenfuchs, M./Kohler-Koch, B. (Hg.), Europäische Integration; Opladen; S. 249–280.

EIRMA (European Industrial Research Management Association) (1978): Workshop Technology 88; Paris, 15.–17.3 1978; Paris.

EIRMA (European Industrial Research Management Association) (1982a): The Role of RTD in the Innovation Process. Working Group Reports N° 27; Paris.

EIRMA (European Industrial Research Management Association) (1982b): Industry's Needs for Basic Research. Working Group Reports N° 23; Paris.

EIRMA (European Industrial Research Management Association) (1983a): The Role of Industrial RTD in the 1980s. Proceedings of the EIRMA Annual Conference, Interlaken, 18.–20.05.1983. Conference Papers Vol. XXVIII; Paris.

EIRMA (European Industrial Research Management Association) (1983b): Technological Challenges to European Industry Today, Special Conference, Brussels, 22./23.09.1983. Conference Papers Vol. XXIX; Paris.

Europäischer Rat (1984): Texte, die den Beratungen des Europäischen Rates zugrunde lagen und dem Rat in seinen verschiedenen Zusammensetzungen zur Orientierung dienen könnten: abgedruckt in: Generalsekretariat des Rates (1989): Europäischer Rat. März 1975 bis Dezember 1988 – 1. bis 40. Tagung – Schlußfolgerungen; S. 175–186.

European Council (Europäischer Rat) (1980): Schlußfolgerungen des Vorsitzes (18. Tagung, 01.–02.12.1980; Luxemburg), abgedruckt in: Generalsekretariat des Rates (1989): Europäischer Rat. März 1975 bis Dezember 1988 – 1. bis 40. Tagung – Schlußfolgerungen; pp.137–140.

European Council (Europäischer Rat) (1982): Schlußfolgerungen des Vorsitzes (22. Tagung, Brüssel, 29. –30.03.1982) abgedruckt in: Generalsekretariat des Rates (1989): Europäischer Rat. März 1975 bis Dezember 1988 – 1. bis 40. Tagung – Schlußfolgerungen; pp.150–153.

European Council (Europäischer Rat) (1983a): Feierliche Deklaration zur Europäischen Union, verabschiedet am 19. Juni 1983 in Stuttgart; abgedruckt in: Generalsekretariat des Rates (1989): Europäischer Rat. März 1975 bis Dezember 1988 – 1. bis 40. Tagung – Schlußfolgerungen; pp.167–172.

European Council (Europäischer Rat) (1983b): Schlußfolgerungen des Vorsitzes über die Arbeit des Europäischen Rates (26. Tagung, 17.–19.06.1983, Stuttgart), abgedruckt in: Generalsekretariat des Rates (1989): Europäischer Rat. März 1975 bis Dezember 1988 – 1. bis 40. Tagung – Schlußfolgerungen; pp.162–165.

Freeman, Ch./Clark, J./Soete, L. (1982): Unemployment and Technical Innovation. A Study of Long Waves and Economic Development, London.

Freeman, Ch./Soete, L. (1985): Informationstechnologie und Beschäftigung; Sussex.

Fusfeld, H. I./Haklisch, C. (1979): Science and Technology Policy: Perspectives for the 1980s; New York.

Fusfeld, H. I./Haklisch, C. (Hg.) (1982a): Industrial Productivity and International Technical Cooperation; New York u.a.

Fusfeld, H. I./Haklisch, C. (1982b): Foreword; in: Fusfeld, H. I./Haklisch, C. (Hg.), Industrial Productivity and International Technical Cooperation; New York u.a.; pp.IX-X.

Fusfeld, H. I./Haklisch, C. (1982c): Foreword; in: Fusfeld, H. I./Haklisch, C. pp.(Hg.), Industrial Productivity and International Technical Cooperation; New York u.a.; pp.3–10.

Genscher, H.-D. (1984): Die technologische Herausforderung; in: Außenpolitik. Zeitschrift für internationale Fragen 35 (1); pp.3–18.

Giersch, H. (ed.) (1982): Emerging Technologies: Consequences for Economic Growth, Structural Change and Employment. Symposium 1981, Institut für Weltwirtschaft Kiel; Tübingen.

Grande, E. (1994): Vom Nationalstaat zur europäischen Politikverflechtung. Expansion und Transformation moderner Staatlichkeit – untersucht am Beispiel der Forschungs- und Technologiepolitik, Habilitationsschrift Universität Konstanz; Konstanz.

Grewlich, K. W. (1981): Technologie – die Sicherheit Europas; in: Außenpolitik 32 (3); pp.211–225.

Grewlich, K. W. (1984): EG-Forschungs- und Technologiepolitik – eine besondere Verantwortung für das wirtschaftlich-technologische 'Flaggschiff'?; in: Wesels, W./ Hrbek, R. (Hg.), EG-Mitgliedschaft – ein vitales Interesse der Bundesrepublik Deutschland?; Bonn; pp.223–271.

Grewlich, K. W. (1985): Informationstechnologien – Europas Antwort; in: Außenpolitik, 36 (2); pp.127–135.

Guzzetti, L. (1995): A Brief History of European Union Research (Commission of the European Communities; DG XII); Brussels.

Haas, P. M. (1993): Epistemic Communities and the Dynamics of International Environmental Co-Operation; in: Rittberger, V. (Hg.), Regime Theory and International Relations; Oxford; S. 168–201.

Henderson, D. (1988): The State of International Economic Cooperation; in: The World Today 11; pp.213–215.

Henderson, D. (1993): International Economic Cooperation Revisited; in: Government and Opposition; pp.11–35.

Von Hippel, E. (1978): A Customer-Active Paradigm for Industrial Product Idea Generation; in: Research Policy 7; S. 240–266.

Hohn, E.-J./Klodt, H./Saunders, C. (1985): Advanced Machine Tools: Production, Diffusion and Trade; in: Sharp, M. (Hg.), Europe and the New Technologies; London; pp.46–86.

IFO (Institut für Wirtschaftsforschung/Institute for Economic Research) (1980): Technischer Fortschritt – Auswirkungen auf Wirtschaft und Arbeitsmarkt, 3 Bände; München.

Kaiser, K. u. a. (1983): EG vor der Entscheidung. Fortschritt oder Verfall; Bonn.

Kalka, P. (1984): Die Genese einer gemeinsamen Forschungs- und Entwicklungspolitik in den Europäischen Gemeinschaften; Polnische Weststudien 3 (2); pp.315–51.

Keck, O. (1986): Gesellschaftliche Steuerung der Technik – ein institutioneller Ansatz, in: Bechmann, G./Meyer-Krahmer, F. (Hg.), Technologiepolitik und Sozialwissenschaft; Frankfurt am Main; New York; S. 17–41. Kingdon, J. W. (1984): Agendas, Alternatives and Public Policies; University of Michigan.

Kline, St./J; Rosenberg, N. (1986): An Overview of Innovation; in: Landau, R./ Rosenberg, N. (Hg.), The Positive Sum Strategy. Harnessing Technology for Economic Growth; Washington DC, S. 275–306.

Kohler-Koch, B. (1998): Bundeskanzler Kohl. Baumeister Europas? Randbemerkungen zu einem zentralen Thema; in: Wewer, G. (Hg.), Bilanz der Ära Kohl. Christlich-liberale Politik in Deutschland 1982–1998. Zeitschift für Gegenwartskunde; Sonderheft 1998; pp.11–25.

Kooiman, J. (1993): Governance and Governability: Using Complexity, Dynamics and Diversity; in: Kooiman, J. (ed.), Modern Government. New Government – Society Interaction; London u.a.; pp.35–51.

Kuhlmann, St. (1998): Politikmoderation. Evaluationsverfahren in der Forschungs- und Technologiepolitik; Baden-Baden.

Lau, E. E. (1978): Interaktion und Institution. Zur Theorie der Institution und Institutionalisierung aus der Perspektive einer verstehend-interaktionistischen Soziologie; Berlin.

March, J. G./Olsen, J. P. (1984): The New Institutionalism. Organizational Factors in Political Life; in: American Political Science Review 78; pp.734–749.

March, J. G./Olsen, J. P. (1989): Rediscovering Institutions; New York.

March, J. G./Olsen, J. P. (1994): Institutional Perspectives on Governance; in: Derlien, H.-U./Gerhardt, U./Scharpf, F. W. (Hg.), Systemrationalität und Partialinteresse. Festschrift für Renate Mayntz; Baden-Baden; pp.249–270.

Mayntz, R./Scharpf, F. W. (1995): Steuerung und Selbstorganisation in staatsnahen Sektoren; in: Manytz, R./ Scharpf, F. W. (Hg.), Gesellschaftliche Selbstregulierung und politische Steuerung. Schriften des Max-Planck-Instituts für Gesellschaftsforschung, Köln, Bd. 23; Frankfurt am Main, New York; pp.9–38.

Meyer-Krahmer, F./Kuntze U. (1982): Innovationsförderung bei kleinen und mittleren Unternehmen. Wirkungsanalyse von Zuschüssen für Personal in Forschung und Entwicklung; Frankfurt/M., New York.

Moravcsick, A. (1991): Negotiating the Single European Act; in: Keohane, R. O./ Hoffmann, St. (Hg.), The New European Community. Decision-making and Institutional Change; pp.41–85.

Narula, R. (2000): Explaining the Growth of Strategic RTD alliances by European Firms; in: Journal of Common Market Studies 4 (37); pp.711–723.

Nelson, R. R. (ed.) (1982): Government and Technical Progress. A Cross-Industrial Analysis; New York et al.

Nelson, R./Winter, S. G. (1977): In Search of A Useful Theory of Innovation; in: Research Policy 6; S. 36–76.

Nelson, R. R./Winter, S. G. (1982): An Evolutionary Theory of Economic Change, Cambridge u. a.

OECD (Organization for Economic Cooperation and Development) (1980): Technical Change and Economic Policy; Paris.

OECD (Organization for Economic Cooperation and Development) (1981a): Science and Technology Policy for the 1980s; Paris.

OECD (Organization for Economic Cooperation and Development) (1991): Background Report Concluding the Technology/Economy Programme (TEP); Paris.

Pavitt, K. (1976): The Choice of Targets and Instruments for Government Support of Scientific Research; in: Whiting, A. (ed.), The Economics of Industrial Subsidies. Papers and Proceedings of a Conference on the Economics Industrial Subsidies held at the Civil Service College, Sunningdale, February 1975; London; S. 113–138.

Perez, C. (1983): Structural Change and Assimilation of New Technologies in the Economic and Social System; in: Futures, 14 (5); pp.357–375.

Peterson, J. (1995b): EU Research Policy: The Politics of Expertise; in: Rhodes, C./Mazey, S. (eds.), The State of the European Union: Building a European Polity?; Boulder/CO; S. 391–412.

Royal Swedish Academy of Engineering Science (IVA) (1979): Technical Capability and Industrial Competence; Stockholm.

Ruyt de, J. (1989): L'Acte Unique Européen. Commentaire; Brüssel.

Sandholtz, W. (1992): High Tech Europe. The Politics of International Co-operation; Berkeley u.a.

Schneider, R. (1986): ESPRIT und EUREKA – Europas Antworten auf die pazifische Herausforderung? – Europäische Technologiepolitik zwischen Technologiegemeinschaft und High-Tech-Unternehmen; inh: WSI-Mitteilungen 39 (14); pp.679–688.

Schneider, R./Welsch, J. (1990): Europäische Forschungs- und Technologieförderung zwischen Industriepolitik und gesellschaftlicher Zukunftssicherung; in: Weizmüller, R. (Hg.), Marktaufteilung und Standortpoler in Europa; Köln; pp.225–272.

Science Council of Canada (1979): Forging the Link. A Technology Policy for Canada. Report 29; Ottawa.

Seitz, Konrad (1985). SDI – die technologische Herausforderung für Europa; in: Europa-Archiv/Folge 13; pp.381–390.

Wallace, H. (1983): Negotiation, Conflict, and Compromise: The Elusive Pursuit of Common Policy; in: Wallace, H./Wallace, W./Webb, C. (Hg.), Policy-Making in the European Community, 2. Auflage; Chichester; S.43–80.

Wallace, W. (1996): Government Without Statehood: The Unstable Equilibrium; in: Wallace, H./Wallace, W. (eds.), Policy-Making in the European Union, 3. Auflage; Oxford; pp.429–460.

Wendt, A. (1992): Anarchy is What States Make of It: the Social Construction of Power Politics; in: International Organization 46 (2), S.391–427.

Working Party TGE (1983): Technology, Economic Growth, Employment. Report of the Working Party 'Technology, Economic Growth, Employment'; set up by a decision by the heads of states and governments at their summit in Versailles, June 04. to 06.1982 published by Bundesministerium für Forschung und Technologie (BMFT); Bonn.

Chapter 13

Conclusion: Policy Changes, Actors, Institutions and Learning

I am sure that the power of vested interests is vastly exaggerated compared with the gradual encroachment of ideas. John Maynard Keynes (1936): The General Theory of Employment, Interest and Money London: Macmillan

At this point we shall revisit the questions posed in the introduction and try to find answers to them on the basis of the case studies which form the book. Indeed, in the beginning of the book we laid out four sets of questions. Firstly, we want to see how policies have changed in the cases that the authors in this book have studied. The main question, as stated in the introduction, concerned how the new ideas have been absorbed by the institutional set-up of the respective systems. Informed by the neo-institutional literature on path-dependency phenomena and institutional inertia, we are interested in the way changes in RTD policy were brought about during the 1990s. Our questions relate to whether the new paradigm has been perceived as an alternative or complementary to the previous paradigm of technology policy, to the viability of the new ideas in the institutional set-up, and whether the policy change has been shallow or deep.

Secondly, we want to know more about the forces enabling changes – a much more actor-centered question. What kind of persons, groups, parties or other forms of institutions are responsible for the changes in the policy field we have been studying. Here, both the national and international dimensions are of interest to us. Both levels are subject to constant evaluations by a large number of actors with respect to the economic and political viabilities related to various policy solutions. In this context, we also want to learn about the reflexive-symbolic dimension of these policies.

Thirdly, we want to evaluate the case studies presented in this book as a whole, with respect to the patterns of policy diffusion and policy learning. As was stated in the introduction, policy learning is essentially a single-country social and political process shaped by its own specific business and administrative traditions. Yet, on the basis of the previous two questions, general remarks can be made about the nature of the learning processes in the case studies analysed. Policy diffusion refers to the extent to which and in what way the new policy paradigm has spread over in Europe and the US.

Finally, and this is very much connected to the last set of questions, we want to risk looking into the future of innovation policy-making. How likely does it seem that there will be a convergence of policies what might be the role of policy tools such as benchmarking and what is the relation of national and supranational levels in this policy-field?

13.1 Absorption of new ideas

There is extensive evidence in the cases examined that the new perspective on science, technology and innovation started emerging in the late 1980s. Concerns about competitiveness in world markets have worked as a linchpin for national economic policies since the 1970s. The novelty in the 1990s is that competitiveness is no longer related to technological development as such, but to a much wider understanding of the innovation process. Hence, the policy focus moves during the 1990s from supporting 'strategic technologies' to a wider and much context-oriented approach that looks at science, technology and innovativeness as a whole. The buzz-word became 'innovation' rather than 'technology' or 'science'. Issues like innovative SMEs, risk-venture capital, exploitation of knowledge, organizational adaptability and horizontal co-ordination of policy areas like education, research and industry came to the fore in policy circles. Several national documents and reports from 1990 to 1995 have enshrined these issues, ushering in a first step transforming the policy trajectory. Examples are the 1990 report of the Science and Technology Policy Council of Finland, the report 'Vision 2000' by the government of Malta in 1992, and the Netherlands' 'Economy with open borders' document in 1990. It seems as if the start of the new decade has stimulated strategic endeavors, mostly from the ministerial administrative side, under the uncertainty conditions of the political and economic situation of the late 1980s-early 1990s. This period included important incidents such as the fall of the iron curtain and the subsequent break-up of the Council for Mutual Economic Aid (COMECON), the economically weakened USA, the 2nd Gulf War, the burst of the Japanese 'bubble economy' and the economic weakening of Germany as an effect of the reunification.

Despite this generalized transformative spur at the beginning of the decade, national experiences differed considerably as to the extent to and the way in which this new approach resulted in a revamping of the policy instruments and organizational structure. Countries like Finland, the Netherlands and Denmark openly and fully embraced the 'innovation paradigm' in the early 1990s and have re-designed their policy instruments and administrative structure accordingly. Consequently, we might call this group 'first movers', in chronological terms. For a second group, France, the UK, Italy and Austria, the innovation paradigm does not seem to have resulted in major policy transformations until the end of the 1990s. Despite occasional initiatives (like the UK's foresight exercises, the Austrian green book on science policy, the French and Italian governments' new incentive schemes for networks) the innovation paradigm produced slender policy transformations in these countries throughout the 1990s, showing more convincing evidence of change only at the very end of the decade. We might call this group 'late comers', indicating interesting moves towards the innovation policy paradigm in the final years of the decade. For a third group, Malta, Slovenia and Hungary, policy change seems to have held promise in the context of a general administrative reshuffling along the transformation of the political system, where the 'innovation paradigm' would appear to offer a way to 'westernize', 'Europeanize' and modernize industrial policy – although the actual policy changes were frequently not so extensive. This group might be labeled 'discursive reformers', which catches the notion that innovation policy transformations have been inserted within major administrative and economic changes in the country, anchored as well in a wider political discourse context.

The United States and the EU Brite program are two cases which stand on their own. As for the US, the innovation paradigm has found its way into policy documents in a most skewed fashion through initiatives such as the national information infrastructure, (vulgo 'information highway'), the Advanced Technology Program or several initiatives targeting small business. All these initiatives are very much influenced by the innovation paradigm. However, they are not openly declared technology or innovation policies, troubled by the ideological disposition of the country's political mainstream, which foresees a relatively weak role for the state in economic and technology policy. Therefore one might say that the US has an undeclared technology or even innovation policy, which nevertheless has signs of being indirectly influenced by the innovation approach in a rather unarticulated and unspoken manner. The EU Brite program is a case of its own for another reason. Launched by the EU in the mid-1980s, this program can be characterized as one of the first moves towards the current innovation policy in the 1990s. Financed and administered at this supra-national level,

Brite opened up a new era of the EU RTD programs (clustered into the so-called Framework Program) put in place by a combination of shared ideas and interests among member States. Brite has some new interesting and innovation-like elements, such as, research co-operation among firms, and obligatory cross-boundary research projects. This might suggest that Brite and the other EU-RTD programs stopped, partly, the move towards new forms of RTD and innovation policies.

13.1.1 The policy rationale: alternative or complementary?

In the introductory chapter of this book we briefly described how evolutionary institutional economics has challenged the theoretical premises of neo-classical equilibrium economics. We examined also how these differences are reflected in their alternative understanding of the innovation process: neo-classic theory assumes a linear causal relationship between scientific advances and economic growth; whereas evolutionary theory looks at innovation as a complex social process embedded in an institutional context. It is then not surprising that the different theories arrive at different normative statements about the government's role in this respect: whereas for neo-classical economists governmental intervention should only be based on 'market failures', evolutionary economists stress that governmental action should be conceived more widely and be directed towards the system as such and towards the different aspects of the innovation process (the innovation-system approach).

From the case studies analyzed earlier, it is our belief that two main factors have eased the gradual adoption of the evolutionary-institutionalist perspective and of an 'innovation policy' approach in the 1990s. The first of these is the fact that most national policy-makers have seen the 'systemic approach' as complementing (rather than substituting) the previous 'market failure' rationale. Practitioners seem to have focused more on the overall message and worldview provided by the evolutionary theorists than on the theoretical foundations of it. Intuitively, the 'system approach' is a wider approach that 'naturally' includes, rather than excludes, the previous policy rationale directed towards market disfunctionalities, technological bottlenecks, and (subsequent) strategic choices. By subsuming previous rationales into the new one the transition towards innovation policy has been relatively smooth because it has avoided open confrontation with previous policy approaches at the discursive-cognitive level. This is the case of the 'first movers'. The transition of Finland, Denmark and the Netherlands towards an 'innovation rationale' took place in the early 1990s, and was generally perceived as the logical continuation of the technology-strategic approach of the 1980s. As Christiansen points out, the Danish ministry of industry has never abandoned the 'market failure' rationale, but, focusing on the coherence of the national innovation system, has allowed the integration of the 'old' rationale with the new one about 'system failures'. However, the issue of gradual adaptation resulting from the notion of complementarity, is perhaps mostly visible in 'late comers'. Austria, the UK, France and Italy, have introduced some innovation-policy elements within their existing technology policy frameworks. Here the transition is obviously gradual, since previous schemes seem to enjoy continuity, but nevertheless within a context of interesting new innovation-inspired initiatives. As for the case of 'discursive reformers' the impact of the new innovation policy rationale came within a whole constellation of rationales for transforming the politico-administrative and economic system. Even if one might expect a more 'radical' type of change, the corresponding chapters show elements of continuity, especially referred to the central role of science and knowledge-producing dimension of policy, while innovation-initiatives were also partly introduced.

The second factor that in our view has a significant effect on the adoption of the innovation policy is the fact that institutionalist-evolutionary theorists have not produced an all-encompassing policy rationale and a detailed course for subsequent policy action. The relative indeterminacy of the 'system-innovation approach' in terms of clear-cut normative statements for policy-makers at the early 1990s eased as well the adoption of the new approach in the different national contexts. The lack of 'ready-made solutions' was the best open door for adapting the new vision into very diverse institutional contexts, normative environments and 'state philosophies'. It opened up for a broad interpretation in policy terms, offering wide possibilities to develop policy programs within distinct political contexts and administrative traditions. Influential documents and studies at the beginning of the decade were mainly those focusing on 'national systems of innovation' – arguably the most influential were the books produced and edited by Lundvall in 1992 and Nelson in 1993. Their normative statements were interesting, but broad. Neither of the volumes came with a pre-determined clear-cut normative statement about policy recommendations. Rather, they introduce important notions for policy action in a rather open way. On the other hand, influential documents with more clear policy statements and courses for governmental action have been produced during the second half of the 1990s (European Commission, 1995; Metcalfe, 1995; Dodgson and Bessant, 1966; Lundvall and Borrás, 1998;

OECD, 1998) at a time when the 'innovation policy rationale' had already become dominant (at least at a discursive-cognitive level) in most advanced industrialized countries. This paradox shows that the kind of economic ideas which have an impact on policy making are not those with 'ready-made solutions' coming with a new 'package of measures' which should be introduced. Instead, those ideas most likely to foster policy change are those that provide a new understanding of social phenomena (the economics of innovation process in this case), suggesting a new way of tackling them, a new policy approach.

13.1.2 The institutional set-up: the viability of new ideas

The way in which the new ideas of evolutionary-institutionalist economists gradually have resulted in a new approach to innovation policy is strongly related to the political, administrative and economic institutional set-up of each state. Some of the countries studied have been rather quick to adopt the new rationale, others quite slow or dithering, while others still are now taking the first steps. Likewise, some states have taken the full conesquences of the new policy rationale and embarked on a general re-organization and conceptualization of policy goals and instruments, while for others these changes have mainly been at discursive-narrative level without major impact on the existing mechanisms but just a few new (ad-hoc) initiatives.

As we have seen in the introduction of this volume, Peter Hall has addressed this issue by pointing to three interrelated factors for the reception of new ideas in national policies: their economic, administrative and political viability (Hall, 1989).

'The economic viability of economic ideas refers to their apparent capacity to resolve a relevant set of economic problems' (Hall, 1989 p.371). As most case studies have shown, the recession in the early 1990s had an impact on the way in which national governments tackled economic policies. This short-time recession emerged as the result of the financial markets' instability and of the structural problems facing Western countries.[1] Even if the crisis was overcome in a relatively short time-span, this sudden economic crisis showed the high degree of global integration of the financial markets, and the structural weaknesses and interdependence of advanced economies. The recession hit the European economies very differently. And so policy-makers had very different reasons to take heed of a wide innovation matters as a policy response to the loss of competitiveness.

As Lemola puts it, the recession itself did not produce the transition from technology to innovation policy in Finland, but it accelerated significantly the adoption of new concepts and modes of operation. And it did so because, at this point there seemed to be a generalized dissatisfaction about the ability of technology policy of the 1980s to respond effectively to the economic uncertainty. The recession provided the clearest evidence that the efforts on strategic technologies developed along the previous decade were not enough, as they were not producing the expected results in terms of competitiveness and job-creation.

Similarly, the Netherlands reacted rather rapidly to the perceived inappropriateness of available technology policies. The RTD policy changes were part of a larger set of reactions to the dire economic situation the country was in the 1980s – despite the efforts of the different Dutch governments to revamp the political economy of the country with a series of economic and political reforms. Finally, in the 1990s, these efforts were successful not least in terms of their ability to create jobs and flexibility in the work force. We can conclude from all these incidents that there is a role for economic crises in the history of policy changes. However, economic crises are not per se a determining factor. Only when the reform of technology policy was discursively linked to the crises, major and substantial policy change was possible, as indicated by the 'first movers'. Likewise, the case of the EU Brite program shows that the background for the launch of this program was the failure of the previous 'national champions'-strategy to respond effectively to the technologically-based economic crises of the 1970s. However, as Edler points out on several occasions, it was only possible because administrators, industrialists and scientists linked the Brite program discursively to this commonly perceived economic situation.

The *administrative viability* means that new ideas are more likely to be accepted if they 'accord with the long-standing administrative biases of the officials responsible of approving them', and 'seem feasible in light of the existing implementational capacities of the state' (Hall, 1989 p.373). As examined earlier, the generalized attitude that the new policy approach represents a continuity by complementing the previous rationale has been a key issue for the viability of the new approach. However, there have been large differences in the timing and in the modes in which the new policy rationale has penetrated the administrative-organizational structure. Examples for 'late comers' are France and Malta. As Foray shows, in France, an elitist bureaucracy is interlinked with a similarly elitist structure of RTD institutions, which until recently both have been less interested to an adoption of the innovation paradigm. Nevertheless, France has developed new policy initiatives along the innovation-policy paradigm, which indicates the changing attitude of elites about the viability of implementing such new instruments within the context of French politico-administrative structures. Similarly, Harper points at the existing administrative structures in Malta, that by and large prevented an adoption of the policy proposals brought forward by the new Malta Council for Science and Technology (MCST), which were very much influenced by the new policy paradigm. Italy is an interesting case in this regard. Belussi argues that the traditional weakness of the Italian central administration in co-ordinating horizontally the administratively scattered R&D-related competences has impeded a transformation from technology to innovation policy in this country. Nevertheless, innovation-related initiatives have always existed at local level, around the well-known industrial districts. In contrast to this are the cases of the 'first movers' (the Netherlands, Denmark and Finland), where the change of policy approach at national level has taken place during the early 1990s mainly from the thrust of a relatively open and 'pro-active' administrative apparatus in search for new ideas in the context of economic instability.

Last but not least, *political viability* refers to the ability of new ideas to have 'some appeal in the broader political arena, to which the politicians who ultimately make policy are oriented' (Hall, 1989 p.375). Looking at the political viability of the new innovation policy approach links this issue with the overall political situation in the countries examined. Interesting cases are the countries which at the beginning of the 1990s were in transition from centrally planned to market-led economies. Whilst some policy-makers in these countries quickly adopted figures of speech heralding the innovation paradigm, they were more hesitant to introduce policy measures. For both Hungary and Slovenia an important reason for the hesitant adoption of the new innovation policies seems to be the small interest available on the side of the policy-makers and the political elite at large about the ventures of RTD – despite a number of discussions and documents of the first half of the 1990s, which indeed seemed to show an impact of the discussions led in Western European countries about the innovation paradigm. Most political elites did not see the innovation policy paradigm as a politically viable way to 'modernize' their countries. However, another reason for the two countries' policy evolution seems to lie in the general inertia and vested interests of the existing and well-established institutions which tried to block policy changes in fear of losing (even more) resources.

Austria provides another interesting case for the difficulties that the new approach encountered at the political level. As Mayer has put it, the deep-seated Keynesian-corporatist model rendered difficult the penetration of new perspectives in the RTD and other policy fields. Therefore the innovation policy rationale has not arrived at this country until the mid-1990s, and even then only through singular initiatives such as the development of the 'K+' and the 'academics for the economy' programs linking the Higher Education System to the business sector through joint finance of the initiatives by state and industry. The USA has been described before as a case, in which the development of a coherent technology policy is made impossible by the ideological orientation of the public. Thereby, the US might be viewed as a special case, in which the political viability of the new innovation paradigm is hindered by deep-seated ideological predispositions. The UK might enjoy a similar situation. The strong ideological context in which the 1979–1997 Conservative government actions were based upon, earmarked these two decades. In the 1980s industrial policy was based on privatization and liberalization, and when these two programs were successfully accomplished in the beginning of the 1990s, industrial policy was a 'policy by exhortation'. This, argues Sharp, was combined with a strong reform in the science and public research sector, with major transformations in University and research council modes of operation. It was first with the 1997 New Labor government that greater focus has been placed in the development of skills and knowledge capabilities of the system linked to innovation-related activities, a core issue in the innovation policy paradigm.

13.1.3 Deep or shallow policy change?

Hall's three dimensions of viability (economic, administrative and political viability) were conceived as a minimum set of conditions for a state to introduce a new set of economic ideas and a new policy rationale. As has been said before, in all the case studies examined, there seems to have been a general adoption of the new innovation policy rationale under very different circumstances and timing. From the early transformations of Finland and the Netherlands to the 'late comers' like Austria and the UK. And from the stable Netherlands to a transition country like Slovenia. Indeed, another aspect is interesting in this regard, namely, the way in which these adaptations have truly signaled a transformation of the policy instruments and strategies, or have (perhaps for the moment) just accounted for a new discursive-communicative change.

To answer this question we have to examine the correlation between the policy goals established in strategic documents, and the implementation mechanisms set in place to accomplish them. Moving to an innovation policy approach is quite demanding in terms of administrative terms as it implies the launch and/or re-definition of some policy instruments. A key aspect of the new rationale is the stress placed on the co-ordination efforts between policy actions in the field of industrial, education, science, and regional policies. Therefore, we will examine this factor more closely.

As before, we shall briefly discuss the cases by dividing the countries into three groups according to the actual policy changes taking place in these. Denmark, Finland and the Netherlands all have engaged into further reaching changes of their policies. They have all enforced relatively large-scale innovation actions in mutifacetious ways, like for example, networking incentives to firms (especially small and medium-sized enterprises), improving vocational training and human capital directly linked to enhancing the innovation-technology capabilities, improving the availability of risk-capital and venture-capital, reinforcing the position of bridge-building institutions in the innovation system (technological institutes or nodal points like 'centers of excellence'), and enhancing the overall flexibility and adaptability of the diverse institutions within the system (for example public research centers and Universities). Along with this panoply of new policy instruments, the 'first movers' have also made quite an effort to coordinate government actions in all these innovation-related issues. A number of formal and informal groups, platforms and committees have been established in order to deliberate and communicate policy activities among administrators and among those and stakeholders. Apparently, then, the 'first movers' resemble radical change. Their strong move towards the new paradigm might have been able to break more clearly with previous lines of government action. However, evidence in our cases shows that the pillars upon which the new policies could be built were already laid down in the 1980s, years before the change to the new set of innovation policies came about – either by wholesale reforms of the political economy of the country, as in the Netherlands, or by pronounced reform efforts in the fields of economic, industrial and RTD policies as in the case of Finland and Denmark.

In contrast with this determined path that 'first movers' seem to have taken, 'late comers' like Austria, Italy, France and the UK, the transformations were less clear cut in terms of the objectives and means of innovation policy. In these countries the new innovation-policy instruments have been developed in the absence of an overall re-definition of political objectives. Moreover, the administrative co-ordination mechanisms have not been significant in this regard, or have simply proved to be rather ineffective or superfluous. The lack of clear linkage between these new instruments with the overall purposes of governmental involvement in this area is the key reason why 'late comers' have so far only had a shallow policy change. Indeed, these countries show a strong pattern of policy change by path dependency anchored in the specific political-administrative and economic context of science-technology-industrial policies. As regards the co-ordination mechanisms, experiences differ notably. In the Austrian case, coordination mechanisms in RTD policy have existed since a prolonged period of time. Yet the institutions responsible for coordination worked only quite imperfectly and to the extent that they functioned it seemed to have been less the success of these institutions than that of the social partners, which were present in all of the respective organizations. Therefore, when the influence of the Austrian social partners began to wane with the late 1980s, the central coordination mechanism was missing. As Mayer states, with the second half of the 1990s several activities were planned with the ultimate aim of arriving at better coordination of policies – yet none of the envisaged solutions, including the 2000 founded Austrian Council for RTD, did cover the whole range of innovation policy. Nevertheless, a number of initiatives have been deployed in the last years of the outgoing and the first of the beginning century, which are based upon the new innovation policy paradigm. France is a very different case, as policy-making there traditionally has been very centralized and highly coordinated. This is the case for French RTD policy, too, but, as Foray shows, this cannot change the fact that only a small number of policies aiming at the innovation system are in accordance with the new innovation paradigm, mainly for reasons of path dependency. In addition, the French organization of innovation works quite well for a number of policy problems, therefore diminishing the incentives for a wholesale reform effort. As Margaret Sharp points out in the UK chapter, this country has experienced quite dramatic changes in the 1980s and 1990s related to industrial and science policy. The 1993 Waldegrave report was the result of a large consultation process, and came up with a series of reforms that at first glance were little more than re-ordering and clarifying the roles of universities and research councils. However, in the event, these proved to be more far reaching, adding to the significant changes operated in the industrial policy of the 1980s and 1990s with liberalization and privatization programs. However, it seems though, that it is not until the New Labor government of 1997 that the innovation agenda was truly accepted and reinforced, particularly in the issue of training and education, articulated into the Science and Technology White Paper of 2000.

According to Belussi, the Italian central government has put significant emphasis on the question of enhancing the knowledge resources of the overall Italian system at the end of the 1990s, a focus that falls under the innovation policy paradigm. However, the heavily decentralized nature of the Italian system, together with the traditionally weak position of the central administration in RTD-related issues has not proved sufficient to foster truly innovation-policy change at the national level. Nevertheless, it might well be argued that Italy represents a rather special case given the highly successful self-organizatorial tradition at local level regarding industrial and innovative activities. The phenomenon of the 'Third Italy' which has developed since the 1970s has provided endless examples of innovation paradigm solutions at decentralized manner, and the notion that 'proximity matters' in economic industrial development.

Hungary, Malta and Slovenia are the three countries which have arguably felt the least impact of the new policy ideas. Since the fall of the iron curtain Hungary has seen a certain modernization of its RTD policies, partially under the auspices of the OECD, the European Commission and other international organizations. However, there has been no successful attempt to revamp the innovation system according to the new policy paradigm – policy innovations remained always isolated attempts to reform, often being quite limited (Havas, 2001).

This comes with the fact that the RTD policy coordination mechanisms rarely worked since the end of central planning – this being primarily, yet not exclusively, an effect of the missing interest of politicians in the policy field. Slovenia is yet a different case insofar as there have been several efforts to bring policy reform to the country's innovation system. Whilst, similar to Hungary, none of these reforms were far-reaching and the coordination mechanisms of the Slovene RTD policy structure were blocked by political bickering between the involved interest groups and thus proved largely ineffective (Mali in this book, Biegelbauer, 2000). Malta whilst never having experienced central planning, but rather a general backwardness of its innovation system, has seen a clash of the traditional with the new ideas on RTD policy. There, the established, traditional political institutions were not won over by the new MCST, which proposed policies according to the new innovation policy paradigm.

As has been established before, the US provides an exception. It actually has introduced several policies adhering to the new paradigm, but refrains from implementing a full-scale technology policy on ideological grounds. Etzkowitz points to a number of policies, active since the early 1990s, which are induced by the innovation paradigm. Yet the ideological barrier, which lets the US administrations refrain from using the terms 'industry' or 'technology policy', prevents a coordinated effort – which in any case might be difficult given the governmental set-up of the USA and its traditionally divided nature.

13.2 Forces enabling change

Until now we have focused on the interplay between ideas and institutions, that is, the way in which ideas have been institutionalized. The role interests have played has, so far, received less attention. By examining the role bureaucrats, politicians, experts, the scientific community, industry and labor representatives have had on the transition to the innovation policy rationale, we attempt to examine the role interests have had on this transition process. Similarly, addressing the question of the internationalization of the cognitive framework of evolutionary-institutional economics is an interesting point, partly explaining the simultaneous attention towards this economic theory. Finally, the symbolic nature of a new policy rationale will be examined later, in clear relation to the 'political viability' of Hall: the search for new solutions to (old) problems generating a new communicative line, metaphor and chain of ideas, generally related to the popular notion of 'globalization'.

13.2.1 Political actors

After having examined the case studies it seems not adventurous to affirm that in most cases the political actors involved in the (deep or shallow) transformation to the new policy rationale have been relatively few. The interplay between politicians, highly positioned civil servants, and experts (many economists) has generally had the lead fostering the new policy rationale. The convergence between the need that politicians and civil servants have of new cognitive frameworks for the political-economic problems, and the 'availability' of a new set of economic thinking along the lines, is not an exceptional situation in policy development. However, the large diversity of potential interests being mobilized is somehow special in the case of innovation policy vis-à-vis other policy domains. The new rationale of innovation policy predicates a wider approach where industrial, education, science and technology policy are realigned into synergetic efforts for enhancing the innovativeness and competitiveness of the system. Hence, a crucial aspect for the success of the new rationale is that this re-alignment is presented in a way that the major stakeholders do not perceive that their interests are threatened. This is especially relevant for active groups like industrial associations, scientific communities, the educational community and environmentalists. The interplay between experts and the politico-administrative elite on the one hand, and the interplay between the politico-administrative elite and the stakeholders on the other, can assume very diverse forms. We will focus on the second type of relationship, since we have already examined the horizontal co-ordination of administrative departments in the previous section.

The interplay between stakeholders and policy-makers has worked very differently in the case studies presented in this collected volume, partly due to the specific national characteristics of interest-representation mechanisms, and partly to the specific form in which these four sectorial policies are designed in the early 1990s. The governments of Malta and the UK launched ambitious strategies for engaging the stakeholders in the policy discussions. The Malta 'networking' exercises provided the government with valuable information about the organization of innovation activities of the country, and with a direct inter-face with the innovators to involve them in the governmental strategy. Likewise, the large 'foresight' exercises in the UK in the early 1990s succeeded in involving innovators in strategic visions for the innovation performance of the country. Yet, these were exercises for communicative purposes, which did not involve direct policy actions or economic resources. The lack of a technology policy in the 1980s meant that Malta was entering the 1990s without any articulated public funding scheme for science and technology, and therefore stakeholders had nothing to loose and much to gain from a governmental attention on innovation. In the UK, the situation was different. The severe budgetary cuts all through the 1980s affected deeply the overall design of science, technology, industrial and educational policy. Consequently, British innovators in the early 1990s had relatively little public involvement to stake to.

Austrian efforts to include stakeholders in policy discussions in the second half of the 1990s were a bit more limited, insofar as the administrative bodies coordinating the process were lacking internal management structures, a reflection of the missing overall coordinative functions of the Austrian innovation system. Perhaps the most ambitious effort was the '1999+' initiative, which had as a goal to produce a science policy green paper. This policy process was, however, ridden with a specific and hardly foreseeable problem: Whilst the paper was the outcome of a lengthy discussion process, it had only marginal effects on actual policy-making, due to the new government in power since 2000, who rearranged the competencies in technology policy-making. Slovenia features differently. This small country is characterized by a deep divide between the industry and the scientific community. In the Tito-Yugoslavian variant of state socialism, 'users' and 'producers' were required to regularly sit together and develop common RTD projects. Yet with the break-up of the People's Republic of Yugoslavia a large part of the industrial producers were suddenly outside the territory of the relatively small Slovenia. Moreover, due to the specialization Slovenia had in the former Yugoslavia most of the country's scientific community was geared towards basic research. This is the main reason why basic science has a strong role in the current Slovene innovation policy, despite what the small size of the country might suggest (Mali and Biegelbauer, 2000).

In the Netherlands, Denmark and in Finland, the interplay between the politico-administrative elite and stakeholders of the innovation-related policy areas seen in the 1990s was not entirely new. The 'first movers' did actually reinforce and expand the largely already established communication channels – although foresight exercises have later been carried out in both countries. Van der Steen identifies several stakeholders' pressures for change behind the Dutch innovation-policy initiatives of the mid- to late 1990s. Most clearly, the role of universities in the 1990s was changing profoundly – along with the scientific, industrial and societal changes related to globalization. By and large, the Dutch government initiatives like 'centers of excellency', 'technology top institutes' or 'research schools' did not have major problems in coming into being, as stakeholders were positively interested on those, not just for the new organizations, but also because they were economical viable through public funding. In this sense, van der Steen talks about 'interactive policy-making' in the 1990s. Denmark is another example where stakeholders and policy-makers have been quite on the same side, and where the new instruments foreseen by the governmental authorities entailed substantial public funding.

As Christiansen puts it, Denmark reinforced and expanded the number of 'contact-points' between stakeholders and the administration in the 1990s. Besides the traditionally active 'technology council', 'craftsmens' council' and industrial associations, the 1997 Report activated 29 different working groups, and a similar pattern of heavy stakeholders interactions has continued ever since.

In a similar manner, but following a more tripartite model, Finland's key social actors took part in the formulation of the new policy and broad consensus was rapidly achieved. Arguably this has to do with the special geographic and economic situation of the country and with the neo-corporatist tradition of interest intermediation, both influencing the consensus-based approach about innovation as a centerpiece of economic policy. However, Austria might represent here another example, where the traditional tripartite articulation of corporate interests did not foster such a policy renewal. Yet it would be not correct to assume that the neocorporatist policy arrangements in Austria are the prime explanandum for the missing policy dynamics. It was rather the government, which made an effort to reduce the role of the social partners in Austrian politics, yet did not invest enough energy into the RTD policy field so as to supplant the old coordination and policy-finding structures with new ones independent of the Social Partnership.

13.2.2 International dimension of cognitive frameworks

In the gradual adoption of the innovation policy rationale, the interplay between experts and the national politico-administrative elites has had a clear international dimension. In most of the case studies the authors relate to the direct or indirect role that international organizations like the OECD, the EU and UNESCO have had in the definition of economic policies. The OECD has played an important role in the development and diffusion of the new innovation policies since the 1980s with an influential set of general and country-specific reports on many issues, especially on technology-innovation and education. These reports have invariably had an effect in the national contexts. Lemola mentions, for example, the direct effect that the documents of some evolutionary-institutionalists and the TEP report of the OECD (1991) had on the re-definition of the Finnish policy towards a systemic-innovation perspective. In other cases, the influence has been more indirect, but equally important. In this sense van der Steen points out the impact of this international organization on the matter of the re-organization of the Dutch higher education system. Indeed, almost invariably all the cases exposed earlier refer to key analytical reports about technology policy, about general economic developments or about statistical trends from the OECD. In Hungary, the OECD technology audits of the early 1990s did not lead to large scale policy-reforms – although such a development seemed to be possible then. In any case, the OECD experts' work led to widespread discussions on nature and functions of RTD policy, which by itself was already a worthy outcome of the discussion process (Biegelbauer, 1994).

The EU involvement in RTD policy in the mid-1980s has also certainly influenced the way in which individual member countries have gradually structured and re-designed their respective policies. On the one hand, the creation of the framework program, a funding mechanism for trans-European research projects on a 50–50 basis, has enhanced national –

corresponding – co-funding schemes. On the other hand, the gradual centrality that the issue of competitiveness and innovativeness in the EU has acquired (Commission, 1994), has enhanced the systemic-innovation perspective on policy design not just at EU level but also at national level (Commission, 1995). The current efforts of Malta's government towards innovation policy are framed within the expected near-future membership. Arguably, Finland was already 'tuned' into the EU mainstream approach to innovation policy and hence had little to change and adapt to (Lemola in this book, and Hakala, 2001), while Malta is moving now towards this direction because its transformations in the 1990s were not as clear-cut as the Finns', and because the innovation approach is being perceived as an important aspect of its preparations for membership. UNESCO seems to have had an impact on Malta's technology policy at the end of the 1980s, but only to some degree, as Harper argues that, at least on paper, most of the technology-oriented suggestions were overcome at the early 1990s by a more innovation-oriented strategy. No evidence of longer-lasting UNESCO influence is available for other non-EU members such as like Hungary, with the exception of the very early transformation period, when UNESCO provided statistical know-how and methodologies to the transition countries.

13.2.3 Reflexive-symbolic function of policy

The relevance that innovation policy has gained in countries like the Netherlands, Denmark and Finland has to do with the centrality of political concerns about competitiveness. Here the symbolism related to innovativeness and modernization has been at the forefront of political debates. Arguably, this has to do with the perception by elites of the economic characteristics of the state in terms of innovative capabilities, and of the role that technology and innovation have in the overall economic performance. In Finland, the self-perception of being a small country in the geographic periphery of Europe, the willingness to find alternative markets to the previously dominant USSR, together with the world-wide presence of Nokia, are three factors that might explain the centrality of technology (especially ICT) in the visions of the future for the country. Likewise, the fears of loosing ground with the welfare state triggered the political attention in the Netherlands and Denmark to matters of technology in the 1980s, and later of innovation and knowledge-based economy in the 1990s.

Apparently, though, in other countries, this matter does not seem to have been so central in political terms. In Hungary and Slovenia technology and science by a few decision-makers were seen as means of enhancing the transition to the market economy. The high expectations placed on the market, and its ability to deliver a technology-push were later – to a degree – followed by a more realistic picture of the dynamics of the innovation process, and the deficiencies inherited from the previous system. Yet these concerns were never systematically translated into policies, due to a shared understanding of a majority of politicians that RTD are not an important means of bringing the country to the level of the EU. The case of Malta shows that the thrust of the late 1980s was not followed by adequate institutional set up or economic resources. This might indicate that the issue was moved on to the sidewalk of the governmental interest.

The UK is another case. The strong liberalizing policies of the 1980s placed the emphasis on the market forces to solve industrial bottlenecks, and hence understood that technological development was about to emerge if optimal conditions for industry were in place. Concerns about competitiveness were mostly focused on issues like deregulation and privatization, rather than on technological capabilities. However, the Blair government, in the late 1990s, linked the issues of globalization and competitiveness placing more emphasis on education and knowledge-base.

Austria has neither placed technology nor innovation at the core of governmental issues. The reason might be the 'conservatism' of government and major corporate interests, which have focused on traditional issues, partly disregarding the potential that innovation has to economically sustain the welfare state. Interestingly, this is the case although the issues of science and technology have been part of most major government statements since the mid-1990s the latest. Yet, these statements often remained lip-service, as neither government spending was increased significantly, nor coherent programs devised and deployed.

Italy and France are two other cases where the technology-innovation matters have not been at the foreground of political debates and attention in the 1990s for different reasons.

France's success in big science areas (like nuclear energy, aerospace and transport system) has provided few incentives to move away from its eminently 'mission-oriented' technology policy style. Arguably, this has prevented the political self-reflexive discourse in the 1990s about the need to move from technology to innovation policy, keeping technology policy away from wider public debates. In Italy, a similar situation emerges, but anchored in different context.

The traditionally successful and active innovation-like initiatives undertaken at the local level, combined with the structural weakness of the national Italian technology policy, meant that a national discourse moving from technology to innovation policy was not an issue, since it already existed in a decentralized manner.

13.3 Policy learning and policy diffusion

Taking collectively the cases in this book, it seems that at the end of the 1990s and beginning of the 2000s there has been a clear tendency to adopt the innovation policy paradigm. However, there are large differences as to the degree and the form in which this new paradigm has been adopted. Reading the cases carefully it is easy to reach the conclusion that each country has followed very specific patterns of policy change and policy learning. This is due to the fact that change is bound to take place within a specific institutional context, anchored in the different administrative economic, social and political traditions of each country, and within larger and recent events, such as the transition to market economy and democracy. The three-headed typology developed at the beginning, 'first movers', 'late comers' and 'discursive reformers' aims at putting together groups of counties by their rapidness and in-depth adoption of reforms. This typology serves our purposes in answering the questions related to what has characterized the transition from technology to innovation policy in the 1990s. Nevertheless, it should not be seen as an absolute categorization of the countries mentioned. Policy change and policy learning are complex social processes deeply embedded in the specific national context where they take place. As Foray puts it, the past success of French's 'mission-oriented' policy instruments in areas like nuclear energy or aerospace, constrain institutionally the introduction of the more broad-oriented and decidedly less 'big-science' perspective of the new innovation policy paradigm. Hence, the resilience of the French model has to do with this rather successful line of policy strategy, and the particular historical tradition of French public administration and state structure. Therefore, it is not adventurous to affirm that this tradition is bound to continue in the future, and as the French political elite moves more decidedly into the innovation policy paradigm, the new instruments and rationale will be adopted within previously given patterns of policy-action. In other words, the innovation policy rationale will be interpreted and adopted in a specific French-manner. Italy is another interesting case. As we have seen in this chapter, and in the corresponding chapter written by Belussi, the heavily decentralized model of the Italian national system of innovation, and the relative weakness of central administrative structures in the implementation and co-ordination of single-defined policy goals, is unlikely to change in the near future. This is so because the relative success of the Italian model resides in the dynamic local and regional levels. The innovation policy paradigm has never been explicitly articulated in Italy, but has for long worked successfully in the numerous industrial districts of the 'Third Italy'. Therefore, learning, as a collective political and social phenomenon, is most likely to take place in Italy following this decentralized tradition, rather than a learning that comes from the deliberative process of the central-administration in Rome. Needless to say that other cases of this book illustrate this point in a very similar manner: institutional set-ups and the socio-political traditions are bound to continue, and be the basis where the new paradigm will be inserted, re-interpreted and adopted, in a singular manner.

Despite all these individual patterns of policy learning, the cases in this book also show a certain degree of more simple policy diffusion. The new innovation policy rationale was never formulated in a neat and clear ex-ante form. This has provided the new rationale with a notorious flexibility in terms of how to translate, in practical terms, all the suggestions from the evolutionary economic theorizing, thereby favoring the rapid diffusion of this new policy paradigm. Moreover, this process has been reinforced by the active role that some economy-related international organizations have acquired lately in this area of policy. Most notably is the case of the OECD, which has openly supported and encouraged its member states to adopt the new rationale, and has accordingly generated a valuable amount of studies providing directly comparable data, and has organized seminars on some specific issues related to innovation. The EU has recently developed a similar line of policy entrepreneurship towards its member states through socio-economic research and through the new benchmarking method. The benchmarking lines of action in the late 1990s and first decade of the 2000s will certainly foster this trend further. The US is perhaps a case apart in this regard, since it has not endorsed these new trends discursively, despite some interesting novelties of its science and technology policy lately.

13.4 What policy issues for the years to come?

Apart from their overall tendency to introduce innovation policy instruments, the case studies above share some challenges ahead. This section has a twofold purpose. Firstly, it will identify and discuss some of the upcoming issues directly related to innovation policy that lie ahead for each of the three groups of countries defined above. After that, it will place this into the context of the European integration process, by relating it to the recent ERA initiative (European Research Area) and by relating it to other significant innovation-related initiatives in the EU context like the emerging EU intellectual property rights regime, risk capital markets, and EU-wide standardization/regulation.

13.4.1 Upcoming issues

For 'late comers' and 'discursive reformers' the challenges ahead in innovation policy seem to be to articulate more effectively the new policy paradigm and to develop accordingly a coherent set of policy instruments. As we have seen in a number of country cases, this is easier said than done. Institutional inertia makes it difficult to implement ex-novo a set of instruments, which are so different from what used to be the standard policy descriptions in the field until a decade ago. Of course, a number of new policy instruments have been put in place in most countries. However, more far-reaching initiatives like the reallocation of responsibility among governmental departments placing innovation in the forefront seem to have been rather limited. Consequently, the main policy issue for the 2000s and 2010s would appear to be a further reaching implementation of the new policy rationale in a way that policy addresses the systemic dimension of the innovation process.

Nevertheless, and independently of to what extent the 'first movers', 'late comers' or 'discursive reformers' have already embraced the innovation policy paradigm, there are a set of challenges for the new policy agenda that are common to them all. One first challenge is the need to foster the enhancement of labor skills, not just by the goal of an educational system that provides the right skills accurately following the market-requirements, but mainly by educating and training people in a way that they are prepared to engulf in life-long learning. In other words, it is not a question of finding the optimal equilibrium between the demand and the supply of skills at a given point in time. It is essentially a matter of designing an educational system that socializes the people into the need to learn constantly, and that stimulates openly creativity, autonomous thinking, and entrepreneurship at any level.

Another challenge for future innovation policy is to foster the ability of firms to be adaptive to a rapidly changing business environment that is becoming increasingly internationalized. Some topics in this regard are: rapid, reliable and simplified information channels for firms, more flexible and open labor market regulations able to integrate different needs from the firms and from important social groups (i.e. women, disabled, immigrants), and fostering less-hierarchical organizational structures in the firms. Firms' adaptability is especially relevant for SMEs.

A third set of issues for the future of innovation policy is mainly the need to foster the availability of risk capital, in their different forms: second-tier markets or venture capital industry. This seems essential for fostering innovation. Despite the efforts and attention that the innovation policy paradigm poses in this issue, there is still much to be done. More bold policy initiatives in this regard will certainly be the trend in the coming years, not just for the capital markets at local and national level, but also at EU level.

A fourth set of issues is related to some wider economic dynamics. Innovation is not just a matter of high-tech in the manufacturing sector. Innovation is also a matter of low and medium-tech sectors producing, acquiring and adopting new knowledge in a manner that enhances their productivity and generates better products to the changing market. And innovation is also taking place in the service sector, related to the possibilities offered by ICT and by business-organizational innovation. This means that the future innovation policy in the 2000s and 2010s should also look at this, understanding that it has to actively support the development of new competences and the adaptability of these other non high-tech manufacturing sectors.

Last but not least, future innovation policy has to place knowledge in a central position. This relates as much to the question of knowledge production (research, science, education of the workforce), as to the question of adequate appropriation regimes (mainly through flexible and innovation-friendly intellectual property rights), and to knowledge diffusion (ranging from technology transfer centers, to popular science diffusion channels).

13.4.2 The future European context for innovation

All the cases presented in this book, with the exception of the US, are European. This calls for a brief percourse around the upcoming issues related to the innovation policy at EU level. The European Union has been integrating rapidly during the last two decades. This is particularly true for innovation-related issues, which have received great attention during the last few years. Six initiatives deserve our attention. One is the so-called 'European Research Area' which aims at generating a single space for research and knowledge production in the EU. A second important initiative is the creation of a single EU intellectual property rights regime, which means EU-wide property rights like patents, copyrights or trademarks. A third one is the goal of creating a truly single capital market in the EU, where there is also place for more integrated risk capital markets. A fourth one is not that new, namely the fostering of common standardization bodies generating EU-wide compatible standards, with an important effect upon technological trajectories and upon market-making. Fifth, the introduction since the Lisbon Summit in Spring 2000 of the 'open co-ordination method' which is reflected in the RTD field by benchmarking exercises of EU's members research systems. Last but not least, the initiatives related to e-Europe aim at introducing more the usage of ICT in business and social life, fostering organizational change at firm level and public administration level.

Starting with the first, the 'European Research Area' (ERA) initiative was launched in early 2000 by the European Commissioner for Research, Philippe Busquin. A number of policy instruments were proposed, which were all geared towards the openness and liberalization of the national research systems in company with a more pronounced and deeper-reaching cooperation of researchers and institutions across the EU. These include, for example, the idea that national funds are to be available for researchers coming from other EU countries, or the creation of Centers of Excellence to be financed directly by the EU. The full implementation of all these initiatives is still in the pipeline. But, regardless of how successful the ERA might become in the end, the dynamics of EU RTD programs as such have (started in the mid-1980s) by themselves had had some impact on the knowledge production structures of the member states and accession candidates alike. Examples of these impacts are the introduction of new research funding lines at national level (in specific technologies or techno-societal problems) eventually matched by EU-funds; or the usage of certain policy instruments like foresight exercises and consensus conferences.

In the second half of the 1990s the EU has developed spectacularly a single EU regime of intellectual property rights. Following the logic of the single market, the creation of such property rights is a step forward in this direction by simplifying and rendering less costly the appropriation of knowledge in the EU area. Besides, further legal security will be granted due to the hierarchical organization of EU laws' judicial interpretation. Furthermore, intellectual property rights will no longer be used as technical barriers in intra EU trade. The EU enjoys today of single EU trademarks, copyrights, industrial designs, and utility models (petty patents). Most important for innovation process, though, is the legal figure of patents, mainly because they protect innovators from unfair copies of their inventions, and allow them to appropriate in monopolistic terms the benefits of their capital investments. With the forthcoming community patent, the

EU will for the first time have a single-patent system for the 15 member states.[2] This new legal figure will possibly have a large impact on the innovation scenario in Europe. Patents will be cheaper and clearer to enforce than before. However, it is difficult to predict whether it will altogether help fostering the innovation performance of the European economy. The reason is that an optimal patent regime should strike the balance between the private appropriation of knowledge and its diffusion, in a manner that the benefits granted to the patent-owner do not undermine the overall innovative performance of the system. And this is as much related to the attitudes of economic actors (aggressive-defensive patenting, over-patenting, etc), as to the judicial interpretation of central legal caveats, mainly the conditions for 'compulsory licensing'.

The third issue in EU innovation policy that has important implications for member states is the attention that risk capital has acquired recently. Moved by the notion that in Europe there is relatively less availability of this type of capital than for example in the USA, the European Bank of Investment has recently launched the i2i initiative aiming, among other things, to stimulate the creation of venture capital funds that provide seed capital and more conventional risk capital. At the same time, the second-tier equity markets have grown rapidly in Europe. Today the London based AIM[3] and the network called Euro-NM (an association of Paris, Frankfurt, Milan, Amsterdam and Brussels high-tech stock markets), share a great part of the European market of small high-tech firms' stocks. Finally, it is worth pointing to the fact that the advent of the single currency is expected to encourage capital mobility in the Euro-zone, and subsequently also the venture capital sector.

Standardization is the fourth area of EU innovation policy of interest here. Standardization came into the European agenda in the mid-1980s directly related to the single market project of Delors. Standard-setting bodies at EU level are today in charge of defining voluntarily common standards by the close co-operation between governmental, producer and consumer representatives. These are convertibility standards that allow a larger market of products by defining their technical specifications. One of the most well-known successes is the GSM open standard in mobile telephony that today operates all through Europe. The impact of convertibility standards in the innovation performance is obvious: it might have positive effects since it creates larger markets for technological products (minimizing prices by increasing competition, and by generating compatibility in larger technological systems). But it might also have negative effects if the standardization level is too high as to de facto hinder the development of alternative and superior technologies (the so-called technological lock-in), or if it works as technical barriers to trade from third country products. Hence, the formalized standardization procedures in Europe are invariably shaping technological trajectories, which have a direct impact on market-creation and on innovative performance.

Benchmarking is the fifth policy issue. As was mentioned above, this is a very new policy tool of the EU which came into being since the Lisbon Summit in Spring 2000 (Lundvall/Tomlinson, 2001, Kastrinos et al, 2001). The benchmarking instrument has been largely used by the OECD since the mid-1980s. With the extension of this instrument to the EU realm, we could expect an acceleration of the diffusion of innovation policy measures in Europe in the coming years. Nevertheless, at the end of the day, it all depends on the willingness and interest from national policy-makers to make use of the data emerging from the detailed comparative analysis and best-practices available.

The last, and perhaps newest initiative within the EU innovation policy is the so-called 'e-Europe'. This is the latest generation of a series of EU policy initiatives devoted to the field of Information and Communication Technologies (ICTs) since the mid-1980s, which started with the liberalization of the telecoms market, the research programs to ICT industry, and were followed by the information society agenda in the mid-1990s. More diffuse than the previous ones, e-Europe covers a wide spectrum of ICT-related issues, willing to introduce the use of this technology in all spheres of European life, advancing organizational flexibility and accessibility.

The multi-level governance form of the EU should be understood as a result of the overwhelming complexity of addressing issues in a vast number of policy areas, all of it in a political system with an increasing number of actors with large institutional diversity. This process is ongoing without any previously designed 'master plan' or teleology other than the very vague words of 'ever closer Union'. Nevertheless, when examining in detail the nature and overall impact of its policy outputs, the EU has undoubtedly assumed a state-like form. Concerning the innovation policy, the six different initiatives examined above indicate clearly that the context where innovative firms and national innovation policies operate is changing dramatically. A new division of tasks might emerge, where national policies are devoted to knowledge-production and competence development tasks, whereas the EU level is in charge of creating a single EU context for the appropriation, exploitation and diffusion of knowledge.

It will be interesting to observe what the impact of the European developments will have on the USA. Although the US as the remaining super-power is an equally large and dynamic country, so as to create its own policy dynamics, discussions on public policy show that US policy-makers constantly compare their country with the other two partners of the global triad, the EU and Japan. This scanning of the international environment is much stronger than it used to be some two or three decades ago. Therefore it seems likely that if a policy measure employed in Europe proves successful, it is to be tried out in the US, too – if under another name and, perhaps, with some adaptations made.

Notes

1 These again resulted from a number of factors, most importantly the rapid rise of new technologies and the need to react to the rearrangement of the world economy due to globalization in general and specifically the fall of the iron curtain.

2 Proposal for a Council Regulation on Community Patents COM (2000) 412.

3 London Exchange's Alternative Investment Market.

References

Andersson, T. (1998): 'Managing a Systems Approach to Technology and Innovation Policy.' STI – Science Technology Industry Review (22): 9–29.

Biegelbauer, P. (1994): 'Evaluation of the Effects of the OECD Report on 'Science, Technology and Innovation Policies in Hungary' on the Country – Report for the 'OECD Technology Audit for Hungary'. OECD internal report.

Biegelbauer, P. (2000): 130 Years of Catching Up With the West – Success and Failure of Hungarian Industry, Science and Technology Policies Since Industrialization. Ashgate Publication.

Dodgson, M./Bessant, J. (1996): Effective Innovation Policy: a New Approach. London, International Thomson.

Edquist, C. (1999): Innovation policy – A Systemic Approach. Linköping, Linköping University.

European Commission (1994): Growth, Competitiveness, Employment. The Challenges and Ways Forward into the 21st Century. Luxembourg, Office for Official Publications.

European Commission (1995): Green Paper on Innovation.

Hakala, J. (2001): 'Finnish Research System and EU RTD Policy', Paper presented at the Autumn Workshop of the Working Group on Politics and Technology of the German Political Science Association in Cooperation with the Fraunhofer Institute for Systems and Innovation Research (ISI), Karlsruhe 'European Research Area' or National Innovation Competition? Technology Policy in the European and Comparative Perspective', November 9th to November 10th, 2001 at Karlsruhe, Germany.

Hall, P. (1989): Conclusion: The Politics of Keynesian Ideas. The Political Power of Economic Ideas. Keynesianism Across Nations. Hall, P., Princeton, Princeton University Press.

Kastrinos, N. (ed.) (2001): Special Issue on the Benchmarking of RTD Policies in Europe. Science and Public Policy, August 2001, Volume 28, Number 4.

Lipsey, R. G./Fraser, S. (1998): 'Technology Policies in Neo-Classical and Structuralist-Evolutionary Models.' STI – Science Technology Industry Review (22): 30–73.

Lundvall, B.-Å. (ed.) (1992): National Systems of Innovation: Towards a Theory of Innovation and Interactive Learning. London, Pinter.

Lundvall, B.-Å./Borrás, S. (1996): Science and Technology Policy Council of Finland. Finland: A Knowledge-based Society, EDITA, Helsinki.

Lundvall, B.-Å./Tomlinson, M. (2001): Policy Learning Through Benchmarking National Systems of Competence Building and Innovation – Learning by Comparing'. Report for the 'Advanced Benchmarking Concepts' Project. March 2001.

MCST (1992): Vision 2000: Developing Malta as a Regional Hub Through Communications Technology (Malta: Poulton's Ltd).

Metcalfe, S. (1995): The Economic Foundations of Technology Policy: Equilibrium and Evolutionary Perspectives. Handbook of the Economics of Innovation and Technological Change. Stoneman, P., Oxford, Blackwell.

Metcalfe, S./Georghiou, L. (1998): 'Equilibrium and Evolutionary Foundations of Technology Policy.' STI – Science Technology Industry Review (22): 75–100.

Nelson, R. R. (ed.) (1993): National Innovation Systems. A Comparative Analysis. Oxford, Oxford University Press.

Netherlands Ministry for Economiy Affairs (1990): 'Economie met Open Grenzen', Second Chamber 1989–1990, no. 21670, Ministry of Economic Affairs, The Hague: SDU Publishers.

OECD (1991). TEP-The Technology Economy Programme: Technology in a Changing World. Paris, OECD.

OECD (1998). 'Special ISSUE on New Rationale and Approaches in Technology and Innovation Policy.' STI 22.

Science and Technology Policy Council of Finland (1996), Finland: A Knowledge-Based Society, EDITA, Helsinki.

List of Authors

Belussi*, *Fiorenza, Assistant Professor at the Faculty of Statistics, University of Padua, Italy.

Biegelbauer*, *Peter S., Assistant Professor at the Department of Political Science, Institute for Advanced Studies in Vienna, Austria.

Borrás*, *Susana, Associate Professor at the Department of Social Sciences, Roskilde University, Denmark.

Cassingena Harper*, *Jennifer, Manager at the Policy Development Unit, Malta Council for Science and Technology.

Christensen*, *Jesper Lindgaard, Professor at the Department of Business Studies, Roskilde University, Denmark.

Edler*, *Jakob, Senior Researcher at the Department for Technology Analysis and Innovation Strategies, Fraunhofer Institute for Systems and Innovation Research, Karlsruhe, Germany.

Etzkowitz*, *Henry, Professor at Purchase College, State University of New York, USA.

Foray*, *Dominique, Professor at the Institut pour le Management de la Recherche et de l'Innovation (IMRI) of the University of Paris-Dauphine in Paris, France.

Lemola*, *Tarmo, Programme Manager in the Technology Department, Ministry of Trade and Industry, Finland.

Lundvall*, *Bengt-Åke, Professor at the Department for Business Studies, Aalborg University, Denmark.

Mali*, *Franc, Assistant Professor at the Faculty of Social Sciences, University of Ljubljana, Slovenia.

Mayer*, *Kurt, Senior Researcher at the Department of Sociology, Institute for Advanced Studies, Vienna, Austria.

Sharp*, *Margaret, Senior Researcher at the Science Policy Research Unit, University of Sussex, UK.

van der Steen*, *Marianne, Senior Policy Advisor in the Directorate for Technology Policy, Ministry of Economic Affairs, The Hague, Netherlands.

Index

Note: The letter n following a page number indicates a reference in the notes.

For Product Safety Concerns and Information please contact our EU representative GPSR@taylorandfrancis.com Taylor & Francis Verlag GmbH, Kaufingerstraße 24, 80331 München, Germany

T - #0173 - 270225 - C0 - 218/163/18 - PB - 9781138717855 - Gloss Lamination